Piracy in Somalia

Piracy in Somalia sheds light on an often misunderstood world that is oversimplified and demonized in the media and largely decontextualized in scholarly and policy works. It examines the root causes of piracy in Somalia as well as piracy's impact on coastal communities, local views about it, and measures taken against it. Drawing on six years' worth of extensive fieldwork, Awet Weldemichael amplifies the voices of local communities who have suffered under the heavy weight of illegal fishing, piracy, and counter-piracy; he makes their struggles comprehensible. He also exposes complex webs of crimes within crimes, of double-dealing pirates, fraudulent negotiators, duplicitous intermediaries, and treacherous foreign illegal fishers and their local partners. *Piracy in Somalia* will help to inform regional and global counter-piracy endeavors, to avoid possible reversals in the gains made so far against piracy, and to identify the gains that still need to be made against its root causes.

Awet Tewelde Weldemichael is Associate Professor and Queen's National Scholar in the Department of History at Queen's University, Ontario. He is also an Associate of the Indian Ocean World Centre at McGill University. He has previously worked for international organizations and held teaching and research positions at universities in Africa, Europe, and the United States. He holds a Ph.D. in History and the LL.M. in Public International Law and is the author of *Third World Colonialism and Strategies of Liberation*. He is former refugee goatherd and is currently a stateless person.

Piracy in Somalia

Violence and Development in the Horn of Africa

Awet Tewelde Weldemichael

Queen's University, Ontario

CAMBRIDGE
UNIVERSITY PRESS

CAMBRIDGE
UNIVERSITY PRESS

University Printing House, Cambridge CB2 8BS, United Kingdom

One Liberty Plaza, 20th Floor, New York, NY 10006, USA

477 Williamstown Road, Port Melbourne, VIC 3207, Australia

314–321, 3rd Floor, Plot 3, Splendor Forum, Jasola District Centre,
New Delhi – 110025, India

79 Anson Road, #06–04/06, Singapore 079906

Cambridge University Press is part of the University of Cambridge.

It furthers the University's mission by disseminating knowledge in the pursuit of
education, learning, and research at the highest international levels of excellence.

www.cambridge.org
Information on this title: www.cambridge.org/9781108496964
DOI: 10.1017/9781108683425

First published 2019

Printed in the United Kingdom by TJ International Ltd. Padstow Cornwall

A catalog record for this publication is available from the British Library.

Library of Congress Cataloging-in-Publication Data
Names: Weldemichael, Awet Tewelde, author.
Title: Piracy in Somalia : violence and development in the Horn of
Africa / Awet Tewelde Weldemichael.
Description: New York : Cambridge University Press, 2019. | Includes
bibliographical references and index.
Identifiers: LCCN 2018039874 | ISBN 9781108496964
Subjects: LCSH: Piracy – Somalia. | Fishery management – Somalia. |
Fishing – Corrupt practices – Somalia.
Classification: LCC HV6433.786.S58 W45 2019 | DDC 364.164096773–dc23
LC record available at https://lccn.loc.gov/2018039874

ISBN 978-1-108-49696-4 Hardback
ISBN 978-1-108-73928-3 Paperback

To Miriam, whose love sustains me.

To Farris, who reanimates my transience through the minutia of planetary here and now.

To Eyl, a jewel along the Somali coast, that took me in as one of its own.

Contents

List of Figures   *page* viii
Preface and Acknowledgments   xi

Introduction: Locating Somali Piracy in Space
and Discourse   1

1   Global Root Causes and Local Circumstances
    of Early Piracy in Somalia   22

2   From Cascading Troubles of Somali Fisheries
    to the Onset of Predatory Piracy   64

3   The Epic Spiraling of Ransom Piracy   99

4   Local Consequences of and Responses to Piracy   133

5   International Counter-Piracy as a Means and an End   171

    Conclusion: IUU Fishing Is Back! Will Piracy Return?   196

Bibliography   205
Index   229

Figures

P.1. A 2012 Somalia country profile map available
at the Perry-Castañeda Library Map Collection. (Courtesy of
the University of Texas Libraries, University of Texas at
Austin.) *page* xx

1.1. A dilapidated refrigerator truck in the center
of Eyl is one of many reminders of the bygone
days of the lucrative fisheries sector in the historic fishing
village. (Photo by the author.) 42

1.2. A Middle Eastern fishing dhow off the coast
of Hafun around the tip of the Horn. (Courtesy
of PDRC.) 57

1.3. FV *Al-Amal*, the Yemeni fishing vessel with
an illegal fishing license, which in August
2015 went aground near Eyl. (Courtesy of PMPF). 59

1.4. One of two self-contradicting fake licenses
under which the FV *Al-Amal* was operating. (Courtesy of
PMPF.) 61

2.1. Lobster exports by private Somali fishing
companies. (Compiled by the author from
data provided by the three companies.) 68

2.2. On any given day since the collapse of fisheries
and expulsion of the pirates, the beach in Bedey
(the coastal half of Eyl) is littered with such disused boats.
(Photo by the author.) 69

2.3. Piracy incidents, both actual and attempted, 1994–2004.
(Compiled by the author from IMB annual reports.) 74

2.4. Comparison of piracy incidents (both actual
and attempted attacks), 1994–2004 and 2005–2015.
(Compiled by the author from IMB annual reports.) 83

2.5. Survey of popular views about causes of piracy. (Compiled by
the author.) 87

3.1. Indian Ocean range rings around Somalia from
     a 2012 country profile map available at the
     Perry-Castañeda Library Map Collection.
     (Courtesy of the University of Texas Libraries, University of
     Texas at Austin.)   101
3.2. Percentage of piracy incidents that resulted in successful
     hijackings, 2005–2015. (Compiled by author from IMB
     annual reports.)   104
3.3. In one of its earliest active operations against
     piracy, in December 2012 the Puntland Marine
     Police Force (PMPF) freed the sailors of MV
     Iceberg I after nearly three years of pirate captivity. (Courtesy
     of PMPF.)   124
4.1. Percentage increase in price index for basic
     consumer goods in Puntland. (Compiled by the author from
     MOPIC data.)   136
4.2. Puntland's livestock export. (Compiled by the
     author from government figures.)   140
4.3. Local views about solutions for piracy. (Compiled
     by the author.)   142
4.4. A pirate skiff ferrying supplies to pirates holding
     an unidentified captive vessel near Gara'ad. Another captive
     vessel is seen at a distance in the background. (Courtesy of
     a confidential source.)   153
4.5. Abdirahman Mohamed Mohamoud "Farole,"
     former president of Puntland (2009–2013), played a crucial
     role in reining in piracy against all odds, domestic and foreign.
     (Photo by the author.)   160
4.6. Total number of incidents and hijackings, 2005–2015.
     (Compiled by the author from IMB annual reports.)   166
C.1. The congested port of Bosaso is the only formal
     port across Puntland. (Photo by the author.)   203

Preface and Acknowledgments

The capital of knowledge that an individual scholar has to offer is small. Admission (of one's shortcomings) saves from censure. Kindness from colleagues is hoped for. It is God whom I ask to make our deeds acceptable in His sight. He is a good protector.

Ibn Khaldun, *The Muqaddimah*, 9.

In 2011, I had the good fortune of holding the Hiob Ludolf Guest Professorship at Hamburg University in Germany, lecturing on piracy, terrorism and insurgency. During that year, a court in Hamburg started to hear the piracy charges against ten Somali men, who attacked the German vessel MS T*aipan* in April 2010.[1] The pirates' capable pro bono lawyers valiantly fought a losing battle, arguing that their clients were fighting for survival and in self-defense against foreign plundering of their marine resources and destruction of their livelihoods. After more than 100 days of hearing the case, in October 2012 the court found all suspects guilty and meted out to them varying prison sentences.[2]

After one of the court's adjournments in July 2011, I went to a series of events that regularly takes place across Germany in the summer in celebration of Klaus Stortebeker, the fourteenth-century Hanseatic League (northern German) pirate. The myth of Stortebeker's feats and the lore surrounding his name is particularly salient in Hamburg, where there is a life-size bronze statue of him and there are restaurants on the shores of the Elbe River, music bands, and songs (including a techno mix) bearing his name, among many others.

---

[1] Captured by a Dutch warship, the ten were handed over to Germany because the ship belonged to a Hamburg-based company. "Dutch Marines Abseil on to a Hijacked Cargo Vessel to Rescue Its Crew and Arrest 10 Somali Pirates," *Daily Mail*, 7 April 2010: http://www.dailymail.co.uk/news/article-1263960/Dutch-marines-abseil-deck-ship-MV-Taipan-freeing-crew-Somali-pirates.html.

[2] "Verdict in Somali Hijacking Case: Court Rules in Germany's First Modern-Day Piracy Trial," *Spiegel Online*, 19 October 2012: http://www.spiegel.de/international/germany/hamburg-court-hands-down-somali-pirate-sentences-a-862350.html.

As I took my students on an alternative boat tour of the Hamburg inner harbor to discuss the city's past and present with piracy,[3] the idolization of Stortebeker stood in sharp contrast to the confinement of the ten Somalis being tried in the same city. The irony of celebrating a long-dead outlaw was living testimony to a popular pirate quote widely attributed to British philosopher Bernard Williams: "The average man will bristle if you say his father was dishonest, but he will brag a little if he discovers that his great-grandfather was a pirate." Popular movies, pirate-day shows, and the popularity of pirate paraphernalia as Halloween costumes reflect the romanticizing of pirates elsewhere in the West.

Only some pirates were afforded such posthumous celebration in Western popular culture, however. Not only did that tradition exclude the pirates off the coast of North Africa, or "Barbary" Coast, but on the contrary many towns in the United States are named Decatur after the American captain who led the final 1815 onslaught on the North African states that harbored the notorious Barbary pirates. The perpetuity in the discourse of Muslim and African infractions, on the one hand, while, on the other hand, the same past criminality of non-Muslims and non-Africans are celebrated and their contemporary similar crimes are either shrugged off or given no more than lip service, is glaring. The treatment of the short-lived piracy phenomenon off the coast of Somalia has not been free from the same historic double standard and has also been a subject of eerie comparisons with Barbary piracy to the detriment of a proper understanding of – and sustainable solutions to – its root causes.

In a simplistic sketch of the eighteenth–nineteenth century piracy off the coast of North Africa, *The New York Times's* Africa correspondent Jeffrey Gettleman drew specious parallels with the piracy off the coast of Somalia and called for similar solutions.[4] Just as US military bombed the Barbary Coast and pounded the bravado out of "a bunch of knife-sucking thugs in blousy pants,"[5] Gettleman had no scruples about a similar remedy in Somalia: "[P]ound the bravado out of the pirates by taking the battle to them where it hurts most – on shore."[6]

Although Gettleman's wide readership makes his shallow, warlike point of view disconcerting, his is by no means unique or first. Renowned French historian of the Mediterranean World, Fernand

---

[3] A small group of social and environmental justice activists in Hamburg organized the tour.

[4] Jeffrey Gettleman, "Lessons from the Barbary Pirate Wars," *The New York Times*, 12 April 2009.

[5] Thomas Jefferson is widely believed to have similarly characterized pirates off the coast of North Africa thus: "When they sprang to the deck of an enemy's ship, every sailor held a dagger in each hand and a third in his mouth, which usually struck such terror in the foe that they cried out for quarter at once."

[6] Gettleman, "Lessons from the Barbary Pirate Wars."

Braudel, had noted how the West traditionally "encouraged us to see only the pirates of Islam, in particular Barbary corsairs"[7] when in fact maritime predation (conveniently dubbed privateering when perpetrated by one's side and piracy when done by rivals or enemies) had dominated the relations between both sides of the Mediterranean. European fortune hunters and renegades particularly crowded Mediterranean privateering/piracy with – and without – the protection of the North African states of the time.

As Tunisian scholar Lotfi Ben Rejeb had deduced, the exclusive association of the once useful and widespread practice with North African states, and the separate dehumanization of the Muslim practitioners of the trade reflected the changing power relations not only between the powers to the north and south of the Mediterranean but also among powers farther afield.[8] Much as the twenty-first century maritime predation off the coast of Somalia is real, mainstream journalist accounts, scholarly narratives and policy discussions around it are similarly emblematic of far-off hegemonic power relations.

This book takes to task the prevalent linear narratives that have smothered meaningful debate about – and helped preclude lasting solutions to – piracy in Somalia. Based on extensive field research in piracy-affected areas in that country, it sheds light on an oft-misunderstood world, oversimplified and demonized in the media and largely decontextualized or inadequately contextualized in scholarly discourse and policy. For the root causes of piracy off the coast of Somalia, its impact on local Somali communities, and the latter's views about and measures against it are by and large missing in the current one-way conversation. The book amplifies the voices of local communities against illegal fishing, piracy and counter-piracy; it makes their legitimate responses comprehensible on their own terms; and it documents their misconceived remedial measures all the while exposing the rationalized criminality around them.

I am hopeful that examining the root causes of piracy, exposing its inner workings, and documenting its consequences and the struggles of its victims will help avoid the risks of possible reversals in the gains so far made against that scourge. I am equally hopeful that this book will bring into sharper focus the parallel gains that await to be made against illegal exploitation of maritime resources in present-day Somalia as a microcosm of the broader imbalances that the Global South suffers. The stories thus documented do help in identifying potential allies to the quest for lasting

[7] Fernand Braudel, *The Mediterranean and the Mediterranean World in the Age of Philip II.* Vol. 2 (New York: Harper & Row, 1972), 754–755.
[8] Lotfi Ben Rejeb, "Barbary's 'Character' in European Letters, 1514–1830: An Ideological Prelude to Colonization," *Dialectical Anthropology.* vol. 6, no. 4 (June 1982), 345–355.

solutions (at sea and on land) to the ongoing crimes, solutions that are homegrown, locally driven and internationally supported.

While, in the spirit of Ibn Khaldun's words,[9] I concede the limitations of my work and accept sole responsibility for the shortcomings that readers will undoubtedly find in this book, I acknowledge the invaluable support I received from its inception to its completion. When this project was no more than an idea on paper, Hamburg University granted me an exploratory fund that enabled me to travel to Kenya and Somalia (Puntland) in the summer of 2011 to test the waters. Research on the project picked up momentum during my Fernand Braudel Fellowship at the University of Paris Diderot (Paris VII), when I was simultaneously wrapping up a previous project.

The Gerda Henkel Stiftung, a Dusseldorf-based not-for-profit research funding organization, awarded me the most generous and crucial funding that enabled me to travel to the field twice. On learning of that award, the University of Kentucky (UK), whose job offer I had accepted, gave me a semester-long leave of absence to enable me to take advantage of the grant and advance my research. The UK College of Arts and Science also awarded me summer research support in 2013.

As funding sources appeared to dry up before the end of my research, I moved to Queen's University in 2014–2015 where I was offered a Research Initiation Grant (RIG) that could not have come at a better time. Another advantage of being at Queen's was the fact that its University Research Grants (URG) scheme enables faculty members to borrow against their future salaries. To the utter amazement of my family and research partners, and to subsequent personal financial hardship, I took two large URGs in 2015–2016 and 2016–2017 to complete the research. As this book goes to press, I continue to pay back that debt. Finally, the Faculty of Arts and Science at Queen's awarded me a discretionary grant to see the project through. To all my funders, I register my utmost gratitude as I do to my family that tolerated me and made do with shrunken family finances.

Beyond funding, this project could not have been possible without the support of a network of institutional and personal backing at every corner. The support of my departments at the University of Kentucky and at Queen's University has been solid. I am especially thankful for the course releases I was afforded at Queen's. The former and current chairs, Jamey Carson and Rebecca Manley, respectively, have been extremely understanding, actively supportive and always caring. The intellectually

---

[9] Ibn Khaldun, *The Muqaddimah: An Introduction to History*, Franz Rosenthal (trans.) (Princeton and Oxford: Princeton University Press, 1969), 9.

vibrant, socially healthy and collegial environment that they led went a long way to making my joining of the Queen's community stimulating and all-around meaningful, for which I also thank my colleagues.

In Nairobi, a network of friends helped facilitated a mutually beneficial arrangement with the regional office of Interpeace, the International Alliance for Peace. I am especially thankful to my cousins Bereket Goitom and Titi Asefaw, my friends Berkti Hagos, Johan Svensson, Asia Abdulkadir and Ulf Terlinden for their friendship and guidance in navigating not only the Nairobi NGO scene but also the Somali political and research environment. The Interpeace regional director, the late Abdurahman Raghe, took especial interest in me as a person hailing from that region choosing to partake in such a project, knowing full well the challenges. I hope, more than anything else, he is looking down at this project with satisfaction in the risk he took with me. Johan, Ulf and Jean Paul Mugiraneza, who succeeded Raghe as Interpeace regional or Somali program directors, were similarly unfailing in their support; I am especially thankful to Asia, Ulf and Johan for that critical and subtle holding of the hand that even seasoned researchers need when venturing into new fields. It is thanks to these friends and mentors and Interpeace's decisive support throughout the project that my research gained traction and reached the level that it did.

On the ground in Somalia, Interpeace's network of regional partners proved equally decisive both at the personal and institutional levels. The attention and support that Abdulrahman Osman "Shuke" gave me (and my project) in Garowe matched that of Raghe's in Nairobi. The stature of these two elders restrained and calmed nerves, opened doors, and paved ways with the hostile, hesitant and/or unenthusiastic government officials, individual Somalis and communities that I dealt with throughout my fieldwork. I was affiliated with the Garowe-based Puntland Development and Research Center (PDRC, latterly renamed Peace and Development Research Center), an independent think tank-type research institution. In its main office, I had access to its extensive research and audiovisual resources with which Muctar Hersi, Ahmed Adam, and Amina Abdulkadir were extremely generous.

I traveled extensively across Puntland with the fearless researchers and peace activists of PDRC's Mobile Audiovisual Unit (MAVU): Abdinasir Yusuf (MAVU leader); cameramen and researchers Abdirisak Abdulkadir, Abdiladif Abdirahman and the late Ismail Hajji Harash; drivers Mohamed Abyan, Abdirizak, Abdulkarim, Awad "Nairobi" and the late Jibril Yare; and the many armed guards who had to accompany me/us wherever we went. In all my travels, I received the invaluable help of local interlocutors and language assistants, who themselves are capable researchers and analysts, among them Sakaria Abdulrahman and Ahmed Mohamed. Among all these unassuming but formidable and brave young men, I was no more than an average student, not only regularly schooled on the local do's and don'ts but also engaged in vigorous methodological and substantive debates – and, in a few instances, even quarrels – which carried hefty consequences to our safety and to my project. All along, the always-alert PDRC deputy director Ali Farah's watchful attention to regional developments proved a useful thermometer to my research travels. I equally benefited from his long experience (at a senior level), gained in the Somali government's fisheries authorities before the civil war, which gave him unique perspective to the topic of my own research.

In Somaliland, Interpeace's and PDRC's counterpart, the Hargeisa-based Academy for Peace and Development was forthcoming with its resources and contacts. I am especially thankful to its director, Mohamed Farah, and staff, who welcomed me with open arms and were unfailingly encouraging. My thanks also go to Mohamed Osman Ahmed, the executive director of Somaliland Counter Piracy Coordination, for his candor and support.

During one of the court hearings in Hamburg in summer 2011, I met the American-German writer Michael Scott Moore and discussed over lunch our respective plans to travel to piracy-affected parts of Somalia for research. Because our travels (his first leg and my second leg) were going to overlap in early 2012, we tentatively agreed to meet either in Nairobi or in Somalia and exchange notes. On asking mutual contacts in Nairobi about Michael's whereabouts in mid-January, I learned that he was in Galkayo, Somalia, and was expected back in Kenya at any time. A few days later, I arrived in Garowe, Somalia, to the news that Michael had just been kidnapped. That news had the worst chilling effect on me as I was about to embark on my first extensive data-gathering travels. During his two-and-half years of captivity, [10] I actively tried to track his whereabouts; his ordeal, which I could only imagine, remained one more reminder of my grim research environment.

Nevertheless, thanks to the staunch support, reassuring friendship and warm hospitality in my Somali network, the specter of my being harmed remained a distant possibility. For a number of reasons, I cannot mention by name many of the Somali men and women who looked after me and actively supported my work, including my interviewees, to all of whom I am grateful. But I cannot pass without acknowledging with thanks the

---

[10] Michael has since written an account of his captivity in fascinating detail, which came out too late for me to use in my current book. See Michael Scott Moore, *The Desert and the Sea: 977 Days Captive on the Somali Pirate Coast* (New York: Harper Wave, 2018).

support, hospitality and friendship of Ahmed Abbas Ahmed, Fatuma Mohamed, Buraale, Sharmarke Ali, Mohamud Abdulkadir "John," the late Abdisalam Hassan, Abdirizak Mohamed Dirir, Abdirizak Ismail Hassan, Abdi Farah Saeed "Juha," Isahak Ahmed, Burhan I. Hassan, Mohamud Hamid Hamid and Professor Mohamed Samantar. Along with my above-mentioned research partners in the field, these friends and many others formed what proved to be an impenetrable safety shield around me wherever I went. After initial doubt, the community in Eyl took me in as one of their own and the officials, elders and activists there always made me feel at home.

Although they did not quite know it and their assistance may seem brief, I received invaluable encouragement, and important maritime scientific pointers and advice from my Eritrean former colleagues at the University of Asmara who went on to become globetrotting, top-notch marine scientists and experts in sustainable Blue Economies: To Dr. Marco Pedulli, Dr. Dawit Tesfamichael, Dr. Mebrahtu Ateweberhan, Dr. Zekeria Abdulkerim, Dr. Iyob Tsehaye and Dr. Essam Emnay Yassin, thank you.

It is interesting to note that Ethiopian intelligence agents trailed me wherever I went in Somali towns. Where they could not physically watch me in far-off villages, I could not help but notice that they kept indirect tabs on my movements. My Somali colleagues and I chose not to acknowledge their presence by design and they did not visibly interfere with our work, which one would imagine to be of little to no danger to their political, economic and/or security interests in the Somali region (the northeast and northwest). The United Nations Office on Drugs and Crime (UNODC), like many similar international and regional organizations, such as the Intergovernmental Authority on Development (IGAD) that were involved in the topic of my research, practically kept me at arm's length or completely shut their doors on me. My repeated attempts to meet UNODC personnel and to consult their resources went unanswered except in one instance when a newly arrived junior official (who, interestingly, attended Queen's University School of Law) came to meet me outside their regional headquarters in Nairobi with their publicly available, expensive-looking brochures – glossy, colorful and in high resolution. Only after he left UNODC was I able to meet and exchange notes with retired British soldier and former military attaché, Col. John Steed, for which I am appreciative.

Upon its completion, my mentor Ned Alpers, and senior colleagues Marc Epprecht, Colin Duncan, Ghirmai Negash, Sandra den Otter, Anthony Lee, Bettina Ng'weno, and Patricia Schneider, and my graduate student Samuel Tsegai read the manuscript in part or in full and offered invaluable feedback for which I thank them heartily. My other graduate student, Daniel Asante Boamah, helped assemble statistical data on piracy, which he, my sister Natsinet and my better half Miriam assisted in aggregating and analyzing along with other relevant quantitative material I was able to gather. I am grateful to all of them. Studying public international law greatly facilitated my understanding of the legal aspects of the story. That also benefited from constructive consultations with my friend, colleague and supervisor Joshua Karton and classmates Ekaterina Antsygina, who is an expert in maritime (continental shelf) law, and Gary Lutton, a seasoned diplomat and expert in treaty laws.

My thanks also go to Cambridge University Press's impressive editorial team (Maria Marsh, Abigail Walkington and Cassi Roberts) and their efficient production partners at Integra (Karthik Orukaimani and Faye Roberts). I would especially like to thank Maria for taking active interest in my book and seeing it through the most critical phase; to Cassi for ably shepherding it through production; and to Faye Roberts for the meticulous copyediting. I am extremely grateful to the anonymous peer reviewers of my manuscript who gave me valuable feedback.

In ways emblematic of the structurally rigged system of knowledge production, doing this research as a black African and moving around on an Eritrean passport made my research travels unnecessarily complicated and taxing (physically, emotionally, financially and time-wise). The indignity of being especially quizzed and of having one's documents closely examined many times over (by the all-powerful airline employees and immigration/customs officers) at various international departure/ entry points are a fraction of the hefty, invisible prices of doing independent research of which only a few researchers even know, much less endure. The withdrawal, by the Dean of the Gujarat National Law University in Ahmadabad in India, of a fellowship offer upon receiving my passport page for visa purposes (hence seeing my face) best epitomizes who, even in the Global South, is considered a credible producer of legitimate knowledge about a topic of scientific research.

As if that, and the physical strain and security risks involved in the research were not enough, perhaps most humiliating, physically exhausting, and draining (financially and in terms of time) was the fact that I was rendered stateless toward the end of my research. Early prospects to acquire an African passport fizzled when the need to bribe officials at key positions became apparent and morally indistinguishable from the uniquely Eritrean circumstances that had, in the first place, left me stateless. Appeals to Canadian authorities have not yielded an outcome in spite of the fact that I have lived, worked, and paid taxes in Canada for four years and counting – and I hold an enviable position at a prestigious national institution.

This book is written despite all the hardships and because of the support of many Somali and non-Somali personal friends, colleagues, siblings and family far and near.

Awet T. Weldemichael

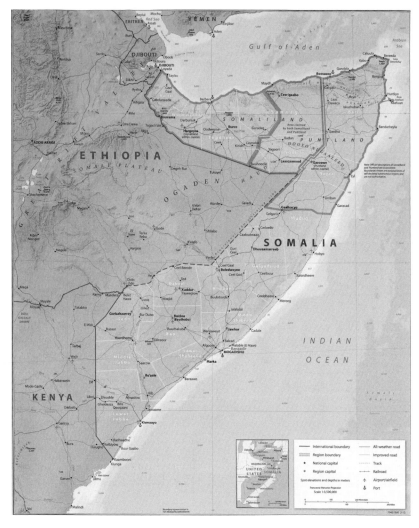

Figure P.1. A 2012 Somalia country profile map available at the Perry-Castañeda Library Map Collection. (Courtesy of the University of Texas Libraries, University of Texas at Austin.)

Introduction: Locating Somali Piracy in Space and Discourse

Maritime piracy off the coast of Somalia subsided in 2012/2013 as dramatically as it exploded between 2005 and 2007.[1] Many local and foreign actors and stakeholders celebrated the end of the scourge. Maritime insurers redrew the high-risk area and shrunk the maritime space where they charged heightened insurance premiums.[2] While some of the international counter-piracy armada departed upon the expiration of their mandates in late 2016, the departure of others seems to be within sight.[3] Nevertheless, the gains against piracy remain precarious so long as its overland and maritime root causes and contributory factors are intact, and its effects on Somalia and Somalis remain unattended.

The process of getting the Somali state back on its feet is proceeding at an agonizingly slow pace. Its security apparatus and administrative structures are still in shambles. Many of the pirate linchpins and their highermost networks are freely roaming and investing their ill-gotten money within the country and beyond. The reservoir of potential recruits looms large because of rampant unemployment and abject poverty. Most importantly, illegal, unregulated and unreported (IUU) fishing, intensified on the heels of receding pirate activities, is increasing the risks of the return of piracy. Averting a relapse to the pre-2012 rate of attacks and ridding the region of the scourge of piracy calls for a proper understanding of – and attending to – the root causes, dynamics and consequences of the crime.

---

[1] The International Maritime Bureau (IMB) recorded fifteen attempts in 2013, which is a significant drop from seventy-five in 2012. Of the fifteen attempts only two were successful hijackings. *ICC IMB Piracy and Armed Robbery against Ships – 2013 Annual Report*, January 2014.

[2] "Marine Insurers Re-draw High Risk Area in the Indian Ocean," *Mint*, 16 December 2015: http://www.livemint.com/Politics/S54MpWbxufH1TKUrdtcDXN/Marine-insurers-redraw-high-risk-area-in-the-Indian-Ocean.html.

[3] "NATO Ends Anti-Piracy Mission in Indian Ocean," *Voice of America*, 24 November 2016: http://www.voanews.com/a/nato-ends-anti-piracy-mission-in-indian-ocean/3609724.html.

Various United Nations bodies and independent analysts agree with many local actors that the nexus between hazardous waste dumping and illegal fishing prompted Somali piracy.[4] Whereas waste dumping took place secretly in remote overland and maritime spaces, often under the cover of darkness,[5] illegal fishing happened routinely in broad daylight and at night, in proximities close to and far off shore.[6] At least since the collapse of the Somali state in the early 1990s, IUU fishers plundered the country's marine resources. Foreign dhows from the region, and industrial-scale fishing vessels from distant water fishing nations (DWFNs) especially took advantage of the deep coastal waters to fish in traditional preserves of local artisanal fishermen.

Somalis directly observed and experienced the damages such illegal fishing caused on the marine environment, the livelihoods of coastal communities and the lives of fishermen. Faced with a threat and without a government to appeal to for protection, Somali fishermen took the defense of their fishing grounds into their own hands and directly, though not always successfully, confronted illegal foreign fishing vessels. Within a decade, their impromptu defensive measures took a life of their own and became the epic, predatory enterprise of ransom piracy of the twenty-first century. What started as a legitimate Somali phenomenon metastasized into a multimillion-dollar, international problem, spanning the breadth of the Indian Ocean and, according to industry estimates, draining the global economy of billions of dollars in ransoms, increased insurance premiums, security arrangements and associated costs. Inflamed by widespread claims of hazardous waste dumping, the sense of righteous indignation among the coastal fishing communities helped rationalize the criminal actions of a few.

---

[4] Abdirahman Jama Kulmiye, "Militia vs Trawlers: Who Is the Villain," *The East African Magazine*, 9 July 2001; S/2008/769, UN, Somalia Monitoring Group (Report), 10 December 2008, Para. 125; Ken Menkhaus (2009), "Dangerous Waters," *Survival*, vol. 51, no. 1 (2009), 21–25; Mohamed Abshir Waldo, "The Two Piracies in Somalia: Why the World Ignores the Other?" *Wardheer News*, 8 January 2009. Accessible at: http://somalitalk.com/2009/april/waldo.html; Ishaan Tharoor, "How Somalia's Fishermen Became Pirates," *Time*, April 18, 2009: http://www.time.com/time/world/article/0,8599, 1892376,00.html; S/2010/91, UN Somalia Monitoring Group (Report), 10 March 2010, Para. 127.

[5] Debora MacKenzie, "Toxic Waste Adds to Somalia's Woes," *New Scientist*, 19 September 1992; Mahdi Gedi Qayad, "Assessment Mission to Somalia in Connection with Alleged Dumping of Hazardous Substances," 10 May–8 June 1997; S/2008/769, UN, Somalia Monitoring Group (Report), 10 December 2008; Greenpeace, *The Toxic Ships: The Italian Hub, the Mediterranean Area and Africa* (Greenpeace Italy Report, June 2010), 20–29. Also accessible at: https://www.greenpeace.org/italy/Global/italy/report/2010/inquinamento/Report-The-toxic-ship.pdf.

[6] Kulmiye, "Militia vs Trawlers." Many firsthand observers of the Somali coast similarly describe their observations of the coast as mobile cities of light.

The preeminent Somalia scholar Ken Menkhaus succinctly captured this phenomenon as a "textbook case of a shift in the motives of an armed group from grievance to greed."[7] Further explication of this shift and an examination of its dynamics and inner workings have been difficult due to, among other factors, the challenging research environment that made fieldwork particularly daunting. Moreover, Menkhaus noted how the country was "without government but not without governance," because the various Somali regions and communities gradually devised mechanisms of managing their day-to-day affairs after the collapse of the state in 1991. As a result of such "governance without government,"[8] wanton criminality was "much better contained than in the early 1990s, when egregious crimes could be committed with impunity."[9] An essential question, an answer to which also forms the basis of this book, arises as to why and how the restraining role of governance without government gave way to escalating criminal ransom piracy in the new millennium.

The tendency to lump together all forms of maritime predation in Somalia and to cast aspersions on local responses has contributed to obscuring the complex evolution of piracy and remedies thereof. As Scott Coffen-Smout astutely observed, the "international community encourages local Somali administrative entities to take responsibility for governance of the region, but when authority is exerted over coastal waters the individuals are labelled pirates."[10] Following Stig Jarle Hansen's groundbreaking fieldwork in some of the pirate-dominated regions of Somalia, leading expert of maritime and naval studies Martin N. Murphy offered an initial way out of the complexity by arguing that there appeared to exist defensive and predatory piracy in Somalia. Whereas defensive piracy is linked to "local fishermen defending what they regard as their fishing grounds" against IUU fishers, predatory piracy "has been present from the beginning. It [only] increased in frequency in 2005."[11]

Murphy then raised important questions pertinent to the nature of what appeared to be defensive and predatory forms of piracy and the

---

[7] Ken Menkhaus, "Dangerous Waters," *Survival*, vol. 15 no. 1 (February–March 2009), 21–25 [here 23].

[8] Menkhaus, "Governance without Government in Somalia: Spoilers, State Building, and the Politics of Coping," *International Security*, vol. 31, no. 3 (Winter 2006/07), 74–106.

[9] Menkhaus, "Somalia and Somaliland: Terrorism, Political Islam, and State Collapse" in Robert I. Rotberg (ed.), *Battling Terrorism in the Horn of Africa* (Cambridge, MA: World Peace Foundation, 2005), 23–47 [here: 27].

[10] Scott Coffen-Smout, "Pirates, Warlords and Rogue Fishing Vessels in Somalia's Unruly Seas," 1999: http://www.chebucto.ns.ca/~ar120/somalia.html.

[11] Martin N. Murphy, *Somalia: The New Barbary? Piracy and Islam in the Horn of Africa* (New York: Columbia University Press, 2011), 12–17.

validity of the distinctions between them. He went on to ask what caused those distinctions and: "Why did the predatory form increase its range so substantially, grow so quickly starting in 2005 and resume with even greater virulence in 2007? Did the defensive form remain distinct or did the two forms merge or overlap?"[12] Although the inevitable confusion between the two, especially where the predatory pirates claim to be self-defense "coast guards," is not lost to Murphy; he deferred a conclusive answer for these and other questions to a later date when researchers could find safe avenues for conducting research on the ground.

Taking advantage of a unique set of favorable factors that eased the difficulty of doing long-term research in the region, this book examines the root causes of – and contributory factors to – piracy in Somalia. Based on extensive fieldwork in the Somali region in general and the semiautonomous Puntland State of Somalia in particular, and drawing from extant scholarly and policy works, this book documents the advent, dynamics, and consequences of the criminal enterprise and its defensive predecessor. In so doing, it gives nuances to piracy in Somalia and situates it in its proper historical and contemporary contexts, challenging and better informing scholarly and civic communities as well as local and international policy makers.

To begin with, this book challenges broad-brush coverage of piracy in Somalia by expanding on Murphy's preliminary typology in order to clearly differentiate and analyze the various forms of maritime predation in the country. Abdi Samatar, Mark Lindberg and Basil Mahayni introduced and identified "political, resources, defensive and ransom" piracies as distinct but interrelated categories.[13] Accordingly, political piracy was a strategy that the rebel Somali National Movement (in present-day Somaliland) pursued to block supplies from reaching the embattled government in Mogadishu; it ceased when that government collapsed in 1991. Resource pirates are the foreign IUU fishers, whose unbridled plundering of the Somalis' marine environment and resources undermined their moral economy of subsistence guarantees. Defensive pirates are former coast guards and fishermen vigilantes who rose to fend for themselves and chase out the resource pirates. Finally, ransom pirates are those criminal elements who came for the extorted ransoms.

Second, while maintaining that the chaos, lawlessness and poverty on land that precipitated and followed the collapse of the Somali state contributed to the emergence of maritime piracy there, one of this book's core

---

[12] Murphy, *Somalia: The New Barbary?* 17.
[13] Abdi Ismail Samatar, Mark Lindberg and Basil Mahayni, "The Dialectics of Piracy in Somalia: the Rich versus the Poor," *Third World Quarterly*, vol. 31, no. 8 (2010), 1377–1394.

contentions is that the latter was not an organic extension of the former. This book holds that the few cases of pirate attacks off the coast of Somalia throughout the 1990s and early 2000s are indicative of the fact that the relationship between the civil war-related criminality on land and armed robbery at sea was at best tenuous. Somali pirate attacks in those years did not stand out from – and in some years they in fact paled in comparison to – those in any given part of the world where piracy existed. Incidents of maritime predation by criminal gangs remained so few throughout the 1990s that Hansen wrote: "[I]n 1992 there were simply no recorded piracy attacks in Somalia. In 1993, there were fewer recorded incidents of piracy in Somalia than in Italy."[14]

State decay and collapse contributed to the start of piracy only to the extent that it incapacitated the country from reining in foreign corporate crimes in its maritime spaces and from responsibly regulating local exploitation of its marine resources.[15] The intensity and methods of foreign IUU and local fishing especially destroyed the marine habitat, contributed to the deterioration of the quality and quantity of the catch, and further eroded the long-term sustainability of Somali fisheries. These aftereffects of state failure forced a necessity upon those genuinely seeking to rid their waters of resource theft and they subsequently offered a fertile ground for those merely claiming to be doing so.

And finally, this book will demonstrate that a combination of several factors transformed piracy from its defensive beginnings to its criminal, predatory ends. In the order of their significance, these factors are: foreign fishing vessels' continued illegal operations; their alacrity to pay rising fines-cum-ransoms to secure expeditious release when captured; the advent of unscrupulous criminal elements with business, military and technical knowhow; the abundance of unemployed youth living in abject poverty; and the continued absence of effective law enforcement. Once localized maritime predation evolved into a profit-seeking vulturine enterprise, it capitalized on the government vacuum and attendant breakdown of law and order on land to overtake – in fact and in discourse – its defensive progenitor in spite of the restraining power of governance without government.

---

[14] Hansen, *Piracy in the Greater Gulf of Aden*, 20.

[15] Although J. Peter Pham considers the questionable claim about shipwrecking to be among "historical antecedents" to piracy as do others, he correctly traces contemporary Somali piracy to the inability of the failed state to "impose a government's writ on the Somali people" and "to assert their sovereignty" over their rich waters. See J. Peter Pham, "The Failed State and Regional Dimensions of Somali Piracy," in Bibi van Ginkel and Frans-Paul van der Putten (eds.), *The International Response to Somali Piracy: Challenges and Opportunities* (Leiden and Boston: Martinus Nijhoff Publishers: 2010), 2.

Thus differentiating the ebb and flow of the various types of maritime predation as well as physical and structural violence in Somalia and locating each in its appropriate place and time, the scope of this book spans piracy's global causes, inner workings, and local consequences. In so doing, it takes to task the current conventional wisdom that is suffused with contemporaneous, heavyweight power politics in the region and beyond. The book also reveals and demystifies the inner workings of some of the Somali pirates' criminal underworld within the country's dysfunctional political economy of conflict. It brings to light complex webs of crimes within crimes of double-dealing pirates, fraudulent negotiators, duplicitous intermediaries, and treacherous foreign illegal fishers (and their local partners in crime). It particularly lays bare details of a few notorious pirate cases that could inform future local and international counter-piracy measures.

History of the Somali Tragedy in Brief

An adequate understanding of the above dynamics calls for a brief historical overview of Somalia and its relevant regions leading up to the advent of piracy there. Located next to the important maritime chokepoint at Bab el Mandeb and along a stretch of more than 3,000 kilometers of the Gulf of Aden and the western Indian Ocean coastlines, Somalia is strategic to global maritime navigation and trade in the region. Tens of thousands of vessels funnel up and down the Bab el Mandeb strait and the Gulf of Aden ferrying some 20 percent of global trade, about 90 percent of which is oil and gas from the Middle East to the west. Progressive erosion of the Somali state since the late 1970s, the country's descent into a bitter civil war in the late 1980s, and the disintegration of its government in 1991 did not augur well to the safety and security of maritime navigation in its waters – although that threat did not transpire forthwith nor was it immediately apparent.

Following the assassination of elected President Abdirashid Ali Sharmarke in 1969, General Mohamed Siad Barre came to power in a bloodless coup that ended one of the earliest democratic experiments in postcolonial Africa.[16] Although his government promised national unity under scientific socialism, he set up a two-decade-long military dictatorship aligned first with the Soviet Union (until 1977) and then with the United States. Somalia made significant cultural, educational and infrastructural advances early on during those twenty years, but the

---

[16] Abdi Ismail Samatar, *Africa's First Democrats: Somalia's Aden A. Osman and Abdirazak H. Hussen* (Bloomington: Indiana University Press, 2016).

Siad Barre dictatorship grew increasingly repressive and predatory. While barring people from identifying themselves by their clans, for example, he relied on his clan and family loyalists to ensure his security and hold on to power. Official corruption, unbridled tribalism and proliferation of weapons gnawed at what was left of the state.[17] Ultimately, in the parlance of Alex de Waal's political-marketplace analysis of contemporary Somalia, "the price of loyalty went up" on Siad Barre, debilitating his "security rentier kleptocracy."[18] The country imploded when none of his quarreling, armed opponents in the civil war or foreign interveners could afford to enter, or stay for long, in that marketplace to keep it together.

Ebbing and flowing since the late 1970s and throughout the 1980s, opposition to the Siad Barre government took many forms that largely reinforced the regime's tribalization of the Somali society. Prominent armed opposition included, chronologically, the Somali Salvation Democratic Front (SSDF) based in the northeast and among the Mejerten sub-clan of the Darod, the Somali National Movement (SNM) based in the country's northwest among the Issaq clan of present-day Somaliland, and the United Somali Congress (USC) based in central Somalia and composed of members of the Hawiye clan. None proved strong enough to overthrow the regime on their own until regional and global configurations changed. At the same time that the two decades of domestic mismanagement and abuse reached their limits, the end of the Cold War abruptly ended the foreign support that had sustained the government.[19] What remained of the postcolonial state edifice unraveled shortly afterwards in January 1991 on the throes of the destructive fratricidal war that Lidwien Kapteijns has characterized as "Clan

---

[17] There is a sizeable corpus of excellent scholarship on Somalia's troubles since independence. For a sample, see I. M. Lewis, *A Modern History of the Somali: Nation and State in the Horn of Africa*, 4th ed. (Athens: Ohio University Press, 2002); Ahmed I. Samatar, *Socialist Somalia: Rhetoric and Reality* (London: Zed Books, 1988); Abdi I. Samatar, *The State and Rural Transformation in Northern Somalia, 1884–1986* (Madison: University of Wisconsin Press, 1989); Said S. Samatar, *Somalia: A Nation in Turmoil* (London: Minority Rights Group, 1991); Afyare Abdi Elmi, *Understanding the Somalia Conflagration: Identities, Political Islam and Peacebuilding* (New York: Pluto Press, 2010); Mark Bradbury, *Becoming Somaliland* (London: Progressio, 2008); and Lidwien Kapteijns, *Clan Cleansing in Somalia: The Ruinous Legacy of 1991* (Philadelphia: University of Pennsylvania Press, 2013).

[18] Alex de Waal, *The Real Politics of the Horn of Africa: Money, War and the Business of Power* (Chichester: Polity Press, 2015), 111, 113.

[19] Elizabeth Schmidt, *Foreign Intervention in Africa: From the Cold War to the War on Terror* (Cambridge: Cambridge University Press, 2013); Okbazghi Yohannes, *The United States and the Horn of Africa: An Analytical Study of Pattern and Process* (Boulder, CO: Westview Press, 1997); Peter J. Schraeder, "US Foreign Policy in an Altered Cold War Environment," *Middle East Journal* 46 (Autumn 1992), 571–593.

Cleansing,"[20] in which entire groups of people were otherized along clan lines and made into an enemy to be eliminated.[21]

Wars and perennial search for water and pasture had long dictated the mobility of the largely pastoral, nomadic Somalis and accordingly influenced their habitation across the country, although the major Somali clan-families have specific territories they call their own. Several other historic factors spurred movements of people that rendered the contours of Somali human geography complex.[22] The fact that Somali coastal towns – from Zeila, Berbera, Mogadishu and Marka down to the Swahili coast – were integral parts of the vibrant Indian Ocean world meant that diverse nomadic and farming communities came to supply these port towns with their food needs and to gradually settle in or near them.[23] European colonialism (and concomitant capitalist modes of exploitation and militarist control) caused its share of population movements and settlements. "By the beginning of the twentieth century," wrote Lee Cassanelli,

pastoral migration, uneven demographic growth, and political conflict has led to the dispersal of the components of these clan-families throughout the [Somali] Peninsula. Thus segments of the Daarood, the largest clan-family, could be found spread from the northeast tip of the Horn to the western Ogaadeen, and from the Gulf of Aden coast to the wells of Wajir in northern Kenya. The Hawiyya, though concentrated in the central plains and eastern coastal regions of the Peninsula, were represented by clans that had made their way to pastures west of the Jubba River . . .[24]

---

[20] For details of the valorization of some clansmen in spite of their previous loyalty to the Barre dictatorship and the targeting of others, who even actively opposed the Barre regime, because of their roots in different clans, see Kapteijns, *Clan Cleansing in Somalia*, 132–146.

[21] Kapteijns (*Clan Cleansing in Somalia*, 73–75) is, nonetheless, careful to not take these clan identities as fixed and unproblematic referents of the Somali society. Lee Cassanelli offers another compelling perspective in which the declared clan identities of the actors (and their victims) during the post-Barre conflicts were no more than a camouflage for their crude endeavor to "gain access to productive land, port facilities, and urban real estate, which in turn could be used to sustain networks of patronage and support." See Lee V. Cassanelli, "Explaining the Somali Crisis" in *The Struggle for Land in Southern Somalia: The War behind the War*, Catherine Besteman and Lee V. Cassanelli (eds.) (London: Westview Press, 1996), 13–26 [here 15].

[22] Lewis, *A Modern History of the Somali*, Chapters 1 and 2 offer an overview of this long history.

[23] Lee V. Cassanelli, *The Shaping of Somali Society: Reconstructing the History of a Pastoral People, 1600–1900* (Philadelphia: University of Pennsylvania Press, 1982), 27; Edward A. Alpers, *East Africa and the Indian Ocean* (Princeton: Markus Wiener, 2009); Alpers, *The Indian Ocean in World History* (Oxford and New York: Oxford University Press, 2014); Michael Pearson, *The Indian Ocean* (London and New York: Routledge, 2003).

[24] Cassanelli, *The Shaping of Somali Society*, 17–19. In the second chapter of his book (38–83), Cassanelli offers an expanded treatment of these dynamics.

Finally, following independence, many Somalis left their hamlets, villages and smaller towns, and flocked to the big towns, especially the capital Mogadishu, in pursuit of better opportunities – business, education, careers, salaried jobs, et cetera.

Although the formation of the Somali nation–state in 1960 defied clan differences and the colonial imposition of arbitrary divisions of the Somali people, the fast-decaying state reified those cleavages and, during its final decade, lived off actively pitting them against each other.[25] Those opposing the Siad Barre dictatorship largely emulated its clan parochialism. In the wake of the dictator's flight, rival political camps clashed head-on in Mogadishu and quickly slipped into the old Bedouin adage: "I against my brother; my brother and I against my cousin; my brother, my cousin and I against the world." Clan and individual militias proliferated, each fending for itself or claiming to be doing so, reducing the cosmopolitan national capital into heavily fought-over blocks of clan and sub-clan territories.[26] Residents hailing from "other" clans were chased out and flocked to "their" clan territories, where they found relative safety buttressed by fledgling political formations. Northern rebel movements carved out such clan territories and prioritized the consolidation of their hold in their respective home turfs over fighting for the control of the seat of central government in Mogadishu.[27]

In May 1991, SNM announced the annulment of the 1960 union between Somaliland and the former Italian Somalia, and unilaterally declared Somaliland independent. Clan elders and traditional leaders jumped in to aid SNM's sluggish progress in state formation. Somaliland has since been making steady progress in its administrative structures, proper functioning of the state, and provision of basic services such as security in spite of its many challenges.[28] The strides that it made, especially the role of traditional leaders and elders, was a template that Puntland later followed, although its political goal fell short of the pursuit of unilateral independence.

---

[25] For a critical firsthand account of highest-level political dynamics of Somalia, see former Prime Minister Abdirazak Haji Hussein's memoir: Abdisalam Issa-Salwe (ed.), *Abdirazak Haji Hussein: My Role in the Foundation of the Somali Nation-State, a Political Memoir* (Trenton, NJ: Africa World Press, 2017).

[26] For a critical examination of the categories of actors, see Roland Marchal, "Warlordism and Terrorism: How to Obscure an Already Confusing Crisis? The Case of Somalia," *International Affairs*, vol. 83, no. 6 (November 2007): 1091–1106. For a broader reading on the tragic turn that Somalia took in the 1990s, see among others: Elmi, *Understanding the Somalia Conflagration*; Bradbury, *Becoming Somaliland*; Kapteijns, *Clan Cleansing in Somalia*.

[27] Kapteijns, *Clan Cleansing in Somalia*.

[28] Lewis, *A Modern History of the Somali*, 282–286; Bradbury, *Becoming Somaliland*.

As soon as SSDF wrested control over what, seven years later, became Puntland, the region that was least affected by the turmoil suddenly faced two major challenges. The Islamist Al-Itihad Al-Islami briefly controlled the port city and commercial capital of Bosaso in 1992, and apprehended SSDF leaders. Not long after an up-swell of grassroots resistance overcame Al-Itihad, a contest over the control of the multi-clan Mudug region erupted with the town of Galkayo at the center of it. That conflict pitted the USC and its allied Habar Gidir sub-clan of the Hawiye against the SSDF-led Mejerten sub-clans of the Darod.[29] Although SSDF forces under Colonel Abdullahi Yusuf prevailed over General Mohamed Farah Aideed's USC forces, the two settled in 1993 on splitting the city of Galkayo and the region of Mudug along a north-south axis with the Mejerten in the north and the Habar Gidir in the south.[30]

As the intensifying civil war in south and central Somalia caused the flight of targeted clan "outsiders" and the displacement of minority groups, the relative peace and stability that ensued in Puntland attracted many of the uprooted because it offered succor to some of the internally displaced minority groups. Those who had originally migrated from Puntland or only had clan ties with the groups there found safety "back home" among their clan folk. In spite of the slow-forming administration and policing functions of SSDF, the overall conditions in Puntland following Siad Barre's overthrow also attracted many of the Puntland diaspora back. The knowhow, entrepreneurship, labor and opportunities that existed on the ground in Puntland combined with the professional skills, investment capital, and entrepreneurship of the newly arrived-cum-returned helped jumpstart basic services and local businesses mushroomed. The fishing sector especially thrived in Puntland following the collapse of the central government in Mogadishu. Before the end of the 1990s, there emerged dozens of jointly or individually owned private fishing companies.

By contrast, the rest of Somalia (southwards from southern Mudug) persisted in vicious cycles of conflict and several false starts at state formation. In central Somalia, until the formation of Central Regions State as a federal unit in 2014, clan and sub-clan disputes over access to water and pasture, among many other reasons, and Islamist insurgents and Islamist counterinsurgents had held back any meaningful state formation. In 2006, south Mudug and Galgadud provinces formed the state

[29] Axmed Yusuf Farah, "Somalia: Modern History and the End of the 1990s," in WSP Somali Programme, *Rebuilding Somalia: Issues and Possibilities for Puntland* (London: HAAN Associates, 2001), 12–17; Lewis, *A Modern History of the Somali*, 286–290.
[30] PDRC, *Dialogue for Peace: Peacemaking at the Crossroads. Consolidation of the 1993 Mudug Peace Agreement* (Interpeace, September 2006).

of Galmudug with south Galkayo their capital. Two years later Himan and Heeb declared statehood with a capital at Adado further west. With rival Islamist forces of the moderate Ahlu Sunna Wal Al-Jamaa and radical Al-Shabaab vying for control of some of their territories, neither of these self-declared states nor the successive national governments in Mogadishu exercised any semblance of effective authority. Feuding individuals and groups brought their cases to clan and religious leaders for adjudication in both regions as in most part of the rest of the country. Ransom pirates operated in Hobyo-Haradere with little-to-no interference from the Galmudug authorities; and many took their loot to the inland town of Adado and splurged without the restraining effect of the Himan and Heeb authorities. In fact, some leaders of both these aspiring states were implicated in the illicit activities, including piracy that afflicted their regions.[31]

In tandem with such a long succession of self-inflicted destruction, conflicts and paralyzing rivalry on land, foreign actors – with and without Somali partners – descended on Somalia's waters and plundered its marine resources. With the central government non-existent, regional authorities were unable to secure their waters from foreign plunderers or to regulate its local use. In the early 1990s, former coast guards joined vigilante fishermen and, with SSDF's green light, fought off foreign vessels illegally fishing in Puntland waters.[32]

That organized effort, which also fought against local maritime criminality, was short-lived due to paralyzing divisions within SSDF that also briefly stalled its state-formation endeavors. By 1994, two factions of SSDF emerged into the open (one under its military commander Yusuf and another around the former police chief General Mohamed Abshir, who was the formal SSDF Chairman); on at least one occasion, they were involved in a gunfight. The active role of the traditional leaders helped SSDF get the state-formation process back on track; that, with the enduring role of Yusuf, ushered in the autonomous Puntland State of Somalia in August 1998, becoming a template for the future reorganization of the country.

SSDF formed a government on the basis of fluid power-sharing among the sub-clans that until now had hamstrung effective governance due to

---

[31] President Mohamed Adan "Tiiceey" of Himan and Heeb, for example, joined Afweyne, when Belgian police lured them into traveling to Brussels in late 2013 in order to purportedly consult on a film. They were both arrested on arrival and sentenced to prison terms. See Laura Yuen, "Former Minnesotan Arrested on Suspicion of Assisting Pirate Ringleader," *MPRNews*, 23 October 2013: https://www.mprnews.org/story/2013/10/23/mohamed-aden-arrested-belgium.

[32] Conversations with Abdiwahid Mohamed Hersi Jo'ar (Bosaso, Hargeisa and Garowe between 2012 and 2017) and interview with Lieutenant Colonel Abdirizak Ismail Hassan (26 and 27 February 2012, Galkayo).

the need to maintain clan balance over the capacity of the office holders. Moreover, nepotistic award of lucrative tasks and widespread irregularities in the administrations of security and finance held Puntland back – especially when compared to the strides that Somaliland made. Whereas some powerful businessmen were granted privileged fishing rights, clan and political loyalties dictated the award of maritime security tasks to private companies. These and subsequent measures by successor administrations neither combated the scourge of illegal fishing, contained local maritime criminality, nor averted the threat of maritime predation (both defensive and criminal) from spiraling to full-fledged predatory piracy.

Out-and-out predatory pirates took advantage of the grievances of local fishermen and camouflaged their selfish criminality behind the local communities' violent reactions against foreign fishers. The outside world's disinterest in the resource pirates and indiscriminate treatment of the defensive and ransom piracies spurred the local communities' "indignant attitudes toward the world's concern with ransom piracy."[33] In 2011, Mogadishu-based parliamentarians even rejected external pressure to criminalize piracy and enact an antipiracy law because they believed that the international community had granted foreign IUU fishers free rein while demanding that Somali authorities contain local responses against them.[34] In the end, concerted domestic and foreign pressure, combined with spiraling negative consequences of piracy on the ground, swayed nearly all Somali political actors to get on board with local and international antipiracy endeavors.

The Landscape of the Scholarly and Policy Literature

Scholars have broadly identified the factors that cause – or contribute to – the emergence of piracy and make pirate operations possible.[35] Without

---

[33] Samatar, Lindberg and Mahayni, "The Dialectics of Piracy in Somalia," 1387.

[34] "Somalia Parliament Rejects Anti-Piracy Legislation," 19 January 2011: http://jurist.org/paperchase/2011/01/somalia-parliament-rejects-anti-piracy-legislation.php; "Somalia: Parliamentarians Accuse Foreign Warships of Supporting Pirates," 19 January 2011: http://allafrica.com/stories/201101190499.html

[35] Jon Vagg, "Rough Seas? Contemporary Piracy in Southeast Asia," *British Journal of Criminology* vol. 35 no. 1 (Winter 1995), 63–80; Carolin Liss, "Maritime Piracy in Southeast Asia," *Southeast Asian Affairs*, vol. 2003: 52–68; Donna Nincic, "State Failure and the Re-Emergence of Maritime Piracy," presented at the 49th Annual Convention of the International Studies Association, 26–29 March 2008, San Francisco, CA. Reproduced as "Statskollaps og sjørøveriets tilbakekomst." *Internasjonal Politikk* 67(1) (January 2009). "Piracy," wrote Murphy for his part, "is only sustainable in places that offer a combination of rewarding hunting grounds, acceptable level of risk and proximate safe havens." See Murphy, *Small Boats, Weak States, Dirty Money: Piracy and Maritime Terrorism in the Modern World* (London: Hurst & Company, 2010), 30.

dismissing the significance of objective conditions to the emergence of piracy, Samatar, Lindberg and Mahayni offered a synthesis of what they called the "'predations-resistance' frame," in which modern-day piracy is attributed to poverty, joblessness, provocative contrasts between the pirates' impoverishment and the plenty surrounding them, and resource theft by the state and corporations that spur local resistance.[36] Within these two frameworks, there is a general consensus among experts on Somalia and the broader Indian Ocean region that, unlike the stealing of shipwrecked cargo in the nineteenth century, the predatory initiatives and thieving intentions of modern-day piracy are new in the Somali scene.[37] The fact that the term *burcad badeed*, the Somali phrase for piracy that literally means "bandits of the sea," entered the lexicons of daily Somali life no more than two decades ago is indicative of piracy's recent advent into the country's conflict-ridden political economy.[38] Nevertheless, the nature, timing, effects and remedies of this two-decade-old Somali phenomenon are disputed in the current scholarly literature, policy works, and journalist reporting.

Different scholars and analysts vaguely imputed piracy in Somalia to a permissive cultural environment that – among other factors – enabled the criminal enterprise to thrive. Whereas many have left such claims veiled,[39] Donna Nincic elaborated on the notion of "cultural acceptance" of piracy as occurring in African settings "when respect for state authority is low, and citizens turn their loyalties toward those who are better able to provide for them, be they other legitimate social actors . . . or criminal groups."[40]

Others have variously drawn direct links between piracy and state collapse.[41] Murphy reiterated the contention that piracy in Somalia emerged out of the civil war when new war elites "came gradually to realize that what worked so well for them on land, kidnapping and

---

[36] Samatar, Lindberg and Mahayni, "The Dialectics of Piracy in Somalia," 1378–1379, offer a concise synopsis of these and other scholarly explanations for the emergence of piracy.

[37] See Alpers, "Piracy and the Indian Ocean;" and Schnepel, "Piracy in the Indian Ocean (ca. 1680–1750)." Also see Stig Jarle Hansen, *Piracy in the Greater Gulf of Aden: Myths, Misconceptions and Remedies* (Norwegian Institute for Urban and Regional Research, NIBR Report 29, 2009), 10.

[38] Numerous elderly interviewees have indicated that the term appeared after the state collapse, coined for specific reference to maritime outlaws.

[39] For example, Pham, "The Failed State and Regional Dimensions of Somali Piracy," 42–43.

[40] Nincic, "State Failure and the Re-Emergence of Maritime Piracy."

[41] Menkhaus, "Dangerous Waters," 23; Jatin Dua and Ken Menkhaus, "The Context of Contemporary Piracy," *Journal of International Criminal Justice* 10 (2012), 749–766, [here 758–759].

extortion in particular, could work for them equally well, if not better, at sea" because the maritime targets were larger in number and worth more.[42] The United Nations Security Council (UNSC) similarly traced piracy to the still-ongoing instability in Somalia.[43] Just as the causes of piracy were deemed to have been found on land, so too were the solutions.[44] An array of experts of security studies and/or with security backgrounds took this point farther by locating the solution to piracy in the restoration of the Somali state.[45]

Nevertheless, the fact that piracy remained very minimal throughout the 1990s has puzzled observers and analysts of Somalia and piracy. Menkhaus himself pondered why it took more than a decade and a half of statelessness and chaos for piracy to explode when "the basic act of piracy is surprisingly low-tech, and could have been achieved at any point since 1991."[46] A leading scholar of maritime affairs and contemporary piracy in Africa, Nincic located the answer to the puzzle in the fact that state failure was not a sufficient condition for piracy, merely a necessary one.[47]

What then contributed to – or took advantage of – this insufficient but necessary condition and ushered in the epic piracy phenomenon? As previously noted, some experts and commentators have blamed the nexus between hazardous waste dumping and IUU fishing, and regarded piracy and pirates – at least in their earliest manifestations – as driven by legitimate grievances against these corporate crimes.[48] Samatar, Lindberg and Mahayni have argued that Somali grievances were not so much about foreign fishing operations in their waters as they were about

---

[42] Murphy, *Somalia: The New Barbary?* 2.

[43] UN Security Council Resolution 1950, S/RES/1950 (2010), 23 November 2010, paragraph 2; UN Security Council Resolution 1976, S/RES/1976 (2011), 11 April 2011, paragraph 2.

[44] Brittany Gilmer, *Political Geographies of Piracy: Constructing Threats and Containing Bodies in Somalia* (New York: Palgrave MacMillan, 2014), 40–41.

[45] Freedom C. Onuoha, "Piracy and Maritime Security off the Horn of Africa: Connections, Causes, and Concerns" *African Security*, 3 (2010): 191–215; Peter Chalk, "Somali Piracy All about Economics," *USA Today*, 10 October 2013: http://www.usatoday.com/story/opinion/2013/10/10/captain-phillips-somali-pirates-column/29623 29/; Kraska, *Contemporary Maritime Piracy: International Law, Strategy and Diplomacy at Sea* (Santa Barbara, CA: Praeger, 2011), 54.

[46] Menkhaus, "Dangerous Waters," 23.

[47] Nincic, "State Failure and the Re-Emergence of Maritime Piracy."

[48] Mahdi Gedi Qayad, "Assessment Mission to Somalia in Connection with Alleged Dumping of Hazardous Substances," 10 May 10–8 June 1997; Kulmiye, "Militia vs Trawlers;" United Nations, Somalia Monitoring Group (Report), S/2008/769, 10 December 2008, Paragraph 125; Mohamed Abshir Waldo, "The Two Piracies in Somalia;" U. Rashid Sumaila and Mahamudu Bawumia, "Fisheries, Ecosystem Justice and Piracy: A Case Study of Somalia," *Fisheries Research* 157 (2014): 154–163.

the moral economic consequences of their theft of resources without regard to local livelihoods.[49]

Others have rejected grievance and legitimate defense as genuine impetuses for piracy and held the latter to be nothing more than greed-driven criminality that took advantage of available opportunities (location, ships, government vacuum and absence of rule-of-law, poverty, et cetera).[50] Industry estimates of the staggering global economic costs of piracy in general and piracy in Somalia in particular (including aggregates of estimated ransoms) helped ingrain greed as a – if not *the* – principal driver behind Somali piracy.[51]

The presumed ubiquity among Somalis of the benefits of piracy reinforced assertions about the centrality of its profit motive to piracy in Somalia,[52] notwithstanding the incalculable local damages that the criminal enterprise caused. In a 2012 Chatham House report evocatively titled "Treasure Mapped," Anja Shortland argued that piracy had "a large interest group behind its continuation" because "pirate incomes have widespread and significant positive impacts on the Somali economy."[53]

---

[49] Samatar, Lindberg and Mahayni, "The Dialectics of Piracy in Somalia," 1389: "It is not that Somalis are objecting to non-Somalis fishing in their waters; rather, because the loot of the fish pirates has been on such an egregious scale, they are objecting to the fact that it endangers their livelihoods. In the language of the moral economy it is not the exploitation of the fisheries per se that offended Somalis but resource pirates' callous ransacking of resources without consideration of the livelihood needs of the local population that triggered the attack on foreign fishing trawlers."

[50] For a representative sample, see Hansen, *Piracy in the Greater Gulf of Aden*, 10; Hansen, "The Dynamics of Somali Piracy," *Studies in Conflict and Terrorism*, 35, 7–8 (2012): 523–530; Chalk, "Somali Piracy All about Economics," *USA Today*, 10 October 2013: http://www.usatoday.com/story/opinion/2013/10/10/captain-phillips-somali-pirates-column/2962329/. J. Pham, "Putting Puntland's Potential into Play," *World Defense Review*, 24 September 2009; Kraska, "Freakonomics of Maritime Piracy," *Brown Journal of World Affairs*, Vol. XVI, Issue II (Spring/Summer 2010), 109–119.

[51] Anna Bowden et al., *The Economic Cost of Maritime Piracy, 2010*, One Earth Future Working Paper, December 2010: http://oceansbeyondpiracy.org/sites/default/files/attachments/The%20Economic%20Cost%20of%20Piracy%20Full%20Report.pdf; Geopolicity, "The Economics of Piracy: Pirates Ransoms and Livelihoods off the Coast of Somalia," May 2011: http://oceansbeyondpiracy.org/sites/default/files/geopolicity_-_the_economics_of_piracy_-_pirates__livelihoods_off_the_coast_of_somalia.pdf; Anna Bowden and Shikha Basnet, *The Economic Cost of Somali Piracy 2011*, One Earth Future Foundation Working Paper: http://oceansbeyondpiracy.org/sites/default/files/economic_cost_of_piracy_2011.pdf; Jonathan Bellish, *The Economic Cost of Somali Piracy 2012*, One Earth Future Foundation Working Paper: http://oceansbeyondpiracy.org/sites/default/files/attachments/View%20Full%20Report_3.pdf.

[52] Kaija Hurlburt, *The Human Cost of Somali Piracy*, One Earth Future Foundation, June 2011, 24–26: http://oceansbeyondpiracy.org/sites/default/files/human_cost_of_somali_piracy.pdf.

[53] Anja Shortland, "Treasure Mapped: Using Satellite Imagery to Track the Developmental Effects of Somalia Piracy" (Chatham House Africa Programme Paper: AFP PP 2012/01), 3, 9.

According to Shortland, piracy "offset the loss of purchasing power of local wages after the 2007/2008 food price shocks"[54] because pirates purportedly provided "local governance and stability, the side-effect of which has been to help other entrepreneurs to trade more easily."[55] In spite of its innovative methodology, such sweeping claims could not have been more wrong, as earlier works had shown.

In early 2011, the UN Secretary-General's legal advisor on piracy, Jack Lang, had reported how piracy was depriving the affected areas of "job-creating investments in a context of widespread insecurity, and the destructive effect of piracy on Somali society which creates a vicious circle."[56] The current book builds on Lang's findings to show that the vast majority of Somalis suffered because of piracy in spite of staggering sums of ransom money that the pirates collected and contrary to widespread claims that Somalis benefited as a result. Even though the negative consequences of piracy, as a criminal enterprise, were not immediately felt, it became the proverbial last straw that broke the camel's back in terms of worsening the communities' economic and security conditions. As a result, the affected local communities organized counter-piracy campaigns at the same rate that they mobilized to confront foreign illegal fishers. Their campaigns, coordinated with the limited security measures of local administrations, took time to gain momentum and traction but proved effective, however precarious their successes.

Methodology

Consistent with the near consensus among scholars of the Indian Ocean world that maritime phenomena are shaped by what happens on land as much as the other way around, Michael Pearson emphasized the "needs to be amphibious, moving easily between land and sea" when accounting for events in the maritime arena.[57] Explaining Somali piracy accordingly will have to balance the relevant overland and maritime developments and become amphibious.[58] While making utmost use of the available secondary literature and policy work, this project relied on primary

---

[54] Shortland, "Treasure Mapped," 3.
[55] Shortland, "Treasure Mapped," 7. Also see The World Bank, "The Pirates of Somalia: Ending the Threat, Rebuilding a Nation," (2013), 27.
[56] Jack Lang, *Report of the Special Adviser to the Secretary-General on Legal Issues Related to Piracy off the Coast of Somalia* (January 2011), 14.
[57] Pearson, *The Indian Ocean*, 5.
[58] Kraska, for his part, posits that much as the conditions on land are important in determining what happens in the nearby waters, and "although piracy emerges from the land, its effects reverberate throughout the seas." See Kraska, *Contemporary Maritime Piracy*, 2.

research in the field in Somalia – among the licit and illicit seafarers (fishermen and pirates) as much as the townspeople and security personnel.

This book draws particularly heavily from: local Somali voices through open-ended individual interviews with largely reliable oral informants; ethnographic and participatory-action research involving groups of elders, youth, women and professionals; and different sets of surveys randomly administered among young Somali men and women in Puntland's three major towns of Garowe, Galkayo and Bosaso.[59] In total, I sat with close to a hundred interviewees; I held more than ten focus group meetings involving at least three resourceful individuals at a time (young, elderly, men, women, professionals, unemployed, former pirates, non-pirates, religious or traditional authorities, and government officials); and I consulted informally with numerous others across Somalia and beyond.

An affiliation with the Nairobi-based regional office of the International Peace-Building Alliance (Interpeace) made travels to the Somali region possible and offered the opportunity for mutually beneficial partnerships with local Somali institutions – mainly with the Peace and Development Research Center (PDRC) in Puntland and to a small degree with the Academy for Peace and Development (APD) in Somaliland. PDRC researchers helped facilitate nearly all focus group meetings and many of the one-to-one interviews across Puntland with the expressly stated purpose of informing my research. With the exception of a few known pirate linchpins, who demanded cash in return for information, all of the participants in this research, including former pirate kingpins and/or financiers, neither asked for nor received money for their information.

Since an exploratory trip in the summer of 2011, I traveled to the Somali region more than a half dozen times, spending between two and ten weeks in the field on each leg. I especially flew into Puntland and Somaliland, and traveled extensively by road in the former. With the exception of my 2016 and 2017 trips when I traveled alone with an assistant and/or interlocutor, I greatly benefited from my travels and collaboration with PDRC's Mobile Audiovisual Unit that campaigned against piracy through grassroots awareness-raising in many of the affected areas – from Bosaso to Gara'ad. During these travels that

---

[59] Between late January and early March 2012, I prepared and administered three different basic surveys: 1) to gauge youths' perceptions about piracy, 2) to assess the relationship between khat vendors and the piracy phenomenon, and 3) to gather women's views and experiences with piracy. The original questions were translated to Somali and back to English for accuracy and administered in times and areas deemed to be safe, as in schools (high schools and colleges), workshops, and peaceful places where youth gather.

stretched over a six-year period, I held more than a hundred structured and unstructured, formal and informal consultations (individual interviews and focus group meetings) with Somalis from different walks of life and of different ages and roles in their respective communities; I observed many pirates and pirate-associates splurge while some were more restrained. As exhilarating as that experience was, it was not without its challenges and hazards, which is a subject for future reflection.

I presented myself to my Somali research participants as a storyteller and not as a judge of their stories, all the while cross-examining what I heard in a bid to avoid imbibing everything told to me. My colleagues, assistants and I devised participant-action research and observed rural coastal communities and their urban counterparts during their day-to-day routines and deliberations over issues relevant to my research. We probed elderly and young fishermen about their story lines, cross-checked with existing data, and came back with more questions. We challenged pirates on the criminality of their trade and government officials about corruption and complicity in related criminal acts.

Amplifying previously unheard voices and taking dominant narratives to task flows from justifiable confidence in one's material. That power of personal conviction demanded that I not shy away, accepting simple or simplistic answers, but probe sketchy stories and untenable narratives. The vast majority of my project's research participants afforded me as much courtesy as my local assistants and colleagues (from PDRC and non-PDRC) supported and challenged me at the same time. My colleagues compelled me to raise hard questions and to probe for honest details while the participants tolerated my doing so. The fact that the vast majority of my assistants, colleagues and interviewees did not question my intentions – and many actively supported my project – ensured my physical safety and the completion of my project in its current form.

This book also makes good use of the burgeoning scholarship, policy works, and publicly available industry and intelligence reports on piracy. Piracy has attracted a new cadre of thematic scholars and analysts with established Somalia scholars addressing the phenomenon within a broader context of their scholarship on the country. Think tanks, international organizations, and local and regional organizations have also variously produced or commissioned relevant policy reports on the topic. By far the most extensive and variable reporting and examination of piracy cases used in this book came from two entities: first the United Nations Security Council-sanctioned Somalia and Eritrea Monitoring Group (SEMG) and the International Chamber of Commerce's Kuala

Lumpur-based International Maritime Bureau (IMB)–Piracy Reporting Center.[60]

In spite of many substantive errors and methodological flaws in its voluminous reports, SEMG offers as reliable analysis and data of salient cases of piracy as is possible for a fluid, fast-moving phenomenon. Likewise, IMB–Piracy Reporting Center's monitoring of global maritime incidents offers extensive reporting on piracy off the coast of Somalia and serves as an important jumping-off point for statistical data, although IMB-PRC is not known for crosschecking signals from ships or correcting for false alarms. Others include the Colorado-based Oceans Beyond Piracy project that has, since 2010, continued to produce useful substantive and analytical reports annually on different aspects of the maritime phenomenon, and has commissioned additional substantive reports and publications. Managed by Robert Young Pelton with funding from Blackwater founder Erik Prince, the open-source intelligence outlet, *SomaliaReport*, also provides uniquely reliable reports and piercing analysis of both piracy and the evolving context within which it operates.[61] Through an integrated analysis of these disparate resources, the chapters of this book offer a unique window into the broader context, inner dynamics and local consequences of piracy off the coast of Somalia.

Layout of the Current Book

The book is divided into three chronological chapters and two thematic ones (one on local effects and responses, and another on international counter-piracy). Following the temporal sequence of developments, some names and events/processes appear in multiple chapters as they progress across time, which has caused some overlapping, slight repetitions, and some inevitable going back and forth. Although the thrust of the book revolves around specific developments during the two decades (from the 1990s to the 2010s) that followed the collapse of the central

---

[60] The International Maritime Organization (IMO) also produces regular reports on piracy, but for purposes of consistency and convenience the data in this book comes from IMB-PRC.

[61] Ian Shapira, "Blackwater Founder Erik Prince Goes to War against a Former Business Partner," *The Washington Post*, 1 January 2015: https://www.washingtonpost.com/local/bl ackwater-founder-erik-prince-goes-to-war-against-a-former-business-partner/2015/01/01 /23385e8a-6f39-11e4-893f-86bd390a3340_story.html?utm_term=.f7a8712056c8;   Ian Shapira, "Blackwater Founder Erik Prince Prevails in Legal Battle with Ex-business Partner," *The Washington Post*, 8 December 2017: https://www.washingtonpost.com/loca l/blackwater-founder-erik-prince-prevails-in-legal-battle-with-ex-business-partner/2017/1 2/08/e0f3d26a-dbc9-11e7-a841-2066faf731ef_story.html?utm_term=.72ea5487b63b.

Somali government, it selectively goes back in time in order to offer adequate background where necessary and to hone its analysis. With that in mind, the first chapter examines the role that waste dumping and IUU fishing, along with local partners and enablers, played in precipitating and perpetuating the causes of piracy off the coast of Somalia. It does so against the backdrop of a short history of Somali modern fisheries and of a Somali maritime legal framework that – however weak and ultimately dysfunctional – pivoted around African and international legal-normative evolution.

The second chapter spans from the mid-1990s to the mid-2000s and documents the rise of a lucrative local fisheries sector after the collapse of the central government. It traces the beginnings of local vigilante responses and how the fishermen vigilantes were manipulated by a few unscrupulous business people for criminal and greedy ends, holding vessels and sailors hostage and demanding ransoms for their release. Once ransom piracy took the center stage, it overshadowed its defensive predecessor. By bringing to light the inner mechanics of Somali ransom piracy and examining some of the cases, the third chapter (which covers from 2007 to 2012) documents previously unknown – or little known – details of a few notorious pirate cases, peeling off their glamorous veil and showing them for what they truly were, a criminal enterprise full of excesses, lies, deceptions, double crossing, human casualty and material loss.

Chapter 4 offers an extensive account of the widespread deterioration of the local conditions associated with piracy as they are locally perceived and as can be demonstrated based on available data and direct observations. It also documents the local communities' antipiracy initiatives and important gains that the rest of the world either did not notice and appreciate or distrusted and ignored because of negative perceptions about Somalis. The chapter challenges some popular, policy and scholarly points of view that apply a broad brush and either consider Somalis as criminals or as accessories and beneficiaries of the crime of piracy. It demonstrates that Somalis carried a heavy brunt of piracy and that they also faced the negative impact of the presence of foreign antipiracy armada in their waters.

Like the chapter before it, Chapter 5 breaks the chronology by documenting international counter-piracy measures since their inception following the intensification of the predatory enterprise in 2007. This chapter also examines the motives of foreign counter-piracy missions, some of their actions and their local impact. And finally, the conclusion brings the various strands of arguments of the book together to highlight the heightened risk of the return of piracy because of the aggressive resumption of illegal fishing in Somalia. It reiterates that addressing the maritime root causes of piracy, especially IUU fishing, and proper recognition and appropriate support of yet-uncelebrated Somali successes in combating it on land, would help stem the prospects of its future return at sea.

1 Global Root Causes and Local Circumstances of Early Piracy in Somalia

Global history of violence at sea may be as old as maritime navigation itself.[1] And throughout time and geography, different individuals and groups resorted to maritime violence for different reasons.[2] Piracy, on the other hand, is an historically contingent conceptualization of that phenomenon that contemporary international law locates in the high seas and makes a subject of international jurisdiction.[3] As such, piracy off the coast of Somalia can be ruled out – in the parlance of international law – until 2005 when Somali maritime violence started to take place in international waters.[4]

Although Somali maritime predation before 2005 is best cataloged as armed robbery at sea, a mundane criminality subject to national

---

[1] As Martin N. Murphy, *Small Boats, Weak States, Dirty Money. Piracy and Maritime Terrorism in the Modern World* (London: Hurst & Company, 2010), 1, puts it, "when the maritime Abel slipped his boat into the water for the first time, Cain was close behind."

[2] "Most people," wrote James Kraska, "living in seaside communities along the shores of the Adriatic Sea, the Black Sea, and the Mediterranean Sea practiced, either deliberately or in self-defense, what we would consider as 'piracy.'" Kraska, *Contemporary Maritime Piracy: International Law, Strategy and Diplomacy at Sea* (Santa Barbara, CA: Praeger, 2011), 10.

[3] United Nations Convention on the Law of the Sea (UNCLOS), 10 December 1982, Article 101. Leading scholar of maritime law Douglas Guilfoyle, for example, shows that it is only within a composite legal framework that pulls together the 1979 International Convention against the Taking of Hostages, the 1988 Suppression of Unlawful Acts against the Safety of Maritime Navigation (SUA Convention) and other international legal conventions and jurisprudence that Somali maritime predation and hostage-taking are best captured and not under the 1958 High Seas Convention or UNCLOS of 1982. See Guilfoyle, "International Law and Counter-Piracy in the Indian Ocean," in *Maritime Terrorism and Piracy in the Indian Ocean Region* edited by Awet T. Weldemichael, Patricia Schneider and Andrew C. Winner (London and New York: Routledge, 2015), 96–112. For additional accessible exposition of the international legal framework on piracy across time, also see Kraska, *Contemporary Maritime Piracy*, 105–137.

[4] The International Maritime Bureau (IMB) reported in 2005 that Somali pirate attacks were reported as far as 400 nautical miles offshore and advised ships that are not sailing to Somalia to stay at least 200 nautical miles away from the Somali coast. ICC International Maritime Bureau, "Piracy and Armed Robbery against Ships: Annual Report, 1 January – 31 December 2005," 15.

jurisdiction akin to armed robbery in city streets, the collapse of the state made such a clear-cut position untenable. The consequent government vacuum in an otherwise globally strategic waterway that demanded concerted international attention and effort rendered piracy a global security issue and latterly a security–development one. More accurately, as Brittany Gilmer demonstrates, it became a problem of insecurity and underdevelopment.[5] The indiscriminate branding of Somali maritime violence as piracy is, however, symptomatic of the hegemony of the powerful to label its target – legitimately or not.[6] Because all forms of Somali maritime predation have thus become synonymous with piracy, it is convenient for purposes of this book to use the International Maritime Bureau's functional definition: "An act of boarding or attempting to board any ship with the apparent intent to commit theft or any other crime and with the apparent intent or capacity to use force in the furtherance of that act."[7]

This chapter lays the broader structural challenges of global waste dumping and of illegal, unregulated and unreported fishing and it documents the phenomena in Somalia. These violations constitute the external root causes of piracy, perpetrated by corporate actors with the active or passive complicity of states – in their home countries and/or countries serving as staging and landing bases closer to their target dumping and fishing grounds. In order to fully appreciate their significance, this chapter analyzes the modern history of Somali fisheries up until the implosion of the central government and examines the subsequent local conditions and actors that helped perpetuate the externally driven violations before the advent of piracy and throughout the piracy years.

The Nexus between Waste Dumping and IUU Fishing

The international crimes of toxic waste dumping and illegal, unreported and unregulated (IUU) fishing are not unique to Somalia or even to

---

[5] Gilmer, *Political Geographies of Piracy*, 33–35.

[6] Newer and emerging Western powers have historically used trumped up or exaggerated claims of local piratical attacks to rationalize their use of force against coastal polities and set up bases in areas of their economic and commercial interests. On the Arabian Gulf of the late eighteenth century and early nineteenth century, for example, see Sulṭan Ibn Muḥammad al-Qasimi, *The Myth of Arab Piracy in the Gulf* (London and Dover, NH: Croom Helm, 1986). Jatin Dua similarly relates an interesting case of a nineteenth century Somali leaders, "rulers of Barawa," who branded the British pirates and sought alliance with the Qawasim of Ras al-Khaimah and Sharjah in order to eject them from their waters. See Dua, "A Sea of Trade and a Sea of Fish: Piracy and Protection in the Western Indian Ocean," *Journal of Eastern African Studies* 7, no. 2 (2013): 353–370 [here 353].

[7] ICC International Maritime Bureau, "Piracy and Armed Robbery against Ships: Annual Report, 1 January–31 December 2005," 2.

Africa as a whole. They occur wherever opportunities arise; the weaker a state the more likelihood of their taking place and the more devastating their impact. Taking advantage of Somalia's weakness, waste dumpers rushed in to dispose of hazardous waste in its spaces and IUU fishers pirated its maritime resources.

Waste Dumping

The global challenge of toxic waste emanates from jarring human incapacity to sustainably manage the byproducts of highly industrialized – or fast-industrializing – and wasteful practices. The international community tardily awoke to the hazards of unregulated disposal of such wastes. Until the early 1970s, waste, including radioactive waste, was dumped at sea with limited restrictions.[8] Gradually, international conventions and codes of conduct came to admonish states and non-states alike to adhere to responsible disposal of toxic substances.[9] Nonetheless, negligent disposal of hazardous refuse remains a daunting global challenge, differently affecting countries depending on their governance capacities. To make matters worse, the waste management business has been sufficiently "easy to enter and lucrative to control" for the Mafia and other organized criminal entities.[10]

Southern Italian mafias – namely the Camorra in the region of Campania and the 'Ndrangheta in Calabria – are particularly notorious for irresponsible disposal of hazardous waste in their own regions in Italy as well as overseas. In 1997, a junior Mafia boss confessed to Italian authorities that his branch of the Camorra had dumped tons of toxic waste in the area stretching between Naples and Caserta that polluted the underground water system in the region.[11] Authorities kept the confession secret until 2013, but the associated health hazard triggered public outcry. The US base in Naples was compelled to conduct its own

[8] See Kirsti-Liisa Sjoblom and Gordon Linsley, "Sea Disposal of Radioactive Wastes: The London Convention 1972" *IAEA Bulletin*, 2 (1994), 12–16, available at: https://www.iaea.org/sites/default/files/publications/magazines/bulletin/bull36-2/36205981216.pdf.

[9] United Nations Environmental Program (UNEP), "Basel Convention on the Control of Transboundary Movements of Hazardous Wastes and their Disposal," 22 March 1989. The treaty that entered into force in May 1992 is only one of several similar international agreements.

[10] Michelle Tsai, "Why the Mafia Loves Garbage: Hauling Trash and Organized Crime," *Slate*, 11 January 2008, available at: www.slate.com/articles/news_and_politics/explainer/2008/01/why_the_mafia_loves_garbage.html.

[11] Gianluca di Feo and Claudio Pappaianni, "Bevi Napoli e Poi Muori, l'Inchiesta-Choc Degli USA," *l'Espresso*, 13 November 2013: http://espresso.repubblica.it/inchieste/2013/11/13/news/bevi-napoli-e-poi-muori-1.141086?refresh_ce.

two-phased "Public Health Evaluation" between 2008 and 2009. It released its compelling findings in three volumes between 2010 and 2011.[12] As recent as 2014, Italian authorities were uncovering illicit landfills where all sorts of hazardous waste was buried.[13] The criminal actors were not Italians only. Nor was Italy the only source and destination of waste.

The dumping of radioactive, industrial, medical, and electronic and other waste has been taking place wherever opportunities presented themselves. A joint investigation carried out by UK's *The Independent*, Sky News, and the international environmentalist group Greenpeace uncovered that British e-waste was being shipped to West Africa where there are functional governments. "On the pretext of re-use," an expert told *The Independent*, "equipment which is clearly not suitable for any type of re-use is effectively being dumped in developing countries."[14] Although the UK is considered the highest-per-capita producer of such waste in western Europe, it is not the only source of e-waste dumped in developing countries.

In 2010, EU countries produced 8.6 million tons of electronic waste, 36 percent of which was properly handled. INTERPOL reported that the remaining 5.5 million tons disappeared into "complementary streams."[15] With some 50 million tons of global e-waste generated in 2012 and dumping in poor Third World countries continuing unabated, the problem only got worse with time.[16] Many African countries have been the destination for hazardous radioactive, industrial, hospital, electronic, and other waste generated in advanced countries of the West.[17]

---

[12] United States Navy and Marine Corps Public Health Center, "Naples Public Health Evaluation, Volume III: Public Health Summary," May 2011.

[13] Jim Yardley, "A Mafia Legacy Taints the Earth in Southern Italy," *The New York Times*, 29 January 2014.

[14] Cahal Milmo, "Dumped in Africa: Britain's Toxic Waste: Children Exposed to Poisonous Material in Defiance of UK Law," *The Independent*, 17 February 2009: www .independent.co.uk/news/world/africa/dumped-in-africa-britain8217s-toxic-waste-1624 869.html.

[15] Report of the Secretary-General on the Protection of Somali Natural Resources and Waters, S/2011/611, 25 October 2011, 13, footnote 48.

[16] John Vidal, "Toxic 'E-waste' Dumped in Poor Nations, Says United Nations," *The Guardian*, 14 December 2013: www.theguardian.com/global-development/2013/d ec/14/toxic-ewaste-illegal-dumping-developing-countries.

[17] For a recent overview of waste export (especially e-waste) to Sub-Saharan Africa, see Chukwunonye Ezeah and Jak A. Fazakerley, "Extended Producer Responsibility as a Tool for Managing E-waste in Sub-Saharan Africa: Key Issue," pp. 37–54 in Onyanta Adama and Chidi Nzeadibe (eds.), *Dealing with Waste: Resource Recovery and Entrepreneurship in Informal Solid Waste Management in African Cities* (Trenton, NJ: Africa World Press, 2017).

For more than two decades, Somalia has been a particular locus of such crimes of international corporate greed and the victim of global governance loopholes and neglect. In spite of the secrecy that continues to shroud the details of waste dumping, it is now established that as early as 1992 – possibly even earlier – toxic waste was being disposed of in Somali territorial waters (and undisclosed locations inland).[18] Initially these cases of dumping were reportedly carried out in return for weapons provided to one or the other of the warring factions in Mogadishu. It is believed that waste dumping continued even after any semblance of local partnerships disappeared in the hodgepodge of rival claimants to government power, armed political dissidents, and criminal gangs.[19] It is important to briefly review the little that is known and that has been said and done – or not – in order to show its significance to the piracy story.

According to the Italian chapter of Greenpeace, there is some trail of evidence dating as far back as December 1991 that shows Italian waste-trading companies (some possibly fictitious) and known Swiss financiers making deals to export solid waste to Somalia and to build waste storage facilities there.[20] Upon learning about the deal, the then-outgoing Executive Director of the United Nations Environmental Program (UNEP), Egyptian scientist Mostafa Tolba, blew the whistle in September 1992 and shared some of the signed documents with the media. Whereas UNEP convened an inconclusive meeting with the Italian and Swiss governments that "aimed at stopping millions of tonnes of European toxic waste being dumped in strife-torn Somalia,"[21] only in 1997 did the UN dispatch a consultant, Mahdi Gedi Qayad, on an assessment mission.[22]

Documenting the scattered waste drums and canisters along the Somali coastline, the assessment mission reported how "some Somali fishermen underlined that they sleep and wake with fear, sorrow and unpromising future due to the presence of such unclassified tank in their fishing area." Moreover, "tankers routinely discharge oily waste" in Somali waters with detrimental effects on the marine environment and

---

[18] Debora MacKenzie, "Toxic Waste Adds to Somalia's Woes," *New Scientist*, 19 September 1992; Greenpeace, *The Toxic Ships: The Italian Hub, the Mediterranean Area and Africa* (Greenpeace Italy Report, June 2010), 20–29: https://www.greenpeace.org/italy/Global/italy/report/2010/inquinamento/Report-The-toxic-ship.pdf.

[19] Ibid.   [20] Greenpeace, *The Toxic Ships*, 20–29.

[21] MacKenzie, "Toxic Waste Adds to Somalia's Woes."

[22] The closest anyone had come to discovering the truth about illicit operations (IUU fishing and toxic waste dumping) in exchange for weapons was Ilaria Alpi, the young Italian journalist who was murdered in broad daylight in Mogadishu in 1994. Peter H. Eichstaedt, *Pirate State: Inside Somalia's Terrorism at Sea* (Chicago: Lawrence Hill Books, 2010), 37–44.

resources. UNEP had estimated as early as 1992 that passing ships discharged 33,000 tons of such waste in Somali waters.[23]

As the Qayad report failed to generate any attention, the release of such waste by passing vessels was worsening due to two interrelated factors peculiar to the Gulf of Aden and the western Indian Ocean regions. According to Sam Bateman, a leading expert in maritime safety and security, these factors are the poor quality of many of the ships that sail in those waters, and the lack of waste management facilities in the region's ports. Significantly stricter regimes of Port State Control (PSC) in the developed world have relegated a higher concentration of old, deficient and wasteful ships to waters off the less-developed coastal states with weak or altogether non-existent PSC mechanisms. Not only do these unseaworthy vessels pose significant risk to sailors, ports, and the environment but they also face higher risks of maritime predation.[24]

To make matters worse, until 2007 the countries along the northwestern and western Indian Ocean (including the Gulf of Aden) were unequipped to handle the waste of the vessels that called at their ports.[25] What that meant was that the tens of thousands of ships that annually traversed those waters had nowhere to dispose most of the waste that they generated on a daily basis other than in the water. Whereas the weakness of the countries in the region and the collective ineffectiveness of their PSC regimes may have encouraged the ships to handle such waste irresponsibly, the virtual absence of maritime authorities in Somalia – hence no risk of bearing the consequences – removed any deterrent function that even weak states serve.

Ali Farah Ali, who was a long-serving senior fisheries official in Somalia before the collapse of the government, cautions against foolhardy claims about hazardous waste dumping. He argues that had the waters off the coast of Somalia been polluted by toxic waste, there would not have been parallel escalation of foreign illegal fishing by companies that exported their catch to advanced countries.[26] While logical, this claim assumes that

---

[23] Qayad, "Assessment Mission to Somalia."

[24] Sam Bateman, "Maritime Security and Port State Control in the Indian Ocean Region," in *Maritime Terrorism and Piracy in the Indian Ocean Region*, Awet T. Weldemichael, Patricia Schneider and Andrew C. Winner (eds.), (London and New York: Routledge, 2015), 82–95.

[25] Bateman, "Maritime Security Implication of the International Shipping Recession," *The Australian Journal of Maritime and Ocean Affairs*, 1, no. 4 (December 2009), 109–117.

[26] Conversations with Ali Farah Ali, Garowe, Puntland, 2011–2017. During my fieldwork in Puntland, I partnered with the Puntland Development Research Center (recently renamed as the Peace and Development Research Center), which Ali Farah helped run as a deputy director and then as an acting director. As such, during my travels, I have had the opportunity to hold open and extended conversations with him when he shared his

greedy, foreign IUU fishers are conscientious about such hazards to their end consumers, and it overlooks the fact that they do not typically declare the sources of their catch. Ali Farah does, however, agree that the worst environmental pollution was – and is being – done by the release of ballast water of passing vessels into Somali waters that has left the long coastline filled with tar.

In spite of the fact that ocean currents transport maritime pollution beyond the borders of individual countries, neither the discharging of heaps of ship-generated refuse nor the deliberate dumping of hazardous waste in Somali waters drew sustained attention of the international community. Not until the December 2004 tsunami washed more of the waste canisters up the beaches was toxic waste dumping in Somalia thrust back into public discourse – albeit fleetingly. In the immediate aftermath of the tsunami in Somalia, the international community dispatched investigative missions and released reports that were, at best, inconclusive. UNEP's early 2005 fact-finding mission found out that the tsunami had

stirred up hazardous waste deposits on beaches around North Hobyo and Warsheik, south of Benadir. Contamination from these waste deposits has thus caused health and environmental problems to the surrounding local fishing communities. Many people in Somalia's impacted areas are complaining of unusual health problems including acute respiratory infections, mouth bleeds and skin conditions.[27]

Shortly afterward, in May 2005, another technical fact-finding mission composed of multiple UN agencies spent four days in Puntland, i.e., north and northeast of the locations that UNEP had inspected. Four months later the Nairobi-based highest UN official for Somalia reported back with their findings: "the mission had found no traces of toxic waste from the samples taken in the three coastal locations and tested in Nairobi."[28] According to the same news flash, the Resident/Humanitarian Coordinator pointed out the fact that there existed an urgent need "for a more comprehensive assessment of the natural environment of Somalia, which would include further investigations of alleged toxic waste sites on land, and dumping of toxic waste at sea."

experience and knowledge of the operations of the Somali Ministry of Fisheries and Marine Resources. He also read relevant chapters of this book and offered useful feedback.

[27] United Nations Environmental Program (UNEP), "After the Tsunami: Rapid Environmental Assessment," (2005), 11: https://wedocs.unep.org/bitstream/handle/20 .500.11822/8372/-After%20the%20Tsunami_%20Rapid%20Environmental%20Asses sment-20053636.pdf?sequence=3&isAllowed=y.

[28] "Somalia: UN Mission to Puntland on Toxic Waste in the Coastal Areas of Somalia," 7 October 2005: http://reliefweb.int/node/186918.

In mid-2008, UN Special Envoy for Somalia Ahmedou Ould Abdallah blew the whistle yet again on illegal fishing and toxic waste dumping off the Somali coast. Convinced that "there is dumping of solid waste, chemicals and probably nuclear" waste and that it was "a disaster (for) the Somali environment, the Somali population," the Mauritanian diplomat claims to have asked international NGOs to investigate, to no avail.[29]

Only in 2011 did the UN Security Council take public notice of this matter. On 11 April 2011, the Security Council demanded an investigation into why "allegations of illegal fishing and dumping of toxic waste in Somali waters have been used by pirates in an attempt to justify their criminal activities."[30] Seven months later, the Secretary-General responded with a report that reviewed the allegations against the backdrop of existing conventions and prohibitions. The report concluded that "prevailing security and resource constraints have limited a thorough examination of the evidence" and that "more robust investigations need[ed] to be carried out" in order to ascertain the allegation.[31]

Such recycling of reports, hesitant claims, assertive counter-claims, and repeated calls for further study by the United Nations system reveal international duplicity in the commission of these globally consequential infractions. As a result, no one has to this day ascertained many aspects of the export of waste to – and dumping in – war-torn Somalia: the exact source(s) and levels of toxicity of the hazardous material, and how much of it was dumped where in Somali territory and waters. Meanwhile, individual cases of waste dumping continue to take place. In November 2012, for example, the newly operational Puntland Marine Police Force (PMPF) caught a North Korean vessel, the MV *Daesan*, dumping expired cement in Somali waters.[32]

Whereas waste dumping took place secretly in remote overland and maritime spaces, often under the cover of darkness, illegal fishing took place routinely in broad daylight and at night, in proximities close to and far offshore. Somali responses to waste dumping have consequently been subdued because they have had limited direct interaction with the practice. Nevertheless, impressive Somali capacity – as an oral society – to spread news and retain information has made the claims of toxic waste

---

[29] "UN Envoy Decries Illegal Fishing, Waste Dumping off Somalia," AFP, 25 July 2008: https://www.hiiraan.com/news4/2008/July/7409/un_envoy_decries_illegal_fishing_was te_dumping_off_somalia.aspx.
[30] UN Security Council Resolution 1976, S/RES/1976, (11 April 2011).
[31] UN Security Council, *Report of the Secretary-General on the Protection of Somali Natural Resources and Waters*, S/2011/611, (25 October 2011).
[32] "Somalia: Puntland Captures North Korean Flagged Vessel Dumping Waste," *Garowe Online*, 18 November 2012: https://www.somalinet.com/forums/viewtopic.php? t=317824.

dumping in Somalia household stories across the country. Not only do stories of waste dumping evoke strong feelings among Somalis, but they also offer grounds for anyone to rise up against these reported violations or serve as justification for those who merely claim to be doing so. By contrast, Somalis directly observed IUU fishing and experienced the damages that it caused on the marine environment, the livelihoods of coastal communities and the lives of fishermen.

Illegal, Unreported and Unregulated (IUU) Fishing

As in the case of waste disposal, the world was slow to wake up to the dangers of unregulated fishing. International conventions and codes of conduct subsequently called on states and non-states to adhere to sustainable fishing. Like toxic waste dumping, however, IUU fishing persists as a daunting global challenge, affecting countries differently depending on their capacities to control and monitor their maritime space and to mitigate the consequences of failing to do so.[33]

In the case of Somalia, however, many experts have either questioned or altogether dismissed the illegality of foreign fishing on the grounds that Somalia had not declared its exclusive economic zone (EEZ). Without attention to chronology, Jack Lang, Stig Jarle Hansen and many others argued that instead of declaring an EEZ to the United Nations, Somalia claimed 200-nautical-mile territorial waters. Lang best represented this view when he wrote: "In the absence of delimitation in accordance with international law, Somalia is legally deprived of a territorial sea and an exclusive economic zone. . . [A]ction cannot be taken until the legal issue of the delimitation of ocean space has been resolved."[34] Similarly, Hansen contended that because Somalia failed to make such a declaration, it forfeited its rights and that foreign actors (states or private companies) could fish in its waters without being in violation.[35]

Chronological flaws aside, claims about Somalia's lack of legal rights to the waters adjacent to it fail to make sense of the lack of recognition of its EEZ parallel to the de facto recognition of its territorial waters when both have become customary international law. In February 2008, the Security Council received a request from the Permanent Representative of the

---

[33] This book adopts FAO's definition of IUU fishing as stipulated in paragraph 3 of the 2001 *International Plan of Action to Prevent, Deter and Eliminate Illegal, Unreported and Unregulated Fishing*.

[34] Jack Lang, *Report of the Special Adviser to the Secretary-General on Legal Issues Related to Piracy off the Coast of Somalia*, S/2011/30, January 2011, 30 (paragraph 89).

[35] Hansen, "Debunking the Piracy Myth: How Illegal Fishing Really Interacts with Piracy in East Africa," *The RUSI Journal*, vol. 156, no. 6 (December 2012): 26–30.

weak Transitional Federal Government of Abdullahi Yusuf, seeking the assistance of foreign navies to combat piracy in Somali waters. Favorably receiving that request, hence recognizing Somalia's right to do so, the Security Council not only authorized a robust international counter-piracy mandate but also made it imperative on foreign navies to secure Mogadishu's green light before entering Somalia's waters.[36] An explication of the postcolonial African (and Somali) state positions on and interactions with the evolving international law of the sea will shed further light on the flaws of the above contentions and help set the record straight.

Market-driven and politically backed growth of the fishing industry, technological advances, and governments' subsidies toward the expansion of their fishing sectors accelerated the fishers' capacity to fish.[37] While the unsustainable trend unnerved the environmentally conscious, who feared its worrisome impact on the marine habitat, Third World countries begun to jealously stake larger claims to their adjoining waters in order to fend off the expanding capacities of advanced countries to exploit maritime resources far and near. Latin American countries led the charge with a 1951 tripartite agreement between neighboring Chile, Ecuador and Peru.[38]

The United Nations convened the United Nations Conference on the Law of the Sea (UNCLOS I), the first of three conferences on the law of the sea, in Geneva in 1958. The ensuing Geneva Convention on the Territorial Sea and the Contiguous Zone stipulated that the "sovereignty of a State extends . . . to a belt of sea adjacent to its coast, described as the

---

[36] UN Security Council Resolution 1816, S/RES/1816 (2008), 2 June 2008: paragraph 9. Subsequent authorizations followed similar requests from the successor TFG of Sheikh Sharif Sheikh Ahmed and similarly stipulated the need for Mogadishu's green light.

[37] By examining post-WWII strategic pursuits of the United States and the economic interests of the American fisheries sector, Carmel Finley offers a compelling analysis of how powerful countries (mainly the US and to some degree Great Britain) triggered the rush to lay sovereign claims to expansive territorial waters. They did so, according to Finley, by limiting national claims to adjacent waters in a bid to secure access rights for themselves. She also shows the early alignments of localized fisheries interests with the national political interests that culminated in the start of states' fisheries subsidies. See Carmel Finley, *All the Fish in the Sea: Maximum Sustainable Yield and the Failure of Fisheries Management* (University of Chicago Press, 2011); Carmel Finley and Naomi Oreskes, "Food for Thought. Maximum Sustained Yield: A Policy Disguised as Science," *ICES Journal of Marine Science,* 70: 245–250.

[38] By Article 2 of what came to be known as the Santiago Declaration on the Maritime Zone (of 18 August 1952), the countries jointly "proclaim[ed] as a norm of their international maritime policy that they each possess exclusive sovereignty and jurisdiction over the sea along the coasts of their respective countries to a minimum distance of 200 nautical miles from these coasts." Although the declaration was not registered with the UN until 1976, it became a precedent setter for regional and international agreements on international law of the sea.

territorial sea."[39] That stipulation rested on the agreement at the conference on the *ab initio* doctrine whereby the rights of coastal states were recognized as pre-existing and whose conferral did not rest on actions of those states. While adjudicating the Libya v. Tunisia case on the continental shelf, the International Court of Justice (ICJ) explained the purpose of the *ab initio* principle "as a means of protecting coastal States which had not made a proclamation of their continental shelf rights and had no means of exploring or exploiting their resources." According to the ICJ's rendition of the 1958 Convention, "the acquisition *ab initio* of sovereign rights [is not subordinated] to actual exploitation or occupation, or even to a proclamation of these rights."[40]

Nevertheless, both the 1958 and the 1960 Geneva conferences (UNCLOS I and UNCLOS II respectively) ended without an agreement on the breadth of coastal countries' territorial waters and fishing zones. The failure to reach an agreement left the poorer and less technologically advanced countries in the Global South anxious. Taking advantage of their growing numbers, they started to exert pressure in the international arena to assert their interests as a bloc and succeeded in moving the UN to action. The growing number of newly independent countries joining the UN General Assembly gave these countries sufficient clout to push through Resolution 1803 (XVII) of 14 December 1962 and Resolution 2158 (XXI) of 25 November 1966, asserting their "permanent sovereignty over natural resources," as the resolution was called.[41] They staked increasingly bigger claims to their adjoining maritime spaces against expanding capacities of advanced countries.

The urgency with which countries of the Global South moved to assert their rights, mitigate foreign infringements, and assuage persistent pressure from environmental concerns led to a succession of regional and international agreements. The Organization of African Unity (OAU, the predecessor to the African Union, AU) adopted a resolution on maritime resources and maritime boundaries. During their seventeenth regular session held in 1971, OAU foreign ministers took note of the fact that

---

[39] "Geneva Convention on the Territorial Sea and the Contiguous Zone," Resolution 1307 (XIII), 10 December 1958, Article 1.

[40] Quoted in Lea Brilmayer and Natalie Klein, "Land and Sea: Two Sovereignty Regimes in Search of a Common Denominator," *New York University Journal of International Law and Politics*, vol. 33, no. 703 (2000/2001), 703–768 [here 711]. Reproduced in Faculty Scholarship Series, Paper 2523 (2001): http://digitalcommons.law.yale.edu/fss_papers/2523.

[41] United Nations General Assembly Resolution 1803 (XVII), "Permanent Sovereignty over Natural Resources," 14 December 1962: www.ohchr.org/EN/ProfessionalInterest/Pages/NaturalResources.aspx and United Nations General Assembly Resolution 2158 (XXI), "Permanent Sovereignty over Natural Resources," 25 November 1966: www.worldlii.org/int/other/UNGA/1966/25.pdf.

"non-African fleets" have been going on "illegal and clandestine exploitation" of the finite fisheries off the coast of the continent, confirmed "the inalienable rights of the African countries over the fishery resources of the continental shelf surrounding Africa," and urged African governments to "take all necessary steps to proceed rapidly to extend their sovereignty over the resource of the high seas adjacent to their territorial waters and up to the limits of their continental shelf."[42] In the absence of a uniform OAU standard, however, different African countries claimed varying sizes of territorial sea and economic zones, as they were called before UNCLOS of 1982.[43]

Somalia was among the first countries to heed the OAU's call on its members to stake claim to as large an area as they possibly could in order protect their maritime resources.[44] In September 1972, the military government in Mogadishu issued a "Law on Somali Territorial Sea and Ports" that claimed Somalia's territorial sea as extending to 200 nautical miles offshore.[45] Individual African countries followed suit in seeking to implement that OAU resolution but the extent of their claims varied, Somalia's being on the larger end of the spectrum.

Nearly decade-long parallel international deliberations culminated in the December 1982 United Nations Convention on the Law of the Sea (UNCLOS) that entered into force in 1994. Article 3 of UNCLOS expanded coastal states' sovereignty over 12 nautical miles of territorial waters, and Article 57 recognized their exclusive economic zone (EEZ), where they have exclusive economic rights, as not exceeding 200 nautical

---

[42] The Organization of African Unity, "Resolutions and Declarations of the Seventeenth Ordinary Session of the Council of Ministers Held in Addis Ababa, Ethiopia from 15 to 19 June 1971," Document CM/Res. 250 (XVII), "Resolution on the Permanent Sovereignty of African Countries over Their Fishery Resources off the Shores of Africa": https://au.int/sites/default/files/decisions/9586-council_en_15_19_june_1971_council_ministers_seventeenth_ordinary_session.pdf.

[43] For a dated but relevant continent-wide examination of this legal development in Africa, see Nasila S. Rembe, *Africa and the International Law of the Sea: A Study of Contribution of the African States to the Third United Nations Conference on the Law of the Sea* (Alphen aan den Rijn, the Netherlands: Sijthoff and Noordhoff, 1980), 90–96.

[44] In a unique study of little-known evolution of Somalia's maritime law, Afyare Elmi and Ladan Affi demonstrate how Somalia remained actively engaged in international maritime deliberations, and how Mogadishu's actions and legislations were consistent with contemporaneous African and global trends. See Afyare Elmi and Ladan Affi, "Barriers to Developing Anti-Piracy Law in Somalia," (Al Jazeera Centre for Studies, November 2014): http://studies.aljazeera.net/en/reports/2014/11/2014112010310522448.htm.

[45] Article 1.1. states: "The Somali territorial sea includes the portion of the sea to the extent of 200 nautical miles within the continental and insular coasts . . ." The President of the Supreme Revolutionary Council, *Law No. 37 on the Somali Territorial Sea and Ports of 10 September 1972.* Also available at www.un.org/Depts/los/LEGISLATIONANDTREATIES/PDFFILES/SOM_1972_Law.pdf.

miles – both of which have become customary international law.[46]
By Articles 16.2 (for territorial waters) and 75.2 (for EEZ), UNCLOS
placed an expectation on coastal states to declare their claims:
"The coastal State shall give due publicity to such charts or lists of
geographical coordinates [of its claims] and shall deposit a copy of each
such chart or list with the Secretary-General of the United Nations."[47]
In practice, however, many countries did not follow suit with this expectation until recently whence remained lingering uncertainties about the
different maritime zones and varying coastal state powers therein.[48]

As a measure of its active involvement in these deliberations since its
independence in 1960, Somalia immediately signed UNCLOS and ratified
it six years later by Decree No. 14 of 9 February 1989. The second article of
the decree established: "The above mentioned Convention and its
Annexes shall have the force of Law in the Territory of the Somali
Democratic Republic."[49] This instrument of ratification has in effect
annulled the 1972 unilateral declaration and brought Somalia's treaty
rights and obligations within internationally accepted standards.
Although its failure to make specific declarations of Somalia's territorial
waters and EEZ does not make it an exception, its incapacity to impose a de
facto EEZ and its lacking enforcement (per Article 73 of UNCLOS) made
foreign exploitation possible. The UK's Foreign Office, for example, did
not recognize Somalia as having an EEZ,[50] when the UK itself had been
exercising EEZ rights long before formally declaring its EEZ in 2013.[51]

In June 2014, Somalia too at long last formally declared its EEZ.[52]
Recognizing the handicap of not doing so, the Somali state and its semi-
autonomous regional authorities agreed to harmonize their maritime
management policies and practices, and mandated Mogadishu to officially establish the country's exclusive economic zone (EEZ).[53]

[46] United Nations, *United Nations Convention on the Law of the Sea*, 10 December 1982. Also
see Brilmayer and Klein, "Land and Sea"; and the International Court of Justice case on
the continent shelf in the dispute between Tunisia and Libya: *Continental Shelf (Libyan
Arab Jamahiriya /Malta)*, Judgment, ICJ Reports 1985, para. 34 (p. 33).
[47] United Nations, *United Nations Convention on the Law of the Sea*, 10 December 1982.
[48] Gemma Andreone, "The Exclusive Economic Zone" in Donald R. Rothwell et al.,
The Oxford Handbook of the Law of the Sea (Oxford University Press, 2015), 163–164.
[49] The Presidency of the Somali Democratic Republic, Decree No. 14, "Instrument of
Ratification," 9 February 1989. (A copy is available from the author).
[50] Hansen, "Debunking the Piracy Myth," 26–30.
[51] Andreone, "The Exclusive Economic Zone," 164.
[52] Federal Republic of Somalia, "Proclamation by the President of the Federal Republic of
Somalia, dated 30 June 2014."
[53] Somali Maritime Resource and Security Strategy, Fisheries Working Group,
"Communiqué of the Somali MRSS Fisheries Working Group," 2–6 April 2014, Beau
Vallon, Seychelles. Available at: http://oceansbeyondpiracy.org/sites/default/files/attach
ments/Apr-6-Somali-Fisheries-Working-Group-Communique.pdf. According to this

Confirming its 1989 ratification of UNCLOS, in June 2014 the Somali federal government accordingly proclaimed an exclusive economic zone, which was immediately communicated to the United Nations.[54] Mogadishu also joined the Indian Ocean Tuna Commission around the same time.[55] But violations continued unabated.

Neither unilateral actions by weak states to extend their claims nor their ratification of treaties and customary international laws that recognized their rights has mitigated foreign illicit activities in their waters or violations by foreign state and non-state actors who exploited the procedural wrinkle of Articles 16.2 and 75.2. Moreover, the African post-colony had to contend with the near impossibility of exercising effective control over such maritime spaces. With a coastline of no less than 3,300 km and an exclusive economic zone (EEZ) of about 1.2 million km^2, Somalia remained especially unable to secure its vast waters. Its challenges became impossibly daunting when the country's previously intermittent civil war intensified and the state collapsed in 1991, removing the limited deterrent function that even a weak state could have on illicit operations in its sovereign spaces – as discussed later in this chapter. Even though Mogadishu's signing and ratification of UNCLOS effectively rolled back its 1972 claim to 200 nautical miles of territorial sea, the unmet expectation that a coastal state declares its maritime claims presented a convenient excuse – in the absence of the state – for foreign interests to violate its maritime spaces and plunder the resources therein with impunity.

Global unequal state-to-state relations and attendant predatory corporate practices have rendered these difficulties particularly intractable for weak, poor countries around the world. Because states actively and passively abet it, the corporate crime of IUU fishing intensified parallel to national claims to vast swaths of the world's seas.[56] Developed Distance Water Fishing Nations (DWFNs) have "placate[ed] their disgruntled fishermen who have been rendered jobless due to the limited-

---

communiqué, the regional states would manage demersal fish, and the federal government would manage highly migratory fish in the offshore waters.

Another agreement signed by Somalia regional and federal authorities in February 2018 has since replaced the 2014 MoU. See, "Somalia Leaders Reach Deal on Fishing and 2020 Polls" *Garowe Online*, 11 February 2018: www .garoweonline.com/en/news/somalia/somalia-leaders-reach-deal-on-fishing-and-2020-polls.

[54] Federal Republic of Somalia, "Proclamation by the President of the Federal Republic of Somalia, dated 30 June 2014."

[55] Indian Ocean Tuna Commission, "IOTC Circular 2014-59," 31 May 2014.

[56] The two principal UN agencies, namely the Food and Agriculture Organization (FAO) and United Nations Environmental Program (UNEP), have long been on the forefront of promoting sustainable practices and environmental protection as well as warning about the lack thereof.

entry fishery policies enforced in those countries" by turning a blind eye to their illegal exploitation of less-developed countries' marine resources.[57]

Astronomical subsidies to their respective fishing sectors are another crucially consequential mechanism through which national governments and intergovernmental organizations enable IUU fishing. These subsidies come in different forms, among them is "the purchase of access rights by governments in the [Global] North . . . that has negative consequences for resource biomass and food security for people in the [Global] South."[58] A lion's share – hence more consequential – of these subsidies is directed toward improving the capacity of the already over-capacitated private fishing fleet.

A 2005 study of the UK-based Maritime Resources Assessment Group (MRAG) identified the interlock between the criminal enterprise's relative advantages, on the one hand, and the subsidies from the home governments and the lack of opportunity in their closely guarded waters, on the other. Those advantages and subsidies led many DWFN's fleets to go about plundering vulnerable, far-off environments and communities with impunity. Establishing that economic considerations drive IUU fishing, it stated that

IUU fishing vessels have lower costs and fewer social responsibilities than licensed fishing vessels, which drives them to exploit resources irresponsibly. The current overcapacity of the world fishing fleet, both in terms of numbers of vessels and technological power, which was created largely through subsidies to the fishing sector in developed countries, has contributed to the problem. Many vessels have no fishing opportunities within regulated fisheries.[59]

In 2012, the United Nations Special Rapporteur on the right to food reported that "the capacity of the global aggregate fishing fleet is at least double that which is needed to exploit the oceans sustainably."[60] Building on an earlier similar recognition of the "relationship between subsidies, overcapacity and overfishing," researchers at the University of British Columbia's Fisheries Centre estimated that as early as 2003,

---

[57] Kulmiye, "Militia vs Trawlers."

[58] U. Rashid Sumaila et al., "A Bottom-up Re-estimation of Global Fisheries Subsidies," Fisheries Centre, University of British Columbia, Working paper # 2009–11 (2009), 19.

[59] The Maritime Resources Assessment Group Ltd. (MRAG), "Review of Impacts of Illegal, Unreported and Unregulated Fishing on Developing Countries. Synthesis Report," July 2005, 5.

[60] United Nations General Assembly, "Interim Report of the Special Rapporteur on the Right to Food," A/67/268, 8 August 2012: 6. Available at www.srfood.org/images/stories/pdf/officialreports/20121030_fish_en.pdf. Also see Anne Schroeer, Courtney Sakai, Vanya Vulperhorst and Andrzej Bialas, "The European Union and Fishing Subsidies," September 2011: http://oceana.org/sites/default/files/reports/EU_Subsidies_Report_FINAL_FINAL-1.pdf.

USD 27 billion had been handed out in subsidies, with USD 16.2 billion of that allocated to capacity enhancement.[61] Based on analyses of 148 coastal countries from 1989 to 2009, the researchers found out that economically advanced western countries as well as Japan, China and South Korea are the principal subsidizers of their respective fishery industries with substantial capacity enhancement components.[62]

Moreover, not only are the publicly disclosed subsidies a fraction of the actual figures, but subsidies have also gone directly to companies with proven records of violations around the world. In Europe, for example, OCEANA discovered that EU subsidies to its fishing sector in 2009 alone exceeded EUR 3 billion, which is three times more than the publicly circulated figure. With subsidies exceeding the value of the fish catch in more than a dozen EU countries, the international environmental group concluded that such grants were uneconomical even to Europe.[63] According to another European group, fishsubsidy.org, in many cases, the EU gave subsidies under the EU Common Fisheries Policies to vessels and companies with proven records of violations, abetting them to go on with their violations. The study claimed that between 1994 and 2006, seventy-five law-breaking Spanish and French fishing vessels received over EUR 20 million in subsidies, and that fourteen of them did so after their violations.[64] The International Consortium of Investigative Journalists found that in the first decade of the century, EU subsidies to the Spanish fisheries (including to companies facing court cases for illegal fishing) amounted to some USD 8 billion, which constitutes a third of the entire sector's value.[65] Some of these companies are believed to have operated in waters off the coast of Somalia.[66]

---

[61] Sumaila et al., "A Bottom-up Re-estimation," 17.

[62] Sumaila et al., "A Bottom-up Re-estimation."

[63] Schroeer, Sakai, Vulperhorst and Bialas, "The European Union and Fishing Subsidies," September 2011: http://oceana.org/sites/default/files/reports/EU_Subsidies_Report_FINAL_FINAL-1.pdf.

[64] "When Crime Pays: How the EU Subsidises Illegal Fishing," Fishsubsidy.org, 8 March 2011: http://www.pewtrusts.org/about/news-room/press-releases-and-statements/2010/03/11/when-crime-pays-how-the-eu-subsidises-illegal-fishing;
"The EU Subsidizes Illegal Fishing," 25 March 2011: www.slowfood.com/slowfish/pagine/deu/news/dettaglio_news.lasso?-idn=19.For a long list of subsidy-receiving vessels that committed violations of different categories, see "Identified Infringements," http://fishsubsidy.org/infringements/;
Christopher Pala, "Billions in Subsidies Prop Up Unsustainable Overfishing," IPS, November 8, 2012: www.ipsnews.net/2012/11/billions-in-subsidies-prop-up-unsustainable-overfishing/ (accessed 18 November 2012).

[65] International Consortium of Investigative Journalists (ICIJ), "Spain Doles Out Millions in Aid Despite Fishing Company's Record," 2 October 2011: https://www.huffingtonpost.com/2011/10/02/spain-doles-millions-fishing-company_n_989246.html.

[66] During the heated debates triggered by the capture and release of the Spanish fishing vessel in late 2009, some observers mentioned in passing that Alakrana itself received millions of dollars in EU subsidies.

The consequent financial and environmental damages of IUU fishing have been astronomical. A 2006 study by an international High Seas Task Force estimated that between USD 4 billion and USD 9 billion were lost annually to IUU fishing.[67] A few years later, a rare worldwide study indicated that, besides its environmental effects, the monetary value of the losses due to the practice ran between USD 10 billion and USD 23 billion.[68] Conservative estimates indicated that sub-Saharan Africa loses about USD 1 billion a year, nearly a quarter of its annual fisheries export.[69] Several other reports corroborated these findings and tracked subsequent developments.[70] Somalia's share of this loss is staggering. Estimates of a 2015 study by the Secure Fisheries Project of the One Earth Future Foundation put Somalia's annual losses at a little over USD 300 million.[71] To fully comprehend these losses in Somalia – beyond the dollar figures – one has to first consider the fisheries sector in that country, and then turn to its dynamic interaction with foreign IUU fishing.

Somali Fisheries in Perspective

Although the nostalgia of the aggrieved tends to paint a rosy picture of the past, the short history of fisheries in Somalia is anything but that. As many experts have attested, the sector had been plagued by perennial shortages of reliable data to enable accurate planning, and lacked the skilled workforce and necessary infrastructure to execute projects. Somali "fisheries legislation . . . [remained] both vague and insufficient for the needs of the

---

[67] High Seas Taskforce, "Closing the Net: Stopping Illegal Fishing on the High Seas. Final Report of the Ministerially-Led Task Force on IUU Fishing on the High Seas," March 2006: https://www.oecd.org/sd-roundtable/papersandpublications/39375276.pdf.

[68] David J. Agnew et al., "Estimating the Worldwide Extent of Illegal Fishing," *PLoS ONE* 4(2) (2009): www.plosone.org/article/info:doi/10.1371/journal.pone.0004570.

[69] High Seas Taskforce, "Closing the Net: Stopping Illegal Fishing on the High Seas. Final Report of the Ministerially-Led Task Force on IUU Fishing on the High Seas," March 2006: https://www.oecd.org/sd-roundtable/papersandpublications/39375276.pdfhttps://www.oecd.org/sd-roundtable/papersandpublications/39375276.pdf.

[70] See the following for an overview: Maritime Resources Assessment Group Ltd. (MRAG), "Review of Impacts of Illegal, Unreported and Unregulated Fishing on Developing Countries. Final Report," July 2005: http://webarchive.nationalarchives.gov.uk/20090422181306/http://www.dfid.gov.uk/pubs/files/illegal-fishing-mrag-report.pdf;

Maritime Resources Assessment Group Ltd. (MRAG) and Fisheries Ecosystems Restoration Research, *The Global Extent of Illegal Fishing*. Fisheries Centre, University of British Columbia, April 2008: www.yumpu.com/en/document/view/37696458/the-global-extent-of-illegal-fishing-international-mcs-network; Sumaila et al., "A Bottom-up Re-estimation."

[71] Sarah M. Glaser et al., *Securing Somali Fisheries* (Denver, CO: One Earth Future Foundation, 2015).

industry, on some crucial points it is totally absent."[72] And the sector remained beholden to the ideological orientations and shifting alliances and partnerships of the government with foreign governments and corporate entities.

Since the final years of Italian rule in Somalia (present-day Somaliland aside), state and private enterprises started to develop the marine potential of the country, especially around the tip of the Horn between Las Qorey and 'Aluula.[73] Many local fishermen and administrators proudly mention these fish processing plants with excitement – what they were and what they could be.[74] But experts have documented their abysmal record and unpromising prospects. Haakonsen, for example, argued that the plants in Las Qorey, Habo and Qandala, "have operated only sporadically in the last few years with great losses, and none at all are operating at this moment [1982/1983]. The same is the case with the only freezing plant in the north, Bolimog."[75] Accordingly, World Bank data show that, by the late 1980s, the Somali fisheries sector contributed less than one percent of the GDP at around USD 10.4 million, which comprised 10 percent of the country's total export along with frankincense and myrrh.[76] The 2005 FAO country report mentioned earlier similarly estimated that in 1990 fisheries accounted for two percent of the Somali GDP. Subsequent surveys, however, indicated that whatever the estimates of the harvest, they only constituted a small part of the potential.[77] Abdirahman Jama Kulmiye, who as a young graduate started his career as an inspector in the Somali Ministry of Fisheries, argues that the harvest in the pre-civil war years made up a paltry 4 percent of the estimated potential of hundreds of thousands of metric tons.[78]

---

[72] Jan Haakonsen, "Somalia's Fisheries: Case Study" (Food and Agriculture Organization of the United Nations (FAO), Rome, Italy, 1983), 176.

[73] Sarah M. Glaser et al., *Securing Somali Fisheries* (Denver, CO: One Earth Future Foundation, 2015), 11.

[74] Interviewing local officials and fishermen, I have repeatedly came across the fact that in the Habo/'Aluula area, for example, Italians built the fish processing plant (at Bolimog) and a landing strip specifically aimed to service that plant by flying its export to Middle Eastern markets.

[75] Jan Haakonsen, "Somalia's Fisheries: Case Study" (Food and Agriculture Organization of the United Nations (FAO), Rome, Italy, 1983), 174. Also see Glaser et al., *Securing Somali Fisheries*, 11.

[76] "Somalia: From Resilience towards Recovery and Development. A Country Economic Memorandum for Somalia," (January 2006), 13-14: www-wds.worldbank.org/external/default/WDSContentServer/WDSP/IB/2006/02/10/000012009_20060210093908/Rendered/PDF/343561SO0REV0pdf.pdf.

[77] See P. J. Fielding and B. Q. Mann, "The Somalia Inshore Lobster Resource. A Survey of the Lobster Fishery of the North Eastern Region (Puntland) between Foar and Eyl during November 1998," (IUCN Eastern Africa Programme: June 1999).

[78] Abdirahman Jama Kulmiye, "Militia vs Trawlers: Who Is the Villain?" *The East African Magazine*, 9 July 2001.

Independent Somalia's first serious attempt to harness this maritime potential had to wait until the devastating cycles of drought and famine of the first half of the 1970s. Since the establishment of the Ministry of Fisheries and Marine Resources in 1971, the government took incremental steps – at least at the policy level – to ensure environmental protection, marine resource sustainability, and employment opportunities for Somalis, among other lofty goals. Jan Haakonsen summarizes the 1974–1978 Five Year Development Plan as aiming: "to maximize the output and gross income of fisheries in order to raise the income level of fishermen; create new employment in the fisheries sector; earn more foreign exchange . . . and to encourage increased consumption of fish within the country."[79]

To combat the drought and famine of the 1970s, the military government of General Mohamed Siad Barre launched an ambitious program of resettling some fifteen thousand of the most affected nomadic communities of the interior to coastal settlements to eke out a living off the sea. In 1974/75, four such settlements emerged, which were autonomous from pre-existing nearby villages and towns; many others also resettled in pre-existing coastal communities and fishing villages.[80] The state offered subsistence guarantees and many of the settlers were inducted into the fishing sector that sold to the state on fixed prices while others took on other trades.[81] The newly resettled nomads-turned-fishermen were integrated into nearly twenty fishing cooperatives – in almost two dozen fishing and landing locations – that had been set up in 1971 to foster and prop up the fishing industry.

According to Haakonsen, the number of full-time and active fishermen in Somalia between the late 1970s and early 1980s ranged from 2,600 to 4,000; and at least 90,000 people (about two percent of the population) depended fully or in part on fisheries along the coast. These vastly artisanal fishermen, who accounted for about a third of the country's known fisheries output, had been using different fishing methods (hand lines, troll lines, cast nets, beach seines and traps) and more than 2,000 traditional, non-motorized oar or sail boats (*badan*) ranging from 2 meters to 12 meters in length. The use of the traditional wooden boats started to decline with the introduction and distribution of hundreds of

---

[79] Haakonsen, "Somalia's Fisheries," 175.

[80] Mohamed Yassin, "Somali Fisheries Development and Management" (June 1981): http://ir.library.oregonstate.edu/dspace/bitstream/1957/6400/1/Mohamed_Yassin_ocr.pdf.

[81] Roberto Antoniotto, "The Fishing Settlement at Baraawe: Notes on Cultural Adaption" in Hussein M. Adam, *Somalia and the World. Proceedings of the International Symposium Held in Mogadishu, October 15-21, 1979* Vol. Two (Mogadishu: Second Haglan Publication), 237–250. Also see Elizabetta Forni, "Woman's New Role and Status in the Baraawe Settlement" in Adam, *Somalia and the World*, 251–264.

motorized fishing boats in the 1970s.[82] There was a short-lived uptick in the fisheries sector as a result. According to one FAO report, with "the introduction of 500 mechanized boats in the early 1970s, the annual catch increased from about 5,000 tonnes to a peak of 8,000 tonnes in 1975."[83]

Nevertheless, because of their poor quality, shortage of skilled operators and lack of maintenance (mechanics and parts), many of the distributed boats deteriorated and quickly fell into disuse. Mohamed Yassin wrote in 1981: "Of 234 motor boats supplied to Brawe, Cadale, and Badey, only 78 (33.3%) are in working condition . . . This problem is common to all the cooperatives."[84] The effect was immediate. "By the late 1970s," reported FAO in 2005, "annual fish production was back to 5,000 tonnes."[85] N.P. van Zalinge's 1988 report indicates that the Somali artisanal fishermen's annual landings between 1978 and 1982 were in fact lower, ranging between 3,580 and 4,390 tons.[86] Due to the parallel and unregulated return of many of the nomads to their previous lives and the state's subsequent prioritization of agricultural resettlements, the fishing villages gradually disappeared or became fully integrated into nearby pre-existing villages.

The military government's initial active attention to fisheries, nevertheless, marked the expansion of artisanal subsistence fishing and the rise of gradually industrializing commercial fisheries in Somalia in partnership with foreign governments and companies. The full picture of Mogadishu's joint ventures with foreign governments and companies is still hazy except in its broad contours. Besides limited issuance of licenses to industrial fishing vessels from DWFN, the Siad Barre government entered into joint ventures first with the Soviet Union and then Italy. Until the 1977 Cold War realignment of the countries of the Horn of Africa, whereby the USSR displaced the United States in Ethiopia and dropped Somalia as a client, a joint Soviet-Somali company called SOMALIFISH briefly operated ten deep-sea factory trawlers. A Somali-Italian joint company

---

[82] Jan Haakonsen, "Somalia's Fisheries: Case Study" (Food and Agriculture Organization of the United Nations (FAO), Rome, Italy, 1983), 173.

[83] FAO, "Fishery Country Profile: The Somali Republic" (January 2005). N.P. van Zalinge reported in 1988 that artisanal landings in 1974 totaled 3,950 tons; 7,900 in 1975 and 7,040 in 1976 before dropping back to 5,280 tons in 1977 and continuing to drop for the subsequent three years before starting to rise again until 1983 when it was back at 5,280 tons. N.P. van Zalinge, "Summary of Fisheries and Resources Information for Somalia," (Rome: FAO, 1988). Prior to Zalinge, Haakonsen had offered those figures as guesses. See table in Haakonsen, "Somalia's Fisheries," 175.

[84] Mohamed Yassin, "Somali Fisheries Development and Management" (June 1981), 8: http://ir.library.oregonstate.edu/dspace/bitstream/1957/6400/1/Mohamed_Yassin_ocr.pdf.

[85] FAO, "Fishery Country Profile: The Somali Republic" (January 2005).

[86] N.P. van Zalinge, "Summary of Fisheries and Resources Information for Somalia," (Rome: FAO, 1988).

Figure 1.1. A dilapidated refrigerator truck in the center of Eyl is one of many reminders of the bygone days of the lucrative fisheries sector in the historic fishing village. (Photo by the author.)

called SOMITFISH then stepped in from 1981 to 1983 and resumed in 1987 as Somali High Seas Fishing Company (SHIFCO) with Italian-built and refurbished trawlers.[87] Persson et al. report that in 1989, Somalia "transferred its territorial fishing rights to China" in what they dubbed a "'guns-for-fish' agreement."[88] Not only does the full extent of the last arrangement remain unknown, but former fisheries officials say that Somalia did not have any fisheries agreement with China. Licenses that were issued to Taiwanese companies were withdrawn upon discovering that their ships pair-trawled and dredged, in violation of the terms of their license agreement.

In tandem with this quick succession of experiments with a series of such joint ventures, the government monopoly gave way progressively to

[87] Mohamed Yassin, "Somali Fisheries Development and Management" (June 1981), 9: http://ir.library.oregonstate.edu/dspace/bitstream/1957/6400/1/Mohamed_Yassin_ocr .pdf; Haakonsen, "Somalia's Fisheries," 174; Food and Agriculture Organization of the United Nations (FAO), "Fishery Country Profile: The Somali Republic" (January 2005); Lo Persson et al., "Failed State: Reconstruction of Domestic Fisheries Catches in Somalia, 1950–2010" (Fisheries Centre, University of British Columbia: Working Paper #2014–10, 2014), 4–5: http://publications.oceans.ubc.ca/webfm_ send/348.

[88] Persson et al., "Failed State," 5.

the rise of Somali private enterprises in the sector. The small-scale fishing cooperatives that, since their establishment in 1971, had been selling their catch to the government, aggregated their operations into a sizable private fishing business around 1988.[89] Especially active in the export of lobsters, shark fins, tuna, mackerel, and other types of fish, this fledgling and briefly lucrative sector faced a critical crossroads with the intensifying civil war. It disintegrated in some parts of the country, while coming to full life in others – the damages and deterioration of government facilities notwithstanding, as we will see in the next chapter.

As if to trivialize the impact of IUU fishing, some Somalia watchers have variously remarked that not many Somalis eat fish in spite of their abundant sea.[90] The situation has been slowly but steadily improving and received a major boost in the mid-1970s as noted earlier. The 2005 FAO fishery country report for Somalia estimated that by 2003, on average a Somali consumed 1.6 kg per year.[91] Although there are indicators that fish consumption has lately been on the rise with many fish stores in Somaliland and Puntland towns "selling out of the entire catch, sometimes even by mid-day,"[92] local consumption remains low compared to other parts of the world. Nevertheless, as we will see in the next chapter, fish have progressively become Somalia's prized cash crop, especially in some parts of the country following the collapse of the central government. This vibrant source of livelihood, employment and profits encountered and clashed with foreign IUU fishing in the country.

IUU Fishing in Somalia

According to Ali Farah, the director of the Fisheries Development Department in the Somali fisheries ministry in Mogadishu between 1980 and 1990, the government restricted industrial-scale fishing to no more than eighteen vessels at a time per its calculation of maximum

---

[89] Conversations with Jo'ar (14 and 15 February 2012, Bosaso).

[90] Indeed many seasoned Somalia experts and dated research attest to that fact. According to Mohamed Yassin, for example, "Somali nomadic culture despises fish as food and fishing as a profession." Jan Haakonsen similarly stated that "only a small minority of the population has ever been engaged in fishing, and fishermen have always occupied the lower end of the social status scale." See Mohamed Yassin, "Somali Fisheries Development and Management" (June 1981): http://ir.library.oregonstate.edu/dspace/bit stream/1957/6400/1/Mohamed_Yassin_ocr.pdf; Haakonsen, "Somalia's Fisheries," 171.

[91] Food and Agriculture Organization of the United Nations (FAO), "Fishery Country Profile: The Somali Republic" (January 2005).

[92] Kaija Hurlburt and Boberta Spivak, "The Fishing Sector in Somalia/Somaliland," Shuraako, January 2013, 9: retrieved from http://shuraako.org/sites/default/files/docu ments/The%20Fishing%20Sector%20in%20SomaliaSomaliland.pdf.

sustained yield (MSY).[93] Upon arriving in Somali ports, fishing vessels were subject to inspection of their fishing gear. They were required to take on board a Somali inspector from that ministry for the duration of their fishing in Somali waters. At least 30 percent of the workforce of a vessel – during its fishing sojourn in Somali waters – were expected to be Somalis from the Ministry's employee roster. Upon either filling up their hold or finishing their agreed-upon time, fishing vessels were required to call at their closest Somali port whereupon another official different from the inspector would go on board to inspect the catch and the vessel's log book. Only then were the fishing vessels expected to sail off to their landing destinations or to off-load their catch on a factory ship.[94]

Violations of these and other government regulations started to emerge before the collapse, but got out of hand progressively with the intensification of the civil war from the late 1980s onwards. According to at least one source, in the final years before its collapse, Somalia's central government collected a lump sum of USD 5,000 per vessel per month for three months for highly migratory fish during the time that they passed Somali waters. All other fishing vessels were charged a USD 2,000 license/permit fee and then 23 percent of the catch, calculated at a royalty price (some 30 or 40 percent lower than the market price).[95] Even before the collapse, however, the violations were apparent although not as blatant as after the collapse. Ali Farah recalls a case when about fifty Japanese vessels came for the highly migratory tuna, but only fifteen of them were licensed in Somalia.

The central government and the local communities were unable to do anything about many such violations. Some of the reasons included the African post-colony's perennial inability to exercise simultaneous and effective authority over its sovereign spaces and Somalia's lack of an effective navy to even attempt to do so. The other major factor, which in later days also aided the pirates, was the remoteness and inaccessibility (by land) of the coastal area adjacent to the rich fishing grounds that illegal foreign vessels frequented. The onetime fisheries inspector and subsequent marine researcher and Puntland state minister of fisheries, Abdirahman Jama Kulmiye, best captured this enduring difficulty:

Access to the many fishing settlements that dot the coastline is hampered by impassable roads and non-existent telephone and postal services. So if, say, pirate ships are spotted fishing illegally offshore of one of these settlements, it can take

---

[93] Conversations with Ali Farah. MSY this was a politically driven, controversial formula that was claimed to help sustain yield and preserve the environment. For the genesis of and controversy surrounding the MSY formula, see Finley and Oreskes, "Food for Thought."
[94] Conversations with Ali Farah.   [95] Conversations with Ali Farah.

several days before the relevant authorities in the bigger towns are notified. Because of the remoteness and/or the inaccessibility of the administrative posts bordering the rich fishing grounds, coupled with the navy's inability to monitor and patrol the entire coastline, *there has always been some pirate fishing in Somali waters* [emphasis added].[96]

With the progressive decay of the state and breakdown of law and order on land, the operators of some licensed foreign vessels started to openly bribe Somali inspectors in order to bypass government regulations, while others started to show up without licenses. The ministry's stations and refrigerators along the entire Somali coastline broke down; the one in Berbera was destroyed during the fighting; and the employees and the population at large were uprooted because of the conflict. Foreign industrial-scale vessels from DWFNs and smaller-scale fishing vessels and dhows from the Middle East and East Africa came in large numbers and year round, plundering Somali waters with impunity.

Somalis and non-Somalis quickly reported the violations and called for international support to halt them. In late 1993, for example, the future president of the semi-autonomous Puntland region of Somalia, Abdirahman Mohamed "Farole," highlighted the IUU fishing by foreigners and the lack of support to the local fisheries sector as some of the main impediments to rehabilitation and economic self-sufficiency of the region. In his own words, "In the fishing sector, lack of fishing gears, spare parts, boat repairing centres, and *looting and destruction of maritime resources by foreign trawlers using illegal methods*, are the main problems" [emphasis added].[97] Shortly afterwards in early 1994 Associated Press journalist Michael Phillips became one of many to report that "dozens of fishing boats from Italy, France, Taiwan, Japan, South Korea and elsewhere are raiding the rich lobster grounds and tuna schools in the Gulf of Aden and the Indian Ocean [i.e., Somali waters]. They're plundering what any functioning government would send its coast guard to protect."[98] A succession of activists, consultants, UN reports and scholars concurred.

---

[96] Kulmiye, "Militia vs Trawlers."

[97] The Delegation of the Nogal Region, Somalia, "Objective Discussions and Views on the Five Papers Prepared by UNOSOM for the Fourth Humanitarian Conference for Somalia in Addis Ababa on 29 November to 1 December 1993." (A copy is available from the author.) Farole presented this paper and took part in the deliberations in his capacity as governor and chairman of the Nugaal Regional Council that had been established in the wake of Mogadishu's collapse.

[98] Michael Phillips, "Intrigue and Lobster in a Peaceful Corner of Somalia," Associated Press (February 2, 1994) quoted in Todd Jennings, "Controlling Access in the Absence of a Central Government: The Somali Dilemma," in *Ocean Yearbook Online*, vol. 15, no. 1 (2001), 407.

In 1997, United Nations consultant Mahdi Gedi Qayad found out that "the absence of a national government and the availability of huge natural marine resources in Somali waters attracted the international poachers and also motivated the illegal fishing and the damaging of the previously unpolluted ecological system."[99] Although Qayad's mandate and the bulk of his findings centered on waste dumping as we have seen in the previous section, his warning on resource theft was on mark as other researchers subsequently demonstrated. Nearly a decade later, the High Seas Taskforce reported that an estimated "700 foreign-owned vessels are engaged in unlicensed and unregulated fishing in Somali waters, exploiting high value species . . . It is highly unlikely that these resources are being fished sustainably."[100] FAO followed up thus:

This illegal, unregulated, and unreported (IUU) fishing in the offshore, as well as in the inshore waters, with the difficulties it causes for legitimate Somali fishermen, causes great problems for monitoring, control and surveillance (MCS) of the Somali EEZ. It is impossible to monitor their fishery production, in general, let alone the state of the fishery resources they are exploiting.[101]

Two important factors attracted foreign industrial vessels into the traditional preserve of artisanal Somali fishermen: the abundance of lucrative fish stocks and the deep waters close to shore. First, foreign ships took advantage of the fact that the underwater continental prolongation around Somalia "is seldom more than 10–15 km wide" along significant parts of the coast, and it is as narrow as 2–5 km in some areas.[102] This means that the seabed close to shore drops sharply to the deep ocean floor, enabling large vessels to fish close to the coast without the risk of running aground. Second, the seasonal (from March to May, and September to November) upwelling of highly migratory schools of fish (e.g., tuna) along the northern Somali coastline made the lucrative fish easy to catch in abundance.[103] Coming as close as they could to shore, the blaring music from the fishing vessels was audible on land as their lights were visible to the naked eye, according to local accounts.

[99] Mahdi Gedi Qayad, "Assessment Mission to Somalia in Connection with Alleged Dumping of Hazardous Substances," 10 May–8 June 1997.

[100] High Seas Taskforce, "Closing the Net: Stopping Illegal Fishing on the High Seas. Final Report of the Ministerially-led Task Force on IUU Fishing on the High Seas," March 2006: www.illegal-fishing.info/uploads/HSTFFINALweb.pdf.

[101] FAO, "Fishery Country Profile: The Somali Republic" (January 2005).

[102] Haakonsen, "Somalia's Fisheries," 172.

[103] According to Ali Farah, the abundance of small pelagic fish, especially sardines, which feed off the rich nutrients stirred up to the surface by the changing monsoons, attract large pelagic fishes like tuna that feed on the sardines. Tuna fishing vessels then follow the monsoon winds–nutrients–small pelagic–large pelagic migratory pattern.

Abdirahman Jama Kulmiye wrote that the concentration of hundreds of illegally fishing vessels on any given night (during the fishing season) lit stretches of the coastline like a metropolitan city.[104] Somali officials and international personnel of UN agencies and other organizations also likened the sight to Paris or New York.[105] "As a result," continued Kulmiye, "once productive swathes of seabed have been transformed overnight into marine deserts."[106]

Somali experiences with these mobile cities of light fluctuated between disinterested descry and collaboration before taking an ugly turn; local responses shifted in more-or-less equal measure until they all went awry. During the first few years of the central government's collapse, large-scale foreign and artisanal Somali fishermen peaceably co-existed in the same fishing grounds and even assisted one another. There are stories in coastal Puntland of local fishermen in the early 1990s supplying foreign fishermen with basic provisions after the latter had run out of theirs, and of foreign sailors offering technical assistance. A Somali journalist who had once done stints as a fisherman in those years recalls how, between late 1992 and early 1993, local fishermen around Eyl needed to get one of their boats welded. They could hear the sound and see the flashing sparks of welding on board a Korean trawler a few miles off the coast. Upon asking for assistance the next morning, "the Koreans lifted the broken boat to their deck, welded, tested and put it back on water." The Korean crew also offered the Somali fishermen some lunch.[107] When around the same time armed Somali thieves attacked and robbed foreign fishermen, many among the coastal communities lamented the innocence of the victims and condemned the crime of the attackers.

Over time, however, foreign industrial-scale fishing vessels' encroachment into the inshore Somali waters intensified. Somalia's commercially oriented, small-scale, artisanal fishing became one of the main casualties of the intensification of foreign IUU fishing. Losing lives and livelihoods, the local fishermen grew increasingly resentful of the foreign fishermen. Whereas generalized claims across Somalia that illegal trawlers fished the Somali waters empty have to be scrutinized against the backdrop of fast-

---

[104] Kulmiye, "Militia vs Trawlers." Many firsthand observers of the Somali coast similarly describe their observations of the coast as mobile cities of light.

[105] According to Kulmiye, for example, foreign fishing vessels "crowded off some stretches of the Puntland (northeast) coast that the glow that emanates from their combined lights at night can be mistaken for a well-lit metropolitan city." Kulmiye, "Militia vs Trawlers;" conversation with former Deputy Minister of Interior of Puntland Ali Yusu Ali "Hoosh" (31 January 2012, Garowe, Puntland).

[106] Kulmiye, "Militia vs Trawlers."

[107] Conversations with Burhaan Daahir (Garowe, 13 November 2012).

shrinking fish stocks and catch across the Indian Ocean,[108] the methods of the trawlers in Somali waters are beyond recourse.

As with their numbers and frequency, it is hard to establish with certainty the fishing methods of foreign vessels operating in far-off Somali waters. Local oral narratives have well documented the destructiveness of those in the close-by traditional preserves of artisanal fishermen. With a capacity in the range of 20 tons (and some as small as 5-ton capacity), Yemeni fishers are, for example, known to dangle thousands of hooks down into the sea and to dredge them across the delicate habitat, destroying underwater crevices, indiscriminately extracting fish, and producing significant by-catch that is then tossed back into the water. Using such destructive methods, "a 20-ton boat filled up in two days," fumed a knowledgeable fisheries official in Bosaso. The level of destructiveness that the Iranian fishing vessels fail to achieve through their methods, continued the same Puntland official, they make up for with their bigger numbers and larger capacities (80–120 tons), which is unsustainable.[109]

Other more industrialized fishers from DWFNs operating in Somali coastal waters used even more destructive methods. Unrelated fishermen consulted from Bandar Bayla to Eyl and Gara'ad (in Puntland) are consistent in their description of the ships' fishing methods that included dynamiting underwater crevices and coral reefs in order to more easily catch the crustaceans and demersal fish. The environmentally conscious fishermen were furious about the implications of the humming, vibrations and frequent explosions that kept them awake at night. "It is one thing to steal the resource" said a fisherman from the Gara'ad area; "nature has its ways of replenishing itself. But to destroy the environment! These people were also endangering the future of the following generations."[110]

Artisanal fishermen along the entire Somali coast complained that foreign trawlers had fired at them or doused them with hot water. Others reported that foreign fishing vessels had destroyed or stolen their fishing gear, resulting in significant financial cost to replace it.[111]

---

[108] Dennis Rumley, Sanjay Chaturvedi, and Vijay Sakhuja, "Fisheries Exploitation in the Indian Ocean Region," in Rumley, Chaturvedi, and Sakhuja (eds.) *Fisheries Exploitation in the Indian Ocean: Threats and Opportunities* (Singapore: ISEAS Publishing, 2009), 1–17.

[109] Confidential conversations with Puntland fisheries official (February 2012, Bosaso).

[110] Interview with Mohamud Abdulkadir (aka John) (27 February 2012, Galkayo). Note: In previous publications I made the error of referring to this source as Mohamed Abdulkadir.

[111] Asha Abdulkarim Hersi (Interview: 24 February 2012, Eyl) says that their losses of fishing gear were worsened by their wasting a lot of time, fuel and energy searching for the missing nets and traps only to conclude that they had been "taken away" by the trawlers. And according to the Mayor of Eyl, Musa Osman Yusuf (Interview: 24 February 2012, Eyl), replacing lost gear could cost up to USD 1,000, which was too expensive for the artisanal fishermen to afford on their own.

According to information gathered at a workshop organized in 2001 by the then-Puntland Development Research Center (PDRC, currently Peace and Development Research Center),

> [F]ishermen of the coastal settlement of Laamiye, located between Bender Beila and Hafun, were infuriated by trawlers destroying their nets. They mobilised themselves and, using motorized boats, attacked the foreign ships with small arms. The bigger trawlers retaliated the next morning by attacking the fishing boats in the area using heavy weapons and shelling the coastal settlement of Laamiye, inflicting heavy losses. The fishermen were powerless to fight back, nor could the Puntland administration help, as it lacked coast guard equipment and capacity.[112]

The losses of the local fishing communities were not limited to material damages as sources indicate that some of the big fishing fleet ran over artisanal fishermen or that the latter's small boats were damaged or submerged in the waves of the passing trawlers. In 2007/2008, residents of the coastal village of Gaba'e witnessed from the mountaintop overlooking the sea a big fishing vessel sailing directly into a small artisanal boat that had been fishing there. The three fishermen aboard the latter were seen jumping into the water just before the small boat submerged upon contact with the trawler.[113] Similar stories abounded during the years I traveled in the Somali region to conduct research for this book.

Charlotte de Fontaubert and Alex Forbes noted that the "international community has moral and legal obligation to safeguard the Somali marine and coastal resources for the immediate and long-term benefit of the Somali people. These moral and legal obligations are intrinsic within a number of regional and global conventions and treaties that have been ratified by a majority of States with interests and activities in Somalia."[114] In the absence of a legitimate sovereignty-wielding national government granting licenses, Todd Jennings argued, "all foreign fishing is also technically illegal."[115] Coffen-Smout and Jennings boldly called for an international management of Somalia's maritime

---

[112] Puntland Development Research Center (PDRC), *Somali Customary Law and Traditional Economy: Cross Sectional, Pastoral, Frankincense, and Marine Norms* (Garowe, Puntland: PDRC, 2003), 95–96.

[113] This story was repeated to me several times during a visit to the Eyl District in February 2012, but no one could say who those fishermen were nor did I encounter any fisherman who claims to have survived the incident.

[114] Charlotte de Fontaubert and Alex Forbes, "Overview of the Legal Framework Concerning the Somali Coastal and Marine Environment," *The Protection and Sustainable Development of Somali Marine Environment, Seaports and Coastal Seas* (UNDP Project, IOM, March 1998) quoted in Jennings, "Controlling Access in the Absence of a Central Government," 416.

[115] Todd Jennings, "Controlling Access in the Absence of a Central Government: The Somali Dilemma," in *Ocean Yearbook Online*, Vol. 15, Issue 1 (2001), 417.

space;[116] this was not unlike the administration of Somali airspace by the International Civil Aviation Organization (ICAO), which was itself latterly mired in controversy.[117]

International legal imperatives and treaty obligations fell by the wayside because internationally mandated maritime space management was not a pressing security concern to powerful countries. More importantly, doing so would preclude lucrative access to uncontrolled resources. As one expert told Jennings, the "declaration of the waters of the former Somalia as a protectorate would take UN Security Council action and since the violators are from UN member countries and there is big money at stake the reality is that no such action would be allowed."[118] Various United Nations missions to Somalia were neither mandated to protect Somali marine resources and environment nor have they so far succeeded in fully restoring a state capable of doing so.

Not until 2009 did the United Nations Security Council acknowledge "Somalia's rights with respect to offshore natural resources, including fisheries," and call for the assurance of "coastal and maritime security, including combating piracy and armed robbery at sea" off the coast of Somalia.[119] And only in April 2011 did the Security Council Resolution 1976 (also repeated in Security Council Resolution 2020 of November 2011) urge states and competent international organizations "to positively consider investigating allegations of illegal fishing and illegal dumping, including of toxic substances, with a view to prosecuting such offences when committed by persons under their jurisdiction."[120] Little, if at all, has so far been done. While many, including lawyers in the Contact Group on Piracy off the Coast of Somalia, argued as late as 2014 that Somalia's failure to declare its waters was the root cause of the problems,[121] waste dumping and IUU fishing continue under the nose of the very international bodies that ought to prevent them.

[116] Coffen-Smout, "Pirates, Warlords and Rogue Fishing Vessels in Somalia's Unruly Seas," 1999: www.chebucto.ns.ca/~ar120/somalia.html; Jennings, "Controlling Access in the Absence of a Central Government," 416.

[117] See Abdisalam Warsame Hassan and Awet T. Weldemichael, "Somalia Airspace and Waters' Control Must Be Reclaimed: UN May Owe Millions in Unaccounted for Air Navigation Charges," *African Argument*, 114, June 2012: http://africanarguments.org/2012/06/14/somalia-must-reclaim-control-over-airspace-and-waters-as-un-may-owe-somalia-millions-in-unaccounted-for-air-navigation-charges-by-abdisalam-warsame-hassan-and-awet-t-weldemichael/.

[118] Jennings, "Controlling Access in the Absence of a Central Government," 420.

[119] UN Security Council Resolution 1897, S/RES/1897 (2009), 30 November 2009, paragraph 5.

[120] UN Security Council Resolution 1976, S/RES/1976 (2011), 11 April 2011, paragraph 8; and UN Security Council Resolution 2020, S/RED/2020 (2011), 22 November 2011, paragraph 24.

[121] Conversation with a source who attended one of CGPCS meetings in 2014.

In violation of international law, in contravention of their layered treaty obligations to Somalia and to the protection of Somali marine biodiversity, and hidden from the public eye, powerful countries continue to subsidize the piratical activities of their private fishing fleets in Somali waters (while using international instruments to respond to Somali reactions in the open). As in the case of dumping, two decades of ineffectual reports, claims, counter-claims, and calls for further study froze the international community into inaction. Such blatant disinterest about hazardous waste disposal and direct and indirect support of IUU fishing vis-à-vis repeated and categorical international condemnations of transgressions of Somali actors have only helped fortify the righteous indignation that Somalis share.

IUU fishing in Somalia, as elsewhere, has negatively affected the local communities in multiple other ways. Because it is generally done on an industrial scale, it reduces job opportunities and denies localized fishing sectors the needed catch and revenue to hire labor. In other words, IUU fishing destroys pre-existing livelihoods without creating new alternative employments or sources of income at the local level. Because it is illegal, it is impossible for the state to tax and generate revenue from it. Because it is unregulated, it is impossible to ascertain that its conduct is consistent with sustainability imperatives of the fish stocks. Because IUU fishing is highly lucrative, it survives and even flourishes in environments rife with corruption; and where corruption does not exist or is limited, local partners can readily be found to do its corrupt bidding.[122]

The Local Factor in Foreign IUU Fishing in Somalia

Whereas it is hard to account for foreign industrial-scale IUU fishers in Somalia's far-off exclusive economic zone,[123] many of their counterparts who fished the country's territorial waters did so in collusion with local partners, exploiting the permissive domestic government vacuum. In the absence of any authority to legislate, monitor and regulate their activities, some kept outdated copies of onetime legitimate fishing licenses; others photocopied or forged licenses; and many did not even bother to keep any

---

[122] Environmental Justice Foundation, *Pirates and Profiteers: How Pirates Fishing Fleets Are Robbing People and Oceans* (London: Environmental Justice Foundation, 2005), 6-7; Maritime Resources Assessment Group Ltd. (MRAG), "Review of Impacts of Illegal, Unreported and Unregulated Fishing on Developing Countries," 5.

[123] In a unique show of unity of purpose, albeit one that quickly faltered, Somalia's regional and federal authorities recently came together and filed with the Indian Ocean Tuna Commission a report documenting foreign IUU fishing in the Somali EEZ. See Somalia, "Report on Presumed IUU Fishing Activities in the EEZ of Somalia," 27 April 2015: www.iotc.org/documents/report-presumed-iuu-fishing-activities-eez-somalia.

form of documentation. Likewise, nearly all – if not all – artisanal and small-scale Somali fishing took place without regulation or reporting of any kind.

Individual Somalis used their former roles in Somalia's state-run fisheries sector to abuse the licensing process/method or to deploy national maritime resources for personal gain. In at least one well-known case, the former manager of the state-owned fishing company deployed its vessels as his personal business. When the government collapsed in January 1991, the five fishing trawlers and a refrigerated transport vessel of SHIFCO (the last in a long line of joint ventures between the Somali government and its foreign partners) became private ventures of the company's last manager, Hassan Munyo (variously spelled as Monya and Munye).[124] Operating out of Yemen, the vessels fished Somali waters without licenses or under suspicious arrangements and, in the process, clashed with local fishermen, vigilante pirates, and regional authorities.[125] Munyo and "his" ships fished for more than a decade preceding the explosion of piracy until the ships purportedly became unseaworthy, owed Yemen and Yemeni businesses millions of dollars, and are now waiting to be turned into scrap in order to repay the owed sum.

The Somali government separately owned and operated two trawlers named *Awdal* and *Ras Asir* that also fell into private hands following the escalation of the civil war. Whereas the circumstances of the sale of *Ras Asir* shortly after the collapse of the government remains unknown, several confidential sources claim that the first officer of *Awdal*, Captain Isse Haji Farah, converted it into a collector and transport vessel for private use. Joining his older brother's lobster fishing business that had been operational since the 1980s and that later became the Northeast Fishing Company (NEFCO),[126] Captain Isse helped expand the family business through partnership with foreign fishing companies; this is discussed later in this chapter.

During the highly contested interim government in Mogadishu (starting in January 1991), both the interim president Ali Mahdi and his arch rival General Farah Aidid and their respective associates are believed to

---

[124] These were three large trawlers that were refurbished by the Koreans with Italian foreign assistance before resuming operations in 1987; two smaller trawlers that were freshly acquired when SHIFCO was about to resume working; and a large mother ship with a refrigerated hold capacity of more than a thousand tons. Whereas the mother ship is believed to have been sold to Argentina under unknown circumstances, the trawlers were operational at least until the year 2000.

[125] In the year 2000, Puntland's privatized marine force and Munyo had a short-lived rapprochement. See Brian Scudder, "Pirate King Turns Law Enforcer," *African Business*, Issue 256 (Jul/Aug 2000).

[126] The *Awdal* reportedly became their collector vessel until 1994 when it was sold to a foreign company.

have continued to issue licenses. The proceeds of these sales of permits went either to private ends or to aid their war efforts against each other.[127] Likewise, former officials of the Somali Ministry of Fishery and Marine Resources are believed to have stolen stacks of printed licenses and reproduced their own (including on plain, government letterhead paper) and sold them for profit to foreign companies and their local partners who were often cash-strapped warlords. Scott Coffen-Smout reported that in 1996, "43 purse seiners and 61 longliners were licensed to fish under this arrangement."[128] Besides regional trawlers from Yemen and Kenya, Persson, et al. added that "four Saudi-Arabian trawlers and some Pakistani vessels occasionally fished along the coast, and three Sri Lankan vessels based in Berbera fished for sharks."[129]

The above and other fishing vessels could only have operated under one of three arrangements: by securing such licenses as were issued by officials in Mogadishu and later by a London-based licensing company, Somaliland licenses or Kenyan licenses; as completely unlicensed but with their own security arrangement or a feeling of security by operating far off shore; or by partnering with powerful local leaders and business-men who offered protection.

In May 2006, the UN Monitoring Group reported that regional adminis-trations as well as individual warlords sold access rights to individual vessels and companies, sometimes on plain sheets bearing the seals of the strongmen.[130] In the group's own words, the right to exploit Somali natural resources "is being sold off by Somali warlords and businesses, sometimes through the services of foreign commercial companies that act as agents and intermediaries for the acquisition of fishing permits and, more recently, exploitation rights for seabed resources."[131] While this seems to hold true across Somalia, Puntland offers compelling examples of how the local factor played itself out with regard to foreign fishing in Somali waters.

---

[127] Hassan Munyo's SHIFCO trawlers are believed to be among the vessels licensed by the Farah Aidid faction, which followed from or explained the two men's close relationship. Confidential Somali sources claim that the Italian journalist Ilaria Alpi was murdered in 1994 because she discovered some evidence linking one of SHIFCO trawlers with weapons shipments from Ukraine to Aidid in Mogadishu.

[128] Scott Coffen-Smout, "Pirates, Warlords and Rogue Fishing Vessels in Somalia's Unruly Seas," 1999: www.chebucto.ns.ca/~ar120/somalia.html. It is important to note that these are European and Asian industrial-scale vessels.

[129] Persson et al., "Failed State," 6. Also see Jennings, "Controlling Access in the Absence of a Central Government," 411. Also see Coffen-Smout, "Pirates, Warlords and Rogue Fishing Vessels in Somalia's Unruly Seas."

[130] Report of the United Nations Monitoring Group on Somalia, S/2006/229, 4 May 2006, Paragraphs 71–75.

[131] Report of the United Nations Monitoring Group on Somalia, S/2006/229, 4 May 2006, Paragraphs 71.

Powerful local leaders and businessmen partnered with foreign companies and hired local militia for protection to exploit coastal fishing resources without licenses or with dubiously acquired ones. They secured licenses for their foreign partners' large fishing ships through newly set up local front companies or by piggybacking them on pre-existing companies like NEFCO, TARIFCO or TAR. They also granted protection to the foreign partners during their fishing of Somali waters. According to several officials and fishermen interviewed, these powerful individuals and their companies hail from the inaccessible tip of the Horn (around the areas of 'Aluula, Qandala and Ras Hafun) and they have allegedly brought to the region a large number of Iranian and Yemeni boats under such arrangements. A seemingly exasperated government official, for example, blurted the name of a leading businessman from Qandala as being responsible for up to 75 percent of the Iranian vessels that fished Somali waters at any given night during the high fishing season.[132]

In 1996, for example, Captain Isse Haji Farah of NEFCO is believed to have secured the permission of Colonel Abdullahi Yusuf, leader of the Somali Salvation Democratic Front (SSDF), to bring Ukrainian fishing vessels to the region. Farah recruited ten men as guards from Qandala for his first ship, *Sealion I*, and another ten from 'Aluula for his second, *Sealion II*.[133] NEFCO's initial venture grew into a large family business with sister companies, changing foreign partners but with an unchanging green light from the government. All Puntland administrations since Abdullahi Yusuf's granted to them, and hence to their foreign partners, the license to fish; this was even the case during the strict refusal of the Farole government to issue fishing license to others.[134] The younger brother of NEFCO owner, Shire Haji Farah, who entered politics and held ministerial posts in the regional government in Puntland, vehemently argues that NEFCO chartered the foreign fishing vessels for its own business, dutifully paid all necessary fees and generated handsome revenues to all the successive Puntland administrations.[135]

---

[132] Confidential Interview with a government official with intelligence and fishing knowledge (February 2012, Bosaso).

[133] Confidential Interview with a knowledgeable government official (August 2015, Galkayo).

[134] Interview with former president of Puntland, Abdirahman Mohamed Farole (14 August and 12 September 2015, Garowe). Former Puntland Minister of Finance under 'Aadde Muse's government. Mr. Mohamed Ali Yusuf "Gagab" (Interview: 11 September 2015, Galkayo), however, said he always had a fight with Captain Isse about his illegally bringing dozens of foreign vessels.

[135] Interview with Puntland Minister of Planning and International Cooperation Shire Haji Farah (28 March 2017, Garowe).

Nevertheless, widespread corruption at the highest levels of Somali authorities and the active evasion of regulations by business people have been documented. In July 2011, the Monitoring Group observed that "the sale of licences to foreign vessels in exchange for fishing rights has acquired the features of a large-scale 'protection racket,' indistinguishable in most respects from common piracy."[136] More specifically, that Security Council body went on to say the following about four South Korean vessels that operated in Puntland waters with NEFCO as their local agent:

[S]ince May 2009, four fishing vessels of the Republic of Korea [FV *Aurola No.7*, FV *Aurola No.9*, FV *Golden Lake 808* and FV *Ixthus No.7*] have been frequently and repeatedly observed fishing off the coast of Puntland and delivering their catch to Bosaaso port. Notwithstanding Somali pirate rhetoric claiming to protect Somali marine resources, those vessels operate confidently in Somali waters, broadcasting automatic identification system signals and remaining in visual distance from the shore with slow speed, lowered stern ramp and no obvious precautionary measures. According to information received by the Monitoring Group, the companies operating the vessels have been issued 'approved licenses to fish' in Puntland territorial waters. None of the vessels has ever reported an attack by Somali pirates – a finding that appears to validate the Monitoring Group's previous observation.[137]

As we will see, this curious phenomenon climaxed in 2014 when the same company, agent and at least one of these vessels became the center of an open internal dispute within the Puntland government.

Official corruption in Mogadishu and the regional states and the continued lack of coherent national policy and practice contributed to the intensified return of IUU foreign fishers following the drastic decline of piracy incidences. In July 2013, the central government signed two suspicious agreements, the implementation and effectiveness of which is unknown. First it signed away a lion's share of its rich fisheries to a certain Somalia Fishguard Ltd. (registered in Mauritius) in return for the latter setting up a Somalia Fisheries Protection Force.[138] It then granted the Netherlands-based Atlantic Marine and Offshore Group a contract to serve as coast guard in Somali waters.[139] Three days later,

---

[136] Report of the UN Monitoring Group on Somalia and Eritrea, S/2011/433, July 2011, paragraph 118.
[137] Ibid.
[138] Ilya Gridneff, "Somalia Questions Deal Giving Ex-U.K. Soldiers Fish Rights," *Bloomberg Business*, 23 December 2014: www.bloomberg.com/news/articles/2014-12-2 3/somalia-questions-deal-giving-ex-u-k-soldiers-all-fish-rights.
[139] Khalid Yusuf, "Somalia Government Signs Landmark Coastal Protection Contract," *Horseed Media*, 30 July 2013: https://horseedmedia.net/2013/07/30/somali-government-signs-landmark-coastal-protection-contract/.

Puntland's Minister of Maritime Transport, Ports and Counter Piracy rejected the latter: "The recent contract signed on the 30th July, 2013 . . . that hands over the power of Somali Nationals to Foreign Company over our territorial waters, marine resources, Ports and Trade is unacceptable, inapplicable and unsuitable in Puntland State."[140]

Meanwhile, the autonomous Puntland region experienced heightened foreign fishing operations without generating corresponding revenue from them because of alleged local collusion and corruption. The problem of foreign IUU fishing so confounded President Abdiweli Mohamed Ali "Gas," that he declared it a "national disaster" shortly after he took the helm of the regional government in Garowe in 2013.[141] Nevertheless, foreign illegal fishing intensified under his watch and, according to some sources, it did so with the active facilitation and complicity of corrupt officials at the highest levels of the Puntland government.

In March 2014, Puntland's Ministry of Fisheries and Marine Resources decreed to delegalize all fishing licenses that had been issued before and placed a three-month moratorium on issuance of new licenses.[142] The government then retained the old registration and licensing regulations and pricing (discussed in Chapter Two) but introduced what it claimed was a tamper-proof license. Because Yemeni fishermen had historically come in large numbers without licenses, the Puntland government, as part of reforming its fisheries regime, decided to make a special arrangement in order for the Yemenis to fish legally while generating revenue stream for the state.

In 2014, a high-level Puntland delegation traveled to Yemen for ministerial level negotiations. They settled on a lump sum payment of USD 2,000 per ship (as small as 6-ton capacity and as large as 20 tons) for those that fish on their own and USD 800 per ship for those that come to buy from local fishermen. That deal required Yemeni vessels to come to Puntland and pay the fee before going off to fish and then sailing back home. The agreement was scrapped when Yemeni vessels failed to show up for registration but continued to fish illegally as they had done before.[143]

[140] Ministry of Maritime Transport, Ports and Counter Piracy, "Press Release," 2 August 2013: http://radiosahan.org/2013/08/3502/.

[141] "Somalia: Puntland Leader Speaks Out on Illegal Fishing, Calls It 'A National Disaster,'" Garowe Online, 2 June 2013.

[142] Andy Hickman, "Somalia Cracks Down on Illegal Fishing," Al Jazeera, 24 Sept 2014: https://www.aljazeera.com/news/africa/2014/09/somalia-cracks-down-illegal-fishing-2 01492320535275716.html.

[143] Interview with State Minister Dr. Abdirahman Jama Kulmiye (11 September 2015, Galkayo). That failure, says Puntland State Minister of Fisheries and Marine Transport, Dr. Abdirahman Jama Kulmiye (Interview: 11 September 2015, Galkayo), spurred the Puntland government to contract a private ship from Ali Tar to combat illegal fishing in

Figure 1.2. A Middle Eastern fishing dhow off the coast of Hafun around the tip of the Horn. (Courtesy of PDRC.)

Their potential for greed aside, Yemeni officials, fishing companies and fishermen may not have taken the Puntland authorities and their scheme seriously because of alleged rampant corruption within Puntland. Between 2014 and 2015, Yemeni fishermen complained to their Somali partners that they had been awash with solicitations to buy ready-made fishing licenses. It turned out, sources claim, when Puntland officials went to Yemen on official business, some of them traveled with briefcases full of original licenses and used local interlocutors to go door to door and sell those licenses. These license-retailers approached fishing companies and known individual fishermen alike, twisting arms and promising security.[144]

Moreover, during and after the moratorium there was at least one exception that caused rifts within the Puntland Ministry of Fisheries and triggered a flurry of formal letters from the director general for fisheries, the deputy minister, state minister, minister, and ultimately the president himself. Dated between 14 June and 18 August 2014, these letters reveal that the Bosaso-based Northeast Fishing Company

conjunction with the PMPF. Current and past PMPF officials, however, say that they neither recognized that private security ship nor worked with it.

[144] Confidential interview (August 2015, Galkayo).

(NEFCO), working as an agent of the United Arab Emirates (UAE)-based ARA Fisheries, had secured for the latter's four South Korean vessels (*Baek Yang 37, Ixthus 7, Ixthus 8,* and *Ixthus 9*) permission to continue fishing in Puntland waters throughout the moratorium. Then, a few days after the moratorium lapsed, they were granted licenses for forty-five days (from 14 June to 30 July 2014), which was later extended for six months.[145]

As noted earlier, this was not the first time that some of these and other South Korean vessels of the same company had fished in Puntland waters unmolested by piracy or local vigilantes because their local agent guaranteed their security. The dispute within the Puntland government over them, however, gave them undesired negative publicity that the company, the local agent, and Puntland officials wished to avoid. To that effect, they reflagged the vessels as Somali to the satisfaction of many of those involved.[146] Officials who found that unacceptable for any number of reasons were shown the way out (of the regional government). Those privy to the inner workings of the governments in Garowe and Mogadishu claim that reflagging of the Korean ships only showed the parallel level of corruption and collusion at the level of the national government in Mogadishu.

Shire Haji Farah, Puntland cabinet minister and the younger brother of NEFCO's owner Isse Haji Farah, rejects allegations of wrongdoing and insists that the four fishing ships were not Korean to begin with. According to him, they were family-owned but had to be Korean-registered in order to be able to export to the more lucrative European markets. Given the negative attention that they drew, however, Captain Isse decided to scrap their Korean registration and register them in Somalia with fishing licenses in Puntland. By doing that, says the regional minister, the company lost 50 percent of its profits and now remains restricted to Asian and Middle Eastern markets that accept Somali products.[147] Given that conflict situations incubate many half-truths, and as many untruths and conspiracy theories about resources, Shire's claims can be accurate. Nevertheless, several additional cases that have now become public seem to add credence to allegations of collusion and

---

[145] An undisclosed source delivered the letters to the author long before their circulation in wider circles.

[146] Somalia, "Report on Presumed IUU Fishing Activities in the EEZ of Somalia," 27 April 2015: www.iotc.org/documents/report-presumed-iuu-fishing-activities-eez-somalia. According to this report, *Baek Yang 37* has been renamed *Haysimo 2, Ixthus 7* is named *Butiyalo 1, Ixthus 8* is now *Butiyalo 2,* and *Ixthus 9* is *Haysimo 1*. These are names of mountains in the inaccessible tip of the Horn from where the business family hails.

[147] Interview with Puntland Minister of Planning and International Cooperation Shire Haji Farah (28 March 2017, Garowe).

Figure 1.3. FV *Al-Amal*, the Yemeni fishing vessel with an illegal fishing license, which in August 2015 went aground near Eyl. (Courtesy of PMPF.)

corruption that seem to pervade the formal fisheries sector across Somalia today.

On 11 January 2015, the FV *Poseidon*, a South Korean fishing vessel, ran out of fuel and made a port call at Mogadishu for refueling. The Somali coastguard impounded it on grounds that its USD 2-million-worth (by local estimates) of fish cargo had been illegally caught in Somali waters. The Somali Auditor General Nur Farah faced death threats and was a target of an assassination attempt as he tried to investigate the ship.[148] Around the same time, a Yemeni fishing vessel, the *Al-Amal*, was apprehended by the coast guard on the same charges and brought to the same port.[149] Not long after their capture, while the auditor general's

---

[148] "Auditor-General's Life at Risk Following Investigations into Illegal Fishing," 21 January 2015: https://somaliagenda.com/auditor-generals-life-at-risk-following-investigations-into-illegal-fishing/
Also see, Report of the UN Monitoring Group, "Annex 2.2: The *Al Amal* and *Poseidon*, and the Assault on the Auditor General." S/2015/801, October 2015.

[149] "Exclusive: High-level Corruption in Somalia Facilitates Illegal Fishing," 2 April 2015: https://somaliagenda.com/illegal-fishing/
Also see, Report of the UN Monitoring Group, "Annex 2.2: The *Al Amal* and *Poseidon*, and the Assault on the Auditor General." S/2015/801, October 2015.

investigation was still ongoing, both ships were released under suspicious circumstances and, one morning, sailed to Mombasa.[150]

Seven months later in early August 2015, *Al-Amal* went aground near Eyl, the erstwhile pirate hub in Puntland, while illegally fishing in Somali waters. Ironically, the Puntland Marine Police Force (PMPF) responded to its distress signal and rushed to the scene only to notice some irregularities in its "fishing license." On further scrutiny, the PMPF discovered a second license that was not consistent with the first. They apprehended the sailors and passed the matter to appropriate Puntland authorities, who released the crew a few days later.[151] The Indonesian captain and the first officer were kept behind and taken to court, which found them guilty and sentenced them to pay fines before leaving the country.[152]

Besides the individuals and companies discussed in the chapters of this book, several confidential sources allege that a former minister in the Abdullahi Yusuf government and another businessman – both from the Cape Guardafui region – with local representatives at Qandala and 'Aluula continue to privately sponsor dozens of Iranian vessels at a time, and several times a season. With a capacity ranging between 100 tons and 200 tons each, these vessels pay their Somali agents between USD 8,000 and USD 10,000 per ship, while the former minister is believed to collect as much as USD 15,000 per ship. There are several individuals in the same region who do so at a much smaller scale, with two to three ships at a time.[153]

The successive Puntland administrations typically know these men and often give them the nod to go on with their business, but they neither show serious interest in what and how exactly they do so nor assert their authority to follow up on their payment of taxes and license fees. In some cases, the agents pay for a single license and duplicate it across their ships. In other cases, they bribe officials at nodal positions with a cut of the proceeds of the illicit operations. In one such deal that went bad, a district police commissioner, in return for a share of the proceeds, used his relations with high-level officials in the Puntland government to secure for the Cape Guardafui businessman the green light to bring in Iranian vessels. On failing to receive the promised sum, the police chief sent his policemen after the businessman and, with the assistance of misinformed local PMPF units, had him arrested for at least two months.[154] Other

---

[150] Once in Kenya, the vessels were also accused of illegally fishing in Kenyan waters, a topic that is beyond the scope of the current book.
[151] Consultations with PMPF commander, Admiral Abdirisak (August, 2015, Garowe).
[152] Consultations with John Steed (March-April 2017, Nairobi).
[153] Confidential interviews (August 2015, Galkayo).
[154] Confidential interviews (August 2015, Galkayo).

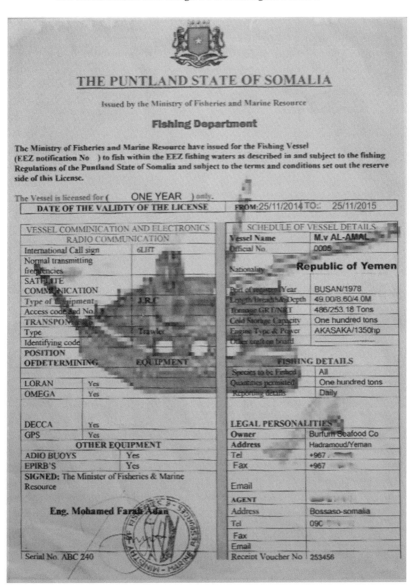

Figure 1.4. One of two self-contradicting fake licenses under which the FV *Al-Amal* was operating. (Courtesy of PMPF.)

than that, these agents spend no more than USD 100 per day for their ten-man security team on board each vessel (the guards pay for their own food); they pay no taxes or fees; and once their ships fill up their holds, they just sail back to their landing bases.

Conclusion

Subsistence self-sufficiency based on – as well as limited commercial exploitation of – the maritime resources in less-developed regions deteriorated as a result of IUU fishing and more so in least-governed, war-torn countries like Somalia. The rising subsidies provided by developed countries to their fishing sectors have enabled IUU fishers to go about plundering already vulnerable coastal communities with impunity.[155] Fractions of the value of the pirated resources are then handed out as development assistance-cum-charity to those who have lost their livelihoods as a result. Complicit western countries have funded such alternative livelihood projects to coastal communities that had once relied on – or supplemented their livelihoods with – income from the fisheries sector.[156] Equally complicit non-western countries have not even bothered to make that gesture.

The immediate aftermath of the collapse of the central government in Mogadishu in January 1991 saw foreign industrial fishers aggressively enter Somali waters as telltale signs of waste dumping started to surface. While many of these corporate violators came to the country with licenses (by all likelihood expired) and agreements, others came on the invitation and with the protection of Somali partners, and still others came with neither. The local factors in the foreign IUU fishing in Somalia posed multi-layered challenges to the successive Puntland governments and threaten to thwart the federal government's future fisheries goals and strategies. First, these local factors laid bare the non-existent deterrent capacity of successive administrations and became bad examples to foreign fishers eager to maximize profit. Second, the geographical expanse of Somali coastline and the sheer inaccessibility of several strategic coastal areas facilitated IUU fishing as much as, later on, it granted pirates much-needed safe havens. Third, clan-based political structures make it

---

[155] Christopher Pala, "Billions in Subsidies Prop Up Unsustainable Overfishing," *IPS*, November 8, 2012: www.ipsnews.net/2012/11/billions-in-subsidies-prop-up-unsustainable-overfishing/ (accessed 18 November 2012).

[156] FAO, for example, acknowledged in 2011 that Spain co-funded its "Fish Is Good for You" campaign to promote local fish consumption and combat hunger in Northeast Somalia (Puntland); as previously indicated, Spain is among the leading countries whose distant-water fishing fleet has long been involved in IUU fishing off the coast of Somalia.

administratively difficult and politically risky for any leader to act decisively in ways that may threaten the established clan balance that many dodgy actors are quick to invoke irrespective of the legitimacy of their case.

The direct and indirect support of IUU fishing by many powerful countries, along with the complex local factors, have thus had dire real-life consequences to the communities that felt compelled to resort to extreme measures. The tough competition from the IUU fishers, compounded with natural disasters, has sent the Somali fishing sector on what seems like an irreversible downward spiral. The callousness of the foreign violators and the scale of their violations spurred impromptu domestic criminal activities that drew international attention; international neglect of the foreign root causes of those crimes has so far contributed to the delay of a sustainable solution. Meanwhile, in spite of the emerging understanding of piracy as "a problem of *underdevelopment* and *security* in Somalia" [emphasis original],[157] the United Nations Security Council treated counter-piracy as a security project (under Chapter VII of the UN Charter). The UN continues to, by and large, ignore maritime policing against piracy's root causes at sea, i.e., foreign IUU fishing and waste dumping. It also relegates developmental remedies of piracy's secondary causes (or contributory factors) to a myriad of inchoate, and in many instances self-replicating, non-governmental organizations without an international mandate.[158]

---

[157] Gilmer, *Political Geographies of Piracy*, 2–3.

[158] For a discussion of the various ways that piracy is treated and its presumed commensurate remedies, see Christian Bueger, "Drops in the Bucket? A Review of Onshore Responses to Somali Piracy," *WMU Journal of Maritime Affairs* 11 (2012): 15–31; Gilmer, *Political Geographies of Piracy*.

2 From Cascading Troubles of Somali Fisheries to the Onset of Predatory Piracy

The Somali fishing sector went from commercial boom to bust in four tumultuous decades, interspersed and ultimately superseded by maritime (and overland) criminality in quick, if convoluted, succession. Incidences of armed attacks and robberies did occur in Somali waters throughout the 1990s but they did not draw much attention because they did not stand out in scale or kind from other overland and maritime robberies around the world.[1] Hansen found no recorded incidents in Somali waters in 1992 whereas 1993 saw fewer of them in Somali than in Italian waters.[2] Also as indicated in Chapter 1, not only did some foreign and Somali fishermen co-exist in Somali waters in the early 1990s but early armed robberies that the former endured triggered condemnation among other Somalis. Somali fishermen saw the foreign fishermen as innocent and forthcoming with help when they encountered distressed Somali fishermen at sea – as local customary law of the sea demands.[3]

A cycle of whirlwind developments caused the short-lived coexistence and cooperation to degenerate into intense rivalry and active conflict. As both foreign IUU fishing and unregulated local fishing intensified to the detriment of the marine environment and sustainability of their catch, the local fishermen started to suffer more. Gradually they came to resent the foreign vessels. Somali fishermen blamed their foreign counterparts for what had befallen them and actively started to attack them. The foreign vessels in turn started to match the firepower – and ultimately to outgun – the local fishermen vigilantes, leading to fierce competition and violent encounters several years before the emergence of larger-scale predatory attacks.

---

[1] According to the International Maritime Bureau's Piracy Reporting Center, there have been a total of just over 150 reported incidents of (actual and attempted) maritime attacks associated with Somalia in the ten years between 1994 and 2004.

[2] Hansen, *Piracy in the Greater Gulf of Aden*, 20.

[3] Puntland Development Research Center (PDRC), *Somali Customary Law and Traditional Economy: Cross Sectional, Pastoral, Frankincense, and Marine Norms* (Garowe, Puntland: PDRC, 2003).

Pervasive foreign bias that discounted Somali perspectives and grievances on the one hand, and the non-permissive research environment on the ground in Somalia on the other, contributed to the indiscriminate treatment of all forms of maritime predation as piracy. This chapter will correct that perception by clearly delineating – both chronologically and substantively – the mundane, everyday robberies, the impromptu defensive responses of aggrieved local fishermen, and the predatory attacks for hostages and ransom. It locates the beginnings of defensive piracy in the dynamic competition and violent confrontations between, on the one hand, Somali fishermen and their small fishing companies and, on the other hand, resource pirates, i.e., the foreign industrial vessels on IUU fishing missions in Somali waters and their local accomplices. The chapter analyzes how the authorities' ill-conceived trials and errors in regulating and securing fisheries helped inflame the situation. It also documents the early beginnings and proliferation of ransom piracy. To better appreciate the effects and long-term implications of all these – IUU fishing, legitimate local responses to that, and criminal hostage taking – it is important to start with a thumbnail sketch of the briefly lucrative, export-oriented Somali fisheries industry since the collapse of the government in 1991.

A Vibrant Sector in the Absence of the State

Peacetime economic activities like commercial fishing, and to some degree even subsistence fishing, came to a standstill in many coastal areas in south and central Somalia as many of their residents fled their homes and became internally displaced persons (IDPs) or refugees in neighboring countries due to the raging civil war.[4] Nevertheless, northern Somalia, i.e., Somaliland and Puntland, was spared the worst of the post-Siad Barre fratricidal chaos that allowed the resumption and expansion of old economic activities and the start of new ones. Those regions also benefited from population inflows because their relative security and stability, combined with limited opportunities, attracted the diaspora back and offered relief and safety to groups that had been otherized and targeted in the clan-based bouts of violence in central and southern Somalia.[5]

---

[4] Afyare Abdi Elmi, *Understanding the Somalia Conflagration: Identities, Political Islam and Peacebuilding* (New York: Pluto Press, 2010); Lidwien Kapteijns, *Clan Cleansing in Somalia: The Ruinous Legacy of 1991* (University of Pennsylvania Press, 2013); Yusuf Mohamed Haid, *Out of Mogadishu: A Memoir of the Civil War In 1991* (N.P.: 2016).

[5] As Aweys Warsame Yusuf demonstrates for the rest of Somalia, such businesses and businesspeople helped stabilize the political situation and provided needed services but, as

In the northeast, i.e., Puntland, the war displaced Somalis – whether they hailed from Puntland, had long ancestral ties there, or were simply seeking refuge from the conflict – and the returning diaspora combined their entrepreneurial, investment and human resources with the capacities and opportunities that awaited them on the ground to kick-start the economy. The richly endowed and under-exploited fisheries sector especially offered lucrative opportunities and absorbed readily available resources. The most entrepreneurial among the returned and newly arrived townspeople found business opportunities, economic sustenance, and alternative livelihoods in the hitherto under-exploited fishing sector, which they quickly capitalized on without regulation – and contributed to its exploitation.

By the mid-1990s, Puntland saw the emergence of more than twenty private companies (individual and shared) with their own fishing component and another component for buying the catch of smaller-scale and individual artisanal fishermen. Stretching between Gara'ad in the south and Hafun in the northeast, these companies had the capacity to collect, freeze, and export their catch – nearly entirely to the Middle East – at various processing stages.[6] Smaller-scale Somali fishermen also sold their catch to "visiting foreign boats calling at ports on both the Gulf of Aden and the Indian Ocean coast to buy mackerel from local fishermen, some of whom . . . entered into partnerships with these visiting boats."[7]

According to some estimates, by 1998 Puntland's lobster and shark fin exports reached USD 3.5 million each and shark meat export reached USD 500,000.[8] The attendant demographic growth saw the number of inhabitants of towns and traditional fishing villages increase in tandem. Between 1991 and 2005, for example, the population of the historic fishing village of Eyl (divided between Da'awad village on the hill facing the ocean and the coastal fishing settlement called Bedey on the beach) is

we will see later in the book, at least some of them also contributed to globally consequential threats to stability and security. See his chapter "Somali Enterprises: Making Peace Their Business," in Jessica Banfield, Canan Gunduz, and Nick Killick (eds.), *Local Business, Local Peace: The Peacebuilding Potential of the Domestic Private Sector* (London: International Alert, 2006), 469–507.

[6] Interviews with owners and executives of East African Fishing Company (February 2012, Garowe); Al-Shaab33 Fishing Company (19 February 2012, Bosaso), and AGfish Company (27 February 2012, Galkayo). All three companies emerged in the early 1990s and still maintain a reduced presence while most of the others went bankrupt under the heavy weight of illegal fishing, tsunami, piracy, and aggressive counter-piracy operations that have made their fishing ground a no-go zone.

[7] Puntland Development Research Center (PDRC), *Somali Customary Law and Traditional Economy: Cross Sectional, Pastoral, Frankincense, and Marine Norms* (Garowe, Puntland: PDRC, 2003), 96.

[8] WSP Somali Programme, *Rebuilding Somalia: Issues and Possibilities for Puntland* (London: HAAN Associates, 2001), 146.

believed to have grown by nearly tenfold and to have reached close to 10,000 people, most of whom lived directly or indirectly off the fishing sector.[9]

The fishing business model that directly or indirectly employed many and generated much profit in the 1990s consisted of entrepreneurs or company owners at the top tier. They invested capital to procure equipment – from nets and traps to fishing boats, trucks, and freezers – for their own companies and to give on credit to smaller-scale fishers. The entrepreneurs also gave out unsecured, competitive loans to other fishermen who would repay their debt with their catch, turning the transaction into a form of localized, small-scale, resource-backed loans. Besides the limited number of permanent employees, these companies hired hundreds – and in some cases thousands – of seasonal employees, both expert divers and laborers. With established routes and networks for exporting the fish in bulk, the bigger companies partnered with independent smaller-scale fishermen and fisherwomen who owned boats and equipment, hired their own limited number of seasonal employees or used family labor, and sold their catch to the bigger companies.

The 1990s thus saw an unprecedented boom of locally owned, export-oriented fisheries business in Puntland and across Somalia. Young men who joined in the rush early on and became divers and skilled laborers started to emerge as a new "class" in their own right, identified by their long, expensive *me'awis* (traditional *sarong*) and crowding together during non-fishing seasons. Their peers envied these fishermen; the young and aspiring looked up to them as role models; and the daring ladies were candid about their desires for them. Whereas school-age boys dropped out of school and ran off to coastal fishing villages,[10] young ladies sang "Are you a diver, so that I may laugh/have fun with you?"[11] Throughout the 1990s, therefore, the private Somali fishing industry did well by most accounts, in spite of the tough competition from industrial fishers and the marine environment that was deteriorating due partially to the intense and unregulated exploitation by both private and industrial fishers.[12]

---

[9] Mayor Musa Osman Yusuf of Eyl (24 February 2012, Eyl).

[10] My driver during my January–March 2012 travels across Puntland was one of those teenage boys who quit school to become fishermen. In my subsequent travels, I encountered many such school dropouts who had largely failed as fishermen.

[11] In Somali the song went: "*Quusoa ma tahay, aan kula qoslee?*"

[12] Interviews with several fishermen and fish exporters indicate that the income of a Somali commercial fisherman reached as high as USD 20,000 per season and that of an average diver reached USD 5,000. There is a good chance that these figures are a little exaggerated but they give an indication of the overall well-being of the trade and of the hope and optimism of the practitioners.

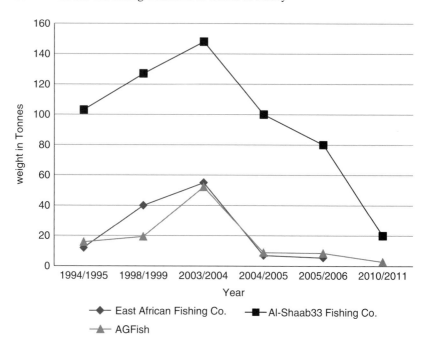

Figure 2.1. Lobster exports by private Somali fishing companies. (Compiled by author from data provided by the three companies.)

By the end of the 1990s and the beginning of the 2000s, however, the private Somali fishing sector had seen its better days. The lucrative enterprise's downward spiral intensified because of natural and man-made causes. IUU fishing, as discussed in the previous chapter, and piracy, as we will see in the next, are among the principal culprits. Based on statistics from three companies with complete data sets, the graph above (Figure 2.1) best demonstrates the dire predicament of the fishing sector in the hands of foreign resource pirates and, subsequently, Somali ransom pirates.

On land too, IUU fishing adversely affected business and employment opportunities for it neither raised local revenue nor offered alternative livelihoods.[13] Many Somali commercial fishermen quit as soon as they observed the steady decline in the face of rising IUU fishing, while others continued operations with rising deficits until nearly all of them went bankrupt and closed up shop. Lacking a government to defend their interests and without insurance arrangements to fall back on, the local Somali fishing companies never recovered from their losses.

---

[13] Environmental Justice Foundation, *Pirates and Profiteers: How Pirates Fishing Fleets Are Robbing People and Oceans* (London: Environmental Justice Foundation, 2005), 6–7.

Figure 2.2. On any given day since the collapse of fisheries and expulsion of the pirates, the beach in Bedey (the coastal half of Eyl) is littered with such disused boats. (Photo by the author.)

Fishermen Vigilantes and Defensive Piracy

Having noted that any country would dispatch its coast guard to protect its marine resources from foreign plunderers, the February 1994 story by the Associated Press journalist Michael Phillips continued: "But since Somalia had no coast guard and no functioning government, clan militiamen are threatening to turn speed boats into gun boats and take matters into their own hands."[14] And that was exactly what they did after their repeated pleas for local and international help to end foreign IUU fishing in their waters fell on either incapable or deaf ears.[15]

The many fishermen vigilante groups remained ad hoc and loose except one, which was staged by recognized and recognizable personalities, had the blessing of the rebel Somali Salvation Democratic Front (SSDF), and was joined by former coast guards in its endeavor. As a young community activist and owner of a family fishing business, the former Director General

---

[14] Michael Phillips, "Intrigue and Lobster in a Peaceful Corner of Somalia," Associated Press (2 February 1994) quoted in Todd Jennings, "Controlling Access in the Absence of a Central Government: The Somali Dilemma," in *Ocean Yearbook Online*, vol. 15, no. 1 (2001), 407.

[15] As we will see in Chapter 5, foreign IUU vessels responded with a hail of bullets to unarmed civilians pleading with them to leave their waters.

of the Ministry of Fisheries and Marine Resources in Puntland, Abdiwahid Mohamed Hersi "Jo'ar," and fishermen activists like him mobilized the communities and appealed to SSDF leaders, Mohamed Abshir and Abdullahi Yusuf. They were especially bitter about Hassan Munyo, who not only freely operated the former SHIFCO trawlers in the inshore waters that had been the traditional preserve of the local artisanal fishermen, but who also allegedly brought other industrial-scale fishing vessels from European and Asian Distant Water Fishing Nations (DWFNs).[16]

Lacking its own coast guard, SSDF granted the fishermen activists the green light to take action whereupon in 1992 they formed a short-lived Organization for the Protection of Somali Coastline (*Ururka Badbaadinta Xeebaha Somaliyeed* or UBAXSO in its Somali acronym).[17] Led by Salah Hashi Arab, a former marine officer turned fisherman, and joined by some former coast guards, UBAXSO alone captured a dozen foreign IUU fishing vessels and brought them to Bosaso where they were fined by SSDF. Jo'ar claims that they also took action against what he called local "thieves," who were attacking non-fishing commercial liners.[18] To the chagrin of Hassan Munyo, UBAXSO units also captured one of the SHIFCO vessels around Hafun; it was later released upon the payment of a fine that was negotiated by the enigmatic Boqor Abdullahi "King Kong," the Qardo-based king of the Darod.[19]

The friction between the two topmost SSDF leaders, their falling out with each other, and the eventual splitting of SSDF into two factions in 1994 (that lasted organizationally until at least 1996) had their own negative effects on maritime security in the Gulf of Aden and the western Indian Ocean. While an attempted excavation of an old shipwrecked treasure vessel off the Horn of Africa triggered fighting between the factions in the mid-1990s, the fishing permit granted by one was not recognized by the other. In 1994, Mohamed Abshir granted fishing licenses to two Italian trawlers with the intermediation of a Bosaso-based Italian NGO. It is reported that one of the guards/inspectors provided by Mohamed Abshir hijacked the trawler and brought it to Bosaso in collusion with someone in the Abdullahi Yusuf faction.

---

[16] Conversations with Abdiwahid Mohamed Hersi "Jo'ar" (Bosaso, Hargeisa and Garowe between 2012 and 2017). Interview with Lt. Col. Abdirizak Ismail Hassan (26 and 27 February 2012, Galkayo).

[17] Conversations with Abdiwahid Mohamed Hersi (aka Jo'ar).

[18] Conversations with Jo'ar. The earliest captured fishing vessels include two Taiwanese ships, *Yue Fa No. 3* and *Chian Yuein No. 232*, that were caught illegally fishing off the tip of the Horn near Bandar Bayla. See "SSDF Group Seizes Two Taiwan Fishing Boats," AFP, 6 April 1992; Bahadur, *Deadly Waters*, 31.

[19] Conversations with Ali Farah; and conversation with Burhaan Daahir (13 November 2012, Garowe).

The Italian NGO helped negotiate a ransom settlement in the amount of USD 245,000, a portion of which has reportedly been used for the upkeep of that faction.

As rival SSDF camps sought to outdo one another, UBAXSO failed to balance between the two and ceased to exist as a result. Further, different groups also sought to take advantage of the leaders' distraction to advance their respective interests, including opportunistic hijackings of ships. Whereas Martin Murphy reports that in 1997 SSDF forces took the Taiwanese trawler MV *Shen Kno II* and collected USD 800,000 in ransom,[20] a confidential source also gives an account of another vessel in the same year in which Abdullahi Yusuf's bodyguards were involved. Yusuf had permitted the unnamed vessel to fish in Puntland waters, giving it an onboard protection team led by one of his own bodyguards known by the vile nickname of *Aakhiradii Wase*. It is reported that upon discovering a stash of USD 40,000 in the vessel's safe while it was in Mombasa, one guard called for assistance from another guard who happened to be Abdullahi Yusuf's nephew. The two then commandeered the vessel out of the port of Mombasa to Gara'ad and stole the USD 40,000 for themselves while their leader Abdullahi Yusuf negotiated an additional USD 300,000 in ransom.[21] Although such money-driven piratical acts existed, they remained fewer than the defensive measures against IUU vessels; both incidences paled in comparison to other piracy-prone places around the world.

Meanwhile, small groups of fishermen vigilantes mushroomed in various localities without a clear leader or a semblance of organization. They exacted fines on captured ships without uniformity or accountability to a centralized authority; this made the exercise susceptible to manipulation by different people as is discussed later in this chapter. In some instances, individual fishermen fired warning shots to alert the large foreign vessels approaching their boats, fishing nets and traps. In other instance, they haphazardly went on impromptu attacks or counterattacks, righteously convinced that blatant violations and violence by the IUU vessels made their responses self-evidently legitimate. They confronted and/or went after foreign vessels upon discovering that the latter – and their likes – had destroyed the nets, traps and boats they had set up at night. By either ignoring the fishermen, deliberately or accidentally ramming their artisanal crafts, dousing the artisanal boats/fishermen with highly pressurized – and sometimes hot – water, or shooting back at

---

[20] Murphy, *Somalia: The New Barbary?* 13. Although his earlier writing referenced Murphy and his figure, J. Peter Pham later claimed that the ransom was in fact USD 1 million. See Pham, "The Failed State and Regional Dimensions of Somali Piracy," 46.

[21] Confidential Interview (February 2012, Bosaso).

them, the foreign vessels' responses only inflamed the situation and escalated the tensions to violent confrontations.

Data on local damages in the ensuing confrontations are hard to come by. Local oral sources are difficult to corroborate, partially because they lack the accuracy of dates, name of vessels, and other essential details. Foreign sources have hardly bothered to systematically document Somali losses. The scattered and sometimes anecdotal accounts are telling, however. Scott Coffen-Smout, for example, reported the damages incurred during the second capture – within one year – of the Italian-owned and Mombasa-based MV *Bahari Hindi*, which had been illegally fishing in Somali waters thus: "In December 1998, the same vessel [i.e., *Bahari Hindi*] and its 33-member crew were arrested and taken in Eyl, northeast Somalia, for allegedly violating Somali territorial waters, destroying local fishing nets, and firing at local fishing boats. A clash occurred before the capture and two Somali fishing boats were destroyed."[22] Todd Jennings, similarly documented an earlier violent encounter: "Late in 1997 fighting broke out between local fishermen and four foreign vessels; seven Somalis were wounded."[23]

Notorious pirate leader Abshir Abdullahi Abdule "Boyah" claims to have lost a fishing boat in 1999 because a large industrial fishing vessel plowed into it – the fishermen on board jumped off in time to save their lives. Although Boyah had been among the fishermen vigilantes since the mid-1990s, he did not instantly turn to ransom piracy.[24] But Khaadar Ahmed, another former pirate in Eyl, said that the loss of his only fishing boat in 2002 was the last straw that pushed him into piracy. He said the very same night he lost his boat, he and his colleagues collected the guns available, boarded another small fishing boat, and went after any vessel that they could find nearby.[25]

The local fishing companies and their smaller-scale suppliers joined in the impromptu responses of the fishermen vigilantes. Their joint protest intensified with the increase in number and scale of foreign industrial fishing vessels and the latter's increasingly violent encounters with local fishermen. "According to witnesses," wrote Jennings, "big vessels looted local nets – a practice Somali fishermen claim is not uncommon. This, in

[22] Scott Coffen-Smout, "Pirates, Warlords and Rogue Fishing Vessels in Somalia's Unruly Seas," 1999: www.chebucto.ns.ca/~ar120/somalia.html.

[23] Todd Jennings, "Controlling Access in the Absence of a Central Government: The Somali Dilemma," in *Ocean Yearbook Online*, vol. 15, no. 1 (2001), 407.

[24] Interview with Abshir Abdullahi Abdule "Boyah" (8 and 15 June 2014, Garowe, Puntland).

[25] Both these former pirates later renounced the trade on the urgings of Puntland former Mufiti, the late Abdulkadir Nur Farah "*Gacmay*" in 2008. Focus group meeting with residents of Eyl on 6 September 2015.

turn, has led Somali fishermen to rig their boats with heavy machine guns, some threatening to destroy every foreign vessel in sight."[26] Mohamud Abdulkadir Mohamed "John" is one of many such fishermen.

With his company's headquarters in Kulub (some 12 km north of Gara'ad), John is open about how he planned to confront the trawlers from the mid-1990s through the early 2000s.[27] He first bought his fishermen weapons and allowed them to use his speedboats to capture the trawlers with the intention of sinking them or burning them with gasoline, which he also provided.[28] By his own account, in the early 2000s John even tried – but failed – to procure sea mines to plant in Somali waters in order to prevent the trawlers from coming into their fishing grounds and to blow them up if they did. "The idea," he said, "was to send a strong message and prevent others from coming to our waters."[29] He was unsuccessful and his declining fishing company continued to struggle into the 2010s until it was no more than a name.

Similarly in Eyl, when an illegal trawler was captured and brought to harbor in 2000, many, including the then-anti-IUU fishing activist and subsequent mayor of the district, wanted to pull the vessel off the water and let it "die" on the beach. That was expected to become a visible reminder to the other illegal trawlers of the fate that awaited them should they continue to pirate Somali resources.[30] The owners of the local Somali fishing companies and the fishermen vigilantes claim not to have been interested in money. They say that they only wanted the foreign industrial fishers to get out of their waters. As we will see later in the chapter, they were outsmarted by, on the one hand, the foreign vessels eager to be freed and ready to pay up to the pleasure of the captors and, on the other hand, the rogue vigilantes who demanded increasingly higher fines-cum-ransoms.

From the many European, Asian and African vessels (both in terms of origin as well as flag) that had been illegally fishing in Somali waters in the 1990s, different writers have variously documented the ones that were captured by vigilante fishermen and the fines (or ransoms) that they reportedly paid for their release.[31] These writers and others, including

---

[26] Todd Jennings, "Controlling Access in the Absence of a Central Government: The Somali Dilemma," in *Ocean Yearbook Online*, vol. 15, no. 1 (2001), 407.

[27] Interview with Mohamud Abdulkadir Mohamed "John" (27 February 2012, Galkayo).

[28] Had "John" succeeded in this scheme, that would not have been the first time that a vessel was set on fire in Somali waters for in 1991 the MV *Naviluck* was reportedly set on fire by pirates aboard three attack boats. See Murphy, *Somalia: The New Barbary?* 12.

[29] Interview with Mohamud Abdulkadir Mohamed "John" (27 February 2012, Galkayo).

[30] Interview with Mayor of Eyl, Musa Osman Yusuf (24 February 2012, Eyl).

[31] Scott Coffen-Smout, "Pirates, Warlords and Rogue Fishing Vessels in Somalia's Unruly Seas," 1999: www.chebucto.ns.ca/~ar120/somalia.html; Todd Jennings, "Controlling Access in the Absence of a Central Government: The Somali Dilemma," in *Ocean Yearbook Online*, vol. 15, no. 1 (2001), 407; Mohamed Abshir Waldo, "The Two

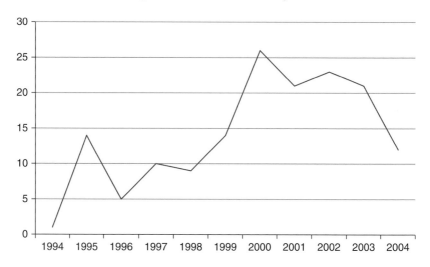

Figure 2.3. Piracy incidents, both actual and attempted, 1994–2004. (Compiled from IMB annual reports.)

the Piracy Reporting Center of the International Maritime Bureau, have also reported that non-fishing vessels too had fallen victim. Somali and Somali-contracted transport and fishing vessels had not been spared either. While Hassan Munyo is reported to have paid for the release of his SHIFCO vessels and crew four times, in 1998 the Isse Mohamud family (a Mejerten sub-clan) of Nugaal captured around Eyl a fishing vessel that had reportedly been under the protection of the Omar Mohamud (another Mejerten sub-clan family) of north Mudug. The tense negotiations that ensued settled on a fine/ransom of around USD 200,000.[32]

The Authorities' Feeble Reentry into Fisheries/Security

While the civil war-induced chaos in southern and central Somalia went on, the attention of the fledgling state of Puntland did not turn toward illegal fishing until the adjudication of a captured fishing vessel in the Gara'ad–Jarriban area (along the border with Galmudug) exposed

Piracies in Somalia: Why the World Ignores the Other?" *Wardheer News*, January 08, 2009: http://somalitalk.com/2009/april/waldo.html.

[32] Focus group meeting with residents of Eyl (5 September 2015). The timing, location and fine seem to suggest that the vessel in question was the MV *Bahari One*. For an account of that boat's illegal activities and capture, see Scott Coffen-Smout, "Pirates, Warlords and Rogue Fishing Vessels in Somalia's Unruly Seas," 1999: www.chebucto.ns.ca/~ar120/s omalia.html; Murphy, *Somalia: The New Barbary?* ; Bahadur, *Deadly Waters*.

a potentially destabilizing political development. Around the same time as the formation of the Puntland State of Somalia in 1998, Gara'ad fishermen captured a Taiwanese fishing vessel in nearby waters and brought the sailors to land where local Omar Mohamud sub-sub-clan elders from the Abdi Isse family held court independently of the newly declared government in Garowe. Unlike traditional courts before and after them, these Abdi Isse elders had declared the Jarriban area as "Coastland," separate from Puntland on the grounds that Puntland's founding president, Abdullahi Yusuf (who was a Reer Mahad, another family of the Omar Mohamud) had purportedly neglected them. "Coastland's" ad hoc court recognized the hijackers as legitimate coast guards and applauded their actions. It found the foreign fishermen guilty of trespassing, of using prohibited fishing methods, and of causing environmental damage. The foreign fishermen were released upon the payment of USD 200,000 in fines, which was divided among the hijackers, local community and court/administration.[33]

The conclusion of this affair in the difficult Mudug region, in complete exclusion of the SSDF/Puntland officials, sent shockwaves through the recently reunited SSDF and its barely established government in Garowe. There were several additional factors that compelled the government to devise a formalized pursuit of maritime security. First, the fledgling Puntland administration, especially Abdullahi Yusuf himself, was concerned about international implications of a possible explosion of piracy. Second, Abdullahi Yusuf's new administration had come under rising internal pressure from its own powerful constituencies to defend the territory's marine cash crop from foreign resource pirates. Perhaps equally important, influential power brokers had been lobbying the new administration to offer them a potentially lucrative security contract to police the region's coastal waters.

The Puntland government contracted with private security providers to serve as its coast guard and aimed to finance the deal by the proceeds it expected from issuing fishing licenses. Garowe entrusted two companies at different times with the responsibilities of both issuing licenses and protecting Somali waters from illegal trawlers: Hart Group (1999–2002) and Somali-Canadian Coast Guard (SomCan; 2002–2005, and 2007–2009). Although the full story of these security companies is still murky, from what a few authors have written[34] and from interviews with informed personalities in Puntland, not only have the security companies

---

[33] Conversation with former Somali journalist Burhaan Daahir (13 November 2012, Garowe).
[34] Hansen, *Piracy in the Greater Gulf of Aden*; Murphy, *Somalia: The New Barbary?* 22–24; Bahadur, *Deadly Waters*, 62–70.

failed to contain illegal fishing but they also exacerbated the conditions that gave rise to – and that continued to be used to rationalize – piracy. In the words of retired Brigadier General Abdirizak Sheikh Osman "Ali Baadiyow," for example, Hart Group "took the licensing idea but did not take the patrolling" component of their contract.[35] Similarly, Jo'ar is quoted as saying that, for its part, SomCan too "was keeping the security of their own licensed ships instead of keeping the security of the sea."[36]

Under the protection of Hart and SomCan coast guards, foreign trawlers continued fishing in inshore waters within earshot of the coast, an area that had traditionally been the exclusive fishing grounds of artisanal fishermen. Except this time the foreign fishers were protected under the authority of the state. In the process, the fishing vessels destroyed local fishermen's gear and in many cases their heavily armed guards, the use of whom was neither legal nor normal practice, fought off community defense vigilantes. Whatever the merits of these security solutions, the local fishing communities did not see the privatized coast guards any differently than they did the armed foreign trawlers that stole their fish almost at gunpoint. In the words of General Ali Baadiyow, "the hungry [Somali] people could see that their own government was involved in illegal fishing: piracy,"[37] in the sense that the government protected illegal fishers. Thus left to their own devices, the local fishermen, among them Abshir Abdullahi Abdule "Boyah," continued to attack and capture foreign fishing vessels.[38]

Meanwhile, the industrial fishers had been arming themselves increasingly and/or had secured the protection of local partners before, during, and after Puntland contracted with privatized coast guards. Scattered – and sometime anecdotal – data suggest that many of DWFN's more technologically advanced vessels have fished in Somalia's EEZ (beyond 12 nautical miles from shore) but, because of their distance from the coast, such vessels have fallen outside the reach or even censure of the weak regional authorities. It is important to underscore the fact that IUU fishers (from DWFNs as well as from the Greater Horn of Africa and the Persian Gulf) have actively flouted the various efforts of Somali authorities to legalize and regulate their operations through the payment of appropriate fees.

The current Puntland government, under President Abdiweli Mohamed Ali "Gas," preserved the licensing and registration costs and the requirement that it inherited from the preceding governments.

---

[35] Interviews with Brigadier General Abdirizak Sheikh Osman "Ali Baadiyow" (February and October 2012, Galkayo)
[36] Quoted in Bahadur, *Deadly Waters*, 65.   [37] Interview with General "Ali Baadiyow"
[38] Bahadur, *Deadly Waters*, 19.

Accordingly, the regional fisheries authorities were to levy USD 1,000 as a flat, yearlong registration fee on foreign vessels. The specific licensing costs differed based on the types of vessels: on a 45-day long fishing trip, trawlers would pay USD 150 per ton, long liners USD 100 per ton, mother ships USD 100, and purse seines USD 300. Although the regulation allowed foreign companies to hire local agents on the ground, it expected the fishing vessels to sail to Bosaso for inspection, among other requirements.[39]

Although IUU vessels did not seek government licenses, those that did and that paid the appropriate registration and license fees were technically eligible for state protection. Accordingly, the Puntland government had one of two security options for the licensed vessels; it offered either to put government-authorized guards on board the ships that it licensed or to grant those vessels the option of contracting with private guards, not to exceed four AK-47-armed guards per vessel. Some foreign vessels that operated close to shore, however, either had fake licenses or secured local protection through those who were fraudulently licensed, as previously indicated. Such vessels came with more armed men and far superior weapons.[40]

Failure to comply with the Puntland state's regulations carried hefty monetary penalties, although the Puntland state lacked the capacity – and its officials lacked the cohesion and integrity – to enforce them, even on captured vessels. The regulation stipulated that unlicensed foreign vessels that were over 50 tons would be liable for USD 400 per gross registered tonnage (GRT) and an additional USD 10,000 for the captain; the use of prohibited gear or fishing in prohibited areas would incur an additional penalty of USD 2,000. Those vessels below 50 tons would be levied with half the above penalties and USD 1,000 for the captain.[41] But the modest fees did not entice foreign vessels or their local accomplices to get legitimate licenses; nor did the threat of hefty penalties deter them from illicit fishing operations.

Confidential sources have, for example, related how powerful businessmen from Qandala and 'Aluula brought foreign vessels to Somali waters without licenses, or with forged or duplicated ones; they regularly contracted with dozens of local gunmen from the region to board the vessels

---

[39] This is according to guidelines printed on the back of the authentic licenses that were in use before 2013.

[40] In early 2012, for example, an Iranian vessel/dhow falsely claimed to be licensed with government protection. Confidential interview with a government official with intelligence and fishing knowledge (February 2012, Bosaso).

[41] This is according to guidelines printed on the back of the authentic licenses that were in use before 2013.

that fished off the tip of the Horn. The armed guards were paid USD 10 per day and up to ten guards were put aboard a vessel. Upon encountering the authorities or facing the threat of pirate attack, these heavily armed private guards would show up and not only claim that the ship was theirs or under their protection, but would actually engage in firefights when necessary. In other instances, the foreign vessels came armed with heavy weapons, either from their home countries or countries not far from their fishing grounds.

The Turning Point from Defensive to Predatory Piracy

In the ensuing militarized competition, the artisanal and small-scale commercial fishermen in Somalia lost to the sheer number of foreign fishing crafts, their fishing capacities, and their firepower. After a few failed encounters, many of the artisanal fishermen vigilantes realized that they had been outgunned and overpowered. "Our boys lost hope when they realized that the trawlers' licensees supplied them with armed militias to overpower opponents," said a fisherman in late 2000.[42] Whereas some fishermen who resorted to force in order to genuinely defend their waters gave up at that point, others took to attacking every vulnerable vessel they encountered at sea.[43]

Neither deterred by the risk of being captured nor dissuaded by the fishermen's pleas, foreign vessels fishing in Somali waters (and the owners of captured trawlers) proved too eager to pay "fines" directly to their captors in order to secure the expedited release of their vessels and crew. It was more economical to do so and to go about their business without the risk of increased insurance premiums, dragged-out court processes that could result in increased labor costs and potential spoilage of the catch, subsequent investigation by the company, loss of client confidence, embarrassment and even a potential lawsuit back at home.[44] For their part, the ordinary fishermen – the divers and laborers – who did the

---

[42] Abdulkadir Khalif, "Somalia: How Illegal Fishing Feeds Somali Piracy," *The East African*, 15 November 2005.

[43] Statistics collated from IMB annual piracy reports and the data collected from the field show a drop of maritime attacks between 2003 and 2004 that inexplicably coincide with the start of a sharp decline in the annual landing of fishing companies in Puntland.

[44] Whereas Carolin Liss reports that as much as 50 percent of piracy incidents may go unreported, in October 2005, the United Nations Monitoring Group on Somalia thus documented some ships' and companies' justifications for their failure to report a hijacking: "The actual extent of piracy is very difficult to gauge; there may have been other cases that have gone unreported, since many shipping companies do not report incidents of piracy for fear of raising their insurance premiums and prompting protracted, time-consuming investigations. The same is true of ransoms paid. Ship owners and companies do not want to divulge any information regarding the amount of money

hijackings and remained in charge of the captured vessels, wanted money. The earliest such incidents are traced to 2000 when the frontline hijackers and the owners of the captured trawlers outmaneuvered the coastal communities' activism and deterrence against IUU fishing by striking deals whereby the hijackers released the trawlers upon receiving undisclosed sums from the foreigner vessels.[45]

The alacrity with which the earliest-captured foreign fishers paid – and local vigilantes' collected – increasing "fines" thus started ransom payments, which lured increasing numbers of pirates into attacking fishing, transport, and luxury vessels alike.[46] As a senior police official put it: "Whenever ten guys get paid ransom money, twenty more pirates are created."[47] An interview that Jatin Dua conducted with a pirate in Puntland confirms the above story:

I was a fisherman in Eyl catching lobster mostly but also snapper and tuna. One day a trawler cut our nets in the middle of the night when we were fishing not far from the coast. A few of us decided enough was enough and we boarded the boat. The captain was a Pakistani. We made him pay USD 1,000 as a tax to fish in our waters. We went back to the village and told everyone about it. Soon the boys started getting on the fiber boats and chasing trawlers to get money from them. This is how we became pirates. After a while, we started going after bigger boats.[48]

This escalating dynamic of exchange between local captors and foreign captives took on a life of its own when local profit-driven actors hijacked and semi-professionalized what many believe were legitimate, impromptu acts of self-defense. Perhaps Onuoha best captured this when he wrote of the "much larger, hidden, long-term costs" of paying ransoms or fines:

[It] encourages old and new groups to partake in the profitable criminal enterprise . . . old pirate gangs will expand and new ones will emerge. . . [I]t provides

---

paid for the release of ships and crews." Report of the United Nations Monitoring Group on Somalia, S/2005/625, 4 October 2005, paragraph. 105. Also see Liss, "Maritime Piracy in Southeast Asia," 55–56; Nincic, "State Failure and the Re-Emergence of Maritime Piracy;" and Murphy, *Small Boats, Weak States, Dirty Money*, 64-71.

[45] According to John, between late January and early February 2000 a Taiwanese fishing vessel was the first to be captured by the fishermen near his company headquarters in Kulub.

[46] I spoke with five commercial fishermen, numerous artisanal fishers, five regional/district administrators, two retired generals, three colonels, and three legal experts including the current Attorney General, and even pirates who blame these early ransom payments as the source of the current problem of piracy.

[47] Quoted in Andrew Harding, "Postcard from Somali Pirate Capital," BBC, 16 June 2009: http://news.bbc.co.uk/2/hi/africa/8103585.stm

[48] Quoted in Dua, "A Sea of Trade and a Sea of Fish: Piracy and Protection in the Western Indian Ocean," *Journal of Eastern African Studies* vol. 7, no. 2 (2013), 353–370 [here 354].

pirates with finance to procure sophisticated weapons and high-tech gadgetry. This has contributed to the frequency of their attacks, the expansion of the range of their onslaught, and the success rate of their forays. This further emboldens the pirates and worsens the situation.[49]

But the critical turning point into full-fledged predatory ransom piracy had to wait until a late-2004 natural disaster, i.e., the "Christmas tsunami," that compounded the cascading troubles of the Somali private fishing sector.

The losses that the Somali fishing companies continued to suffer because of foreign IUU fishing made it impossible for them to continue investing in upgrading their equipment, procuring new equipment, or giving out loans. Their increasingly outdated gear and that of their smaller-scale partners – especially in the face of fierce competition from a large number of medium- and industrial-scale fishers – in turn diminished their catch as well as their capacity to retain their employees. The tsunami that hit the Indian Ocean in December 2004 worsened the downward spiral of the short-lived lucrative sector and sealed its fate.

The tsunami devastated Somali coastal communities and the local fishing companies in many ways.[50] Hermann Fritz and Jose Borrero reported that, in Puntland, the floods caused the loss of around 200 human lives (between the dead and missing), more than 1,500 houses (destroyed or damaged), and close to 300 fishing boats. Of Eyl's 145 fishing boats, 40 were reported destroyed and 70 damaged.[51] The tsunami thus consumed a huge portion of the capital of the local fishing companies that had persisted in the business, caused a drastic decline in their already reduced catch, and pushed even more able-bodied young men into joblessness and despair.[52]

When the tsunami dealt the withering fishing sector a severe blow and devastated the fishing communities along the coast, it served as an immediate precipitant for the evolution of defensive piracy into predatory criminal enterprise. After a decline in attacks in the years preceding the tsunami, piracy returned with a vengeance. It became a full-blown

---

[49] Onuoha, "Piracy and Maritime Security off the Horn of Africa," 202.

[50] BBC, "Somali Tsunami Victim Toll Rises," 5 January 2005: http://news.bbc.co.uk/2/hi/africa/4147097.stm; Hermann M. Fritz and Jose C. Borrero, "Somalia Field Survey after the December 2004 Indian Ocean Tsunami," *Earthquake Spectra*, vol. 22, no. S3 (June 2006), 219–233. The tsunami also washed toxic waste canisters up the Somali coast and thrust the question of waste dumping in Somalia back into public debate, although only fleetingly.

[51] Fritz and Borrero, "Somalia Field Survey."

[52] Confidential interview (February 2012, Garowe). This story was confirmed in several confidential interviews (between January and March 2012 in Garowe and Galkayo) with other fishermen, some of whom turned to piracy.

ransom piracy driven by insatiable greed, notwithstanding the pirates' continued claims to be defensive in intention.

The tipping point from the previously predominantly defensive attacks to predatory ransom piracy occurred in 2005 when a few seasoned but impoverished fishermen from Eyl, with the help of a capable organizer from Haradere, decided to indiscriminately capture vessels for ransom.[53] Hansen, who was among the first foreign scholars to interview some of the early ransom pirates in Somalia, gives all the credit to the administrative, mobilizing and business acumen of Mohamed Abdi Hassan "Afweyne." According to him, these pirates or the "Hobiyo-Haradhere cartel," as he called them,

set the stage for current-day piracy and for putting it on the global map. The group was small, efficient, and multi-clan, and was mainly a product of the efforts of one man – Mohamed Abdi Hassan "Afweyne." Although Afweyne originated from a city with relatively little piracy (Haradhere in the region of Mudug) and a clan that had hitherto not engaged in maritime robbery (the Suleiman clan of the Hawiye family), he was an exceptionally good organizer. Afweyne handpicked his members and carefully designed his cartel to keep cost low, profits high and efficiency maximal.[54]

According to Boyah, however, it was a marriage of convenience. On the one hand, the experienced fishermen from Eyl needed an investor and, on the other hand, Afweyne needed their expertise. Considering what Boyah called their local peers' aversion to the inherent risks and the resistance of their community around Eyl, they were searching for both places where they could take pirated ships and for a local sponsor. Afweyne learned about the exploits of Eyl fishermen vigilantes from Hobyo–Haradere area fishermen who knew Boyah and his colleagues. Those fishermen arranged a radio communication one night, following which they headed to Haradere where Afweyne received them.[55]

Having previously worked in coastal south Mudug as a diver-fisherman, Boyah says that they found the natural harbor at Hobyo and the inaccessible inland hideout of Haradere an ideal base for their prospective criminal enterprise. Unrelated developments in local conditions on the ground aided their planning. A bloody feud between Sa'ad and Saleebaan families (of the Habar Gidir sub-clan of the

---

[53] The fishermen were Abshir Abdullahi Abdule "Boyah" himself (interviewed on 8 and 15 June 2014 and 27 March 2017, Garowe, Puntland), Garad Mohamed, Farah Abdullahi, Abdullahi Abdi Yare, Abdiweli Hared; and their organizer, Mohamed Abdi Hassan "Afweyne." Also see Hansen, *Piracy in the Greater Gulf of Aden*, 25.

[54] Hansen, "Dynamics of Somali Piracy," *Studies in Conflict & Terrorism*, 526.

[55] Interview with Boyah (8 and 15 June 2014, and 27 March 2016, Garowe, Puntland).

Hawiye) had just subsided.[56] The cessation of that conflict made the Hobyo–Haradere corridor ideal for the pioneer ransom pirates from Puntland. Afweyne then introduced an attractive business model in order to harness the enormous potential they saw in hijacking ships for ransom.[57]

With Afweyne proving an effective organizer of pirates and mobilizer of local support and with many enthusiastic volunteers in their immediate vicinity, ransom piracy got off the ground with the capture on 10 April 2005 of the Hong Kong LPG carrier, MV *Feisty Gas*.[58] The pirates commandeered the vessel to the waters off the village of Hobyo and the pirate ringleaders shuttled between the coast and Haradere until the delivery of a ransom. According to the October 2005 report of the United Nations Monitoring Group on Somalia, the ship owners' "agent met the representative of the hijackers at various locations in Mombasa and paid the ransom of USD 315,000 in the following instalments: on 20 April, USD 150,000; on 22 April, USD 150,000; and on 25 April, USD 15,000."[59]

Shortly afterwards in late June 2005, the same group of pirates, including Garad and Boyah, hijacked near Hobyo the United Nations World Food Program (WFP) chartered MV *Semlow* that carried relief supplies destined to Bosaso. The pirates demanded a half-million dollars in ransom but because no large ransom was forthcoming for what Boyah said was a rickety ship crewed by inexperienced Kenyan sailors, he claims that the pirates sold the cargo to a known Mogadishu-based businessman for USD 25,000 and collected USD 80,000 for the ship and its crew.[60] As in

---

[56] This Sa'ad-Saleebaan conflict has to be seen within the broader intra-clan and inter-clan conflicts over meager resources, power (local and regional), and revenge killings that ravaged post-Siad Barre Somalia.

[57] The timing that Boyah gave me (Interview 8 and 15 June 2014 Garowe, Puntland) is off by at least one year from the timing the Norwegian scholar Stig Jarle Hansen attributes to him in 2009. For Hansen's rendition of what happened and when, see *Piracy in the Greater Gulf of Aden*, 23–25 and "Dynamics of Somali Piracy," *Studies in Conflict & Terrorism*, 35, 7–8 (2012): 523–530.

[58] According to the IMB, pirates (possibly the same pirates who later captured the *Feisty Gas*) had earlier that day tried – but failed – to capture a Cyprus-flagged bulk carrier, the MV *Tim Buck*, because the latter's master "took evasive maneuvers, increased speed, sounded whistle, sent distress alert and crew closed all doors and hid inside accommodation." ICC International Maritime Bureau, "Piracy and Armed Robbery against Ships: Annual Report, 1 January–31 December 2005," 20.

[59] Report of the United Nations Monitoring Group on Somalia pursuant to Security Council resolution 1587, S/2005/625 (2005), 4 October 2005, paragraph 104; Boyah (Interview: 8 June 2014, Garowe) claims that they collected USD 300,000.

[60] Interview with Boyah (23 March 2017, Garowe); Donna Nincic, "Maritime Piracy in Africa: The Humanitarian Dimension," *African Security Review* 18.3 (2009), 12, added that the pirates "stole USD 8,500 from the ship's safe, ransacked the crew's cabins . . ." Also see Report of the United Nations Monitoring Group on Somalia, S/2005/625, 4 October 2005, Paragraph 102–103.

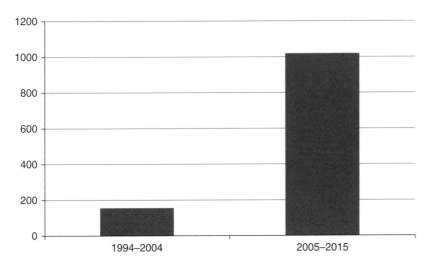

Figure 2.4. Comparison of piracy incidents (both actual and attempted combined) that occurred in the years of 1994–2004 and 2005–2015. (Compiled from IMB's annual reports.)

the case of the vigilante fishermen before them, the activity of the early ransom pirates remained seasonal. Until the widespread use of mother ships, pirates by and large sat out the rough waters along the Somali coast between July and August and between December and January.[61] Yet, between 2005 and 2007, IMB's Piracy Reporting Center recorded more than 120 reported attacks, of which thirty-four were successful hijackings in Somalia, mostly by the Hobyo–Haradere pirates.

The emerging ransom pirates exploited widespread local economic hardship and resentment against foreign illegal vessels to rationalize their attacks on every vessel they encountered. Direct experiences with – or witness accounts of – IUU fishing and stories of waste dumping had evoked strong feelings among Somalis, many of whom felt legitimately aggrieved and resorted to a host of dangerous countermeasures. The pioneers of ransom piracy named themselves "Somali Marines" (Hobyo–Haradere), "National Volunteer Coast Guard" (Kismayo, then Eyl) or "Ocean Salvation Corps" (Eyl).[62]

[61] That is due to the seasonally changing Indian Ocean monsoon winds that blow in a northeasterly direction between November and March and southwesterly currents reverse the trend between April and October.
[62] Report of the United Nations Monitoring Group on Somalia, S/2006/229 4 May 2006, Paragraph 90; Peter Lehr and Hendrick Lehmann, "Somalia – Pirates' New Paradise" in Peter Lehr (ed.), *Violence at Sea: Piracy in the Age of Global Terrorism* (New York:

The pirates had the money to buy not only their logistical needs but also the loyalty of at least a few. They were sufficiently armed and ruthless, especially after 2007, to enforce the acquiescence of many. These two factors combined with pre-existing, widespread, local resentment against foreign illegal fishermen and their vessels to furnish the necessary environment for pirate launching and landing. The fact that pirates had such safe havens where they not only felt secure to negotiate ransom without hiding but were also supplied with every need they had for their money was the most salient feature of Somali ransom piracy that distinguished it from its contemporaries in other parts of the world. Mainstream journalism and scholarship documented the accounts and bravado of these ransom pirates and committed significant energy and space to disprove their claims.[63]

Several ransom pirates, including a few ringleaders, have latterly become candid about the bogus national or regional garb they tried to drape over their criminal acts in order to piggyback on legitimate grievances of local coastal communities and to rationalize their actions to the outside world. Years after his renunciation of piracy and after doing time for his crimes, Boyah (like many other pirates I interviewed between 2012 and 2017) admitted that what they were doing was "haram" (sin) and that they called themselves anything or said anything that got them the support of their people because they could not operate without it: "[W]hen you want to do something and you know it is wrong, you will say anything but that does not make your actions right."[64] Similarly, one of the notorious pirate leaders who hijacked the MV *Rim* in February 2010 recalled how, when he joined the pirates, he came across fishermen who said they went into piracy after the big trawlers destroyed their livelihoods but the vast majority of pirates, including himself, had not even been to the sea before; they only exploited the fishermen's claims.[65]

Routledge, 2007), 3 and 5; Murphy, *Somalia: The New Barbary?* 31–33; Bahadur, *Deadly Waters*, 33–34. The Monitoring Group (paragraph 90 (b)) also reported of little-known "Marka groups" of pirates allegedly led by Yusuf Indohaadde, the self-declared governor and overlord of Lower Shabelle. Nevertheless, not only do other sources contradict this claim, but General Indohaadde's activities have all been land-based.

[63] See, for example, Jeffrey Gettleman, "Q. & A. With a Pirate: 'We Just Want the Money,'" *The New York Times*, 30 September 2008. Sugule Ali, the purported spokesperson of the pirates who hijacked the weapons-laden MV *Faina* in late September 2008, told Gettleman: "We don't consider ourselves sea bandits . . . We consider sea bandits those who illegally fish in our seas and dump waste in our seas and carry weapons in our seas. We are simply patrolling our seas. Think of us like a coast guard."

[64] Interview with Abshir Abdullahi Abdule "Boyah" (8 June and 15 June 2014, Garowe, Puntland).

[65] Confidential interview (November 2012, Garowe).

Their early successes, however, quickly put them on a collision course, albeit briefly, with an emerging alternative power center in southern and central Somalia: the Union of Islamic Courts (UIC). Not long after the UIC vanquished its rival warlords and established its ascendancy in Mogadishu, pirates hijacked a vessel belonging to one of the Courts' most prominent financiers out of the port of El Ma'an, the only operational natural harbor north of Mogadishu.[66] Two months later, around mid-August 2006, the pirates hijacked a Yemeni vessel en route to deliver a sizable cache of weapons to the UIC, which prompted the latter to not only forcefully retake the vessel but also to declare that it would drive the pirates out of their inland hiding at Haradere.[67]

Many give the UIC credit for the decrease in piracy incidents in 2006 when only twenty-two cases of pirate attacks were reported, five (23 percent) of which resulted in successful hijackings.[68] The Monitoring Group, for example, reported that UIC's rise "has had a severe dampening effect on . . . [piracy]. After declaring piracy illegal, ICU took over Harardheere (on the central coast, also spelled *Haradere*). Since the elimination of that pirate group, there have been no acts of piracy along the central and southern coastal area."[69] Nevertheless, UIC's anti-piracy disposition is questionable as are its operations in Haradere and the uniqueness of the overall decline of piracy in Somalia.

To begin with, 2006 saw a worldwide dip in reported piracy incidents; the IMB recorded a total of 239 reported incidents, which was the lowest since 1999 when the total annual average stood at 360 incidents. The claim exaggerates the UIC's influence, effective control, and impact outside of Mogadishu; beyond its rhetoric, it only held effective sway in pockets of southern and central Somalia with the remaining vast swaths of

---

[66] Some analysts claim that the hijacked boat belonged to prominent UIC financier and co-owner of the El Ma'an port, Abubakar Omar Adani, whom the Monitoring Group characterized as a "business cartel boss," Report of the United Nations Monitoring Group on Somalia, S/2006/229, 4 May 2006, Paragraph 136. On the port at El Ma'an, see paragraphs 64–68 of the above report.

[67] According to the Monitoring Group, the Yemeni "dhow contained the following cargo: RPGs – 25 units; DShK – 10 units; PKM machine guns – 90 units; AK-47 assault rifles – 400 units; fuel – 42 drums and a variety of ammunition." Report of the United Nations Monitoring Group on Somalia, S/2006/913, 22 November 2006, paragraph 142.

[68] Thean Potgieter and Clive Schofield, "Poverty, Poaching and Pirates: Geopolitical Instability and Maritime Insecurity off the Horn of Africa," *Journal of the Indian Ocean Region* vol. 6, no. 1 (June 2010), 86–112. This claim constitutes a part of the disputed discourse that the UIC, by restoring a semblance of order in areas it controlled, became the first positive force in Somalia since the escalation of the civil war in 1994.

[69] But it neglected to mention that for pirates not using mother ships, the monsoon winds are too violent in the summer months and do not sufficiently calm and become weak until November/December. Report of the United Nations Monitoring Group on Somalia, S/2006/913, 22 November 2006, paragraph 202.

territory slipping in and out of its control. Not only did the UIC have no control over the vast Puntland coastline that saw some pirate activity in the inaccessible tip of the Horn, but there is no evidence of the UIC driving pirates out of Marka, which was controlled by its loyalists under whose control piracy took place and who, according to some sources, even played an active part in piracy. The claim fails to expound on the above-mentioned direct and immediate reasons for the UIC's banning piracy in areas it controlled firmly or intermittently.

Even if its ban on piracy were effective, the UIC only stayed in power for about four months after its anti-piracy decision; the season and length of those months could not have made a huge difference in the rate of pirate attacks because: i) piracy involving mother ships took place year-round with unpredictable ebb and flow throughout the months; and ii) pirates relying on small boats did not venture out into the ocean when summer monsoon winds rendered the waters too violent for small boats. Finally, the likely enforcers of the UIC's anti-piracy decisions (i.e., Al-Shabaab) entered into a marriage of convenience with the pirates, especially after 2007 – although not to the extent that western security establishments and think tanks made it appear.[70]

Meanwhile, aggrieved at the audacious criminality of foreign fishers, many Somalis had been openly supporting the pirates and others quietly sympathizing with them – at least until the ugly consequences of ransom piracy, as discussed in Chapter 4, started to become manifest. While some Somalis continued to approve of piracy because they believed it was a legitimate response, many others rejected it as *haram*. In a 2012 random survey conducted among 236 youth in Bosaso, Garowe and Galkayo, more than 34 percent said that either illegal fishing (46 respondents) or waste dumping (36 respondents) caused piracy; an equal percentage of the respondents approved of piracy. The numbers of those who "approved" of piracy (33 respondents) and those who "somewhat approved" (45 respondents) corresponded roughly with those who thought piracy was "positive" (26 respondents) or "somewhat positive" (45 respondents). Both the "positive" and "somewhat positive" responses also correspond with those who attributed piracy to illegal fishing and waste dumping.

Compared to pirates in the years after 2007, the early ransom pirates were remarkably unostentatious and left little footprint of their loot or their excesses on the host community. After every successful hijacking,

---

[70] For an accessible exposé on who is/was who in Al-Shabaab, how its leaders wielded significant influence within the UIC (their small numbers notwithstanding), and how they evolved to become the notorious militant organization, see Hansen, *Al-Shabaab in Somalia: The History and Ideology of a Militant Islamist Group, 2005–2012* (London: Hurst & Company, 2013).

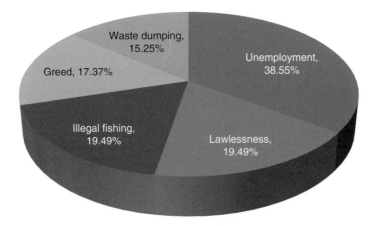

Figure 2.5. Survey of popular views about causes of piracy (Compiled by author.)

they typically went into "hibernation" to enjoy their loot in relative obscurity and only came out to prepare for another operation after exhausting their extorted fortunes. These inter-clan pirates were able to operate in a single clan territory through the payment of a share of the ransoms to the locals. Boyah claims that when they were in Hobyo–Haradere they "donated" 20 percent of the ransom to the community and the needy among them, although it has been hard to establish the recipients and amounts over time.

As the pirates grew in number and diversity, rival pirate groups – like those of Mohamed Abdi "Garfanje," Ahmed "Saneeg" and others – started to emerge in the same area. Meanwhile, ransoms steadily grew in amount and frequency, drawing the envy of different armed local militias who demanded ever-larger shares of the ransom. Afweyne proved unable to protect all of "his" pirates. Nor did the payment to one local militia group shield pirates from additional demands for payment from the same or another militia. In late 2007 when such demands intensified and turned into physical threats and confrontations with pirates hailing from outside south Mudug,[71] the non-local pirates returned to their respective clan territories. They took their criminal enterprise with them and were successful in recruiting new pirates due to worsening conditions in the local communities and the relative financial advantages and successful experience that the pirates accumulated in their new trade. Only

---

[71] Although local extortions of money from pirates were purely greed-driven, clan rivalry and conflict especially between the Seleban/Hawiye and Mejerten/Darod cannot be discounted.

then did pirates start to splurge in order to show off, and to attract and retain followers.

The Proliferation of Predatory Ransom Piracy

The breakdown of the inter-clan business organization among pirates and their dispersal back to their respective home regions led to the rise in Puntland of clan-based and sub-clan-based pirate groupings, although inter-clan pirate groups did not completely cease to exist elsewhere in the country. A pirate organizer best captured the new reality when he said, "We started with friends and relatives and we picked up the best not by skill but by bravery."[72] Boyah, Farah Abdullahi, Bakeyle and others went back to Eyl, which emerged as the new, most vibrant pirate den for the subsequent three years.[73] Garad Mohamed went to Kismayo and briefly rejoined the "National Volunteer Coast Guard" before returning to his mother's native area in Eyl in 2009.

Lesser-known pirate figures started their own operations in Gara'ad before former *khat* trader Abdullahi Yere joined in and overtook everyone. After at least one joint attack with Boyah, Mohammed Mussa Saeed "Aargoosto" returned to his native Qandala and launched his own operations around the tip of the Horn, where he cohabited that region with another Qandala native, Isse Mohamoud Yusuf "Yuluh." The two make up what the United Nations Monitoring Group dubbed "the Qandala – Hafun network" that has reportedly managed to stay in business by morphing into a new, post-piracy role.[74] Further along the Gulf of Aden, Fouad Warsame Said "Hanaano" launched a separate pirate group out of Lasqoray (northwest of Bosaso along the Gulf of Aden) until Hanaano fell to the Yemeni authorities in October 2009.[75]

Around the same time that the original pirate groups underwent a process of purging and the previously described, relatively homogeneous groups emerged in Puntland, several related and unrelated developments occurred to take the criminal enterprise to altogether new heights in the region's waters and across the vast Indian Ocean.

---

[72] Confidential interview (October 2012, Galkayo).

[73] Interview with Abshir Abdullahi Abdule "Boyah" (8 and 15 June 2014, Garowe, Puntland).

[74] "Report of the Monitoring Group on Somalia and Eritrea, Annex 3.1.c: Profiles of Mohammed Mussa Saeed 'Aargoosto', Isse Mohamoud Yusuf 'Yullux' and Abdirahkim Dhuqub," S/2013/413, 12 July 2013, " 108.

[75] Confidential interview (February 2012, Galkayo). Also see Report of the United Nations Monitoring Group on Somalia and Eritrea, S/2010/91, 10 March 2010, "Case Study 3: The Eastern Sanaag Pirate Militia," 40; Report of the United Nations Monitoring Group on Somalia and Eritrea, S/2011/433, 11 July 2011, paragraph 107.

The worsening of Puntland's economic and financial woes, sudden political changes in Mogadishu and Garowe, and the further deterioration of the lot of Somali fishermen attended the return of the earliest ransom pirates to their clan territories. Each of these developments produced its own group of potential recruits for piracy with skills coveted among pirate kingpins and investors – old and new alike.

In October 2004, Abdullahi Yusuf stepped down from the Puntland presidency to take the helm of the newly established Somalia-wide Transitional Federal Government (TFG). When he moved south to lead the TFG, not only did he take with him from Puntland close to 2,000 seasoned soldiers (and an almost equal number of newly enlisted ones),[76] but Puntland also helped finance his administration, first in Jowhar and then in Baidoa and finally in Mogadishu.[77] Besides weakening Puntland's security apparatus, of which the pirates took full advantage, continuing to pay the arrears of the soldiers that the president took with him to the south proved to be a crippling drain on Puntland coffers. Partially because of that, Puntland experienced its worst economic and monetary crisis during the final two years of the administration of General Mohamud Hirsi Muse ('Aadde Muse) in Garowe that succeeded that of Abdullahi Yusuf. 'Aadde Muse's actions and inactions triggered a renewed wave of hyperinflation and led to popular resentment and unrest in Puntland towns after his government failed to pay the salaries of its employees.[78] After several months of going without pay, many soldiers abandoned the defense forces between late 2007 and early 2008, and started searching for alternative means of supporting themselves and their families.

Meanwhile in December 2008, Abdullahi Yusuf lost the presidency in Mogadishu. The following month, the former leader of the Union of Islamic Courts (UIC), Sharif Sheikh Ahmed, succeeded as the new TFG president.[79] Hailing as he does from the rival Abgaal sub-clan of the Hawiye, Sheikh Sharif proved unwilling and/or unable to absorb the large number of Mejerten (a Darod sub-clan) soldiers of his predecessor. The Puntland government was already unable to pay its own soldiers,

---

[76] Interview with one of Abdullahi Yusuf's former bodyguards (28 October 2012, Galkayo).

[77] Interview with Mohamed Ali Yusuf "Gagab" (who was Minister of Finance under 'Aadde Muse before he effectively became the latter's vice president) (11 September 2015, Galkayo).

[78] Ioan Lewis, *Understanding Somalia and Somaliland: Culture, History, Society* (London: Hurst & Company, 2008; 2011 reprint), 104–106. Interview with Mohamed Ali Yusuf "Gagab" (11 September 2015, Galkayo).

[79] As ICU leader, Sheikh Sharif had vowed to fight the invading Ethiopian troops in December 2006 and their allied TFG troops that had come from Puntland as had the former TFG president, whom Sharif succeeded.

much less able to absorb Yusuf's troops that were returning from Mogadishu. These trained and experienced soldiers, including the former president's longest-serving, personal bodyguards mentioned earlier, then returned home empty-handed; they too had to scramble for ways to support themselves and their families.[80] All this took place around the time that the cascading deterioration of fisheries caused rising unemployment of seasoned fishermen and divers.

When recruited into piracy, many of these sets of trained soldiers and seasoned fishermen proved instrumental in transforming the organization and reach of the criminal enterprise. Some of them became successful pirates on their own but kept – and continue to keep – a very low profile.[81] Pirate kingpins, investors in and organizers of piracy operations rushed to outdo their rivals by attracting the better-skilled and bigger numbers of such recruits. They did so by pouring payments – in cash and in kind – in unprecedented amounts to lure the non-pirates into piracy and to retain the committed pirates. Although the majority of such spending was to be repaid upon the new pirates' receipt of their share of ransom, the excessive splurging drew growing numbers of able-bodied men to piracy with adverse long-term local effects that are discussed in Chapter 4.

A pirate recruiter in Bosaso, for example, met an unpaid and disgruntled Puntland soldier who, by his own account, had just quit the military and hoped to buy a typing machine and become a scribe in order to support his family. Seeing this former soldier as a potential recruit into piracy, the pirate recruiter gave him a day's worth of *khat* (the leafy, mildly narcotic drug) to chew, a place to sleep, and USD 1,000 to send to his family. The next day, the recruiter asked the recruit if he were ready to join a group of pirates about to go to the sea. His answer was swift and unmistakable; he was ready to die for them. The former-soldier-turned-pirate-recruit explained his response: "The effect of USD 1,000 on someone like me! . . . USD 1,000 for my family! The next day they asked me if I were ready to go to the sea and I said 'I am prepared to die.'"[82]

Meanwhile, the inability of the local fisheries industry to recover from its cascading troubles (both man-made and natural) had regularly been pushing many more fishermen out of their legitimate line of work. This

---

[80] Interview with one of Abdullahi Yusuf's former bodyguards (28 October 2012, Galkayo).
[81] Confidential interviews, including with one of Abdullahi Yusuf's former bodyguards (October 2012, Galkayo).
[82] Confidential interview (February 2012, Galkayo). Sudden tension descended in the room when I countered that piracy was a crime and how was it that a trained soldier opted to knowingly join a criminal world. The tension was as quickly lifted when the pirate quipped with a cocky smile: "It is also a crime to see one's family starve to death" and his friend and my assistants broke into laughter in response to what they said, a witty way of responding.

reservoir of experienced seamen without jobs and living in abject poverty was the last ingredient for the epic explosion of ransom piracy. The stories of the returned pirates' successful exploits and wealth helped attract new recruits among their own clansmen who had previously been averse to the risk and to what many had rightly regarded as a morally dubious undertaking. The escalation of ransom piracy in turn eroded the fishing sector even more; the two have since developed an inversely proportional relationship. As in the case of defensive piracy, many fishermen turned to ransom piracy of their own volition, others were cajoled into joining, and many were pushed into illegally migrating to greener pastures elsewhere in the Horn of Africa or the Middle East.

Initial financing for the ransom pirates had purportedly come from individuals and groups based in Dubai and Djibouti, as well as from some women *khat* retailers in Somali towns. Following the homogenized proliferation of the criminal enterprise itself and the proven soldiery of its rank-and-file operatives, investing in piracy became increasingly democratized. Increased clan, sub-clan, or family and neighborhood identification with pirate groups assuaged the concerns of many previously reluctant investors who had once wavered or waxed moral but now rushed to offer capital to groups from their own clans, sub-clans or neighborhoods. A onetime pirate and subsequent investor and notorious Galkayo gangster related that upon his return to Garowe from a successful pirate operation in late 2008 "there was this rush by investors who offered money for future missions."[83] The Somali terms of *malgelin* for investment and *malgereye* for investor thus entered the lexicons of the burgeoning piracy industry in Somalia.

Whereas few established businesspeople either knowingly entered the criminal enterprise or found themselves sucked in, there were more widespread instances of investments coming from levels as low as households. A once-legitimate businessman and urbanite trader was among the first major investors who inadvertently got sucked into the criminal enterprise after helping supply foodstuffs to a captured ship. He ended up being the principal financier of pirate attacks from Murayno to Las Qoray and Elio.[84] A certain "Swahili" who had been a successful merchant similarly found himself sucked into piracy funding when he started to finance the expenses of his pirate cousins who brought their captive ship to Bandar Bayla. Upon being repaid in shares of the ransom, he went on to become an active investor in pirate missions.[85] As mentioned above, the onetime

---

[83] Confidential interview (February 2012, Galkayo).
[84] Interview with Lt. Col. Abdirizak Ismail Hassan (26 and 27 February 2012, Galkayo).
[85] Interview with Lt. Col. Abdirizak Ismail Hassan (26 and 27 February 2012, Galkayo).

khat trader Abdullahi Yere started to invest and take active part in pirate missions until he grew to dominate all pirate operations in and around Gara'ad. After the Somali coast came under close international monitoring, he is believed to have started launching attacks from the Yemeni coast by renting Yemeni dhows (especially from Mukalla) for up to USD 50,000 to camouflage his operation.

Smaller-scale organizers or mobilizers of investments in piracy raised the bare minimum of about USD 30,000 for equipment, weapons, and basic food and fuel supplies to launch a mission of no more than ten pirates in a single boat.[86] They worked through layers of smaller-scale "salesmen" or promoters to tap into neighborhood, family and clan networks and friendships to mobilize capital in a tacit, prototypical pyramid scheme. In this way, roughly between 2008 and 2011, a buzz about piracy investment pervaded conversations in urban Puntland, turning the enterprise into a complex crowd-funding exercise of varying opacity.[87] Nevertheless, not all of the small-scale funders knew that they were "investing" in piracy; nor did all the deliberate investors necessarily knew where – or to which pirate group or mission – their money was going.

The majority of the new and smaller-scale investors, who wittingly or unwittingly got involved, were removed from the actual pirate organizers and the farther they were removed, the riskier their investment or loan. Many were thus scammed and others realized where their investment or loan had gone after the accumulated pirate capital was lost in a failed attempt. In some cases, their contact person in the scheme either died, was apprehended or disappeared in the operation, went on *tahriib* (illegal migration), or simply denied that he had collected money from ordinary townsfolk. None of the latter could demand their money back nor speak loudly about it out of fear of stigma and/or legal repercussions. Many lost large sums of money because the pirates did not return or because the organizers swindled the investors.

If pirate missions were successful and agreements were honored, however, then the shares of investment determined the dividends according to an agreed-upon formula. Pirate groups typically allocated shares, or what they called "*saami*," to individual members and to weapons and equipment. Each pirate received such a share and the first one to board the ship during capture at sea received an additional share. AK-47s and RPGs (without rockets) were worth a half share each, whereas an RPG with its

---

[86] Interview with Lt. Col. Abdirizak Ismail Hassan (26 and 27 February 2012, Galkayo).
[87] To that extent, claims that the relatively well-off got involved in piracy in search for quick and large sums of money is not wholly inaccurate.

rockets represented one share. Language experts or translators-cum-negotiators were either paid a negotiated figure regardless of the total ransom or accepted stock shares of the ransom. Negotiators who were contracted for a fixed amount received their payments in a single lump sum ranging between USD 5,000 and USD 50,000 (a few are alleged to have collected as much as USD 150,000). The pay for those who agreed to take shares was determined by the monetary value of a share. That in turn depended on the gross amount of ransom, the cost of the pirate mission, the expenses incurred, and the number of pirate personnel (from investors to security guards on land) as well as their weapons and equipment.

Although split among many actors across the piracy food chain, the sums that individual pirates – from the foot soldiers to the ringleaders – received from a successful piracy operation remained sufficiently large to pay off corrupt government officials and traditional leaders alike. Given that the government of Abdirahman Farole barred active pirates from entering Garowe after he took office, those wishing to travel between Galkayo and Bosaso would disguise themselves as guards or as part of the entourage of important government officials, for which they paid generously. Upon collecting his hefty share of a ransom, notorious pirate Abdirizak Sanof Ina Jental is believed, for example, to have paid a military commander USD 60,000 for safe passage through Garowe.[88] Others either paid handsomely or invoked family and clan ties to secure various levels of protection from ranking government officials.

Ungovernable Terrains and Absent Governments

The fact that Somali ransom pirates chose the Hobyo–Haradere area first and later moved to various locations along the Puntland coastline raises an important issue of why and how pirates in general, and Somali pirates in particular chose their hubs. Whereas some scholars offered economic, geographical, cultural and other explanations, Jatin Dua and Ken Menkhaus have drawn attention to malleable governance. They note how "the hotspots for piracy in Somalia do not line up perfectly with ungoverned spaces,"[89] which led them to conclude that piracy thrived in "an operating environment featuring a weak and corrupt government [that] affords social advantages. Pirates, like mafias, may prefer weak, controllable governments to anarchy."[90]

---

[88] Interview with Lt. Col. Abdirizak Ismail Hassan (26 and 27 February 2012, Galkayo).
[89] Dua and Menkhaus, "The Context of Contemporary Piracy," 756.   [90] Ibid., 757.

The findings of my own fieldwork contradict some of the above points and add nuance to others. If one is to distinguish pirating from ship-wrecking, the former has had no basis or precedent in Somali history and culture. Wherever pirating emerged in Somalia, it had a corrosive effect on the values and peaceable operation of traditional societies – as documented in Chapter 4. Although pirate–government piggybacking on one another and collusion between pirates and at least individual government officials emerged afterwards, my research has shown that piracy exploded in regions without or beyond the reach of government authorities. In that sense, my findings corroborate Donna Nincic's conclusions (her relatively dated data notwithstanding) that in Africa, "the vast majority of pirate attacks (from 62% in 2006 to 83% in 2007) have occurred in the most highly failed states (FSI > 90)" on the Failed State Index (FSI).[91] While Somali pirates did not – and possibly could not – operate in areas of active conflict, they thrived where there existed a government vacuum, which was essential for the distinct features of Somali piracy: commandeering the captured ships and holding their sailors hostage until the payment of ransom.

When the earliest ransom pirates picked the Hobyo–Haradere corridor as their launching pad, the area had just emerged from internecine conflict and had had no government; the weak Galmudug administration had not even been declared on paper much less established on the ground.[92] Later on, local authorities in Galmudug sought to court the pirates in order to both keep them out of Al-Shabaab's orbit and to potentially deploy them against Al-Shabaab.[93] In Puntland especially, where the vast majority of ransom pirates concentrated from 2007 onwards, all pirate hubs were small natural harbors that were remote and inaccessible by land – as were the pirate dens in Galmudug.[94] Many of these hubs had access to telephone networks (that are private in Somalia) that enabled pirate informers to send word of impending attacks long before government forces could make their way to their targets.

Advanced telecommunications and the poor quality – or complete lack – of paved roads gave the pirates ample time either to take defensive

---

[91] Nincic, "State Failure and the Re-Emergence of Maritime Piracy."

[92] However, as Menkhaus argues elsewhere, one has to be careful not to mistake the absence of government authority for the absence of governance. See Menkhaus, "Governance without Government in Somalia: Spoilers, State Building, and the Politics of Coping," *International Security*, vol. 31, no. 3 (Winter 2006/07), 74–106.

[93] Jeffrey Gettleman, "In Somali Civil War, Both Sides Embrace Pirates," *The New York Times*, 1 September 2010.

[94] Their inaccessibility by land explains why construction of roads was adopted as a counter-piracy strategy by the Farole government and its foreign partners, mainly TIS/USAID and the UN agencies.

positions from which to repel incoming forces, to relocate to another, more inaccessible location or simply to put to sea where government authorities could not reach them. When the Puntland Marine Police Force (PMPF) arrived in Bargal in late 2011, the pirates sailed the last remaining hijacked ship to sea and went to Mur'ayo, near 'Aluula, which was Isse Yuluh's base.[95] Pursuing the notorious pirate leader into the remote area around Cape Guardafui, the PMPF started to run low on supplies and was too stretched across an inhospitable terrain. The Farole government used a small airplane, which it had acquired as part of its counter-piracy materiel, to resupply its forces. As a result, the international community severely reproached Puntland for its airborne capacity in violation of the standing arms embargo.[96]

Unlike Galmudug, Puntland authorities did not seek pirate collaboration against Islamic insurgents; however, individual officials in the governments of 'Aadde Muse and Abdirahman Mohamed "Farole" are implicated in piracy, although there is no evidence to suggest that those officials had themselves invested in piracy or dispatched pirate missions. In their characteristic savvy to manipulate their clan and family ties, pirate linchpins typically sought – and often got – the protection and, in some cases, the facilitation of their brethren in government, both in Garowe and Mogadishu. Upon capturing the Libyan-owned MV *Rim* in February 2010, one of the two pirate leaders reached out to an unnamed relative who held a high-level post in Somalia's Ministry of Foreign Affairs to reach the Libyan ambassador in Nairobi.[97]

To justify their acts and lay the ground for the coming-to-power of their sympathizers, some pirates and their supporters claimed and aggressively campaigned that the family of Puntland president Abdirahman Mohamed "Farole" had used piracy money to campaign and win the 2008 election for Puntland presidency. Asserting that "the newly established administration of Abdirahman Mohamed 'Faroole' is nudging Puntland in the direction of becoming a criminal State,"[98] the Monitoring Group also repeated the yet-unsubstantiated claim that Farole "benefited from much larger pirate contributions to his political war chest."[99] Nevertheless, the few notorious pirate kingpins and negotiators, who, like Farole, hailed from the Isse Mohamud sub-clan of the Mejerten, continued to live freely in and around

---

[95] Interview with Mayor of Bargal, Abubakar Ahmed Yusuf (28 August 2015, Galkayo).

[96] Interview with former president of Puntland, Abdirahman Farole (14 August 2015, Garowe).

[97] Confidential interview (November 2012, Garowe).

[98] Report of the United Nations Monitoring Group on Somalia and Eritrea, S/2010/91, 10 March 2010, paragraph 137.

[99] Report of the Monitoring Group on Somalia and Eritrea, S/2010/91, 10 March 2010, 41.

Garowe because they were either granted amnesty under the various anti-piracy campaigns, had the protection of powerful members of their sub-clan, or had served prison terms for their crimes.

Onetime Farole political backers, who subsequently became bitter political foes, said that the former president's family had no money to even build a house much less to invest in piracy. It was the good will of several influential clan and religious leaders and power brokers who took note of Farole's education, long professional career and capacity that sealed the outcome, especially in light of the economic, security and political deterioration during 'Aadde Muse's government.[100] But government counter-piracy policies and measures involved intricate negotiations and prolonged discussions along clan and family lines that pressing conventional security concerns could not afford; hence the impatience of foreign partners, observers and analysts, and local political rivals' exploitation of that impatience.

After the Farole government started to intensify pressure on piracy and its domestic operatives, supporters and sympathizers, Garowe's efforts met a brick wall of clan politics, especially when confronted with ranking members of its government.[101] The relative political stability of Puntland is founded on a delicate equilibrium between the various Harti (a branch of the Darod clan) sub-groups. Among the Mejerten majority, maintaining the precarious balance between the family lines of the three brothers – the Omar Mohamud (Galkayo-Burtinle-Jarriban), the Isse Mohamud (Garowe-Eyl), and the Osman Mohamud (Qardo-Bosaso) – took precedence over all other regional or national concerns. Members of government who represented – and hailed from – the smaller non-Mejerten groups that were scattered from northwest to northeast Puntland had significant clout because of Puntland's rivalry with Somaliland over their territory, the strategic (security and economic) significance of their region – its own poverty notwithstanding – and the extreme inaccessibility of some of their areas (hence government dependence on their good will).[102]

---

[100] The Monitoring Group and other Farole critiques overlook the fact that Farole had served as Puntland's Minister of Finance under 'Aadde Muse. Given the opaque dynamics of Somali politics, it is not inconceivable for him to have amassed the cash he needed for – and spent on – the election campaign in late 2008.

[101] Interview with Mohamed Abdirahman Farole (12 June 2014, Garowe).

[102] Clan-wise, the majority of Puntlanders belong to the Mejerten sub-group of the Harti/Darod, one of the five broad clan divisions of the Somalis. The other sub-divisions of the Darod are the Dulbahante, Marehan, Ogadeni and Warsangeli, among others. For their part the Mejerten majority of Puntland are divided among descendants of three brothers: the Omar Mohamud in Mudug (Galkayo-Gara'ad), Cisse Mohamud in Nugaal (Garowe-Eyl), and Osman Mohamud in Karkar and Bari (Qardo-Bosaso).

Held back by – and beholden to – these intricate clan dynamics, the successive governments were modest in both their developmental and counter-piracy projects. But the pirates were effective in either buying government officials with money and family ties or in manipulating the precarious system by touting government measures as targeting them unfairly. Weariness that the whole system may come apart at the seams scuttled international pressure as well as local desire and preparedness to stamp out support for piracy. That enabled a few government officials to be – or appear to be – in cahoots with pirates who were disguised as their family affairs, or to meddle with piracy under the cover of helping facilitate the release of foreign hostages from pirate activity, or to secure the release of clansmen from capture and incarceration in foreign lands.[103]

Conclusion

The indiscriminate treatment of the few early cases of everyday robberies and the almost knee-jerk-like reactions of aggrieved fishermen on the one hand, and failure to distinguish these robberies and fishermen's reactions from greed-driven predatory attacks for hostages and ransom on the other, have continued to obscure the origins and dynamics of the epic twenty-first-century phenomenon of ransom piracy in Somalia. Data is sparse on the few cases of criminality that resulted in the theft of ships' cargo and/or sailors' valuables (including equipment) that took place throughout the 1990s. In addition to being operationally indistinguishable, both the fishermen vigilantes and subsequent predatory pirates claimed to be fending off IUU fishing; this fact may have also contributed to the confusion in academic and policy circles.

The evolution of defensive piracy to predatory business was helped by many factors that are at the heart of the inability of experienced seamen to sustain themselves and support their families. These include: i) overfishing that, due to lack of alternative or supplementary livelihoods, decreased their catch in inshore waters; ii) IUU fishers' large-scale theft of Somali resources and their plundering of the marine environment at a faster rate than it could recuperate and replenish its resources, which further reduced the artisanal fishermen's catch even in the offshore waters; and iii) the 2004 tsunami that dealt the withering fishing sector an irreversible blow, driving off its remaining employees. All these combined to push many more subsistence and employed fishermen out of legitimate lines of work and into the warm embrace of ransom piracy;

---

[103] Interview with head of Puntland's Counter Piracy Directorate, Abdirizaq "Duceysene" Mohamed Dirir (4 February 2012, Garowe).

townspeople and nomads, civilians and soldiers joined in later on. With all these factors in place, predatory ransom piracy got off to an epic start and exploded due to prevailing security and political environments in Mogadishu, Galmudug, and Puntland.

All along, IUU fishing in Somali waters ebbed and flowed according to the intensity of pirate activities in a given time or area. Just as no remedial action by the various Somali authorities could rein in the foreign IUU operations, neither could they single-handedly bring the pirates to heel. Until 2012, the pirates and the authorities played an epic rat race, with the pirates holing themselves up in the most inaccessible regions or relocating to areas just beyond the reach of the authorities that have been perennially incapable of exerting effective, simultaneous control over their territories. The pirates also hid behind clan and family affiliations with powerful persons and groups that threatened the balance of government and scared the authorities, or they simply bribed ranking government officials and some elders – although the titled, traditional elders remained firmly opposed to piracy from the start.

3   The Epic Spiraling of Ransom Piracy

This book has established so far that piracy was a direct reaction to the latent and manifest violence that illegal, unreported, and unregulated (IUU) fishing meted out to the coastal communities during the years of civil war – with claims of waste dumping further rationalizing the attackers' acts. It has also shown that this relatively recent Somali phenomenon thrived in the context of the vacuum of the shrinking and ultimately collapsed state that, in the first place, enabled foreign corporate theft of the country's resources. In the absence of any semblance of maritime policing, increasingly armed foreign trawlers, coming as close as two miles in some areas and five in others, attacked Somali fishermen, destroyed their gear, diminished their catch, ruined their livelihoods, and cost the lives of some. The coastal communities – from the fishing companies to their smaller-scale suppliers and ordinary fishermen – protested the illegal vessels' violations and violence.

Following the origins of the grassroots resistance – and its abuse – described in the previous chapter, this chapter presents a few cases to illustrate the spiraling of the grassroots resistance into the epic ransom piracy of the twenty-first century. Much as the account in the second half of this chapter shows that there was no formula as to how each case of piracy unfolded or as to its outcome, a broad schema could be deduced on pirate organization, negotiation, and splitting of ransoms, all of which are sketched in the first half of the current chapter.

The Spread of Piracy across the Indian Ocean

We have seen in Chapter 2 how the breakup of the original Hobyo-Haradere group of pirates, the many unpaid soldiers whom the pirates recruited, and the impoverished fishermen who joined them all aided the dispersal of pirates and the proliferation of their bases of operation on land. Although Somali pirates had marauded the international waters long before the deployment of the international antipiracy armada, the latter's heavy naval presence in – and close monitoring of – the Gulf of Aden and the Somali coastline deprived the pirates of these hunting grounds, compelling more and more of them to sail further off shore to avoid the navies. As Kenyan analyst Rashid Abdi put it, the multinational antipiracy patrolling "simply displace[d] the problem. Pirates are now moving farther away . . . to places where the water is less tightly patrolled."[1] Ironically, therefore, the foreign antipiracy navies had the immediate effect of fanning piracy farther away from the nearby waters and into the breadth of the Indian Ocean.

Given the small size, limited capacity, and often poor construction of their boats, pirates increasingly resorted to the use of mother ships. These larger vessels were hijacked or rented, typically dhows from the region capable of sailing in the ocean and carrying the pirate attack skiffs far into the open waters before launching them at unsuspecting prey from a closer range.[2] The idea of mother ships was not an accidental "innovation" that the twenty-first century ransom pirates stumbled upon when a hijacked vessel was incapable of generating the ransom they sought. The earliest such recorded incident dates back to 1998 and involved the freighter *Noustar*.[3]

Explaining the first reported pirate attacks in international waters in 2005, the International Maritime Bureau reported in January 2006 that pirates were "believed to be using 'mother vessels' to launch attacks further away from the coast."[4] Although its claims of pirate intelligence networks, technological sophistication, and hierarchy seem flimsy, the UN Monitoring Group also reported as early as May 2006 the use of fishing vessels and dhows as mother ships.[5] Two years later it repeated: "Some vessels (particularly fishing vessels) have been hijacked with the sole intention of being used as mother ships" and presented documented cases of the use of mother ships.[6] Such ships enabled pirates to strike hundreds and eventually more than a thousand miles from shore. With

---

[1] Rashid Abdi interview, "The Price of Piracy," CNN, 9 May 2011.
[2] According to NATO sources in the region, rental mother ships came from – or at least contracted in – Yemeni (Al Mukallah and Al Shishr, Sayhut, Nishtun and Al Ghaydah) and Somali ports (Bossaso, Aluula and Mogadishu). See, S/2008/769, UN Somalia Monitoring Group Report, 10 December 2008, paragraph 137.
[3] Murphy, *Somalia: The New Barbary?* 14.
[4] ICC International Maritime Bureau, "Piracy and Armed Robbery against Ships: Annual Report, 1 January – 31 December 2005," 15.
[5] Report of the United Nations Monitoring Group on Somalia, S/2006/229, 4 May 2006, paragraph 85.
[6] "For instance," wrote the Monitoring Group, "the attack on the French luxury yacht, *Le Ponant*, on 4 April 2008, was preceded by the hijacking of the Russian-made trawler, FV *Burum Ocean*, some 57 nautical miles south of the Yemen coast. The trawler was

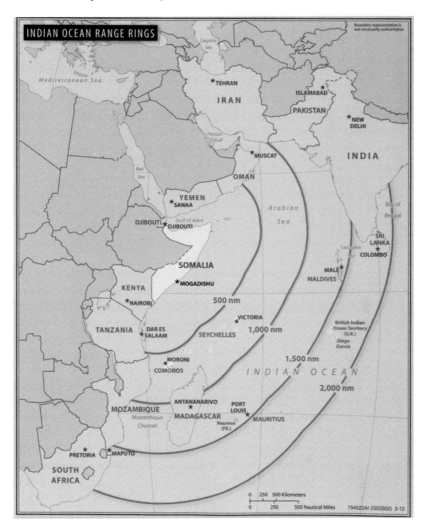

Figure 3.1. Indian Ocean range rings around Somalia from a 2012 country profile map available at the Perry-Castañeda Library Map Collection. (Courtesy of the University of Texas Libraries, University of Texas at Austin.)

reportedly taken to Aluula Puntland, refueled and used as a mother ship to attack the *Le Ponant* and later abandoned. In other cases, such as the MT *Yenegoa Ocean*, hijacked on 4 August 2008, vessels whose owners are unable to meet ransom demands are used as mother ships until ransom is paid." UN Somalia Monitoring Group Report, S/2008/769, 10 December 2008, paragraph 137.

them, pirates also managed to stay at sea for longer, to defy the turbulent monsoon seasons, and to attack faster and bigger vessels than they otherwise would.[7]

Both before and after the advent of mother ships, pirates used grappling hooks and retractable aluminum ladders to scale their prey – large and small alike – from fast pitching, rickety, small boats serving as platforms. The physical dangers of doing so notwithstanding, observers have argued that the disproportionately low risk vis-à-vis the massive gain was an important incentive behind the explosion of piracy incidents. "At its very core," wrote journalist Jay Bahadur, "the solution to piracy lies in basic economic principles: the cost-benefit analysis of these men must be shifted to favour more legitimate pursuits. Naval battle fleets can do their share to boost the 'cost' side of piracy."[8] That observation is accurate for the successful pirate attacks that resulted in ransom payments, but the vast majority of piracy incidents did not lead to the capture of ships much less to the collection of ransom.

Nevertheless, industry experts and proponents of militarized solutions latched on to low-risk, high-profits contentions, claiming to be heightening the risks associated with piracy – and policy followed suit. As late as November 2016, the EU NAVFOR chief of staff, Colonel Richard Cantrill, said: "If you're a pirate, what we've sought to do is raise the cost of you going to sea to commit an act of piracy . . . If you do, you could meet a naval asset. Ultimately you might end up in prison for your crime."[9] Whereas the statistical analysis of successful hijackings relative to the total number of pirate attempts shows the fallacy of disproportionately higher profits compared to the risks involved; ending up in prison may not have been the worst thing for the pirates to fear.

Typically spurred by a khat-induced high (or *merqan*, as it is locally called), pirates get on the attack boat as a one-way ticket to a target, the potential ransom. As they sail farther away from the coast, the *merqan* fades; in its place, fear and the desire to hang on to life with every available thread grip the pirates. If and when a prey vessel is within reach, the rush to

---

[7] In 2010 Monitoring Group reported: "With their extended reach, pirates have also demonstrated their proficiency in attacking larger and faster vessels, such as the MV *Asian Glory*, a United Kingdom-flagged vehicle carrier with a 23-meter freeboard, hijacked 600 nautical miles (1,111 km) off the Somali coast on 1 January 2010, during the north-east monsoon." Report of the Monitoring Group on Somalia, S/2010/91, 10 March 10 2010, paragraph 122.

[8] Jay Bahadur, *Deadly Waters: Inside the Hidden World of Somalia's Pirates* (London: Profile Books, 2011), 23. To his credit Bahadur went on to warn "without the alternative 'benefit' of meaningful occupation on land, no permanent solution on land is possible."

[9] Eoghan MacGuire, "'Resurrection' of Somali Pirate Attacks Feared after Tanker Shootout," NBC News, 20 November 2016: http://www.nbcnews.com/news/world/resurrection-somali-pirate-attacks-feared-after-tanker-shootout-n685731.

onboard it becomes less about striking it big than about making it out alive. The final adrenaline rush and daring to board a large vessel in the high seas thus comes partially from human survivalist urge to escape the dangerously small and unstable boat for the steadiness and safety of the much larger prey.

For the pirates at sea, therefore, the potential gain was purely material while the assured risk was life itself. As Bahadur himself put it, "For the average pirate – ragged, ill-equipped, and often without enough food and fuel to get him home – any ship that floats is a welcome oasis in the desert."[10] Moreover, contrary to claims that pirates had relied on sophisticated intelligence and technology or used witchcraft to lead them to their prey, the targeting of vessels remained random and opportunistic. And in spite of the abundance of ships in the pirate-affected seas and the pirates' survival imperative in open, far-off waters, their low success rates speak to the odds stacked against them.

According to data from the International Maritime Bureau (IMB) Piracy Reporting Center, there were a total of 995 cases of reported piracy incidents between 2005 and 2013. With a total of 217 actual hijackings (and hostage-taking of sailors) in the same time frame, the pirate success rate averaged 21.8 percent. The most successful year was 2008 with a success rate of 41 percent and 2011 as the least successful at 11.8 percent.[11] These figures do not account for the cases in which pirates disappeared at sea before attempting to take a ship, hence an unreported incident. Even then, the low success rates had deadly real-life implications for the pirates in the high seas because their chances – after an unsuccessful chase and/or boarding attempt – of still having enough fuel, food, and energy to attack another ship or to make it back home was very low.[12] Pirate desperation at sea was so dire that many of the pirates interviewed for this book even wished for the navies to "rescue," i. e., apprehend them.

One has to also consider the fact that not all hijackings led to handsome ransoms. Whereas some sailors overpowered the pirates and sailed to

[10] Jay Bahadur, *The Pirates of Somalia: Inside Their Hidden World* (New York: Pantheon Books, 2011), 54.

[11] These numbers are drawn from the annual reports of the Piracy Reporting Center of the International Maritime Bureau.

[12] Taking IMB's figure of 778 unsuccessful pirate attempts to hijack vessels, if we err on the conservative side and assume each of these failed pirate incidents involved a single pirate boat with no more than seven pirates on board, and if we optimistically estimate that 50 percent of these skiffs are either captured or destroyed by the international antipiracy flotilla or make it safely back to the Somali coast, some 389 boats must have disappeared annually during these years. That leads to the conclusion that no less than 2,700 lives were lost at sea between 2005 and 2013, a conservative estimate of more than 300 annually.

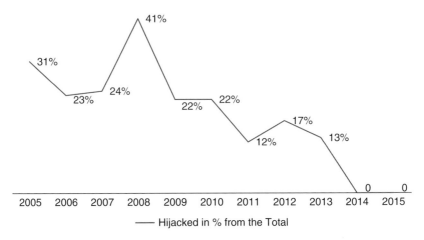

Figure 3.2. Percentage of piracy incidents that resulted in successful hijackings, 2005–2015. (Compiled from IMB annual reports.)

freedom, some sailors were rescued or killed in the rescue attempt (in which the pirates were also killed or apprehended), and some shipping companies abandoned their vessels and sailors. In other cases, fraudulent intermediaries swindled some companies and/or cheated the pirates. As we will see later in the chapter, layered levels of ignorance – not knowing that powerful foreign navies were there and not knowing what they looked like – even led to pirate attempts to hijack warships.

Broad Schema of Ransom Negotiations and Delivery: The Rise of Ancillary Trades

Once teams of seven to thirty hijacking pirates, attacking from one to three boats, board a vessel, there is little that an external rescue operation can do. There is much less the sailors themselves can do without facing the real prospect of serious physical harm to themselves and fellow sailors.[13] In a rush to consolidate their control, the pirates cut off the

---

[13] There are only a handful of exceptions in which seafarers locked themselves in a safe room and disabled the engine until a navy ship came to their rescue and apprehended the pirates. A prominent case is that of the German vessel, MV *Taipan*, in early April 2010. Upon encountering the pirates, *Taipan*'s sailors sent out a distress signal and locked themselves in until the Dutch frigate *Tromp* came to their rescue and marines stormed the vessels and apprehended the pirates. A Hamburg court tried the pirates, found them guilty, and sentenced them to different prison terms. "Dutch Marines Abseil on to a Hijacked Cargo Vessel to Rescue its Crew and Arrest 10 Somali Pirates," *Daily Mail*, 7 April 2010: http://www.dailymail.co.uk/news/article-1263960/Dutch-marines-abseil-deck-ship-MV-Taipan-freeing-crew-Somali-pirates.html; "Verdict in Somali Hijacking

ship's communications (internal and external) and gather all the hostage seafarers into a controllable space. The ship's distress signal is the final independent communication of the hijacked vessel with its owner/manager or ship-tracking and maritime security organizations. The company's communications on the satellite phone are either unanswered or are answered only to confirm the hijacking.[14] Not until the pirates feel secure enough onboard the vessel and reroute it to – and often even reach – their desired pirate hub does the captive ship's communication system go alive again as do the communications to pirate contacts on shore in Somalia.

Successful pirates make contacts with Somalia either on Thuraya satellite phone and/or mobile phones (where there is network coverage) to share the news and make security and logistical arrangements. Contacts made to individuals or organizations believed to be capable of paying the desired ransom are done under strict instructions and monitoring by the pirate leader(s). In rare cases, when one of the pirates speaks English and either he or another pirate on board the captured vessel have the power to call the shots, ransom negotiations start from the moment the pirates take full control of the vessel.[15]

Early on, pirate leaders were part of the attack team; in the later phase of piracy (around 2009 and after), however, most of the pirate kingpins and capable translators stayed onshore. During the early phase of ransom piracy, between 2005 and 2007, Somali pirates went through practically any potential intermediary who called them and whom they felt could deliver the ransom to them: these ranged from well-placed individuals both in and out of the successive central and regional governments in Somalia to individuals and groups across the region. It is possible that the Mombasa-based East Africa Seafarers Assistance Program (SAP) entered the ransom negotiations terrain during the earliest cases of ransom piracy. SAP was founded in 1996 to monitor maritime activities in the Indian Ocean and to offer seafarers assistance at sea and on land. In that capacity, it became a frontline hub for gathering and disseminating

---

Case: Court Rules in Germany's First Modern-Day Piracy Trial," *Spiegel Online*, 19 October 2012: http://www.spiegel.de/international/germany/hamburg-court-hands-do wn-somali-pirate-sentences-a-862350.html; Jan Schwartz, "German Court Convicts 10 Somalis of Piracy," *Reuters*, 19 October 2012: https://www.reuters.com/article/us-ger many-somalia-pirates/german-court-convicts-10-somalis-of-piracy-idUSBRE89I0YX201 21019.

[14] Although the specifics of each case were likely to be different, this general framework is confirmed by the earliest pirate Abshir Abdullahi Abdule "Boyah," in personal interviews on 8 June and 15 June 2014 (Garowe, Puntland) and by numerous latecomers to ransom piracy.

[15] This, for example, was the case of MV *Rim* that was hijacked by pirates in early February 2010.

information on distressed vessels and sailors, and on maritime events.[16] The initial contacts of the captive sailors and pirates with the SAP are still shrouded in secrecy. From early on, SAP started to serve as a go-between connecting the pirates in Somalia and the owners/managers of the captive vessels/sailors around the world.

As families of hostages as well as shipping and insurance companies started to hire professional hostage negotiators, many of the early pirate intermediaries lacked the wherewithal to keep up with the meticulous, methodical and drawn-out process. At the same time some pirates started to complain that SAP was either not being an honest broker or was charging them a hefty percentage for the services it rendered.

Corroborating such pirate claims and the many related conspiracy theories has proven extremely difficult. Andrew Mwangura, SAP's founder and director, does not divulge any detail beyond insisting that his organization got involved and remains so for "humanitarian reasons and not monetary gain."[17] If fragmentary information from pirates and the UN Monitoring Group on Somalia is accurate and can be trusted, SAP and/or Mwangura himself in fact make handsome proceeds for their service. For example, during the first major, successful case of ransom piracy in April 2005 the Monitoring Group reported a total ransom payment of USD 315,000 with the final USD 15,000 delivered separately as a third installment of the total. As already mentioned, however, one of the pirate leaders who hijacked *Feisty Gas* said that they collected a total of USD 300,000 in ransom.

By 2008, there emerged a motley group of Somali and non-Somali intermediaries as go-betweens for the pirates in Somalia and the shipping companies, wherever they were. Conveniently placed in some Middle Eastern or East African cities, the intermediaries briefly outpaced SAP only to see their favored position quickly deteriorate in its turn. On numerous occasions, the pirates felt cheated and even double-crossed by the Somali middlemen who lived far from the pirates' reach. Besides the consequent alleged deaths of some negotiators-cum-translators in the hands of paranoid pirate leaders, the case of three Thai fishing vessels (*Prantalay 11, 12* and *14*) that were seajacked in April 2010 epitomizes the breakdown of trust between pirates and their negotiators – as we see later in this chapter.

As a result of double-crossings and the breakdown of trust, the irony aside, the pirates started to introduce their own negotiators on the

[16] See the Seafarers Assistance Program's webpage: http://www.ecop.info/english/e-sap-n et.htm.
[17] Andrew Mwangura, personal interview, 8 January 2012 (Mombasa, Kenya).

ground – often times English-speaking Somalis, some of whom were returned from diasporas from the west. From the outset, there were some ad hoc or occasional translators who, because of their relative knowledge of the English language, found themselves facilitating – or actively sought to facilitate – the negotiation between their pirate relatives and whomever was on the other side of the line. But there quickly emerged semi-professionalized translators-cum-negotiators, who proved their worth to their bosses by dealing with sophisticated foreign negotiators; the fact that they had an unmatched advantage over any counterpart who cared about the lives of the hostages cannot be overlooked. One successful negotiation brought another until they became invaluable to pirate kingpins and their financiers; in some cases they too invested in piracy.

A few names stand out among the dozens of established pirate negotiators, the few one-off negotiators and the many unsuccessful ones. Only a few negotiators showed the mettle to handle fidgety pirates in pursuit of the big buck and nervous foreign professionals intent on securing the release of hostages for the least possible amount of ransom. Mohammed Saalil Shibin became famous as a negotiator because of his arrest in connection with the hijacking of the *SV Quest* that resulted in the slaying of all four Americans on board the yacht under a murky rescue mission that involved elite SEAL and FBI teams. Although his prior involvement in the piracy industry is unknown, he reportedly returned from Zambia on the request of his pirate relatives who captured the *SV Quest*. Operatives of the US-aligned Puntland intelligence services arrested the multi-lingual Qardo native (i.e., an Osman Mohamud of the Mejerten) in Bosaso and transferred him to Djibouti in order to be extradited to the United States. In April 2012, a US federal court found him guilty in the February 2011 hijacking of the sailing vessel.[18]

Having first come to the attention of the outside world as a capable negotiator in his handling of the German MV *Victoria* case in May 2009,[19] Mohamed Said Baafe "Looyan" is believed to have successfully negotiated the ransom of dozens of pirated vessels. With his overseas experience as a young student in the United Arab Emirates and his work for nongovernmental organizations in Puntland, Looyan shot to fame in pirate circles because of his work for his cousin and first employer, the notorious pirate leader Garad Mohamed. His record of successes led to

---

[18] Ahmed Abdi and Robert Young Pelton, "The Negotiators: The Business Side of Pirate Ransoms," *SomaliaReport*, 3 May 2012: http://piracyreport.com/index.php/post/3308/The_Negotiators.

[19] Jay Bahadur, "Pirates, Inc.," *The Financial Times*, 23 June 2010: https://www.ft.com/content/e5f60614-7d23-11df-8845-00144feabdc0 (last accessed 20 July 2018).

his working, sometimes simultaneously, for different pirate groups in Puntland and Galmudug (i.e., in the Hobyo-Haradere area). By mid-2011 the Monitoring Group listed twenty known cases of pirated ships that he had successful negotiated.[20] He is reported to have successfully negotiated the release in April 2012 of the Italian chemical tanker, the MT *Enrico Ievoli* (captured in late 2011),[21] for an estimated ransom of about USD 9 million, of which he reportedly collected USD 500,000.[22]

Like Looyan, the other prominent negotiators also revolved around a pirate linchpin, in this case Isse Yuluh. From his earliest pirate career, Yuluh seems to have relied on a young negotiator with whom he still had a trusting father-son relationship. In one of the last successful hijackings, on 10 May 2012 Isse Yuluh's pirates captured the Liberian-flagged Greek tanker MT *Smyrni*, which was loaded with 135,000 metric tons (about a million barrels) of crude oil.[23] After drawn-out haggling, the negotiator reportedly secured an agreement for a ransom of USD 9.5 million, the largest recorded, upon the payment of which the ship and its crew were released in mid-March 2013. Sources claim that the same negotiator secured for his boss an estimated USD 9 million in ransom for the simultaneous release of the MV *Royal Grace* that had been under captivity since 2 March 2012.

With a few notable exceptions, like that of the February 2010 hijacking of the MV *Rim* by a multi-lingual pirate leader who led the boarding team, the pirate leaders and capable translators-cum-negotiators generally stayed on shore. That meant that ransom negotiations did not begin until the ship docked at the desired pirate harbor and the pirate leader or investor and translator-cum-negotiator came on board to take charge.[24] In discussing the fate of the American sailing boat, *SV Quest, SomaliaReport* correctly

---

[20] Report of the UN Monitoring Group on Somalia and Eritrea, S/2011/433, 18 July 2011, Annex 4.2.: "Case Study: Loyaan Siciid Barte, Pirate Negotiator," paragraphs 7–21 and Annex 6.1: "Private Security Companies Operating in Somalia," paragraphs 20–23.

[21] "Release of Italian ship the '*Enrico Ievoli*,'" Statement of the Italian Ministry of Foreign Affairs, 23 April 2012: http://www.esteri.it/mae/en/sala_stampa/archivionotizie/comunicati/2012/04/20120423_ievoli.html.

[22] Abdi and Pelton, "The Negotiators."

[23] "Pirates Hijack Greek-owned Tanker off Oman," Reuters, 11 May 2012: http://www.reuters.com/article/us-somalia-piracy-idUSBRE84A0B820120511.

[24] Another partial example is that of notorious pirate kingpin Garad Mohamed's abortive April 2012 hijacking of Panama-flagged, Chinese cargo vessel *Xiang Hua Men* that culminated in the Iranian navy capturing Garad and his men. This is only a partial example because the pirates did not speak English and, had they been successful, it would have been unlikely for them to have started negotiations before arriving in their desired pirate hub. Other pirate leaders who were consistent exceptions included Sanjab and Yuluh. See "Xiang Hua Men Freed by Iranian Naval Commandos: High Profile Pirate Leader Garaad Captured in the Operation," *SomaliaReport*, 6 April 2012: http://piracyreport.com/index.php/post/3219/XIANG_HUA_MEN_Freed_By_Iranian_Naval_Commandos.

pointed out an important factor that led to the tragedy: "It was actually the lack of skilled negotiation that led to the deaths of the four Americans . . . [A]n FBI hostage negotiating team . . . made the fatal mistake of trying to negotiate with the motley crew of amped-up pirates [at sea] instead of the investors" on land through capable negotiators.[25]

The broad schemas of phases and intermediary actors described here – like the ransom delivery methods to be discussed later – were neither linear nor clearly delineated by time, geography, or pirate groups. They sometimes overlapped, especially from the late 2000s when diverse and highly professionalized pirate groups, negotiators, and ransom delivery-men emerged, and some pirate leaders continued to lead the boarding teams in the high seas.

Once agreed upon,[26] ransoms were delivered in one of three ways. Initially, the money was delivered to the local intermediaries, either in person or through wire transfer to Somali (often Mogadishu-based) bank accounts. In their turn, the in-person deliveries of ransoms took two forms. First, the deliveries were by tugboats that often sailed from Kenyan waters and, according to some sources, under the aegis of the Mombasa-based SAP. Second, cash was flown in small, chartered planes, and then transported overland under heavily armed protection of foreign private security companies.

The Canada-registered, Kenya-based private security and risk management company Salama Fikira International was involved in such ransom negotiations and deliveries. It is unknown how long its operations went on before one of its attempted deliveries was exposed and its personnel arrested at Mogadishu's Aden Adde International Airport with USD 3.6 million in late May 2011.[27] But Salama Fikira continued ransom deliveries until at least late March 2012 when it flew in over a million US dollars to pirates in the Galmudug region of Somalia and flew out their British hostage, a tourist kidnapped from Kenya and held in pirate captivity for six months between September 2011 and March 2012.[28]

As tugboat deliveries took a long time and chartered plane deliveries were exposed after Salama Fikira's fiasco, airdropping of ransoms started

[25] Abdi and Pelton, "The Negotiators."

[26] In at least one case, however, the pirates reneged upon receiving the agreed-upon ransom and refused to release the hostages.

[27] "Brits Arrested in Somalia with '£2.2 Million Ransom for Pirates,'" *The Telegraph*, 26 May 2011, http://www.telegraph.co.uk/news/worldnews/piracy/8539542/Brits-arres ted-in-Somalia-with-2.2-million-ransom-for-pirates.html. See also Report of the UN Monitoring Group on Somalia and Eritrea, S/2011/433, 18 July 2011, Annex 6.1: "Private Security Companies Operating in Somalia," paragraphs 20–23.

[28] Dominic Wabala, "Kenya: Ex-UK Soldiers Based in Nairobi Carried Tebbutt Ransom to Adado," *The Star*, 23 March 2012: https://allafrica.com/stories/201203231364.html.

to rise as a preferred method. It is believed that the notorious pirate leader Aden Abdirizak Hussein "Aden Sanjab" (whose final prey was the MV *Iceberg I* held between March 2010 and December 2012) was the first to demand that the ransom for one of his earlier preys be airdropped to the ship. Typically in such instances, a small aircraft would first buzz past the hijacked ship to get a sign of life among the captive sailors, and only then would it parachute the bag of cash into the nearby water, whereupon the pirates dispatched a skiff to fetch it. However it was delivered, the entire ransom amount was brought in front of the pirates (those who had hijacked the vessel at sea and those who guarded it in the inshore waters) and the pirate financiers where it was split according to the formula agreed upon before the launching of the pirate mission and according to the monetary value of the shares.[29]

Some of the ransoms that the pirates collected either stayed outside of Somalia from the get-go or left the country immediately after the partners in crime split their shares. Often those who took their money out of Somalia did so by injecting it into legitimate businesses. In July 2011, the Monitoring Group reported:

[A] large proportion of the ransom money is invested by pirate leaders in the 'qaad' or 'miraa' [the mildly narcotic drug] trade through Somali businessmen in Nairobi. Aircrafts that fly qaad from Kenya into Somalia often return to Nairobi with cash – an important channel for piracy proceeds to leave the country. Pirate leader Mohammed Abdi Hassan 'Afweyne,' for example, is said to run such a business for the piracy network in Harardheere/Hobyo.[30]

Claims also abound that piracy money flooded into Kenya and created a construction and real estate boom in Eastleigh, a Somali-dominated Nairobi neighborhood.

These assertions remain to be substantiated especially in light of the difficulty, if not the impossibility, of establishing the exact ransom figures paid in the first place, as the cases below demonstrate. Moreover, the amount of ransom money that flowed out of Somalia was inherently limited because about two-thirds of the ransoms were generally shared in sums that were too small to cross the border or to have a consequential investment in a foreign country. The majority of piracy's smaller stake-holders, regular foot soldiers and many pirate kingpins squandered their

---

[29] Some experts have called on the need to counter piracy by also following the money trail and have blamed the difficulty in doing so on the telephone money transfer system (Sahal) in Somalia. But the very diffuse distribution of the ransom money and the delivery in cash makes it very difficult to track the money.

[30] Report of the UN Monitoring Group on Somalia and Eritrea, S/2011/433, 18 July 2011, Annex 4.3: "Case Study: Pirates and Finances – the Hobyo-Harardheere 'Business Model,'" paragraph 5.

shares on luxury sports vehicles, prostitution, alcohol, khat, and later (on a few occasions) on more potent drugs.

On their first case of ransom piracy in 2005, Boyah and his pirates demanded a half million dollars to release the MV *Feisty Gas* but received USD 300,000, which was divided according to a pre-arranged formula: 30 percent to the investor, 40 percent to the hijacking team; the remainder reportedly split among the translator, the local area, and donations to the needy. This formula remained by and large unchanged except that, as the hijacking pirates were increasingly emboldened, they insisted on raising their share to 50 percent in many cases. When split among the seven pirates, Boyah's share bordered USD 20,000 but he recalls going broke a few weeks later: "People [shahat] took everything!"[31]

In one of his purportedly final hands-on piracy operations, Boyah joined six other pirates and, on 28 October 2007,[32] hijacked the MV *Golden Nori*, a Panamanian-flagged Japanese chemical tanker. The figures that foreign sources give for the release of the ship and its crew ranged between USD 1 million and USD 1.5 million.[33] Local sources give different and varying figures. A self-declared accountant for that pirate group said that the final ransom was dropped to USD 500,000.[34] Boyah, for his part, said that they collected USD 700,000 for *Golden Nori*.[35] These conflicting figures reflect the difficulty of establishing how much ransom money found its way into Somali hands inside Somalia. Whatever the total ransom figures, the majority of it was spent on harmful, addictive practices and non-productive vocations that had a devastating impact on the local communities – as discussed in Chapter 4.

Around the same time in late 2007, a group of fourteen pirates on board two boats captured a ship (most likely the Danish MV *Danica White*) and held it and its crew hostage for just under three months when they received a disputed figure in ransom. While Lloyd's List put the ransom at USD 1.5 million, one of the pirates put the figure at USD 1.7 million.[36]

---

[31] Boyah, personal interview, 8 June and 15 June 2014 (Garowe, Puntland).
[32] Boyah also had a direct role in the hijacking of the French luxury yacht in April 2008, although he did not join the attack team at sea.
[33] Rob Crilly, "Somali Pirates on 'Benzene Bomb' Threaten to Kill Hostages," *The Times*, 12 December 2007: http://www.thetimes.co.uk/tto/news/world/africa/article2593380.e ce; Mari Yamaguchi, "Seized Crew of Japan Tanker Believed Safe," *The Associated Press*, 11 December 2007, http://www.washingtonpost.com/wp-dyn/content/article/200 7/12/11/AR2007121100098.html; "Somali Pirates Free Japan Tanker," BBC News, 12 December 2007, http://news.bbc.co.uk/2/hi/africa/7139897.stm.
[34] Confidential interview (February 2012, Eyl).
[35] Interview with Abshir Abdullahi Abdule "Boyah" (8 June and 15 June 2014, Garowe).
[36] Captured on 1 June 2007, the MV *Danica White* was released on 23 August 2007 upon the payment of ransom a day or two earlier. One of the pirates who captured this vessel was very specific regarding the number of days that they held the ship captive, which is an

The difficulty of establishing the amount of ransoms in the first place is best shown by Ocean's Beyond Piracy's own self-correction with a 35 percent margin of error in one of its preceding estimates. In the daunting task of establishing the global economic cost of piracy, the Colorado-based think tank first estimated that in 2010 a total of USD 238 million had been paid in ransoms. Its 2012 report corrected that estimate to USD 176 million, which itself is hard to corroborate.[37] The same report's estimates of global economic losses due to piracy in Somalia ranged between USD 5.7 billion and USD 6.1 billion, of which only 1 percent went to "ransom and recovery."[38] The criminality and human suffering of ransom piracy aside, the perturbation that it caused largely involved foreign companies paying one another in the form of insurance and other premiums, and the provision of security personnel and equipment, all of which stayed outside of the piracy zone, in this case Somalia.

The pirates of *Danica White*, like the other pirate groups before and after them, allocated shares or *saami* to individual members and to weapons and equipment. Individual pirates received a *saami* each and the first one to board the captive ship received an additional share. An additional half share each was allocated for an AK-47 or RPG launcher (without rockets), whereas an RPG with its rockets represented a share. Also as in the cases of ransom sharing before and after the *Danica White* pirates, the monetary value of a share varied depending on a number of the factors listed above. In the particular case of the *Danica White*, a share was worth about USD 40,000.

A pirate, who joined this group with his own AK-47, "earned" USD 60,000.[39] But he had incurred a debt of USD 10,000 (in khat, alcohol and women) during the ten weeks that they held the vessel and its crew hostage. Although he consequently left the ship with USD 50,000, he arrived in the nearest urban center of Galkayo with only USD 38,000. By mid-2008, i.e., eight months later, he was left penniless with no one to borrow from. By then, he said, he had already become a "bemboweyne" (the pirates' word for "the insatiable, the guzzler") and was gripped by the urge to go to sea again.[40] This is the most common of pirate stories in

---

important clue when compared to other ships captured around the same time: "For two months and twenty days [that we held the ship], I had no knowledge of my family." Confidential interview (February 2012, Garowe); David Osler, "Svitzer Tug Hijacked off Somali Coast," Lloydslist, 4 February 2008: https://lloydslist.maritimeintelligence.info rma.com/LL073042/Svitzer-tug-hijacked-off-Somali-coast.

[37] See Jonathan Bellish, *The Economic Cost of Somali Piracy 2012*, One Earth Future Foundation Working Paper: http://oceansbeyondpiracy.org/sites/default/files/attach ments/View%20Full%20Report_3.pdf.

[38] Ibid.   [39] Confidential interview (February 2012, Garowe).

[40] Confidential interview (February 2012, Garowe).

Somalia. One-time captors, many pirates later found themselves held captive by their addiction to excesses or by their small-scale lenders. In yet another case of risky venture typical among many pirates, a former fisherman-turned-pirate put in the final USD 13,000 left from his fishing business into a piracy mission, involving seven pirates. His investment equaled nearly a quarter of that mission's stock and was used to buy a bazooka and six AK-47s, a ladder, fuel, food, and a Thuraya phone. On 21 August 2008 the group hijacked a German vessel, possibly the MV *BBC Trinidad*, which was sailing under the Antigua and Barbuda flag.[41] Although Andrew Mwangura of the Seafarers Assistance Program (SAP) reported then that the ship was released after the delivery of a ransom in the order of USD 1.1 million, the main pirate investor said they actually extorted USD 1.3 million from its owners.[42] His personal share of the ransom totaled USD 300,000, a whopping 2,207 percent return on his investment. Like many pirates before and after him, he bought a "new" SUV and drove it, without any prior driving experience (and possibly while under the influence of alcohol and/or khat), until it flipped over and he narrowly escaped with his life and a permanent leg injury.

Piracy investment organizers/mobilizers and pirate recruiters were as greedy and callous as the regular pirates were irresponsible spendthrifts. A pirate organizer who claimed to have captured the Liberian-flagged Greek bulk carrier MV *Eleni P* in January 2010[43] also claimed to have collected close to a half million dollars for putting in a quarter of the USD 40,000 that went into the hijacking operation. He reportedly set up his own "company" and bought four boats (with two outboard engines each), five RPG-7s, three PKM machine guns, twelve AK-47s, and, perhaps most curiously, fifty F-1 hand grenades. In response to my muttering that one could capture a town with these, the pirate said: "Yes, capturing a ship with a bunch of illiterate and ignorant pirates is like capturing a town. When they approach a ship or board it, they don't know what is where and so they fire very indiscriminately and scare

---

[41] The main features that lead me to assume that the pirate was talking about MV *BBC Trinidad* are the facts that it was a German vessel, the general timing was in the second half of 2008, and the proximity of the ransom figure reported by third party sources to the figure given by the pirate himself. Confidential interview (February 2012, Garowe).

[42] "German-owned Ship Paid 1.1. Mln USD Ransom to Somali Pirates," *Xinhua*, 12 September 2008: https://www.somalinet.com/forums/viewtopic.php?t=184311; Confidential interview (February 2012, Garowe).

[43] MV *Eleni P* was actually hijacked on 12 May 2010, 250 nautical miles off the Omani coast and released on 11 December 2010 upon the payment of ransom that the pirate leader said was USD 4 million. See "Somali Pirates Free Greek-owned Bulk Carrier," Reuters, 11 December 2010: http://af.reuters.com/article/energyOilNews/idAFLDE6B A09D20101211.

everyone in the ship."[44] Many pirates who took part in hijackings have separately attested to the pirates' random shootings upon boarding vessels, partially to scare the crew but mainly because of their own fear and nervousness.

That same pirate claims to have dispatched two "rented" mother ships with two skiffs each, none of which returned. Whereas one is believed to have been captured by a British navy ship that deposited the pirates in Seychelles, the other reportedly attacked a different navy ship – possibly the Danish *HDMS Esbern Snare* in May 2011, leaving several pirates dead and the rest injured. Such attacks on warships were not uncommon and pirate recruiters did in fact prefer the least-informed and gullible recruits for pirate attack teams. "The least educated and most physically fit, who cannot even differentiate a warship from a normal ship," one recruiter put it before continuing candidly, "we chose those who were ignorant of the presence of international navies. If anyone knew, we took them off."[45] And between 2009 and 2012, there were at least half a dozen known cases in which pirates actually attacked warships of different sizes with the intention of hijacking them; needless to add, none succeeded.[46]

Although there is no sufficient evidence to suggest the presence of systematic recruitment of such candidates, many of the pirate recruits from 2010 onward were uninformed that piracy was a crime or that powerful navies were out at sea to suppress piracy by force. Young men, who were between their late teens and mid-20s (prime age for pirate foot soldiers) at the time of piracy, had been born and raised in the midst of civil war. Not only had they not experienced basic services, including semblances of justice, security, and the rule of law that modern states ought to offer, but they grew up in an environment where violent power imbalances had been normalized and the powerful got their way – at sea and on land.[47] In addition to several elderly locals who attested to it, two

---

[44] Confidential interview (October 2012, Galkayo).
[45] Confidential interview (October 2012, Galkayo).
[46] Three war ships were attacked in 2009: FGS *Spessart* (German, 29 March 2009); *Nivôse* (French, 3 May 2009); and *La Somme* (French, 7 October 2009). In 2010, the USS *Nicholas* (US, 1 April 2010), USS *Ashland* (US, 10 April 2010), and in 2011, the HDMS *Esbern Snare* (Danish, 12 May 2011).
[47] The turning upside down of normalcy and the breakdown of societal constraints on the dictates of brute force are best represented at the individual level by a people's reliance on themselves and their display of violent power capability, either to induce fear in others or because they fear others. At the height of pirate dominance of the town of Galkayo in early 2012, a well-built young man of no more than five feet, six inches walked past me and four of my colleagues as we stood in a circle planning our day. Several of our security guards stood not far from us. The young man held his AK-47 rifle on frontal assault position (across his body with the muzzle facing down), a finger on the trigger, and three bullet magazines in a magazine holster on his chest (below the gun). Although that image is only slightly different from other similar images and stories in Galkayo and in other conflict

of the pirates interviewed at the Bosaso maximum-security prison claimed that they did not know that piracy was a crime.[48] After two others learned to write and read in prison, they also learned to recite the most basic of Islamic prayers.[49] Whereas these examples are neither the exception nor the rule, many other pirates were aware of what they were doing and that it was forbidden in Islam and the law; they also talked of exiting and pondered post-piracy livelihoods as Jatin Dua demonstrates.[50]

The following cases illustrate some of the common traits already identified but each also represents, in its own unique ways, the layered and tragic dynamics surrounding piracy off the coast of Somalia: the wanton criminality and insatiable greed of the pirates, the illegal practices and criminal neglect of many foreign fishing and maritime shipping companies, the widespread hypocrisy and double dealing of some, and the strength and courage of others.

The Three *Prantalay* Vessels

PT Interfisheries is a Bangkok-based Thai fishing and food processing company whose vessels fished the rich waters along the African side of the Indian Ocean out of Djibouti.[51] On 18 April 2010, while on one such operation, three PT Interfisheries vessels (*Prantalay 11, Prantalay 12*, and *Prantalay 14*) encountered Somali pirates more than 1,000 nautical miles off the coast of Somalia. All three sister vessels and their total crew of seventy-seven Thai and Burmese sailors were commandeered to the Somali coast and arrived at the notorious pirate hub, Gara'ad, on the southern border of Puntland. The greed and illegality of foreign vessels and their local accomplices aside, the tragedy that followed lies at the cross-section of pirate callousness, the fraud and duplicity of negotiators and intermediaries, the complicity of foreign governments (in the region

---

and crime environments, I was particularly struck by the fact that it had been too normalized for any of my colleagues, guards, or others lingering around to even notice him.

[48] Two former pirates serving time in the Bosaso prison interviewed on 20 February 2012, Bosaso, Puntland.

[49] Two former pirates serving time in the Bosaso prison interviewed on 5 June 2014, Bosaso, Puntland.

[50] See Dua, "After Piracy? Mapping the Means and Ends of Maritime Predation in the Western Indian Ocean," *Journal of Eastern African Studies* vol. 9, no. 3 (2015), 505–521; and Dua, "A Sea of Trade and a Sea of Fish: Piracy and Protection in the Western Indian Ocean," *Journal of Eastern African Studies* vol. 7, no. 2 (2013), 353–370.

[51] This seems like an innocuous – even mundane – practice until one takes into account that foreign vessels from European and Asian DWFNs pirate Somali maritime resources by staging their IUU fishing operations from – and landing their catch in – nearby countries in East Africa or the Middle East.

and beyond) that enable IUU fishing, and the treachery of foreign fishing companies themselves.

When the captive *Prantalays 11, 12,* and *14* arrived off the coast of Gara'ad, the pirates brought on board an English-speaking clansman and relative of some of the pirates to help them negotiate the ransom with the company owners. In the ensuing pre-negotiation posturing, the pirates demanded a whopping USD 9 million per vessel – a total of USD 27 million.[52] The company owners, the Thongchai Tavanapong family, for their part insisted PT Interfisheries itself was not worth more than a half million dollars. Moreover the family also insisted that their company was not involved in any illegal activity and that they were captured in international waters.[53] Yet, suspiciously, the names of two Somali men were found in the vessels' records as agents. Although at this point there may not have been hard evidence that the PT Interfisheries vessels were involved in IUU fishing in Somali waters, their operation out of a nearby country and their having Somali agents and representatives was straight out of the rule book for IUU fishers in Somali waters. The illegality or legality of the vessels' activities was, however, of little relevance to the predatory pirates who were only after the ransom money.

When communication started between the pirates and the company, however, the company first told the pirates to communicate with the two men named on the vessels' papers: A Puntlander and former Somali diplomat based in one of the Gulf countries, and an alleged warlord from Galmudug based in Mogadishu. But when the pirates insisted that they were not going to deal with any intermediaries, the company offered the pirates USD 200,000 while retaining its Somali agents as intermediaries. After several weeks of going back and forth, the company agreed to a ransom of USD 1.2 million which represented USD 400,000 per vessel. Three weeks later, the pirates turned that offer down.[54] But the former Somali diplomat assured the fishing company that he would secure the release of the boats for the USD 1.2 million. To that effect, he traveled to

---

[52] V. Narayan "Somali Pirates Wanted USD 27M for Prantalay," *The Times of India,* 9 February 2011: http://timesofindia.indiatimes.com/city/mumbai/Somali-pirates-wanted-27m-for-Prantalay/articleshow/7455661.cms?referral=PM; "Consul-General of Thailand to Mumbai Visits the Original Crews of Vessel *Prantalay 14,*" 9 February 2011, Royal Thai Consulate-General: http://www.thaiembassy.org/mumbai/th/news/44 3/18413-กงสุลใหญ่-ณ-เมืองมุมไบเยี่ยมลูกเรือประมงพรานทะเล-1.html; "The Devil and the Deep Blue Sea: Four Thai Fishermen Watched Their Friends Die and Suffered Brutal Assaults during Five Years of Captivity at the Hands of Somali Pirates," *Bangkok Post,* 22 March 2015: http://www.bangkokpost.com/print/503918/.

[53] SomaliaReport, "Weekly Piracy Report: Thirteen Pirates Killed by US, Drama of Seized Ransom in Mogadishu," 30 June 2011: http://www.piracyreport.com/index.php/post/8 92/Weekly_Piracy_Report.

[54] Confidential interviews (October 2012, Galkayo).

Puntland where he met and communicated with ranking government officials, local elders, and the pirate negotiator in Galkayo.[55] He reportedly told the negotiator that he had come with the agreed-upon USD 1.2 million and offered the negotiator USD 150,000 to help him convince the pirates to accept the ransom and release the boats.

By his own admission, the negotiator tried to pay a gang of assassins some USD 50,000 to kill those who refused to accept the ransom that was on offer; he then wanted to convince his relatives to accept the ransom and release the boats.[56] According to *SomaliaReport*, other pirates attacked *Prantalay 12* "in what might have been a clumsy attempt to liberate the ship after a sum of money was paid to a Somalia middleman."[57] It has not been possible to ascertain if this was the work of the negotiator or that of a different set of hired guns.

The former diplomat proceeded to Bosaso and reportedly met with other powerful men, among them a minister in the Puntland government.[58] Upon discovering the diplomat's meetings, the negotiator told the company that their agents had not paid the pirates the ransom and that the boats would not be released. He also told the pirates that the company had paid the USD 1.2 million ransom, which they had turned down, to their agent, who was refusing to pay them.[59]

Meanwhile, according to sources in Garowe and Bosaso, a Puntland minister reportedly agreed to secure the release of the ships. Under the guise of raising awareness among the elders and youth of the district to set up administrative structures and assist antipiracy initiatives, the minister traveled to the pirate area. He had with him an estimated USD 300,000 to distribute among the elders to win their intercession and to pressure the pirates to release the ships.[60] When the minister's entourage of five vehicles – including three technicals (pickup trucks mounted with heavy machine guns) – arrived on 11 October 2010, they fell into a pirate ambush.

Early that morning, the minister's convoy came under heavy fire from the pirates. As the five vehicles tried to escape, the pirates gave chase, capturing the minister and his men in the afternoon and herding them back to the pirate den of Gara'ad. Intense government pressure and negotiation with the elders secured the release of the ranking government

[55] Confidential interviews (October 2012, Galkayo).
[56] Confidential interviews (October 2012, Galkayo).
[57] "Weekly Piracy Report," *SomaliaReport*, 30 June 2011: http://www.piracyreport.com/in dex.php/post/892/Weekly_Piracy_Report.
[58] Confidential interviews (October 2012, Galkayo); also interviews in Bosaso and Garowe.
[59] Confidential interviews (October 2012, Galkayo).
[60] Confidential Interview with a government official with intelligence and fishing knowledge (February 2012, Bosaso).

officials.[61] The pirates took the tens of thousands of dollars that they found on the person of the minister. But they did not discover the hundreds of thousands more that were stashed away under the passenger seat of the minister's car. On the government's insistence, that car was also returned and its valuable contents were found intact.[62]

Having at this point given up on ransom, the pirates decided to use the boats as mother ships. They formed three groups, each with a vessel, and managed to hijack two other vessels. Nevertheless, the *Prantalay 12* broke anchor and was washed up onto the shore around Gara'ad, where it remains beached. The pirates saw no financial prospects in the crew of that vessel and practically stopped feeding them. An unknown number of the crew are reported to have died and were left to rot until local residents interred them with minimal burial rites. The pirates also left fourteen Burmese sailors, whom they deemed worthless, to wander around until PMPF took them to the regional capital from where they were flown out of Somalia.[63] Several Thai hostages were, however, taken inland; for years few knew the exact number or whereabouts of the remaining survivors until February 2015 when four were released, reportedly upon the payment of a ransom that some say was USD 1 million while others claim was only USD 150,000 to cover expenses.[64]

On its second journey as a mother ship, *Prantalay 14* (with a crew of sixteen Burmese and four Thais) came to the attention of Indian navy warship, the INS *Cankarso*, near the Lakshadweep islands on 28 January 2011. After some resistance from the pirates, the Indian

---

[61] Interview with head of Puntland's Counter Piracy Directorate, Abdirizaq Mohamed Dirir (4 February 2012, Garowe).

[62] Confidential Interview with a government official with intelligence and fishing knowledge (February 2012, Bosaso).

[63] Confidential interviews (October 2012, Galkayo).

[64] "Somali Pirates Release Fishermen Held for Five Years," *Al-Jazeera*, 27 February, 2015: http://www.aljazeera.com/news/2015/02/somali-pirates-release-fishermen-held-years-150227094729606.html; "Somali Pirates Free Thai Fishermen Held for Four Years," BBC News, 27 February 2015: http://www.bbc.com/news/world-asia-31664266; "The Devil and the Deep Blue Sea: Four Thai Fishermen Watched Their Friends Die and Suffered Brutal Assaults during Five Years of Captivity at the Hands of Somali Pirates," *Bangkok Post*, 22 March 2015: http://www.bangkokpost.com/print/503918/; "Consul-General of Thailand to Mumbai Visits the Original Crews of Vessel *Prantalay 14*": http://www.thaiembassy.org/mumbai/th/news/443/18413-กงสุลใหญ่-ณ-เมืองมุมไบ เยี่ยม ลูกเรือประมงพรานทะเล-1.html; "The Devil and the Deep Blue Sea: Four Thai Fishermen Watched Their Friends Die and Suffered Brutal Assaults during Five Years of Captivity at the Hands of Somali Pirates," *Bangkok Post*, 22 March 2015: http://www .bangkokpost.com/print/503918/; Colin Freeman, "Why a Retired British Army Colonel Has Become the Last Hope for Somalia's Forgotten Hostages," *The Telegraph*, 26 March 2015: http://www.telegraph.co.uk/news/worldnews/africaandindianocean/so malia/11495268/Why-a-retired-British-army-colonel-has-become-the-last-hope-for-So malias-forgotten-hostages.html.

navy sunk the ship, rescued the hostages and arrested the pirates. A week later, on 6 February 2011, and in the same vicinity of the Lakshadweep islands, a different Indian navy ship, INS *Tir*, responded to the distress signal of Greek bulk carrier the MV *Chios* that was being chased by *Prantalay 11*. The pirates quickly gave themselves up and another twenty Thai and Burmese hostage sailors were rescued before *Prantalay 11* was also sunk.[65] Fifty-eight of the foreign fishermen have thus been accounted for over a span of five years (forty rescued, fourteen freed by the pirates and local authorities and four ransomed) while the remaining nineteen are presumed dead under the crude conditions of pirate captivity.

Catch-N-Release and Hijack: The MV *Rim*

On repeatedly failing to carve out room for himself as a negotiator or to compete with Looyan in Eyl,[66] a Somali returnee from the United States joined an ill-fated pirate mission. The Danish navy captured but released the pirates after a substantial and healthy meal and a ride that brought them closer to their home around Eyl.[67] The former diasporic then convinced a known pirate financier, Abdulkadir Musse Hirsi "Computer," to give him his own boat. The former diasporic became the co-leader of an inexperienced team of pirates from the Warsangeli sub-clan and sailed off toward the international sea lanes in the Gulf of Aden. After several days of being lost at sea, the boat reached the coast of Yemen. The crew was physically exhausted and without fuel to sail back

[65] SomaliaReport, "Weekly Piracy Report," 30 June 2011: http://www.piracyreport.com/i ndex.php/post/892/Weekly_Piracy_Report; "Consul-General of Thailand to Mumbai Visits the Original Crews of Vessel *Prantalay 14*": http://www.thaiembassy.org/mum bai/th/news/443/18413-กงสุล ใหญ่- ณ- เมือ งมุมไบ เยียม ลูก เรือ ประมง พราน ทะเล- 1.html; "The Devil and the Deep Blue Sea: Four Thai Fishermen Watched Their Friends Die and Suffered Brutal Assaults during Five Years of Captivity at the Hands of Somali Pirates," *Bangkok Post*, 22 March 2015: http://www.bangkokpost.com/print/503918/.

"Navy, Coast Guard Destroy Somali Pirate Vessel," *Deccan Herald*, 29 January 2011, http://www.deccanherald.com/content/133143/navy-coast-guard-d estroy-somali.html; Sanjoy Majumder, "Indian Navy Seizes Pirates' Indian Ocean Mothership," BBC News, 6 February 2011, http://www.bbc.co.uk/news/world-south-asi a-12376695; "Fishermen Freed," *Maritime Security Review*, 16 March 2011: http://www .marsecreview.com/2011/03/fishermen-freed/.

[66] For the overall context in Eyl and specific background of what the said pirate told me, see Bahadur, "Pirates, Inc.," *The Financial Times*, 23 June 2010: https://www.ft.com/con tent/e5f60614-7d23-11df-8845-00144feabdc0.

[67] Confidential interview (November 2012, Garowe). Foreign navies' practice of catch and release has infuriated Somalis opposed to piracy and analysts of maritime piracy have criticized it as emboldening the criminal enterprise. While there are several logistical, procedural, and other issues associated with holding pirates on board a vessel for longer than may be allowed, many impute the navies' catching and releasing of pirates to their lack of seriousness about counterpiracy, which makes their presence questionable.

home or even make it to the crowded international sea lanes. They turned off the boat's engine and spent the night at sea, desperately contemplating their next move as the waves pushed them, one time closer to, another time farther from, the shores. In the early hours of the following morning, on 2 February 2010, the Libyan-owned, North Korean-flagged MV *Rim* sailed straight in their direction without a convoy and far from the heavily guarded Internationally Recommended Transit Corridor (IRTC). Within half an hour of spotting it, the pirates boarded the vessel and took it over.

The international navies responded to the ship's distress signal and arrived shortly afterward. One of the captive sailors, 36-year-old Romanian Virgil Cretu, recalled the moment thus: "We sent an SOS. NATO troops came. [The pirates] asked them to leave. If not, they'd kill us one-by-one."[68] But a pirate source had a more vivid and possibly dramatized recollection of how they repelled the military helicopter that hovered above the ship's deck in front of the bridge: One of the pirate leaders stuck the muzzle of his AK-47 into the captain's mouth and ordered him to take a step out of the bridge for the helicopter to see him while the pirate leader stayed inside. Although not a word more was necessary, the pirate shouted to the helicopter over a handheld loud speaker that this was not a Hollywood film and either they back off or the sailors' deaths would be on them. The helicopter instantly lifted off and left the scene. The pirates commandeered the vessel to Gara'ad where it would remain for four months.[69]

As the MV *Rim* sailed from around the tip of the Horn south to Gara'ad along the coast, one pirate co-leader started to call inland to make security and logistical arrangements while the other, the returnee, started making international calls and demanding ransom. Before the ship reached its destination, the returnee pirate leader managed to piece together the essential story of the ship they had just hijacked. Its Libyan owner had decided to decommission the ship and was about to sail it to India where it was to be turned into metal scrap. A Lebanese-Palestinian businessman contacted the owner on behalf of a Syrian family that wanted to make one last trip with the vessel, to which the owner agreed. The veracity of what the pirate leader was told and what he told me aside, the ship owner had neither a financial interest in the ship nor any contractual obligation to the crew.

The pirates reached out to an unnamed relative, who held a high-level post in Somalia's Ministry of Foreign Affairs, to reach the Libyan

---

[68] Virgil Cretu in an Associated Press video clip available on YouTube: https://www.you tube.com/watch?v=6aQ9rk5oZCg&t=21s.
[69] Confidential interview (November 2012, Garowe).

ambassador in Nairobi. The ambassador promised that the Libyan leader would pay whatever amount the pirates demanded if there were a single Libyan national on board.[70] None of the captive sailors was Libyan and communication between the ambassador and the pirates, which was facilitated by Somali government official in Mogadishu, ended.[71]

From talking to the crew, the street-smart pirate who had returned from the US learned that the *MV Rim* was worth about USD 1 million as scrap. It had previously been maintained and refurbished in Romania under the watch of Virgil Cretu, who was purportedly rewarded afterwards with employment on the ship as a crewmember. With a team of sixteen Syrian sailors, the ship then sailed – to Ukraine according to some and to North Korea according to others – and was reportedly loaded with illicit arms buried under meters of clay, which was the official cargo in the ship's manifest. Therefore, the ship was not insured and there was no entity to step forward and openly claim the cargo. The pirates then went back to the Libyan owner and tried unsuccessfully to cajole him into giving them the USD 1 million that the ship was worth as a scrap. As a last resort, they even had the hostages call home and relate their predicament in a bid to force their families to raise money for ransom.

With his hopes dashed, one of the two pirate leaders later confessed to me his calculations at the time: Threatening to pass the ship, hostages and cargo to Al-Shabaab would not have improved their prospects; trying to strike a deal with – and hand over the purportedly valuable cargo and Muslim hostages to – Western navies would have threatened their own lives at the hands of Al-Shabaab or its loyalists. Although the leader concluded in the first few weeks of the ship's hijacking that no ransom would be forthcoming, he came off the ship and started large-scale borrowing (secured by the pirated ship) from individuals and businesses who were unaware of the ship's dampened ransom prospects.

The pirate leader bought a house on the outskirts of Garowe and had it fully furnished before he arrived with his entourage of pirates in several cars that he had just bought. Thus started nearly three months of splurging, raucous parties and wild sex orgies. The leader delegated the day-to-day provision of essential supplies and security to junior lieutenants and forgot about it. By his own recollection, he blew no less than USD 300,000 – entirely borrowed – during the three months. Then unexpected news came from the coast, leading to his lenders' repossession of every material thing he had left that was worth a penny. A pirate cook, who had

---

[70] Confidential interview (November 2012, Garowe).
[71] Meetings of the highest-ranking Libyan leader with other pirates went on in a different context although, as discussed in Chapter 4, the objective was to end piracy and not to facilitate it.

reportedly been abused by the other pirates, helped the crew overpower and kill the pirates. The crew retook control of the ship and, exactly four months after its capture, on 2 June 2010, they sailed the MV *Rim* out to sea.[72] The EU NAVFOR mission dispatched a military helicopter and a warship to its aid and prevented another pirate group on a different hijacked vessel from chasing it.[73] The sailors of MV *Rim* were transferred to the EU NAVFOR warship *Johan de Witt* and the MV *Rim* has since disappeared from the records;[74] allegedly it was blown up in the high seas.

The MV *Iceberg I*

Like the MV *Rim*, the MV *Iceberg I* can also be considered as among the few vessels that became free from pirate control – even if after extended captivity. Whereas the sailors of the MV *Rim* overtook their captors and sailed out to sea after six months of being held hostage, the MV *Iceberg I* and its crew of twenty-four African and Asian sailors were held hostage for close to three years before PMPF staged a successful rescue operation. In contrast to the MV *Rim* case, however, a more experienced and hands-on pirate leader, Aden Abdirizak Hussein "Sanjab," led a close-knit group of pirates, who hailed from the Omar Mohamud family of the Mejerten, to the Gulf of Aden. The *MV Iceberg I*, a Panama-flagged UAE cargo ship, was owned by a company based in Dubai. On 29 March 2010 it was hijacked and sailed to Eldenane, near Gara'ad. The pirates demanded USD 10 million for the release of the ship and its crew. As late as mid-2011, the Dubai-based company offered no more than USD 300,000. Meanwhile, unsubstantiated stories – ranging from the ship's cargo being

---

[72] Shortly after their escape, the Romanian sailor Virgil Cretu, who sustained bullet wounds in the process, had the following to say to the Associated Press: "This Somalian helped us very much. We had a hidden phone, and he brought us a phone card. A SIM card. I was secretly talking [to people] in Romania, [and] in Syria, [about] the problems I had. The Somalian stole food from the pirates, water, and gave it to us. The Somalian gave me a gun. They, uh, the pirates, were fighting, and they started to take shots at each other. When they saw me with the gun, I fell in the middle, between them, in the crossfire. And then, a bullet hit me." Romanian sailor Virgil Cretu in Associated Press video clip available on YouTube: https://www.youtube.com/watch?v=6aQ9rk5oZCg&t=21s.

[73] Confidential interview (November 2012, Garowe); EU NAVFOR Somalia, "Crew of the Hijacked MV *RIM* Retake Control from Pirates, EU NAVFOR Warship *SPS Victoria* Gives Medical Support," 2 June 2010: http://eunavfor.eu/crew-of-the-hijacked-mv-rim-retake-control-from-pirates-eu-navfor-warship-sps-victoria-gives-medical-support/;

As Virgil Cretu put it: "[After we escaped,] all of the vessels who were with the pirates came after us. I don't know how much time passed. Finally, the Spanish helicopter appeared, from the ship *Victoria*. I contacted him. And the helicopter called the first [pirate] vessel, which was the nearest, to change course. If not, it would open fire."

[74] "MV *Rim* Abandoned," *Maritime Accident*, 4 June 2010: http://maritimeaccident.org/tags/mv-rim/.

toxic materials, to its owner being a Guantanamo Bay detainee, to inces-
sant pirate threats (first to the company and ultimately the families of the
hostages who were being tortured), to killing the hostages unless ransom
was paid – all added to the hysteria surrounding this ship and prolonged
the agony of the hostage sailors.[75]

After several failed rounds of negotiations, not only did the company
managers refuse to make any further ransom offers, but they also denied
ownership of the ship and cut off all communication with the pirates. The
erratic Aden Sanjab grew increasingly impatient and paranoid; he hired
one negotiator after another to restore communication. In one of his
many angry outbursts, he sliced the ear of the ship's captain; also, two
crew members died, one of illness and another under mysterious circumstances. The vessel had long been immobilized by lack of fuel and maintenance, and the crew had run out of clean water.

More than two years had passed by the time I tried to reason with the
pirate leader through indirect contact; I made he points that no ransom
would be coming from any source and that he should cut his losses and
show some compassion to the crew by releasing them. His curt reply was
as swift as it was indifferent: He himself was a hostage of his original
financiers and subsequent lenders and suppliers as much as the sailors
were his hostages. Over the years they had held the *Iceberg I* hostage, the
pirate group had accumulated close to USD 3 million in debt. A voluntary
decision on the leader's part to free the hostage sailors – if he had the
humanity to do so – would have left him responsible for the debt. Several
attempts to identify and reason with his financiers and to mobilize local
elders to back that initiative either met a brick wall of silence or were
dampened in an unending and sometimes circuitous chain of people.

After amassing so much debt for food (for the hostages and hostage-
takers alike), and for the pirates' khat, alcohol, and other luxuries like cars
and women, the hostage-takers themselves become hostages of their
creditors; this perpetuated, at least at the individual level, the cycle of
piracy and its consequences. Typically, the captured ship(s) in the nearby
waters are security for the debt that its captors incur on land. In some
cases, however, the pirates lose the ship(s), either because the crew over-
powers their captors, are rescued or for other unforeseen reason. If this
happens the pirates are not expected to pay the debt they incurred until
the day they lost the ship(s) – but few if any of the local businesses
associate with them afterwards, much less give them credit. Sometimes,

---

[75] "The Saga of the MV *Iceberg*," *Neptune Maritime Security*, 27 June 2012; Colin Freeman,
"Abandoned at Sea – The Forgotten Hostages of the Somali Pirates," *The Telegraph*,
29 August 2012: http://www.telegraph.co.uk/news/worldnews/africaandindianocean/so
malia/9507047/Abandoned-at-sea-the-forgotten-hostages-of-the-Somali-pirates.html.

Figure 3.3. In one of its earliest active operations against piracy, in December 2012 the Puntland Marine Police Force (PMPF) freed the sailors of MV *Iceberg I* after nearly three years of pirate captivity. (Courtesy of PMPF.)

the local businesses and individual investors who lend money to pirates post-hijacking are different from the initial investors who dispatched the pirate team in the first place; each group ends up absorbing its respective losses.[76]

After about thirty-three months of captivity, in December 2012, the pirates holding MV *Iceberg I* were attacked directly by PMPF and presidential guard units on what they dubbed a humanitarian rescue. Upon the failure of the first onslaught, government forces blocked the pirates' supplies and ammunition until the pirates capitulated on the second attempt by the government forces. The offensive left one exit avenue for the pirates in the event they were wise enough to take it and leave the hostages behind. Puntland forces immediately airlifted the twenty-two surviving hostages, first to the capital and then out of the country shortly afterward.[77]

---

[76] Only rarely, especially in 2009 and after, have pirates disappeared after receiving their share of ransom without settling their local debts. When the pirates fail to repay their debts, their lenders are left bankrupt or nearly so.

[77] Interviews with PMPF commander, Admiral Abdirizak Dirie Farah (13 August 2015, Garowe); Mohamed Abdirahman Farole (12 June 2014, Garowe).

The Sailing Yacht *Ing* and the MV *Dover*

A Danish family of five (two parents and three teenage children) and two crewmembers, also Danes, set out on board a sailboat, the SY *Ing*, for a well-publicized journey around the world. Between late 2010 and early 2011, they sailed off Australia and headed west into the Indian Ocean, all the while live-blogging about their adventures on SailBlogs. When they approached the piracy-affected areas, however, they reportedly "ignored warnings that 'pirates are not like Johnny Depp' and sailed into dangerous waters."[78] On 19 February, Jan Johansen, the father of the family, blogged: "We set up an anti-piracy plan to know what to do if we are attacked, and each day we send our position [to the international naval forces monitoring the Indian Ocean] . . . There has never been a [pirate] attack on a sailboat that has followed the recommended route."[79] Unfortunately, they did not fully adhere to recommendations of the international authorities and there had been several attacks on yachts before – some resulting in successful hijackings and others ending in worse tragedies.

Instead of sailing in a convoy, the family sailed alone, believing that it was safer to do so when in fact the opposite was true. Whereas there is no record of vessels – sailboats or cargo ships – being attacked while in convoys, there were several cases of sole-sailing luxury yachts being hijacked by Somali pirates. Almost two weeks before the *Ing* met its fate, Somali pirates had hijacked an American sailboat, the *SV Quest* with four Americans on board; all had been killed in a botched rescue attempt that involved the US Navy. As YachtPals reported, the Johansens seemed to have known about that incident.[80]

Moreover, in late October 2009, Somali pirates attacked and kidnapped a British couple, Paul and Rachel Chandler, who were sailing between Seychelles and Tanzania aboard their yacht, the *Lynn Rival*. The pirates reneged after receiving the agreed-upon sum and held them hostage for a total of thirteen months until a conscientious member of the Somali diaspora in England interceded and secured their release. In early April 2009, Somali pirates hijacked a French sailing yacht, the *SV Tanit*

---

[78] David Charter, "$3M Ransom Paid to Free Danish Yachting Family Held Hostage for Six Months by Somali Pirates," *The Australian*, 8 September 2011: http://www.theaustralian .com.au/news/world/m-ransom-paid-to-free-danish-yachting-family-held-hostage-for-six-months-by-somali-pirates/news-story/39dd68022210eb30f87a7a1efae4a1e6.

[79] Quoted in David Charter, "$3M Ransom Paid to Free Danish Yachting Family Held Hostage for Six Months by Somali Pirates," *The Australian*, 8 September 2011: http://ww w.theaustralian.com.au/news/world/m-ransom-paid-to-free-danish-yachting-family-held-h ostage-for-six-months-by-somali-pirates/news-story/39dd68022210eb30f87a7a1efae4a1e6.

[80] "Danish Family Yacht Captured by Pirates," YachtPals, 1 March 2011: http://yachtpals .com/pirates-dutch-yacht-9206.

with three adults and a three-year-old child on board.[81] More famously, in early April 2008, pirates captured the French luxury yacht *Le Ponant* and held its thirty-strong crew hostage until they collected millions in ransom. Not only was Johansen inaccurate in his assertion, but also in hindsight their security assessment was flawed as their move was risky.

On 24 February 2011, pirates under the still-at-large linchpin Isse Yuluh, hijacked the *SY Ing* and the seven Danes on board. Two weeks later they arrived around Hul Anod (near Bandar Bayla, further north of Hul), declaring that, should anyone attempt a rescue, the fate of their hostages would be that of the four Americans two weeks prior.[82] Undeterred, the Puntland government immediately dispatched an expeditionary Rapid Response Unit of the police. Colonel Abdirizak Ahmed "Gantal" commanded the seventy-five policemen with four technicals. Nevertheless, the pirates were alerted about the force's dispatch (possibly by a member of the dispatched police unit) and held the high ground overlooking the single, narrow path leading to the coast. When the police arrived, they lacked a coordinated effort and, according to Colonel Gantal, some disregarded his command. As one group of police approached the pirate positions against orders to hold their positions, and another group of police chased after the pirates, the pirates opened fire; killing five police officers, injuring six and disabling one of the technicals.[83] With the unit thus thrown into confusion, not only was the planned assault was aborted but the Rapid Response Unit was disbanded shortly afterwards.[84]

The next day, Yuluh's pirates moved the Danish hostages to another vessel the pirates had hijacked, the Panama-flagged Greek tanker MV *Dover* (with twenty-three Asian and European hostages), off the waters of Bargal, northeast of Bandar Bayla, and tethered the *Ing* to the *Dover*. The coastal community in Bargal, as much concerned for their own safety

[81] "Yacht *Tanit* Attacked by Pirates – Sailing Crew Taken Hostage," YachtPals, 7 April 2009: http://yachtpals.com/pirates-yacht-4130.

[82] "Pictured All Smiles on Their Yachting Holiday, the Five Somali Pirates Are Now Threatening to Kill," *Daily Mail*, 2 March 2011: http://www.dailymail.co.uk/news/arti cle-1361691/Somali-pirates-threaten-kill-family-5-pictured-yachting-holiday.html; "Somali Pirates Release Danish Hostages," *The Guardian*, 7 September 2011: https:// www.theguardian.com/world/2011/sep/07/somali-pirates-release-danish-hostages; Robert Young Pelton, "Terrorists, Pirates or Fishermen? Part Two: Land Based Anti-Piracy," *SomaliaReport*, 20 April 2012: http://piracyreport.com/index.php/post/3257/ Terrorists_Pirates_or_Fishermen.

[83] Interview with Colonel Abdirizak Ahmed "Gantal" (26 March 2017, Garowe).

[84] Sources say that President Farole feared that specialized police unit because it had been established by his predecessor and hence was loyal to Farole's political rivals who hailed from the Osman Mahamud family clan. Be that as it may, the Puntland Marine Police Force (PMPF) overtook the antipiracy operations of the Rapid Response Unit.

(from the navies) as for that of the hostages, mobilized against the pirates within a week of the hijacked ship's arrival. Elders urged local businesses to stop dealing with the pirates; their antipiracy militia engaged in a shootout with the pirates, ultimately evicting them from Bargal as well.[85] The pirates relocated again to a small hamlet called Gumba, south of Bargal and inhabited exclusively by Yuluh's sub-clan family.[86] Meanwhile as the local community's hostility and the government's antipiracy operations both intensified, the *MV Dover* sailed out to sea towing the *SV Ing* until the latter broke off in the stormy waters around the tip of the Horn.[87] Although the pirates did not recover the yacht itself, they held all thirty hostages for the next six months, demanding a ransom of USD 5 million. According to some sources, the pirate linchpin Isse Yuluf even offered to release the Danish hostages without further pre-condition if the Johansens were to give him the hand of their thirteen-year old daughter in marriage.[88] Finally in early September 2011, an airplane dropped a reported USD 3 million in ransom that secured the release of the hostages,[89] who were promptly flown out of the country and disappeared from public view.

The MV *Albedo*

Mohamed Abdi Hassan Afweyne's pirates hijacked the Iranian-owned, Malaysian-flagged bulk carrier MV *Albedo* in the Gulf of Aden on 26 November 2010 with twenty-three of its South Asian crew and sailed to Haradere. The pirates initially demanded a ransom of USD 8 million. Unable to come up with so much money without insurance coverage, the Iranian owners offered to raise USD 1 million but the pirates turned that down with derision. In July 2011, the pirates killed one of the two Indian sailors, Rajoo Rajbhar, to send a message. In 2012 Pakistani sources were

---

[85] Confidential interviews (Summer 2014, Garowe); Sue Richards, "Somalia Hostages – Danish Family Free," noonsite.com, 7 September 2011: http://www.noonsite.com/Members/sue/R2011-09-07-1.

[86] Confidential interviews (Summer 2014, Garowe); Robert Young Pelton, "Terrorists, Pirates or Fishermen? Part Two: Land Based Anti-Piracy," *SomaliaReport*, 20 April 2012: http://piracyreport.com/index.php/post/3257/Terrorists_Pirates_or_Fishermen.

[87] Sue Richards, "Somalia Hostages – Danish Family Free," noonsite.com, 07 September 2011: http://www.noonsite.com/Members/sue/R2011-09-07-1.

[88] "Pirate Will Free Family If He Can Marry Girl, 13" *National Post*, 30 March 2011: http://news.nationalpost.com/news/pirate-will-free-family-if-he-can-marry-girl-13; "Somali Pirates Release Danish Hostages," *The Guardian*, 7 September 2011: https://www.theguardian.com/world/2011/sep/07/somali-pirates-release-danish-hostages.

[89] David Charter, "USD 3M Ransom Paid to Free Danish Yachting Family Held Hostage for Six Months by Somali Pirates," *The Australian*, 8 September 2011: http://www.theaustralian.com.au/news/world/m-ransom-paid-to-free-danish-yachting-family-held-hostage-for-six-months-by-somali-pirates/news-story/39dd68022210eb30f87a7a1efae4a1e6.

specific that the sailor had died of cholera.[90] But Colin Freeman and Mike Pflanz's report in 2014[91] and James Verini's 2015 exposé gave grisly details of how, at the behest of a negotiator who could not get through to the company upon the expiration of the one-week deadline he had previously given, pirates took Rajoo Rajbhar and shot him in the chest.[92]

As the pirates kept torturing their hostages so that they would call their families to come up with ransoms, their stories started to gain public attention. Pakistani activists in Karachi formed a Citizen's Police Liaison Committee (CPLC) to coordinate their negotiations. CPLC came up with a creative idea to reimburse the pirates for the expenses that they had accumulated up to the moment of release.[93] The pirates agreed and calculated that they would release all the hostages upon receipt of USD 2.85 million for "expenses" incurred. The two sides agreed that 20 April 2012 would be the deadline.[94] By mid-2012, however, the Pakistani initiative only managed to raise USD 1.1 million. In July 2012, the pirates collected the sum and released seven Pakistani crewmembers.[95] Soon after that, the Iranian owner of the vessel cut off all communications, disowned the vessel, and abandoned the remaining crew to their own fate.[96]

A year later, the *Albedo* started taking water and sunk in early July 2013, taking with it seven pirates and four of its hostage sailors as it went down.[97] The remaining eleven crew members of the MV *Albedo* survived,

---

[90] "As Deadline Approaches, Pak to Raise Money for MV *Albedo* Crew's Release," NDTV, 14 April 2012: http://www.ndtv.com/world-news/as-deadline-approaches-pak-to-raise-money-for-mv-albedo-crews-release-476663; "MV *Albedo* Sinks after Nearly 3 Years in Captivity," MS Risk, 12 July 2013: http://www.msrisk.com/somalia/mv-albedo-sinks-after-nearly-3-years-in-captivity/.

[91] Colin Freeman and Mike Pflanz, "Somali Pirates Release Crew after Nearly Four Years in Captivity," *The Telegraph*, 7 June 2014: http://www.telegraph.co.uk/news/worldnews/piracy/10883414/Somali-pirates-release-crew-after-nearly-four-years-in-captivity.html

[92] James Verini, "Escape or Die: When Pirates Captured a Cargo Ship, Its Crew Faced One Desperate Choice after Another," *The New Yorker*, 20 April 2015: http://www.newyorker.com/magazine/2015/04/20/escape-or-die.

[93] Conversations with Naeem Sarfraz, (25-27 July 2012, Halifax, Nova Scotia). A retired Pakistani naval officer who went on to become a mariner and a businessman, Naeem was privy to the grassroots initiatives and negotiations that helped free the MV *Albedo* hostages.

[94] "As Deadline Approaches, Pak to Raise Money for MV *Albedo* Crew's Release," NDTV, 14 April 2012: http://www.ndtv.com/world-news/as-deadline-approaches-pak-to-raise-money-for-mv-albedo-crews-release-476663.

[95] "Pakistani Crew Held by Somali Pirates Reaches Home," Dawn, 2 August 2012: http://www.dawn.com/news/739203/pakistan-crew-held-by-somali-pirates-reaches-home

[96] Verini, "Escape or Die."

[97] "MV *Albedo* Sinks after Nearly 3 Years in Captivity," MS Risk, 12 July 2013: http://www.msrisk.com/somalia/mv-albedo-sinks-after-nearly-3-years-in-captivity/.

thanks to the nearby FV *Naham 3*, an Omani-flagged Taiwanese fishing vessel that Somali pirates hijacked in March 2012 and tethered to the MV *Albedo* when its engine developed technical problems. The EU NAVFOR sent air and naval assets that cordoned off the area to conduct search and rescue, but they were unsuccessful.[98] The pirates took the surviving hostages from the MV *Albedo* inland to 'Ammaaraa, a ramshackle village in Galmudug a day's drive away from its nearest town, Galkayo. Their conditions remained uncertain until eleven of them managed to escape in early June 2014 – more than three years and six months later.[99] The FV *Naham 3* also sunk a year after its crew rescued the MV *Albedo* sailors. Three of the all-Asian crew of twenty-nine sailors of the *Naham 3* died and the remaining twenty-six were taken inland where they lived in squalid conditions for years until they were freed in October 2016.[100]

The saga of the MV *Albedo* and the many other hijacked ships and hostages is not only one of cruel, greedy villains. It is also a story of heroic acts of survival, solidarity, hope, and risk-taking for others. Besides the sailors' strength to survive the terrifying and harsh conditions of captivity, there are many unsung heroes whose feats of accomplishments remain to be written. Suffice it to mention just a few and to lighten the so far gloomy account.

Whereas families of hostages endured much hardship, many of them – especially Indian and Pakistani mothers and wives of sailors – were on the streets and offices lobbying their governments to do more to protect their mariner sons and husbands. Many other heroes also championed the freedom of forgotten hostages in Somalia. Shahnaz Khan, the wife of Captain Jawaid Khan of the MV *Albedo*, started a vibrant fundraising movement that was supported and quickly joined by experienced seamen and businesspeople. A retired Pakistani naval officer and businessman

---

[98] "EU Naval Force Helicopter Overflies MV *Albedo* And FV *Naham 3*," 18 July 2013: http://eunavfor.eu/update-eu-naval-force-helicopter-overflies-mv-albedo-and-fv-naham-3/; "At Least 11 Dead as Ship Held by Pirates Sinks off Somalia," *Reuters*, 8 July 2013: http://uk.reuters.com/article/uk-somalia-pirate-ship-idUKBRE9670QU20130708.

[99] Colin Freeman and Mike Pflanz, "Somali Pirates Release Crew after Nearly Four Years in Captivity," *The Telegraph*, 7 June 2014: http://www.telegraph.co.uk/news/world news/piracy/10883414/Somali-pirates-release-crew-after-nearly-four-years-in-captiv ity.html; Verini, "Escape or Die." According to Verini, the escape was possible because John Steed and his hostage-negotiations-expert colleague, Leslie Edwards, managed to raise over USD 200,000 that they used to bribe the pirate guard, who cut out the investors and split the money three ways with his two accomplices. Separately, Steed paid and enlisted a minister in the Galmudug regional administration to secure the hostages once they escaped from their captors and to transport them to safety in Galkayo until they were flown out of the country.

[100] "Crew of FV *Naham 3* Released by Pirates after Over 4 1/2 Years in Captivity," Oceans Beyond Piracy, 22 October 2016: http://oceansbeyondpiracy.org/somali-pirates-releas e-crew-fv-naham-3.

Naeem Sarfaz, for example, lobbied internationally to bring to light the fate of neglected hostage sailors in Somalia; he also helped guide the Pakistani grassroots initiative and negotiations with the pirates of the MV *Albedo*.[101]

The United Nations Office on Drugs and Crime (UNODC) in Nairobi has a small, secretive hostage support unit that has accomplished a lot without much fanfare. It tracked the forgotten hostages and quietly negotiated with their captors or sensitized people such as clan elders, religious leaders, and government officials around them toward that effect. John Steed, a retired British colonel and former military attaché in Kenya who once led that unit, now continues the same work outside the UN system; he has played a crucial role in securing the freedom of the last four hostages of MV *Iceberg I*, the eleven hostages of MV *Albedo*, and the twenty-six hostages of FV *Naham III*.[102]

On 22 March 2015, two related pirate groups hijacked two separate Iranian vessels named *Siraj* and *Jaber*. Not long afterwards, *Jaber's* sailors overpowered the four sleepy pirates on board and sailed to freedom and to the pirates' imprisonment in Iran. The pirates of *Siraj* forced its seventeen hostage sailors to an inland hideout in the Galmudug region; there the two pirate leaders had a falling out and split the hostages between them (five with Kerani and twelve under Abdiweli). One of Kerani's five hostages escaped; from Abdiweli's group, four were rescued and four died in captivity. Both pirates continued to hold four hostages each, complicating the negotiations that are likely to become even more difficult because, on the one hand, the hostages hail from poor parts of Iran and the Iranian government has not been forthcoming with financial support. On the other hand, the pirates have demanded the release of the four pirates from FV *Jaber* in addition to an uncertain sum in ransom.

During fieldwork in the spring of 2017, I witnessed Steed, Abdirizak Mohamed Dirir (Puntland's former Director of Counter-piracy) and others hard at work, speaking with the two pirate kingpins and their associates, and with the owner of FV *Siraj*, who had come to Hargeysa to see the negotiation through.[103] As this book goes to press, the situation remains unchanged with Steed and his networks continuing to maintain the hostages with a supply of "food and medicine but it [is] hard to get

---

[101] Conversations with Naeem Sarfaz (Halifax, NS, 25–27 July 2012).

[102] Colin Freeman, "Why a Retired British Army Colonel Has Become the Last Hope for Somalia's Forgotten Hostages," *The Telegraph*, 26 March 2015: http://www.telegraph .co.uk/news/worldnews/africaandindianocean/somalia/11495268/Why-a-retired-Britis h-army-colonel-has-become-the-last-hope-for-Somalias-forgotten-hostages.html.

[103] Personal conversations with John Steed and Abdirizak Mohamed Dirir (January–March 2017).

through and we are trying to negotiate their release. But we have no money and no one is offering to help."[104]

Conclusion

As the criminal enterprise of ransom piracy grew exponentially from 2005, so did its local and foreign victims. Throughout those years of heightened piracy incidents, pirates held for ransom a total of nearly 4,000 sailors for varying lengths of time in various coastal and inland locations across Somalia. At the height of piracy activity in 2011, there were more than 1,100 such hostages, with the longest having been held for almost five years. Some sailors were killed or committed suicide during the hijacking or shortly afterwards. Several others died due to the appalling conditions of captivity and the callous neglect of the pirates. Even the few who were rescued or managed to escape without paying ransoms endured harsh conditions of prolonged captivity; they inevitably live with visible and invisible scars of that traumatic experience. The anguish of their families can only be imagined.

The criminal world of Somali ransom pirates began with a "code"; without that code, that world degenerated into something unrecognizable and uncontrollable by its initiators. With the increasing number of soldiers-turned-pirates following the disintegration of inter-clan pirate groups, that code started to peel away one layer at a time. Pirates began to double cross each other, both across and within clan groupings. They became hostile toward, and on occasion attacked, local communities. A large number of young boys entered the piracy world, a development that, ironically enough, even Boyah and other early pirates lamented. The consequences proved devastating to the local communities and eroded what little support pirates had enjoyed among their hosts.

Meanwhile, having previously sought and received amnesty from local authorities and from the Transitional Federal Government in Mogadishu, "Afweyne" announced his "retirement" in January 2013. He also called on his colleagues to do the same and to exit what he now declared was "dirty business."[105] Although by all accounts his operations had long been passed on to his son, Abdulkadir Mohamed Afweyne, in an exclusive interview with CCTV's "Faces of Africa" program (conducted in April 2013 and aired in 2014), Afweyne the father sought to establish his antipiracy record thus:

---

[104] Personal communication with John Steed (February 2018).
[105] James M. Bridger, "The Rise and Fall of Somalia's Pirate King," *Foreign Policy*, 17 November 2013.

We disarmed 932 pirates, including their commanders. They are being rehabilitated at three different centers. There were armed vehicles posted along the coast to prevent rehabilitated pirates from going back to the sea. I give them food, and I also buy for them a very expensive type of khat called miraa. Every day, I have to pay USD 12,500 at the very least.[106]

The government of Sheikh Sharif Sheikh Ahmed in Mogadishu reimbursed his purported expenses as an antipiracy tsar, but he had not faced justice for his crimes and remained liable to being brought to a court of law. Posing as filmmakers, the Belgian police lured him to travel to Belgium as a consultant on a documentary film about Somali piracy. Upon his arrival there in October 2013, authorities arrested him at the Brussels airport and sent him to jail to await trial.[107] More than two years later, a court in Bruges sentenced him to twenty years in prison for the 2009 hijacking of the *Pompei*, a Belgian dredging ship, among other associated crimes.

---

[106] "Afweyne Big Mouth and the Somali Pirates," CCTV Faces of Africa, 2014.
[107] "Somali Pirate 'Big Mouth' Arrested in Belgium," *Al-Jazeera*, 14 October 2013: http://www.aljazeera.com/news/africa/2013/10/somali-pirate-big-mouth-arrested-belgium-2013101416231617270.html; James M. Bridger, "The Rise and Fall of Somalia's Pirate King," *Foreign Policy*, 17 November 2013.

4 Local Consequences of and Responses to Piracy

The previous chapters have examined the root causes and dynamics of piracy, and have shown the proliferation of pirate gangs across Somalia. In a bid to attract the best men with the most coveted skills, and to retain the already committed pirates from going to rival gangs, pirate kingpins and their mobilizers poured money into recruitment. The consequences proved devastating to the local communities and, in the end, eroded what little support pirates had enjoyed among their hosts. Ransom piracy has since caused more harm to Somalis – in coastal areas and inland towns alike – than is recognized by the outside world and more than can be addressed with quick-fix military solutions on land or at sea. Donna Nincic observed early on how "while maritime piracy in Somalia imposes much-publicized costs on the shipping community, it also extracts a deep toll from the population itself,"[1] concluding that it could not "adequately be addressed and eradicated unless it is seen as both a *cause* of social and economic hardships and an *effect* of social, political and economic destitution as well" (emphasis original).[2]

Although the consequences of piracy were not felt locally until after 2007, Somalis have since taken note of the many direct and indirect ways they have manifested in their lives. Piracy helped destroy the livelihoods of those who depended on the fishing sector; it directly and indirectly contributed to skyrocketing prices of consumer goods; it scared away legitimate businesses and job-creating investments; and it jeopardized the delivery of humanitarian aid. Pirates contributed to the further deterioration of local social fabric, exposed their communities to unprecedented kinds of physical insecurity and violation of societal norms; and became a drain on the meager services that were available to a population already on the edge.

---

[1] Donna Nincic, "Maritime Piracy in Africa: The Humanitarian Dimension," *African Security Review*, 18, no. 3 (2009), 13.
[2] Nincic, "Maritime Piracy in Africa," 15.

Without accounting for other possible contributory factors, this chapter examines the ugly local developments that are associated with ransom piracy in Somalia in general and Puntland in particular. This is because of the concentration of piracy in Puntland after 2007 and the environment that enabled me to research the topic there. Combining the perceptions and experiences of the affected communities with statistical data (where appropriate and available) and with observable facts on the ground, the chapter analyzes the multiple, inter-related and mutually reinforcing negative developments in Somalia that are blamed on piracy. It documents the plight of Somalis under the heavy weight of piracy and, in so doing, it contributes to the quest for lasting land-based solutions to the ongoing crime, solutions that are homegrown, locally driven, and internationally supported.

Collapse of the Fishing Sector

Ransom piracy contributed to the worsening vicious cycle initiated by IUU fishing: diminishing catch; declining income; dwindling capital to reinvest in equipment; hence reduced catch and dissipating employment opportunities. It became the proverbial last straw that broke the back of the Somali-owned, export-oriented, rudimentary-but-lucrative fishing sector and also helped erode what little remained of subsistence fishing. Piracy and fishing have since developed an inversely proportional relationship, the reversal of which bodes well for a sustainable Somali solution to the scourge of piracy.

Even though many companies went bankrupt and closed down, a few surviving companies started to bring laborers from south and central Somalia to make up for their loss of manpower to piracy. Within days of coming to the fishing villages, the fishermen would make contact with pirates, who actively recruited them or provided them handouts of cash, food, drinks, or chew – as they did to a *shahat* or beggar.[3] Even as shahat, the newly arrived laborers ended up making more (in cash and in kind) than they normally would as laborers or divers for the fishing companies that brought them there in the first place. Most of them quit within days and the companies were left scrambling for new manpower.

Somali fishermen have consistently complained about pirates stealing their fishing boats and catch, fighting, and injuring or killing the fishermen in the process. Executives of a fishing company in Bosaso related the

---

[3] Although it literally means "beggar" in Arabic, *shahat* in this Somali context is considered more dignified than a simple beggar.

injuries and deaths their smaller-scale fishermen suffered at the hands of the pirates. A fisherwoman from Eyl lost one of her boats to pirates but intercepted another daring group of pirates pulling her other boat behind their truck and driving fast through Bedey, the coastal half of Eyl.[4] Many other fishermen were not as fortunate; pirates managed to steal their equipment and their catch. A fisherman told *SomaliaReport* that "pirates came to Bargal beach [in late 2011] and seized my friend's boat. They took it to Oman and my friend never saw his boat again."[5] Another fisherman in Lasqorey also told *SomaliaReport* how pirates stole their catch at gunpoint: "One day . . . Somali pirates with a small boat like ours came over and asked us to buy a fish. They didn't have much money so we refused them. Finally, they forced us to give them the fish that we worked so hard to catch."[6]

Inflation and Price Hikes

Prices of basic consumer goods started to rise sharply in the immediate aftermath of the explosion of ransom piracy in 2007 and remained high. In October 2012, the Puntland Ministry of Planning and International Cooperation (MOPIC) released a price index of basic consumer goods in Garowe and Bosaso for the preceding four years with 2005 as a base year. Accordingly, the retail prices of basic necessities like foodstuffs, medicines, and clothing rose by an average of 47.62 percent per year in both towns. Galkayo was not included because MOPIC did not start to compile data on its prices of consumer goods until 2008. Nevertheless, even Galkayo's already high price index witnessed an additional average increase of 15.3 percent per year during the same time frame.[7] Although other factors cannot be ruled out, pirates and piracy contributed to such increases in prices of basic consumer goods in Puntland in at least two easily identifiable ways: pirates' massive borrowing at exorbitant interest rates and skyrocketing of insurance premiums because of piracy.[8]

---

[4] Confidential interview (February 2012, Eyl).

[5] Mohamed Beerdhige, "Pirates Hijack Vessel despite Gov Security Team: Iranian Dhow Fishing Legally with Support of Puntland Government," 25 January 2012: http://piracyre port.com/index.php/post/2618/Pirates_Hijack_Vessel_Despite_Gov_Security_Team.

[6] Ibid.

[7] Professor Mohamed Samantar, the principal macroeconomist in the Puntland Ministry of Planning and International Cooperation who oversees the study, is careful to point out that his ministry and Puntland lacked the resources to investigate what role piracy played in these price hikes, but he believes the analysis in this report to be sound.

[8] That is in addition to the global financial crises and increase in the global price of foodstuffs that are not within the scope of this report.

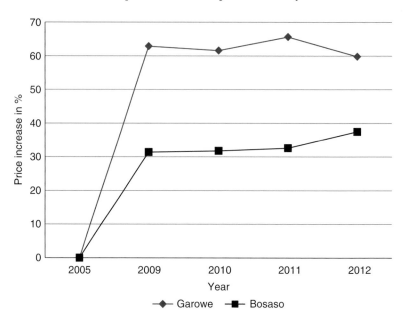

Figure 4.1. Percentage increase in price index for basic consumer goods in Puntland. (Compiled by author from MOPIC data.)

Trickling Down of Insurance Costs and Impediments to Trade

Speaking about the whole of Somalia, a Somali businessman and contractor related how, on top of its being completely unsupported by a state or the international community, the economy suffered due to piracy. Among other things, foreign vessels refused to transport goods to Somalia.[9] Former Somali prime minister and current Puntland president, Abdiweli Mohamed Ali "Gas," speaks similarly of the toll the exorbitant insurance premiums exacted on Somalia. According to him, of the more than 20,000 vessels that sailed past the Gulf of Aden, fewer than 5 percent came under attack by Somali pirates and, at the height of pirate success, 3 percent of the attacked were actually hijacked and their crew taken hostage. But insurance costs increased for all those buying coverage when sailing past the piracy-prone waters; in some cases insurance premiums tripled or quadrupled.[10]

[9] Confidential interview (August 2011, Nairobi).
[10] Interview with former prime minister of the Transitional Federal Government, Abdiweli Mohamed Ali (21 October 2012, Galkayo).

Industry sources in fact show a far more dramatic increase in insurance premiums since Lloyds classified the Somali coastline as "a war risk area" in mid-2008. Londonmaritime.com cited "insurance broker Marsh & McLennan" in reporting that "the cost of insuring ships against piracy has increased 1,900% since [January 2009]." In other words, "shipping firms that were paying 0.05% of the value of their goods for insurance premiums are now paying as much as 0.1%."[11] In 2010 Oceans Beyond Piracy reported that while not all vessels purchase insurance premiums in the four categories that they are offered, war risk premiums alone "have increased 300 fold, from $500 per ship, per voyage; to up to $150,000 per ship, per voyage, in 2010."[12]

More specifically in Puntland, the Bosaso-based Chamber of Commerce shows that piracy hampered Puntland's imports and exports with a direct bearing on prices of basic consumer goods in local markets and export of livestock. Early on, the majority of south Asian-owned dhows that transported goods to and from Bosaso ceased operations as pirate attacks escalated. The ones that continued to operate did so at a significantly increased transportation charge (as much as 30 percent across the board) for the same cargo because of the increased insurance premiums for sailing in piracy-infested waters.[13]

Foreign traders also lost confidence in sending their goods for their Somali partners to sell and send back the money as they had done before piracy. As a result the relationship of Somali business people with foreign partners stopped and many such companies went out of business.[14] That reduced competition among suppliers and gave them significant pricing leverage.

All those costs ultimately trickled down to retail prices that end consumers absorbed without new or additional sources of income. Although the market of consumer goods started to feel the squeeze from piracy, prices did not fully respond until 2009. An immediate jump at that time has since plateaued (except in Galkayo where costs have declined although retail prices of consumer goods there have remained comparable to the other towns). A random visit to any retail store in one of Puntland's towns demonstrates how the consumers absorb these increased costs. According to one pharmacy's rare six-year records (for 2007–2012 inclusive), of most-sold medicines in Garowe, the prices of Paracetamol tablets and antibiotic capsules more than doubled in 2007 and quadrupled in

---

[11] See Maritime London, "Piracy: A Tax for Shipping?" 26 June 2009: http://www
.maritimelondon.com/london_matters29june09.htm#1.
[12] Bowden, *The Economic Cost of Maritime Piracy*, 10.
[13] Confidential interview (February 2012, Bosaso).
[14] Confidential interview (February 2012, Bosaso).

2009. Prices of cough syrups and vitamins also jumped, but to a lesser extent.[15]

Spendthrift Pirates Borrow Massively

Average pirates hardly retained fluid cash before – or long after – the delivery of ransoms. Wherever they went, pirates and their entourage of *shahat* either bought supplies on credit from local businesses or borrowed massively. Given the pirates' typical desperation at the moment when goods were purchased and their alacrity to pay hefty interest afterwards, and given the overall level of risk involved for the retail businesses, the merchants demanded – and in many cases the pirates offered of their own volition – interest rates of as much as 100 percent, which dramatically spiked the prices of commodities for everyone. The risks involved in such lending were not hypothetical.

During the first few years of ransom piracy (especially before 2009) negotiations to free captured ships generally did not drag on for long and ransoms were delivered relatively quickly.[16] During those years, pirates also paid local businesses what they were owed as quickly as the ransoms were received. The speed with which those debts were settled had the immediate effect of doubling the prices of commodities in the pirate dens. That was especially the case because local retailers stocked up on supplies (from the towns) as frequently as the pirates paid their debt. In cases when the ransom was late and debt repayment delayed, larger business counterparts in the towns sold supplies to coastal merchants on credit; doing so was not out of the ordinary in the Somali business context.

This increase in prices was not restricted to coastal villages; those in the towns also showed a commensurate rise. Businesses in inland towns gave credit to their partners at the coast and faced similar risks. They charged interests that were paid as quickly as the ransoms were delivered and pirate debts on the coast were settled. Meanwhile, immediately after the capture of a ship, the attack team of no more than thirty pirates per ship would descend on a nearby town where they went on their own spending sprees on credit secured by the captured ship along the coast. As soon as the ransom was paid and split, the ground/security teams also went to the towns to spend their smaller shares of the ill-gotten fortunes. Even when

---

[15] Confidential interview (February 2012, Garowe). On the pharmacy owner's request for confidentiality, no identifiers of him or his business are disclosed.

[16] On average, ransoms were delivered after about three months of captivity and retailers in coastal pirate dens generally procured supplies a few times a year. In cases when the local retailers did not have cash to pay for their supplies right away, they too bought their goods on credit from the suppliers, hence the distribution of the risks and high interest rate.

they were paying for their purchases up front, pirates were too willing to pay twice the value of the items.

The cumulative effect of these dynamics contributed to a parallel rise in commodity prices across the board in Puntland, making it increasingly difficult for non-pirates to afford the rising living costs. More and more people sank deeper into poverty. Piracy or illegal immigration became the only option available for increasing numbers of ablebodied persons willing to undertake either of the risky ventures. Some pirates ended up migrating illegally, either after accumulating enough cash to pay their way or after losing out in the piracy industry, and were smuggled halfway to their destination from where they called relatives to pay for them.[17]

The Livestock Business Suffered

The export of livestock supports the livelihoods of many Somalis and is an important source of revenue for the Puntland State of Somalia.[18] Statistics from Puntland's Ministry of Livestock and Animal Husbandry indicate the region's export of livestock steadily rose after Puntland's establishment in 1998 and averaged 1.8 million head of livestock annually between 2005 and 2008, with 2008 witnessing the summit figure of 1,926,062 head.[19] But that dropped to an average of 1.4 million head of livestock between 2009 and 2011. In 2012 (the final year of piracy) there was a further drop in livestock exports to about 1.3 million head.[20] The secretariat of the Chamber of Commerce has a nuanced explanation for the dramatic decrease in Puntland livestock exports during the height of piracy.

Before piracy, foreign buyers demanded to have freight on board (FOB) before paying for it.[21] Because piracy endangered the safe delivery

---

[17] For an account of human trafficking and illegal migration in Somalia, see Nimo-Ilhan Ali, *Going on Tahriib: The Causes and Consequences of Somali Youth Migration to Europe* (Nairobi: Rift Valley Institute, 2016).

[18] Although it covers livestock trading between southern Somalia and Kenya, Peter D. Little's *Somalia: Economy without State* (Oxford: James Currey, 2003) offers a fascinating analysis that also captures the general picture of the livestock industry across Somalia.

[19] Per statistics from the Puntland Ministry of Livestock and Animal Husbandry shared with me privately.

[20] Although protracted clan conflicts contribute to the decline of livestock exports when either traders or herders have to traverse the territory of a rival clan, no such conflicts have taken place to significantly affect trade routes since 2007.

[21] For a perspective on how Somali general traders and businessmen in other Somali regions and ports handled their foreign trade or transacted with their foreign partners, see Report of the United Nations Monitoring Group on Somalia, S/2006/229, 4 May 2006, paragraph 63.

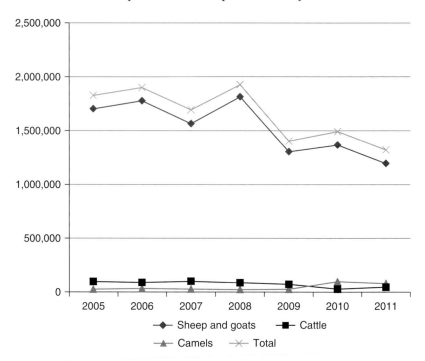

Figure 4.2. Puntland's livestock export. (Compiled by author from government figures.)

of their purchases, foreign companies started to demand that Puntland traders bring their livestock to Djibouti instead of Bosaso.[22] Doing so not only increased the cost and risks that Puntland traders bore because Puntland does not have the Letter of Credit (LC) system but also reduced the revenue that the state would have collected from exports through the port of Bosaso.[23] Meanwhile, although the livestock-supplying nomads were not immune to the inflation that affected Puntlanders from all walks of life, they did not necessarily earn more for their cattle, sheep, goats and camels.

[22] Confidential interview (February 2012, Bosaso).
[23] Given that international trade involves buyers and sellers living under different legal and financial systems and that they may not have face-to-face knowledge of each other, recognized banks mediate their transactions by issuing letters of credit (LC) to guarantee that the supplier or service provider will be paid in time upon the delivery of goods or services.

Lost Job-Creation Opportunities and Endangered Humanitarian Aid

Like other criminal activities, piracy benefited initially from the problem of joblessness across Somalia, and particularly in Puntland, and joblessness became the biggest impediment for a solution. The cascade of economic difficulties associated with piracy directly reduced the creation of local jobs, which in turn made jobless young men available in abundance for recruitment into piracy. As Jack Lang reported in January 2011, the "growing insecurity caused by piracy is depriving the north of Somalia of possible job-creating investments (port operations, fishing, and development of public infrastructure)."[24]

Nevertheless, there is no alternative to job creation as a significant part of the solution to piracy. Not only do many people in Puntland attribute piracy partially to joblessness but even more people believe that job creation is the best solution for eradicating piracy. As shown in Chapter 2, ninety-one of the 236 respondents (38.5 percent) in a 2012 survey thought that youth unemployment was at the root of piracy. And 124 of the same respondents (52.5 percent) believed job creation to be the best solution as shown in Figure 4.3.[25]

Piracy also endangered the lives of many Somalis who had been in dire humanitarian situations; this was especially true of those in central and southern Somalia, although not all of the pirate attacks came from that region. At a time when more than two million Somalis remained dependent on food aid, almost all of which was delivered by sea, pirates attacked vessels that brought life-saving supplies to the poverty-stricken people.[26] According to Donna Nincic, between 2005 and 2009 alone, pirates attacked close to a dozen such vessels,[27] whose slow speed and low freeboard made them particularly vulnerable. One pirate group alone hijacked three vessels chartered to the World Food Program (WFP); the MV *Semlow* in June 2005 was the first, as discussed in Chapter 2. Initially, not even the vessels that were run by Somalis were spared.

In October 2005, the Somali-owned Towfiq Export and Import Company chartered a cargo vessel called *Sembo*[28] to transport supplies

---

[24] Jack Lang, *Report of the Special Adviser to the Secretary-General on Legal Issues Related to Piracy off the Coast of Somalia*, January 2011, 14.

[25] It is important to note that some respondents gave more than one answer to a given question.

[26] Jack Lang, *Report of the Special Adviser to the Secretary-General on Legal Issues Related to Piracy off the Coast of Somalia*, January 2011, 14.

[27] Nincic, "Maritime Piracy in Africa," 10–13.

[28] Although one of the company owners, Mohamed Daylaaf (Interview: 8 August 2011, Nairobi), said the name of the boat was *Sembo*, the details he offered resemble those of

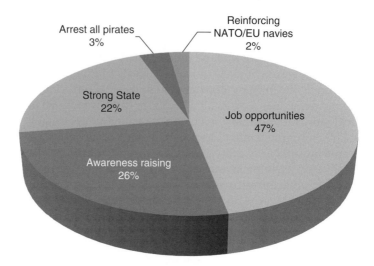

Figure 4.3. Local views about solutions for piracy. (Compiled by the author.)

under contract to the WFP's humanitarian intervention in Somalia. Once at the port of Marka, pirates smuggled weapons on board and commandeered the *Sembo* out of port toward the open ocean. The company dispatched two boats with armed security personnel on board, surrounded the ship, and served the pirates an ultimatum to leave unmolested within twenty-four hours. With nowhere to go, the pirates accepted the offer and escaped in a boat that the company supplied; the ship sailed back to port to offload its remaining cargo.[29]

In May 2007, pirates attacked another cargo ship, the Jordanian-flagged MV *Victoria*, chartered to the same company, under the same WFP contract and from the same port of Marka. The vessel had just emptied its cargo and sailed toward Dar es Salaam in Tanzania. As soon as *Victoria* sent a distress signal, the Somali charterers dispatched a security team aboard two dhows to disrupt the pirate attack. In the ensuing exchange of gunfire, one of the company's security guards (the staff supervisor) was killed before the pirates relented and fled.[30]

MV *Miltzow*, which was briefly hijacked by pirates in October 2005. See Nincic, "Maritime Piracy in Africa," 12.

[29] Interview with Mohamed Daylaaf (8 August 2011, Nairobi).

[30] Interview with Mohamed Daylaaf (8 August 2011, Nairobi); "Somalia: Pirates Attack UN Aid Ship, Prompting Call for Action," UN News, 20 May 2007: http://www.un.org /apps/news/story.asp?NewsID=22609&Cr=Somalia&Cr1#.UTDXW6X3A_M.

Although Somali contractors with the World Food Program chartered foreign vessels to deliver the humanitarian assistance and claimed that they had their own "protection plan,"[31] a rising number of the chartered vessels and their crews refused to sail to Somalia. As a result, in "March 2007 the WFP had over 2,400 tons of food supplies waiting on dock in Tanzania ready for delivery and was having difficulty finding ships to hire."[32] As humanitarian organizations working in Somalia warned of an imminent catastrophe, the WFP Executive Director at the time called for immediate security measures to enable continued delivery of relief aid. He urged "key nations to do their utmost to address this plague of piracy, which . . . if unresolved, will sever the main artery of food assistance to the country and to the people who rely on it for their survival. Unless action is taken now, not only will our supply lines be cut, but also those of other aid agencies working in various parts of Somalia."[33] NATO's timely and effective responses averted the immediate catastrophe as we will see in the next chapter, but the secure delivery of humanitarian assistance remained so compromised that, according to Lang, the WFP was "relying more and more on very costly air deliveries."[34]

Deterioration of Safety and Security and Draining of Resources

With the breakdown of inter-clan pirate groups, the existing "pirate code" dissolved and pirates more frequently double-crossed each other across and within clan groupings. The consequent tension and violence within and among pirate groups led to increased insecurity of local communities. Residents of every town and village that experienced a pirate presence attested without fail to the sudden deterioration of safety and security of previously peaceful communities following the advent of pirates on the scene. The pouring in of unearned cash also led to a worsening erosion of the social and family fabric, and to destabilization of the traditional order that had preserved itself through the years of war. Heavily armed pirates came to previously peaceful and least-armed communities and they did not hesitate to use their weapons against each other and non-pirate local residents alike. The attendant insecurity affected everyone.

---

[31] Interview with Mohamed Daylaaf (8 August 2011, Nairobi).
[32] Nincic, "Maritime Piracy in Africa," 11.
[33] Quoted in "Somalia: Pirates Attack UN Aid Ship, Prompting Call for Action," 20 May 2007: http://www.un.org/apps/news/story.asp?NewsID=22609&Cr=Somalia&Cr1#.UTDXW6X3A_M.
[34] Jack Lang, *Report of the Special Adviser to the Secretary-General on Legal Issues Related to Piracy off the Coast of Somalia*, January 2011, 14.

The exact statistics of security incidents involving pirates or related to piracy are hard to come by. This is because, among other factors, pirates choose to settle disputes outside the justice system as represented by state authorities, however weak those authorities may be.[35] A number of other practical and methodological challenges made it difficult to track pirate-caused security incidents exhaustively. The few documented cases capture, in broad strokes, the combined effects of their activities that are inescapable to the naked eye.

In an open group discussion with Eyl residents (as part of participatory action research) about these and other piracy-related developments, a religious leader from the village of Da'ewad in Eyl quietly mused, "The powerful get angry fast." He had a near-death experience when a pirate, in objection to his preaching against piracy and pirates, fired in his direction. Many other elders and activists were victims of that anger when pirates shot at them randomly. Even mosques were not safe. In at least one incident in Eyl, pirates shot several rounds into the mosque on a Friday in order to stop the antipiracy sermon. A representative of the youth campaigners against piracy in the historic fishing village related how security had so deteriorated that "our wives started to miscarry due to extreme fear."[36] The situation was even worse further south, especially when the hub of piracy moved to the Mudug region of Puntland.

A ranking official in the office of the northern Mudug regional governor related that pirates were into "all night partying and gun fire . . . to a point that we assume that every gun shot is pirate-related."[37] Both pirates and non-pirates similarly characterized the level of pirate-caused disturbances between the inland town of Galkayo and the coastal village of Gara'ad in the same region. An army veteran and ranking police officer in Galkayo compared the pirates' random and wanton shootings to the sound of hundreds of simultaneous suicides: "When they marry, they fire so much ammunition that one thinks a battalion had killed itself."[38]

Security disturbances surrounding intra-pirate rivalries or quarrels and drunken commotions were not the only ills that followed the advent of ransom pirates after 2007. In mid-February 2012, a nineteen-year-old civilian was killed in Galkayo in one such shooting during the wedding of a pirate. The police responded and apprehended the shooter only to face multiple challenges. On the one hand, the family of the victim wanted to

---

[35] According to a one-time investor and pirate organizer in Mudug, the elders whom the pirates corrupted were important in resolving intra-pirate disputes as well as the pirates' disputes with the host communities. (Confidential interview, October 2012, Galkayo).

[36] Confidential interview (February 2012, Eyl).

[37] Confidential interview (February 2012, Galkayo).

[38] Interview (26 February 2012, Galkayo).

avenge the death of their relative and demanded that the killer be handed over to them as was the custom. On the other hand, the pirates wanted to free their colleague and, to that end, they attacked the police station twice. This was not the first time that the Galkayo police came under similar pirate attacks.

Suddenly "enriched" young men owned flashy sports utility vehicles (SUVs) with automatic transmissions (as opposed to the harder-to-drive stick shifts). Driving them under the influence of alcohol and drugs and without prior driving experiences, they caused numerous accidents. The same regional official in Galkayo also blamed pirates for nearly all traffic accidents. "About 99 percent of traffic accidents are pirate-caused," he said, "head-on collisions, over-turning, and knocking down people are among the speeding related accidents."[39] Never-before-seen car accidents shocked the locals and contributed to increased injuries and fatalities.

When asked what had happened to his leg, a pirate who had a limp related the story of the car accident he had because of his "crazy" driving without prior experience. He went on to say that nearly all injuries of young men that are not caused by gunfire are due to car accidents similar to his.[40] A different pirate admitted how, behind the façade of bravado of successful pirates, the horrors of capturing a ship in the high seas chased the pirates on land. In their delirious high-speed race from themselves they caused many accidents.

Like other security incidents, however, pirate-caused car accidents are hard to nail down statistically because pirates do not typically wait until their disputes are reported to the police. However, medical reports give a picture of pirate-caused casualties that have been brought to the few available medical facilities. The emergency medical care that pirates receive is a source of an impassioned debate between two professionals in the field. One medical doctor argued that treating pirates drained the medical resources that would have otherwise gone to the rest of the community, and argued that medical institutions needed to prioritize their meager allocation of resources to the most needy, innocent citizens. Another medical doctor insisted that pirates should receive equal treatment regardless of the circumstances of their injuries and argued that it was not up to medical professionals to establish the guilt or innocence of their patients, especially at a time when many pirates were doing well to chase away resource thieves at sea.

According to information from the Galkayo Medical Center (GMC), up to 60 percent of that center's resources during the years of piracy were

---

[39] Confidential interview (February 2012, Galkayo).
[40] Confidential interview (February 2012, Garowe).

used in treating pirates wounded in car accidents or in intra-pirate fights.[41] Roughly aggregated data from GMC indicate that medical facility treated 912 cases involving pirates between 2010 and 2012; more than half of the cases treated were gunshot injuries (pirate and non-pirate). The numbers reported by the Galkayo General Hospital for the same time frame stands at a staggering 1,562. Both medical facilities also treated a total of 1,877 cases of car-accident-related injuries. What is jarringly absent from these reports are rape cases. Although numerous cases of pirate-perpetrated rape and other forms of sexual violence were mentioned in my interviews, Galkayo Central Hospital did not report any case of rape and GMC reported only three in 2010, two in 2011, and seven in 2012.

At the heart of nearly all of the violations of social norms, religious prohibitions, security incidents, and public commotion in both coastal areas and inland towns is the massive consumption of alcohol and drugs by gunslinging and SUV-driving pirates. As described by a one-time notorious pirate, the hours of the day in Gara'ad were divided into three: khat chewing during the daytime, drinking in the evening, and shooting at night.

Substance Abuse and Attendant Ills

There is a large structure in the outskirts of the regional capital of Garowe that houses some of Puntland's mentally ill persons. It was spearheaded by Mrs. Hawa Ahmed Mohamed who, beginning in 2005, campaigned against the stigma about mental illness and started to care for those who suffer from it. The facility was built on land granted by the Puntland government and with funds raised by the Somali Diaspora in Europe. Called the Garowe Psychiatric Center, the facility catered to more than thirty known pirates who had drifted from sanity due to a mix of substance abuse and violence. By early February 2012, thirteen former pirates had already been treated and discharged. Of the forty-nine inpatients who were in the facility at the time, fifteen were former pirates.[42] In spite of Mrs. Hawa's best efforts and impressive success, the stigma remains pervasive. Also, many young Puntlanders have irreparably damaged their physical and mental health through excessive use of drugs, alcohol and brute violence.

---

[41] Confidential interview (October 2012, Galkayo).
[42] Confidential interview (February 2012, Garowe). The psychiatric facility housed forty-nine and catered to sixty-seven male outpatients and eighty women patients in different affiliated institutions across Puntland.

Tracking the smuggling and consumption of drugs and alcohol into Somalia has been particularly difficult because fierce Islamic prohibition to both drives the illicit trade deep into the underground, even in places where actual consumption of alcohol is as public as participation in piracy. Discrete telephonic consultations with a half dozen alcohol retailers offered a rough estimate of 500 bottles consumed daily across Puntland between 2008 and 2009 during the heyday of piracy. That figure jumped to more than 840 bottles per day in 2009–2010, and increased by an additional 100 to 945 bottles the following year. Noticing my shock at what were considered unlikely figures, one telephone informant volunteered to help: "Have you seen pirates drink this poisonous drink? I have!"[43] He related other occurrences, some of which I had heard before from activists, government officials and pirates. Apparently many pirates simply downed an entire bottle of dry gin and did so as regularly as they could afford to.[44]

The strict Islamic prohibition against alcohol and an entirely Muslim population did not deter the pirates, nor did the exorbitant prices that traders and retailers charged. An example is the cost of Ethiopian gin popular among Somali pirates in coastal areas and towns. In the Ethiopian capital, Addis Ababa, a bottle of Baro's Dry Gin is retailed at no more than ten dollars. In Garowe and Galkayo, it costs one hundred dollars and one would be lucky to get a bottle after going through a chain of trusted connections. Not only did that price double in the coastal areas but gin was traded openly and consumed publicly. There were times when a 75cl bottle of gin cost as much as USD 500 in the Galkayo – Gara'ad corridor.

A fortuitous late-February 2012 lunch with an alleged alcohol trader did not lead to the promised and much-anticipated access to the darker underworld of crime within crime in pirate-dominated Galkayo. But the brief exploratory encounter revealed the profitability of the bustling business. The alleged trader, who appeared to be in his thirties, said his phones rang incessantly day and night with demands for alcohol supplies. Sure enough, he only uttered a few words during our brief conversation before his several phones went off in turn, and sometimes simultaneously.[45]

---

[43] Confidential interview (October 2012, Galkayo).

[44] This makes perfect sense in light of the fact that pirates hardly did anything leisurely. The concept of recreational drinking is unknown to them; they reached the climax of their consumptive capacity as fast as they were introduced to the drink.

[45] A planned follow-up meeting did not take place because the already precarious security suddenly deteriorated due to a reported ransom delivery at the coast and consequent increase in pirate activities in town. Coupled with the escalating suspicion surrounding us, this meant it was time for our immediate departure from the town that government forces were wise to avoid when pirates took control.

Equally devastating is the parallel excessive consumption of the mildly narcotic stimulant leaf, khat; the Kenyan variety is called *mirah* or *meeru* and the Ethiopian one is called *hareeri*. The explosion of piracy saw a parallel increase in the sale and consumption of khat across Somalia and the quadrupling of prices, at least in Puntland. From the 1990s to the first half of the 2000s, a *fer* (a pack of five bundles, weighing about a kilogram) of Kenyan khat or *mirah* cost between one dollar and five dollars in the urban centers.[46] By the mid-2000s, the price jumped to an average of ten dollars which had doubled by 2009. While it was not uncommon to see a *fer* of *mirah* going for up to twenty-five dollars in the towns, it was hard to find it for less than forty dollars along the coast between Eyl and Gara'ad. There were times between 2009 and 2012 when a *fer* of Kenyan khat cost fifty dollars.

These skyrocketing khat prices did not reduce or contain consumption levels because the drug was essential to the piracy picture. Just as khat numbed pirates to the dangers ahead when they boarded the boat and sailed out to sea, it calmed their anticipation when they came back with a pirated ship, and kept them vigilant until ransom was paid – at times for days in a row without any sleep. During their lazy days, pirates consumed khat in large quantities for entertainment purposes to attain a much-craved state of euphoric *merqan* (high).

According to MOPIC estimates, import of khat (both the Kenyan mirah and the Ethiopian hareeri) into Puntland was consistently on the rise and had reached an annual import of 142,944 tons in 2007 when piracy exploded.[47] Many dispute this figure because imports are allegedly reported inaccurately to evade taxation. But this estimate gives a picture of what was to come. In the years that followed, when Galkayo took the unenviable place of being a pirate hub, that town's imports of the Kenyan variety alone nearly equaled the region's total. According to confidential data collection from some of the fifteen or so khat importers (the bulk traders), small cargo airplanes flew in from Kenya with a total of 84,320 tons of khat in 2008; 96,425 tons in 2009; 108,780 tons in 2010; and 111,410 tons in 2011.

A cursory look and brief conversation with khat bulk traders regarding trends confirmed the exponential increase in consumption of khat despite its rising price. The bulk traders took turns in sharing the 100-sack daily imports; two divided the imports one day and another two traders did the same on the following day. The two daily importers then distributed and

---

[46] Prices for khat always doubled or nearly doubled in remote coastal villages like Eyl and Gara'ad.

[47] Ministry of Planning and International Cooperation, *Puntland Facts and Figures*, 4th ed. (Puntland State of Somalia, 2008), 18.

transported the khat to local retailers, often directly but sometimes through yet another level of go-betweens. According to one, who claimed to have been in the business for well over a decade before the advent of ransom piracy, his sales ranged between ten and twenty *fers* during the fishing season – before piracy. After piracy, his sales exceeded 300 bundles (i.e., six sacks and more) per day and business ran year round.[48]

Women became attracted to khat retailing as a lucrative business venture that could be started without capital in spite of the attendant physical and financial dangers, which were especially worsened by the type of clientele. According to an early February 2012 survey, only six of the fifty-one respondents in Galkayo and five of thirty-four respondents in Garowe entered that business between 2005 and 2006. Of khat dealers in Galkayo, 50 percent started in 2007 or after, while 64 percent started in Garowe during the same period. The clearing of pirates from Garowe and the emergence of Galkayo as the principal pirate town in Puntland in 2009 did not alter the rate of khat consumption, although the number of new entrants into its retail business decreased slightly: in 2009 and after, Garowe saw a 44 percent increase in retailers while Galkayo's retailers increased by 29 percent.[49]

What exacerbates the financial, time, and energy drains associated with the widespread consumption of the addictive substance is that it is neither illegal nor socially unacceptable. According to a February 2012 survey among khat retailers (all of whom were women), more than 84 percent of the fifty-one respondents in Galkayo and 41 percent of those in Garowe said their families approved or actively supported their business ventures. In Galkayo, 16 percent reported that their families disapproved of their selling khat while in Garowe 58 percent reported similar disapprovals; in neither city did family attitudes deter the women from continuing their trade. In fact a respondent in Garowe volunteered to relate that her husband threatened to divorce her if she did not stop selling khat; and did exactly that upon her refusal to quit.

As with most other commodities, khat was sold on credit, a factor that was partially responsible for the price hikes. The bulk traders in Galkayo, for example, paid $10 for a bundle of khat at the Galkayo airstrip. They then transported it to the coast and sold it for between twenty and twenty-five dollars to the retailers, who in their turn charged as much as fifty dollars per bundle – often on credit. "I know a single pirate borrowing as much as $40,000 in khat within a period of five–six months," related one

---

[48] Confidential interview (Galkayo, February 2012).
[49] Ministry of Planning and International Cooperation, *Puntland Facts and Figures*, 4th ed. (Puntland State of Somalia, 2008), 18–19.

trader. He continued, "But you have to know that one person takes care of many [*shahat*]." Although not unheard of, defaulting on khat debt is rare, mostly because there are mechanisms of clan protection of one's commercial interests but also because, as the trader related, "in Galkayo there is no forgetting of people who steal from you or abuse you."[50] But in Galkayo – as elsewhere in Puntland or even the rest of Somalia, for that matter – there are countless egregious abuses that only a few care to remember and try to do something about them.

Violated Bodies, Broken Marriages, Fatherless Children

As in many other war-torn societies, Somali women continued to carry the heavier burden of their community's dire predicament, especially owing to their unique, historic position in their societies. Piracy added more difficulties to their wretchedness. Female members of the family typically stepped in to fill the void left behind by their menfolk who were either jobless, imprisoned, killed, or had disappeared. All male government officials, without fail, listed the burden that piracy had proven to be on women across Puntland. But none ventured to give details because, in the words of one official, "We cannot probe that point further because it is a taboo!"

Women in government and in NGOs have been more forthcoming to speak of women's conditions after the eruption of ransom piracy. But even they spoke in generalities because they faced many practical difficulties in giving specifics. An activist and leader of Somali Women Vision perhaps best captured the difficulty of finding the exact details of broken marriages, fatherless children and countless cases of rape: "When we call on victims to share their experiences with us, their responses is: 'yes, I have experienced this or that but what will you do for me?' or 'I am now raising his children because their mother could not raise them and so abandoned them to me . . . Are you going to help me raise his children?'"[51]

In a random survey conducted among twenty-eight women in Garowe, and fifty in Galkayo, 95 percent of the respondents said that piracy negatively affected women economically, emotionally and physically. The effects included the loss of husbands and sons, the explosion of temporary marriages and their dissolution as well as the dissolution of non-temporary marriages (i.e., divorces), rape, torture, and killings. More interestingly, 43 percent of the respondents in Garowe said they

---

[50] Confidential interview (Galkayo, February 2012).
[51] Interview with a Somali woman activist (6 November 2012, Garowe).

had either a daughter, niece, close relative, or close friend who had been affected thus. "One of my daughters married a pirate at the age of sixteen," volunteered one respondent. "After ten days, he divorced her and she was pregnant." Another respondent related how one of the pirates "married my young sister; two months later, he was captured and [he is imprisoned] now in Seychelles."

Prostitution exploded with the spiraling of ransom piracy in previously self-restrained coastal communities. Increasing numbers of women and girls from other regions of Somalia and from neighboring countries were trafficked in and pimped to constantly intoxicated pirates. That undermined the morals of devout, conservative Muslims and offended the sensibilities of the more tolerant ones.

As if the practice itself were not offensive enough to the majority of local women, repeated violations against the sex workers added insult to injury. Any discussion of the condition of women in general and of sex workers in particular abounds with horrifying detail that explains why many self-respecting, devoutly religious men and women choose not to discuss it. Only a few pirates dared to relate, with various expressions of regret (genuine or not), their experiences or what they say is the experience of their colleagues.

Another particular group of victims of pirate violence has been Somalis who were internally displaced. Puntland was least affected by the civil war that bedeviled the rest of Somalia after Siad Barre. As a result, its residents were able to engage in peaceful and productive businesses of their own, to receive back their kin who had fled the civil war, and to host other internally displaced populations (IDPs) belonging to Darod clan or to ethnic minorities. While the dire living conditions of these IDPs left them more susceptible to the allure of the pirates' extravaganza of spending, their lack of the protection of a close-knit family–clan made them vulnerable to the pirates' exploitation and abuse.

Typically located in the outskirts of the main towns and a few along the high ways connecting them, the camps for IDPs became exclusive realms of pirate anarchy with unknown numbers of abductions, rape, and shootings that resulted in injuries and even deaths of the internally displaced. For example, only during the day did government officials in the town of Galkayo visit the camps on the edges of town to distribute food aid and other supplies. Even then, they faced intimidation from pirates who were better armed and equipped and who acted as if they were in turf war with a rival gang. Upon returning from such a food distribution trip to an IDP camp in the outskirts of Galkayo, the deputy governor of the region related his fresh experience: "A car of armed pirates pulled over and lowered their tinted windows, brandishing their guns" in order to ensure that whoever was in the government vehicle saw them.[52]

Children in Piracy

The involvement of underage children in piracy is another troubling phenomenon. Pirates set bad examples for the young but many underage children joined their ranks in one capacity or another. "It's dangerous for our kids," an elderly fisherman in Eyl told the BBC's Andrew Harding in 2009. "These criminals have brought nothing but harm to our town."[53] School dropouts from the towns, nomads from the expansive interior and coastal residents under the age of eighteen have played various roles – from boarding vessels in the high seas, to securing captured ships in inshore waters, to transporting supplies from land to the captured ships, to being "errand boys" for pirate kingpins.

Children between the ages of fifteen and seventeen years are considered ideal candidates for pirate boarding teams as well as for security on the ground. According to an investor and organizer/recruiter, children in this age bracket are sufficiently mature to obey orders to the letter and to know the consequences of not doing so. Yet they are sufficiently gullible, leaving them blissfully ignorant of the real risks they face in the ocean when they are part of a boarding team. Once in it, however, they are sufficiently agile to accomplish the reckless physical feats of boarding gigantic ships from small, fast-moving, unstable skiffs. As security teams on the ground or in the coastal waters, they do not negotiate with hostages or rival groups. Children under the age of fifteen years are, however, considered too young to entrust with the investments that go into capturing a vessel in the high seas or securing a captured one in the inshore waters. But those under fifteen are ideal as errand boys on land or for transporting supplies to the captured vessels in the nearby waters.

There is, however, no evidence of forced recruitment of such children, partially because the overwhelming poverty and lawlessness have made them available in abundance and willing to take part in risky enterprises. Moreover, the years of strife eroded the protective family fabric and parental authority that helps mitigate child exposure to dangerous influences and manipulation. Conversation with several underage pirates revealed that they had in fact insisted on joining piracy against the advice of their kinsmen, threatening to join other groups if their own relatives did

[52] Confidential interview (February 2012, Galkayo).
[53] Andrew Harding, "Postcard from Somali Pirate Capital," BBC, 16 June 2009: http://news.bbc.co.uk/2/hi/africa/8103585.stm.

Figure 4.4. A pirate skiff ferrying supplies to pirates holding an unidentified captive vessel near Gara'ad. Another captive vessel is seen at a distance in the background. (Courtesy of a confidential source.)

not allow them to become pirates. Such misplaced enthusiasm among the young and the absence of coercion do not make their involvement any less an exploitation of child labor and do not reduce their exposure to danger in order to profit adult pirate kingpins.[54]

Erosion of Social Values and Destabilization Traditional Authority of Elders

Piracy has had far-reaching effects on the role of elders and traditional authority across Somalia. Lamenting the erosion of the traditional system, many elders in Puntland consulted for this research blamed pirates

[54] "Convention on the Rights of the Child (1989)" available at http://www.unesco.org/ed ucation/pdf/CHILD_E.PDF, for example, makes multiple stipulations protecting children from "all forms of physical or mental violence, injury or abuse, neglect or negligent treatment, maltreatment or exploitation" (Article 19, paragraph 1, and also Article 36). It also recognizes "the right of the child to be protected from economic exploitation and from performing any work that is likely to be hazardous or to interfere with the child's education, or to be harmful to the child's health or physical, mental, spiritual, moral or social development" (Article 32, paragraph 1).

for their violations of religious prohibitions and perversion of traditional norms and social values. Generally, however, the overall authority of titled traditional elders and elected local officials was compromised when some of their ranks defended local pirates – either because piracy money corrupted them or because of their family ties to pirates – so that the community would not act against them.

The age-old mechanisms of managing intra-clan and sub-clan conflicts that the pirates manipulated in their favor may have restrained local pirates from responding violently to outspoken local elders opposing their criminal activities. When Gara'ad elders told me in a group meeting that they could walk straight up to a local armed or unarmed pirate and slap him for misbehaving, they may not have exaggerated their own experiences.[55] Nevertheless, there are far too many exceptions to such an assertion of traditional authority for it to be the rule with the pirates. In a typical example of such exceptions, in late 2011 a businessman's truck had a fender-bender with a pirate's sports utility vehicle. Without any consideration of whose fault it may have been, the pirate threatened to kill that businessman should the latter not replace the slightly scratched land cruiser with a "new one." "He threatened me, saying 'Do you know how I got this? I spilled a man's blood for it and I am prepared to spill more blood!' No one could do anything about it," complained the businessman. He appealed to the father of the pirate who gave him an exasperated look, having long lost control over his child.[56]

The distance – or the absence – of ancestral/familial ties between pirates and the host communities undermined the limited deterrent function that clan, sub-clan and family ties served. Pirates from other clans and regions resorted much more easily to violence against anyone standing on their way – traditional elders, government officials or community activists. At the height of piracy, the pirate dens in Puntland hosted Somalis distantly related or completely unrelated to the native sub-clans.

Traditional methods of resolving conflicts involving deaths have been particularly tested. According to a high-ranking security official, especially among groups that previously exchanged diya (blood money), when "a pirate kills another pirate, the clan of the deceased goes to the clan of the culprit and demands diya."[57] But some Mejerten sub-clans neither

---

[55] This is not to say that the act of piracy is considered as acceptable; the repertoire of piracy in Puntland – as in the rest of Somalia – is complex as already discussed. But the criminality of piracy did not completely obliterate aspects of age-old traditions and practices that have been an important means of leverage for a homegrown solution to piracy, as we shall see later.
[56] Confidential interview (February 2012, Garowe).
[57] Confidential interview (February 2012, Galkayo).

accepted nor offered blood money until the advent of ransom piracy. They typically avenged the deaths of their kinfolk on those who killed one of their own. When their member killed someone else, they delivered the killer to the family of the victim for that family to do with the killer what they may. Nevertheless, the explosion of piracy compelled the Mejerten sub-clans to reconsider this practice because a large number of their members became pirates and got involved in a staggering number of piracy-related deaths. Nowadays, and especially in piracy cases, not only do these Mejerten sub-clans accept blood money without asking for the perpetrator alive, but they also offer their victims blood money. As if it were not difficult enough to come up with the standard number of camels in blood money (typically 100 head), it was not uncommon for pirates to pay double that amount in cash easily. The long-term effect of the doubling of the amount of blood money paid by pirates was to increase the level of blood money for everyone, which made it difficult for ordinary people to raise such funds and to settle disputes; this led relatives of victims to revenge and perpetuated the cycle of violence.

Pirate-Caused Clan Conflicts

With the erosion of traditional authority, the elders' management of conflicts was also challenged. Like other elders across Puntland, tradi-tional leaders in the Bari region agreed to treat piracy-related deaths as non-eligible for blood money or for settlement through the diya system. But pirates in the region couched their greed-generated conflicts in clan terms and stoked conflict between the Ali Saleban and Muse Saleban (also known as Ugar Saleban) sub-sub-clans of the Mejerten. The three-year-long conflict cost dozens of pirate and non-pirate lives, many more injuries, and loss of property and opportunities.[58]

The bloody outbursts of violence centered around the notorious Ali Saleban pirate leader, Isse Yuluh, who had been collaborating with pirates hailing from the neighboring Muse Saleban. Convinced that his Muse Saleban partners in crime had cheated him during the splitting of a ransom in early 2009, Yuluh went on a shooting rampage against them. Failing to gain the sympathy of his clansmen or to mobilize them in his

---

[58] According to the only authoritative account of the conflict and the mediation process, the non-fatal impacts of this pirate-caused conflict included: the restriction of access to social services for people residing in remote areas; the inability of frankincense farmers to ensure their economic sustenance; the abandonment of shared settlements; family disputes; and separation of spouses hailing from the conflicting groups. See Abdinasir M. Yusuf, *The Rako Peace Process: Intra-clan Reconciliation Progress* (Report of the Mobile Audio Visual Unit of Puntland Development Research Center, April 2012), 7.

defense against imminent revenge from the Muse Saleban, Yuluh allegedly ambushed a random commercial transporter that belonged to his rivals and was in the territory of the Ali Saleban, killing several and turning the conflict into one based on clan–families. Joined by pirates on both sides, the two clan–families mobilized their respective militias and violently clashed.[59]

Previously peaceful transitional territories between the two groups, their shared grazing lands, and neighboring villages turned into active fighting grounds for the next three years until the final showdown of mid-November 2011.[60] At a place called Labida (between Rako and Qodah), the two sides faced off; more than a dozen were killed and many more were injured. "The battleground was too dangerous," wrote PDRC researcher Abdinasir Yusuf, "that for the following 4 days the corpses and the injured could not be accessed." Outraged by the carnage and the subsequent inhumanity, elders from across Puntland spontaneously mobilized to mediate. Led by Sultan Said Mohamed Garase, more than fifty elders inserted themselves between the warring sides. They camped at the very battlegrounds of Labida, buried the dead, dispatched the injured for medical attention, and started a mediation process that took months to settle the dispute.[61] Meanwhile, the Puntland Marine Police Force (PMPF) chased Yuluh and his men from one hard-to-access hub to the next, more inaccessible one.[62]

Yuluh and his likes were able to plunge their communities into extended conflicts and to cause much hardship inland because of the ransom they extorted in piracy. The ill-gotten money enabled them to procure a varied arsenal of heavy and light weapons.[63] Pirate leaders elsewhere in Puntland have been more cautious than Yuluh in resorting to violence but have nonetheless amassed a large cache of weaponry. The results are a new kind of warlords, who flex their muscles in pursuit of personal or group interests of different sorts.[64] The ease with which

---

[59] Yusuf, *The Rako Peace Process*, 6–7. Documenting this and other similar cases, *SomaliaReport* found a total of forty-nine fatalities and sixty-two injuries in incidents involving pirates between October and December 2011 alone. See "Pirates vs the People: Somali Hijackers Turn against Civilians," 23 December 2011: http://www.piracyreport .com/index.php/post/2384/Pirates_vs_The_People (accessed on 15 April 2012).

[60] Ibid.   [61] Yusuf, *The Rako Peace Process*, 8–9.

[62] Puntland Ministry of Security and DDR, "Somalia: Puntland Maritime Police Forces Deploy in Strategic Coastal Towns," 8 June 2012: https://pmpf.files.wordpress.com/20 12/06/pr_08june2012_en1.pdf; Puntland Ministry of Security, "Press Release: Somalia: Puntland Arrests 53 Al Shabaab and Piracy Suspects," 31 July 2012: http://halgan.net /halgan/wp-content/uploads/2012/07/Halkaan-ka-eeg-Warsaxaafeedka-ka-soo-baxay-Wasaarada-amniga-Puntlland.pdf.

[63] Confidential interview (February 2012, Bosaso).

[64] This fear is of particular concern in the border areas of the rival Darod and Hawiye clans, which are in north and south Mudug, respectively. This is where the most successful and

moneyed individuals and groups can procure weapons speaks to the vibrancy of the black market in arms in Somalia in general, and in Puntland in particular.[65]

Local Antipiracy Responses

As early as 2008, many residents of coastal fishing communities across Puntland started raising questions about and protesting against the hijacking of commercial vessels and taking their crews hostage on religious and humanitarian grounds. The pirates' excesses only confirmed the grounds for these initial mutterings and awakened the coastal communities to the peril of the piracy taking place in their midst. They started to object openly to pirate presence in their areas and to mobilize support of everyone in their communities. But their objections to and mobilization against piracy did not have immediate, tangible results.

A number of inter-related factors impeded traction of their efforts, but did not permanently scuttle them. The overall weakness of the regional government in Garowe was a principal impediment. In addition to facing its worst financial crisis, President 'Aadde Muse's government was paralyzed during its final days due to a number of factors. To begin with, as a member of the Osman Mahamud branch of Mejerten, the president had clan disadvantage in the capital Garowe and in the erstwhile pirate hub of Eyl, both of which lay in the territory of the Isse Mahamud lineage of the same clan family. Allegations swirled regarding the government's direct involvement in – or active abetting of – piracy and kidnappings. The president was in a deadlock with the Puntland legislature as he sought an extension of his term in office while they fiercely denied him that "even by a single day," as his successor, Abdirahman Mohamed Mohamoud "Farole," insisted then. Consequently, the coastal district councils, through which Garowe exercised what little authority it could, were either non-existent, weak or had terms that had lapsed. The government was too distracted to set up new administrative councils, to renew or reinstate the ones whose terms had ended, or to strengthen the ones still in existence.

---

notorious pirates emerged and thrived, and many believe that a few of them have become heavily armed warlords in their own right.

[65] Although beyond the scope of this chapter, it is important to note that the alarming proliferation of arms that afflicts Somalia not only bodes ill for that country's long-term stability but also takes place in violation of a two-decade-old United Nations arms embargo. Article 5 of Security Council Resolution 733 (1992) of 23 January 1992 invokes Chapter VII of the UN Charter to impose "a general and complete embargo on all deliveries of weapons and military equipment to Somalia . . .": http://www.un.org/ga/search/view_doc.asp?symbol=S/RES/733(1992).

Moreover, the repertoire of methods used by pirates in leveraging their power over their willing and increasingly unwilling host communities included invoking clan and family ties (hence protection) and corrupting local elders. Their methods also included threatening to resort – and in many cases actually resorting – to violence. Pirates were moved little – if at all – by the pleas and reasoning of the early antipiracy activists. Coastal communities continued to organize campaigns with Eyl leading the charge, as we will see shortly. However weak, the existence and active participation of a regional government remained as vital for the success of Somali counter-piracy as it was for the sensitization and mobilization of the majority of the population.

Initiatives of Successive Regional Governments

In spite of understandable local and international suspicion of, and impatience with, the pace of Somali authorities' actions against piracy, in hindsight they did make modest efforts in the right direction. More specifically, the successive Puntland governments experimented with different security solutions to the problem. Under pressure from Garowe-based civil society organizations, the 'Aadde Muse government contemplated a proactive antipiracy strategy prepared by a consortium of local NGOs. That plan envisaged setting up nine coastal bases from Las Qoray to Gara'ad, each with two speedboats, three technicals and about 100 soldiers, with the aim of both disrupting pirate operations before they were launched and intercepting them at sea in the event that they succeeded in setting sail. At an estimated monthly cost of about USD 300,000, the proposal was for Puntland to cover 40 percent on its own and to seek external assistance for the remaining 60 percent.[66]

Nevertheless, the 'Aadde Muse government was distracted by domestic concerns and failed to garner support for its proposed counter-piracy force. It made feeble and haphazard attempts to fight pirates with government forces that fell back after encountering the least resistance from the pirates. In the end, as we have seen earlier, many well-trained and well-armed soldiers ended up joining the pirates upon the government's failure to pay their salaries for months on end.

Upon taking the helm in Garowe in early 2009, Abdirahman Farole made strategic moves. The president is credited by supporters and opponents alike for restoring a semblance of order in the regional capital, for taking guns off the streets, and for pushing the pirates out of town through negotiation and, at times, by force. His administration simultaneously

---

[66] Confidential interview (February 2012, Galkayo).

reinstated the council, whose term had lapsed during the final days of 'Aadde Muse, in his home district of Eyl. Led by the mayor and deputy mayor, who were elected by their community for their leadership in anti-piracy activism, the resuscitation of the Eyl district council was a cornerstone for a pirate-free Garowe–Eyl corridor. Although pirates had not threatened the Garowe–Bosaso route, clearing the vital commercial capital and port city proved more difficult and remained incomplete at best.

Before government antipiracy moves could be directed south toward Galkayo, a different existential threat emerged in the north to sap Garowe's limited forces and attention. Intensifying international pressure on Al-Shabaab in south and central Somalia culminated in its eventual withdrawal from Mogadishu in August 2011 – and in the loss of Kismayo a year later. When the streak of loses set in, Al-Shabaab rotated some of its resources and leaders to the harsh terrain of northern Puntland's mountainous region, namely the Galgala Mountains of Bari region. Farole's government doubled the efforts of his predecessor 'Aadde Muse in combating Al-Shabaab in the Northeast (ASNE), as it came to be called. The Bosaso area experienced one of Puntland's most aggressive counter-piracy operations precisely because of the danger posed by the specter of a nexus between the two. In the southern part, however, especially in Puntland's northern Mudug region and the town of Galkayo, numerous interviews and informal consultations with Puntland's security and intelligence personnel indicate that counter-piracy remained a distant secondary concern so long as Al-Shabaab remained a threat in the north and the pirates in the south maintained a comfortable distance from them.

Meanwhile, the Puntland government followed suit with at least two United Nations Security Council resolutions calling on states "to criminalize piracy under their domestic law and favourably consider the prosecution of suspected, and imprisonment of convicted, pirates apprehended off the coast of Somalia . . ."[67] In early November 2010, Garowe decreed that piracy was a punishable crime and empowered the weak region judiciary to prosecute suspected pirates and their accomplices.[68]

---

[67] UN Security Council Resolution 1918 of 27 April 2010, S/RES/1918 (2010) paragraph 2 and UN Security Council Resolution 1950 of 23 November 2010, S/RES/1950 (2010), paragraph 13.

[68] Sharci Lr. 6, "Kuna saabsan Xeerka Burcad-Badeed" (Law No. 6, "The Law on Piracy"), 6 November 2010. Published in the *Official Gazette of the Puntland State of Somalia*, No. 12, 18 December 2010. This legislation defined piracy as a crime based on hijacking or kidnapping at sea to get ransom and defined a pirate as someone who takes part in or facilitates such an act by contributing their wealth, vehicles (land, sea and air), weapons or any other equipment. According to the same act, piracy also means the destruction of Puntland marine resources, and illegal and unregulated fishing without the permission of Puntland authorities; a pirate is one who exploits marine resources within Puntland's EEZ without the permission of Puntland authorities.

Figure 4.5. Abdirahman Mohamed Mohamoud "Farole," former president of Puntland (2009–2013), played a crucial role in reining in piracy against all odds, domestic and foreign. (Photo by the author.)

The Farole government also developed a plan similar to that of the previous administration and secured private funding for its implementation. In late 2010, the United Arab Emirates quietly paid for Saracen International to train the Puntland Marine Police Force (PMPF), a government-recruited marine force 1,000 strong.[69] PMPF actively pursued pirates militarily, disrupted their operations and took the captured suspects to court. It negotiated with coastal district councils to establish bases in former pirate hubs or piracy-prone natural harbors and by early 2012 had established five bases along the coast, succeeded in disrupting piracy missions and in chasing pirates out of several hubs.

Working with local communities, religious leaders and titled elders to push back against the pirates in vast parts of the region, the government preserved itself for large-scale and decisive armed action against the pirates in Galkayo. That came in June 2012 when pirates either surrendered in return for amnesty, were captured and jailed, or fled from the government's reach. The government's success was sealed with its rescue

---

[69] Some sources claim that the UAE contracted with Erik Prince's private security company for USD 10 million to conduct the training, for which he subcontracted with a South African affiliate.

of the MV *Iceberg I* in December 2012. Between December 2010 and February 2012, more than 700 suspects were brought to court; more than 250 of these received prison sentences ranging between five and ten years.[70]

One of the main destinations for these long-term prisoners convicted of piracy was the Bosaso maximum-security facility. During the visit in February 2012, it was holding more than 100 inmates above its limited capacity. Of the prison's 390 inmates, 270 were pirates, a limited number of whom had been handed over by international forces.[71] Besides Puntland's own challenges due to meager resources, limited space, and lack of trained personnel to adequately examine evidence and successfully prosecute, those captured by foreign warships were reportedly handed over to local authorities without any supporting evidence to prove that those apprehended were pirates. Puntland's attorney general lamented the international community's lack of sufficient interest in assisting with badly needed resources to combat the legal and custodial aspects of the battle against piracy.[72]

In spite of the UN Security Council's call on Somalia's Transitional Federal Government and on regional administrations to beef up their security and combat piracy,[73] Puntland's efforts to do so drew unfavorable attention for a number of reasons unrelated to the counter-piracy initiative.[74] Its effectiveness notwithstanding, PMPF found itself caught in an ironic vise; it was squeezed between an international community that both expected Puntland to eradicate piracy but at the same time was apprehensive of its growing capacity to do so – a double standard that Coffen-Smout had long observed.[75] To begin with, the importations of weapons and equipment, and the military trainings violated a two-decade-old United Nations arms embargo on Somalia as a whole. Nevertheless, no one asked for or offered an explanation for the potential contradiction between the arms embargo

---

[70] Confidential interview (February 2012 Garowe).
[71] Confidential interview (February 2012, Bosaso).
[72] Interview with Puntland's Attorney General Mohamed Hassan (12 February 2012 Garowe).
[73] UN Security Council Resolution 1976, S/RES/1976 (2011), 11 April 2011, paragraph 4 requested "States, UNODC, the United Nations Development Programme, the United Nations Political Office for Somalia (UNPOS) and regional organizations to assist the TFG and regional authorities in Somalia in establishing a system of governance, rule of law and police control in lawless areas where land-based activities related to piracy are taking place and also requests the TFG and regional authorities in Somalia to increase their own efforts in this regard."
[74] Mark Mazzetti and Eric Schmitt, "Private Army Formed to Fight Somali Pirates Leaves Troubled Legacy," *The New York Times*, 4 October 2012.
[75] Scott Coffen-Smout, "Pirates, Warlords and Rogue Fishing Vessels in Somalia's Unruly Seas," 1999: http://www.chebucto.ns.ca/~ar120/somalia.html.

and Resolution 1976, the implementation of which required training and the import of weapons and equipment.

Regional observers also aired concern that Puntland was arming itself as part of its perennial rivalry and hostility with Somaliland: hence the fear that it may foment further instability in the Somali region. Finally, the fact that Erik Prince, founder of the once-shamed private security company Blackwater, was behind the training led some to allege that the Puntland marine force was a private army of the Puntland president. As a result of the censure, Garowe officially suspended the contract but Saracen operations went on under different guises.

Whereas time has proven these concerns and allegations against Puntland's armed counter-piracy initiatives to have been misplaced,[76] sources privy to the inner workings of PMPF claim that the force remains hamstrung. Despite its effectiveness in arenas of its deployment, it lacks clarity of mandate, structures and command. Although its command structures are staffed by Somalis and Admiral Abdirizak Dirie Farah commands its operations, PMPF does not operate outside the wishes and orders of the junior Emirati officers (captain and below) who are in overall control of the force. Not only is there no coordination with other Puntland security apparatuses, but the Emirati officers reportedly run their own independent intelligence gathering and processing, based on which they determine the operational priorities of the force. As a result of these and other shortfalls, PMPF's actual capacity remains underutilized and its full potential unrealized.[77]

The Grassroots' Earliest Initiatives and Enduring Leadership

Government antipiracy initiatives relied on the active leadership and accomplishments of the coastal communities themselves. Many coastal communities started organized campaigns as early as 2008 with Eyl leading the charge. Having initially supported the attacks against illegal trawlers, the majority of Eyl's residents watched as unscrupulous groups hijacked their legitimate defense and turned it into a lucrative, criminal enterprise. The majority of the people stopped supporting them but, as

---

[76] Upon losing the presidency, Farole handed over the command of the entire Puntland security apparatus to his successor, Abdiweli Mohamed Ali "Gas." PMPF commander Admiral Abdirizak Dirie Farah (Interview: 13 August 2015, Garowe) insisted that the use of PMPF forces and resources to serve the private ends of any individual person had not been in its mandate; nor had he come under any political pressure from Farole to that effect. But other sources say that neither President Farole nor President "Gas" could deploy them as they wished without the Emirati's approval of the mission.

[77] Confidential interviews (March 2017, Garowe).

the mayor of Eyl put it, "Once the pirates became rich and powerful we [the ordinary people] were held hostage."[78] Shaking themselves free of that grip took time because it required cultivating common views by raising people's awareness before using extreme measures against the pirates. "First," said the local religious scholar, "we recognized that we could not fight them militarily. They had guns and a lot of ransom money. So we . . . mobilized school children and women and mobilized the public to chant and carry banners so that [the pirates] could see the public response. We also made sermons in the mosques."[79] Such campaigns were needed because many of piracy's foot soldiers were unaware that their trade was a crime and gravely dangerous.

Two elderly fishermen between Gara'ad and Kulub had related in passing that many of piracy's foot soldiers thought that piracy was one more legitimate line of work. Pirates interviewed at the Bosaso maximum-security prison claimed that they neither knew that piracy was a crime nor that there were powerful international naval forces at sea combating pirates.[80] Pirate recruiters preferred such recruits as their top choice for attack missions; there are many of them in a country still wallowing from decades of general insecurity that sufficiently disrupted or completely halted the provision of the most basic of services. The unscrupulous pirate recruiters proved adaptable but failed to counter increasingly effective local awareness-raising campaigns.

Awareness raising proved to be an effective tool in the hands of anti-piracy campaigners across Puntland. I joined researchers and campaigners from the Puntland Development Research Center (PDRC, recently renamed as the Peace and Development Research Center) as they traversed the territory. Their travels included Eyl and Gara'ad during their worst days of pirate activity. They sensitized residents to the dangers of piracy by showing foreign and in-house documentaries and video footage of captures and burnings in the high seas. The residents repeatedly expressed shock at their blissful ignorance of the mechanics and brute violence of the piracy that had deprived them of their children.[81] Prior to PDRC's awareness-raising campaign, internationally supported local NGOs had tried messages against piracy by radio and in pamphlets and flyers.[82] PDRC's approach changed the medium and message and helped

---

[78] Interview with Mayor Musa Osman Yusuf (24 February 2012, Eyl).
[79] Confidential interview (February 2012, Eyl).
[80] Interview with two former pirates serving time in the Bosaso prison (20 February 2012).
[81] During my extensive travels with PDRC's Mobile Audio Visual Unit (MAVU), I had numerous conversations with the MAVU team itself as well as with other researchers across Puntland.
[82] For a critical insider's perspective on the thinking behind the international funders of such local NGOs, see Gilmer, *Political Geographies of Piracy*.

restore the power and agency of grassroots actors that had been under-estimated both by the pirates and by advocates of military solutions.

Religious and secular traditional leaders from across the region aided the efforts of Eyl's grassroots mobilization directly in person and on the radio. To begin with, in 2008 the late Mufti of Puntland, Sheikh Abdulkadir Nur Farah "Gacmay" gave several radio sermons that showed how piracy was forbidden according to the Qur'an. Those messages were favorably received by many. The highest-titled traditional leader of the Isse Mohamud, Islan Isse, traveled from Garowe and threw his weight behind the counter-piracy awareness-raising campaigns, as did many others. The overall outcome of these peaceful attempts was so successful that the notorious pirate leader Abshir Boyah renounced piracy and became a leading counter-piracy campaigner. Similarly, in one such mobilization in Eyl in May 2009, hundreds of pirates are said to have collectively renounced piracy.

Even more than the number of pirates it won back from piracy, the pressure from the highest religious and traditional authorities of the land undercut the protection offered to pirates by corrupt local elders. As a last resort, grassroots activists in Eyl armed themselves and confronted the pirates.[83] Without the backing or intercession of the elders, whom they had bought with money, many of the pirates vacated Eyl and went south toward Gara'ad. Forewarned to cease and desist, the rest quietly went underground.[84]

Shortly afterwards in 2009, residents of Bandar Bayla started to orga-nize against both the international resource pirates and the local ransom pirates; they were much more successful with the latter. In January 2012, for example, IUU fishers responded to the community's peaceful pleas to leave their waters with a hail of bullets that forced the unarmed protestors back to shore. When the pirates refused to heed their entreaties, however, the people took up arms and confronted them, demanding they either end their trade or vacate their areas.[85] According to Saed Adan Ali, district mayor/commissioner of Bandar Bayla, Puntland government forces came to the aid of the local vigilantes who had started to physically confront the pirates.

After the pirates, who were holding dozens of Yemeni sailors, refused to heed the government official's repeated request to release the hostages, the combined antipiracy forces of community and government faced off

---

[83] Confidential interview (February 2012, Eyl).
[84] That many pirates quietly disappeared into their peaceful communities does not augur well for the permanent eradication of piracy, especially in light of the persistence of the sea-based root causes of piracy in Somalia and the land-based contributory factors.
[85] Interview with Mayor Saed Adan Ali (11 February 2012, Garowe).

against the pirates in March 2011 at a place called Hul, about 15 kilometers north of Bandar Bayla; the mayor called this "the Battle of Hul." Local antipiracy vigilantes came from the sea and government troops from land. Six government soldiers were killed in the process but all the hostages were rescued unharmed and were handed over to the Somali ambassador in Yemen.[86] The district mayor insists that they did everything they could to confront and evict pirates and to free their hostages as long as the Puntland authorities and relatives or governments of the hostages did not ask to desist from involvement. As elsewhere, the Bandar Bayla and Bargal communities were also concerned that pirate presence with their hostages would trigger attacks from the international counter-piracy forces.

Gara'ad, the last stronghold of pirates in Puntland was similarly cleared of pirates. Spearheaded by a group of returned diaspora and local activists, residents of the Jarriban District mobilized against piracy. "Eyl was a role model for us," said one of the activists, a Somali-American native of Gara'ad. Jarriban District raised its own funds and enlisted a force of 300 armed police (at a monthly rate of USD 300 per officer) for a period of a year and a half (until December 2012). What is perhaps ironic, even disturbing, was the fact that the local community sought the assistance of their own kin in piracy to contain the pirates' excesses on land. Active pirates who hailed from that district contributed cash to support a fledgling police force to impose a semblance of order.[87]

While all these moves helped ostracize many pirates, the active role that women played in the antipiracy mobilization marked the death knell of pirate operations in former pirate hubs. For example, women in Eyl – along with men – organized and staged demonstrations, shouting at the pirates to leave them alone. Perhaps most effective was the refusal of women who owned local businesses – especially women food vendors – to do business with pirates.[88] Their counterparts in Gara'ad also joined their menfolk in antipiracy mobilizations. During the heated days of confronting the pirates in February/March 2012, some women were even seen carrying guns and marching alongside the men.

All these local counter-piracy initiatives succeeded in drastically reducing the rate of pirate attacks and many Puntland government officials, lower-level local administrators, activists and ordinary citizens in towns and coastal villages readily take the credit. They confidently say that they knew how to deal with the pirates, if only the international community

---

[86] Ibid.
[87] Some local observers, however, scoffed at the initiative, claiming the local pirate kingpin Abdullahi Yere bankrolled it.
[88] Confidential interview (February 2012, Eyl).

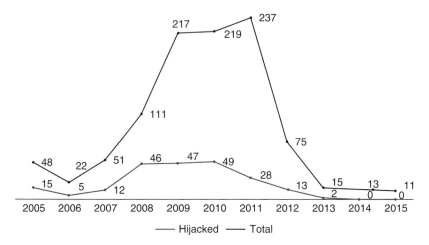

Figure 4.6. Total number of incidents and hijackings, 2005–2015. (Compiled from IMB annual reports.)

had given them the opportunity and followed their lead in pursuit of land-based solutions. "The international navies should learn from us," said one district official who led the local antipiracy campaign. "We have defeated the pirates without heavy weapons; and so we consider ourselves more powerful," he added, half-jokingly. Continued awareness campaigns by religious leaders, titled traditional elders, elected office holders, and an array of activist groups persuaded many pirates to abandon piracy, dissuaded many young men from joining pirate groups, encouraged parents to refuse to marry their daughters to pirates, and warned young women of the real risks of marrying pirates. Somali assertions of their capability to accomplish the task are not farfetched. These antipiracy efforts succeeded in evicting pirates from as far as Bandar Bayla in the north to Gara'ad in the south. Nevertheless, expelling pirates is one thing and ensuring that they do not make a comeback and preventing other crimes from emerging or re-emerging is a different challenge. This became all too apparent following the fast decline of piracy when foreign illegal fishers returned with a vengeance and resumed plundering Somalia's marine resources.

Resumption of the Vicious Cycle of Criminalities

As many pirates either quit piracy of their own volition or were forced by local and international pressure to put an end to their criminal trade, there was a brief uptick in new forms of criminal activities. Robberies, carjackings and associated vandalism noticeably increased in former pirate dens – coastal villages and inland towns alike. Equally alarming and of long-term consequence to local and regional stability was the emergence of organized criminal networks with reaches beyond Somalia itself. Although short-lived, the string of kidnappings spoke to the potential for land-based criminal networks and for activities that, in the absence of alternative legitimate livelihoods, filled – and could fill in the future – the void that piracy left behind.

On June 29, 2012, for example, kidnappers penetrated deep into Kenyan territory and abducted four foreign aid workers at the Dadaab refugee camp.[89] Various government officials and ordinary citizens repeatedly stated that the abductors were pirates who fled the Puntland government's antipiracy offensive earlier that month. The fleeing pirates briefly found refuge in Al-Shabaab-controlled territories in southern Somalia before their hosts reportedly sent them on the short-lived kidnapping mission. Less than two weeks later, on July 11, more than a dozen armed men kidnapped three Kenyan aid workers near the small town of Ba'adwein in Puntland.[90] The kidnappers hailed from the Sa'ad (Habar Gidir, Hawiye) and Omar Mohamud (Mejerten, Darod) sub-clan families that quickly fell out with each other because their joint act triggered clashes with another Darod sub-clan that hosted – hence granted protection to – the victims.

Beyond such localized clashes caused by pirates, however, post-piracy criminality spanned the greater Horn of Africa region. Some of these criminal activities were new while others predated piracy; they included trafficking in humans, arms, and drugs. Perhaps most ironically, because illegal foreign trawlers were at the heart of the plight of Somali fishermen and the rise of piracy that had helped deter IUU fishing, the former pirates reportedly have been colluding with the resumed IUU fishing by providing security to illegal foreign vessels in Somali waters. "In some cases," said Dr. Abdirahman Jama Kulmiye, Puntland's state minister of fisheries and marine resources, "even former pirates are offering security services to IUU vessels."[91] In July 2013, the Monitoring Group reported the employment of former pirates as security guards for foreign fishing companies around the tip of the Horn:

---

[89] "Aid Workers Kidnapped from Kenya's Dadaab Camp near Somalia," 29 June 2012: http://www.bbc.co.uk/news/world-africa-18644745.

[90] "Somalia: Puntland Forces Pursue Aid Worker Kidnappers Linked to Al Shabaab," 12 July 2012: https://allafrica.com/stories/201207130007.html; Mohamed Nuxurkey, "Kenyan Aid Workers Kidnapped Near Galkayo," *SomaliaReport*, 11 July 2012: http://www.piracyreport.com/index.php/post/3509.

[91] Interview with Dr. Abdirahman Jama Kulmiye, Puntland State Minister of Fisheries and Marine Resources (11 September 2015, Galkayo).

Local fishermen from different communities along the Puntland coast between Las Qoray and Hafun have confirmed that the private security teams on board such vessels are normally provided from pools of demobilized Somali pirates and coordinated by a ring of pirate leaders and associated businessmen operating in Puntland, Somaliland, the United Arab Emirates (UAE), Oman, Yemen and Iran. The security teams assist the vessels to cast nets several kilometres long and often open fire on unprotected fishermen in order to drive out competition.[92]

As early as December 2012, those fishermen reported that in a short span of three months such security teams had been involved in "up to 30 incidents . . . firing on unprotected fishermen, crushing their nets and ramming their skiffs."[93]

In the eyes of local communities (fishermen and non-fishermen alike), the aggressive return of foreign fishing ships to their waters made the post-piracy period déjà vu, reminiscent of the pre-2005 bonanza for the illegal fishers. According to local sources along the coast, the sea came to life at night because of the lights of small and industrial-scale vessels; fishermen started to lose the flicker of hope in their trade that they had seen during the piracy period; many lost their lives. In early 2013 in the Cape Guardafui area, three Somali fishermen went out in a small boat to cast their fishing nets, set their traps, and spend the night in their boat. They did not show up in the morning when they were expected. The banged-up tank of their boat was found washed up the beach.[94] Because of such intensification of illegal fishing after piracy, the collusion of powerful local actors, and the alleged corruption of Somali officials, there are palpable signs that former pirates as well as would-be-pirates may be lying in wait until the navies leave. The Monitoring Group reported in October 2014:

Information and communications data seized from arrested pirates also revealed associations with earlier hijacking cases and well-known individuals, such as pirate leaders Mohamed Osman Mohamed "Gafanje," Abdullahi Mohamed Jama "Farahow" and pirate negotiator Abdishakur Mohamud Mohamed "Fred," *indicating that existing pirate networks are continuing to test the waters to assess the viability and possibility of reviving the once highly profitable piracy business* [emphasis added].[95]

Whereas the Somali state and regional authorities are still too weak to exert effective control, the Yemeni turmoil augurs the worsening of the

---

[92] United Nations, Report of the Monitoring Group on Somalia and Eritrea Pursuant to Security Council Resolution 2060 (2012): Somalia, S/2013/413 (July 2013), Annex 3.1: Spoiler Networks in Northern Somalia, 99–129.

[93] Ibid, note 2.

[94] Interview with Mayor of Bargal, Abubakar Ahmed Yusuf (28 August 2015, Galkayo).

[95] Report of the UN Monitoring Groups on Somalia and Eritrea, October 2014, S/2014/726, paragraph 44.

maritime security of the same area that had been affected by Somali piracy. Although not much is known about the identities of the attackers and their actual and potential capacity, the attack against a chemical tanker, the CPO *Korea*, on 22 October 2016 hundreds of miles off the coast of Somalia in international waters,[96] and that on a liquefied natural gas (LNG) tanker, the MV *Melati Satu*, on 26 October around the Bab el Mandeb strait is disconcerting.[97] So are the incidents that unfolded in March 2017.

On 14 March 2017, off the coast of 'Aluula pirates hijacked a tanker, *Aris XIII*; the PMPF surrounded the ship and exchanged fire with the pirates before local elders negotiated a peaceful end to the face-off.[98] Shortly afterwards on 23 March, five young pirates from Eyl and three from Garowe converged at Suuj Garmal, north of Eyl. They commandeered a Somali-owned fishing dhow, *Asayr II*, which had moored there to buy the catch of the local fishermen, and put out to sea. They used *Asayr II* as a mother ship to hijack an Iranian vessel in the Gulf of Aden whereupon they released the Somali dhow.[99] On 3 April, a group of pirates hijacked an Indian cargo carrier in the Indian Ocean and sailed to Hobyo, but under intense pressure from foreign navies the pirates took the hostages on land before releasing them under yet unknown circumstances.[100]

Conclusion

Wherever they went inside Somalia too, ransom pirates left long trails of human and material damages in their wake. In spite of the astronomical ransom figures that pirates collected, and contrary to widespread claims that Somalis benefited as a result, the vast majority of Somali people suffered the consequences of pirates' excesses and recklessness and stories of this were commonplace. The sudden injection of large sums of

---

[96] Jonathan Saul, "Ships More at Risk after First Somali Pirate Attack in Years: Officials," Reuters, 8 November 2016: http://www.reuters.com/article/us-shipping-piracy-somalia-idUSKBN1331UJ.

[97] "Pirates Attack Oil Tanker near Bab al-Mandab," *Al-Arabiya*, 27 October 2016: http://english.alarabiya.net/en/News/middle-east/2016/10/27/Pirates-attack-oil-tanker-near-Bab-al-Mandab.html.

[98] "Product Tanker *Aris 13* Hijacked by Somali Pirates in Gulf of Aden," *Maritime Herald*, 14 March 2017: http://www.maritimeherald.com/2017/tanker-aris-13-hijacked-by-somali-pirates-in-gulf-of-aden/.

[99] "Somalia: Pirates Seize Fishing Ship off the Coast of Puntland," *Garowe Online*, 24 March 2017: http://www.garoweonline.com/en/news/puntland/somalia-pirates-seize-fishing-ship-off-the-coast-of-puntland.

[100] "11 Indian Sailors on Small Boat Hijacked off Somali Coast," *Arab News*, 3 April 2017: http://www.arabnews.com/node/1078481/world.

ransom money destabilized the already precarious local economies. The advent of pirates among previously peaceful coastal communities also had the immediate effect of deteriorating the security of those communities and eroding their social and moral fabric. Typically pirates got high on khat during the day, got drunk in the evening, and randomly shot their guns into the air at night.

This chapter has shown that, contrary to oft-repeated claims that Somalis benefited from piracy too much to make them partners in ending it, the vast majority of Somali people suffered because of piracy. However, they also mobilized their meager resources to fight the pirates and largely succeeded. Religious or ethical morality and the law (Islamic, secular or international) were not the only reasons that compelled the majority to stand up to the few who masterminded piracy. But the criminal enterprise also started to have serious negative consequences for people who were already vulnerable. Pirates undermined social values, violated religious prohibitions, destabilized communities that had lived in relative peace, and threatened their future by setting bad examples for their children. These consequences of piracy were not immediately felt until after the 2007 proliferation of pirate gangs spurred a parallel increase in their excesses. Nor were the reactions of local communities against piracy immediately effective.

As local initiatives against domestic-ransom pirates started to bear positive results, however, the international community's inaction against the foreign resource pirates proved to be a disappointment. As illustrated in Chapter 1, IUU fishing resumed at the same rate that piracy declined, risking a full-blown return of the pirates. Meanwhile, international counter-piracy initiatives have become enduring and geopolitically consequential effect of piracy in Somalia and the region. The broader contours of the advent of private, national and international security forces on counter-piracy missions are laid out in Chapter 5.

5   International Counter-Piracy as a Means and an End

In a sketch of the emerging field of "piracy studies," Christian Bueger notes how "knowledge generation can be organized to address a contemporary problem," i.e., maritime piracy, whereby "a community of inquiry develops, often in close collaboration with practitioners, interpretations of situations, problematizations, solutions and coping mechanisms . . . " to tackle that problem.[1] This is only accurate in so far as it goes. What is gapingly absent in the discourse of nearly all studies of piracy is a reflection of the relationship between such production of knowledge and power. Suffice it to note that the power of knowledge and of knowledge generation frames the mainstream narrative that serves as a basis for internationally legitimized countermeasures by both state and non-state actors.

The study of piracy – especially as it concerns the Horn of Africa and as the subject of this book – has become a site of both blatant and subtle display of such power. Piracy's sudden explosion and expansion in a region of global geopolitical, security and economic significance, has earned international attention as a pressing security problem that has insidiously influenced scholarship into responding to pressing policy imperatives.[2] The views and interests of the powerful have thus taken center stage. Mainstream journalism, the academe, policy fora and popular publications have attended obsequiously in ways akin to what Alex de Waal characterized as "Occidentalism."[3] The circuitous mechanics of

---

[1] Bueger, "Piracy Studies: Academic Responses to the Return of an Ancient Menace," *Cooperation and Conflict* 49, no. 3 (2014), 383–406.
[2] To some degree, the growing repugnance at the human suffering caused by piracy (mainly the suffering of foreign sailors held hostage and not that of Somali victims) may have played a role in at least creating a moral or humanitarian dimension to the debate. But as one lawyer for a powerful stakeholder in the maritime industry put it, if any of the hijacked vessels off the coast of the Horn of Africa were an Airbus A340 commercial jetliner, we would have an altogether different outlook on the matter (Personal conversation, Spring 2011, Hamburg, Germany).
[3] Alex de Waal, "A Social Science in Africa Fit for Purpose," a keynote address for fellows of the 2015–2016 Next Generation Social Sciences in Africa, Addis Ababa, Ethiopia:

power and knowledge have suffused the parameters of intellectual conversation about piracy in Somalia; they have determined – and in some cases even dictated – the course of action available to actors on the ground and afar.

Generally, the international community agreed that eradicating piracy required addressing its root causes, about which there was no consensus. Some scholars and policy makers latched on to that quest to reinforce their position that it was necessary to resuscitate – or establish anew – a functional and effective Somali state.[4] Industry actors had been improvising to minimize or avoid danger by sailing progressively farther from the expanding high-risk areas.[5] They devised mechanisms and advised of ways to avoid, minimize, evade, or resist the threat of piracy on vessels passing through the region. Others, especially those in the security and maritime industries, opted to confront piracy at sea through military means and took punitive measures offshore that also aimed to send a deterrent signal on land.[6] But the all-important grand strategists disguised themselves behind counter-piracy to promote their respective geostrategic interests.

This chapter outlines the broad contours of international responses to Somali piracy and to the driving forces behind them. It shows the pursuit of counter-piracy as an end in and of itself, and as a means to an end. As an end, international responses aimed to neutralize an immanent threat ascribed to underdevelopment and insecurity;[7] those responses quickly

---

http://nextgen.ssrc.org/fellows/spotlight/towards-a-social-science-in-africa-fit-for-pur pose/. Alex de Waal called out western thought, studies and policies on Africa, which are increasingly removed from developments on the ground, on their "tendency to ascribe a cogency to the intellectual and cultural products of the west, that it does not in fact possess." He then went on to say that "Occidentalism also occurs in policy engagement. We shape our analysis to suit our audience, and end up speaking their language. Rather than evidence-based policy, we have policy-based evidence-making. The paradigm of this is engaging with western governments, the World Bank or the United Nations. Much of the policy-related discourse on good governance, post-conflict reconstruction, development, etc., takes place in a fantasyland that exists only in the minds of international civil servants."

[4] As Menkhaus put it, many scholars, commentators and policy makers "seized on [the piracy phenomenon] to plead for a durable political solution to the [then] 19-year crisis of the state collapse in Somalia." Menkhaus, "Dangerous Waters," 21.

[5] The International Maritime Bureau (IMB) progressively modified the distance that ships should sail from the Somali coast until it advised in 2007 "vessels not making scheduled calls to ports in Somalia to keep as far away as possible from the Somali coast . . . " ICC International Maritime Bureau, "Piracy and Armed Robbery against Ships: Annual Report, 1 January–31 December 2007," 22.

[6] For a short synopsis of the divergence between "fixing" Somalia and merely battling the maritime threat, see Ladan Affi and Afyare Elmi, "Avoiding Somalia: What Prevents Onshore Solution to Piracy?" Global Affairs 1, no. 3 (2015), 305–314.

[7] Gilmer, Political Geographies of Piracy, 12.

lent themselves to proactive prevention. Lucia Zedner characterized such a phenomenon as "pre-crime" whereby "the possibility of forestalling risks competes with and even takes precedence over responding to wrongs done." Pre-crime, according to her, "shifts the temporal perspective to anticipate and forestall that which has not yet occurred and may never do so."[8] To that effect, powerful countries dispatched their navies to police Somalia's waters against actual and potential pirates. As a means, international counter-piracy responses served the purposes of counter-terrorism and geopolitics.

International Antipiracy Measures

Since the abortive pirate attack on the luxury cruise ship, *Seabourn Spirit* in November 2005, pressure had been mounting for a robust international response against Somali piracy, but to little effect. That year, the International Maritime Organization (IMO, a specialized agency of the United Nations) formally brought the threat of piracy off the coast of Somalia to the attention of the United Nations Security Council. Then in 2007 the IMO adopted a resolution against piracy, and called for robust antipiracy action on the part of the Somali Transitional Federal Government when the TFG lacked the capacity to provide it. The Security Council was not moved to act decisively until doing so became necessary for the strategic security, economic, and geopolitical interests of the powerful; it restrained itself to escorting humanitarian aid.

In November 2007, the North Atlantic Treaty Organization (NATO) immediately responded to the call of the World Food Program (WFP) for protection with the dispatch of a single French frigate that escorted WFP-contracted vessels that delivered humanitarian aid to Somalia's most needy. Danish, Canadian and Dutch warships successively provided security to such ships following the French.[9] The European Union set up a separate operation and NATO dispatched a new mission in quick succession; all had expanded mandates to counter piracy while protecting WFP vessels. NATO ended its escort of WFP's humanitarian deliveries in December 2008 but launched a counter-piracy operation, Operation Allied Protector, in March 2009; this transitioned to Operation Ocean

---

[8] Lucia Zedner, "Pre-crime and Post-criminology," *Theoretical Criminology*, vol. 11, no. 2 (2007): 261–281 [here 262].

[9] Kees Homan and Susanne Kamerling, "Operational Challenges to Counterpiracy Operations off the Coast of Somalia," in Bibi van Ginkel and Frans-Paul van der Putten (eds.), *The International Response to Somali Piracy: Challenges and Opportunities.* (Martinus Nijhoff Publishers: 2010), 71–78.

Shield five month later.[10] The third NATO deployment ended in mid-December 2016.[11]

In spite of repeated calls from various influential national and international seafarer associations, and of continued lobbying by shipping companies, it was not until mid-2008 that the United Nations Security Council brought some of its weight to bear. Although world powers were not oblivious to the damages of piracy, the threat did seem sufficient to warrant costly military commitments. According to a lawyer for a powerful European shipping association, "[I]f any single one of these hijackings happened to be an Airbus 330, global reaction would be very different. Why then are the lives of sailors and the importance of maritime transport not given the same attention?" According to the lawyer, the economic cost-benefit analysis did not justify a robust military response to Somali piracy. The cost of increased insurance premiums for goods that passed through the piracy-affected waters was inconsequential.[12] Attention – albeit still insufficient – turned toward countering piracy only when doing so also served other, more pressing concerns.

In June 2008 the United Nations Security Council granted foreign navies a mandate to operate in Somali waters. Treating piracy as a threat to global peace and, acting accordingly under Chapter VII of the UN Charter, Security Council Resolution 1816 authorized member states with the interest in – and the capacity for – suppressing piracy to enter "the territorial waters of Somalia" and to "use . . . all necessary means to repress acts of piracy and armed robbery" at sea.[13] Six months later, Security Council Resolution 1851 went even further to authorize countries fighting piracy to seek land-based solutions by undertaking "all necessary measures that are appropriate in Somalia."[14]

---

[10] Geiss and Petrig, *Piracy and Armed Robbery at Sea*, 22–23; Christian Bueger, "NATO's Fight against Somali Pirates: The End of an Unsung Success Story," Piracystudies.org, 21 December 2016: http://piracy-studies.org/natos-fight-against-somali-pirates-the-end-of-an-unsung-success-story/.

[11] "NATO Ends Anti-Piracy Mission in Indian Ocean," *Voice of America*, 24 November 2016: http://www.voanews.com/a/nato-ends-anti-piracy-mission-in-india n-ocean/3609724.html; Bueger, "NATO's Fight against Somali Pirates: the End of an Unsung Success Story," Piracystudies.org, 21 December 2016: http://piracy-studies.org/natos-fight-against-somali-pirates-the-end-of-an-unsung-success-story/.

[12] Confidential interview (July 2011).

[13] UN Security Council Resolution 1816, S/RES/1816, 2 June 2008: paragraph 7. All subsequent UNSC resolutions on piracy off the coast of Somalia retained that authorization and continued to do so under Chapter VII of the United Nations Charter. These include UN Security Council Resolution 1838 of 7 October 2008, paragraph 2 and UN Security Council Resolution 1846 of 2 December 2008, paragraph 10.

[14] United Nations Security Council Resolution 1851, S/RES/1851 (2008), 16 December 2008, paragraph 6. Also see "Security Council Authorizes States to Use Land-Based Operations in Somalia, as Part of Fight against Piracy off Coast,

As the international community commenced deployment of maritime military assets against the pirates in late 2008, some regional experts and observers warned against further militarization of the region. Others, including the UN Monitoring Group, were quick to point out that the aggressive approach in Somali waters was displacing the threat to the uncontrolled vastness of the Indian Ocean with pirates using mother ships to sail out into the ocean where their skiffs would be incapable of venturing alone.[15]

Peter Lehr, a scholar of terrorism studies, foresaw that the deployment of Western naval assets was unsustainable; he counseled instead that "regional navies or coastguards should be encouraged to pool their resources in order to conduct anti-piracy patrols." He also warned that patrolling the Somali coast against pirates would only be half the solution:

The other [half] is to protect Somali waters against illegal fishing, thus giving local fishermen a fair chance to earn a living without turning to criminality. With all the focus on piracy and the 'lure of easy money,' it is all but forgotten that the majority of Somali fishermen do just that – try to earn a decent living against all odds, and now more and more often in the crossfire of pirates and navies.[16]

No analysis subsequent to Lehr's has proven as accurate, reasoned and prescient, but it has gone unheeded.

Undeterred, unilateral and multilateral counter-piracy flotillas followed each other in quick succession. Global superpowers, rival regional aspirants, and countries of little influence even within their coalitions (like Croatia and Montenegro) rushed their warships in to protect their interests – some of which were far-fetched.[17]

The European Union Naval Force dispatched Operation ATALANTA in December 2008 to take over NATO's escort of WFP-contracted cargo vessels and to fight piracy in Somalia's territorial waters.[18] In 2014, the European Union extended the operational mandate of its ATALANTA taskforce to the Somali beaches and their immediate hinterlands, and has

---

Unanimously Adopting 1851 (2008)," SC/9541, 16 December 2008: http://www.un.or g/press/en/2008/sc9541.doc.htm.

[15] Report of the Monitoring Group on Somalia, S/2010/91, 10 March 2010, paragraph 122; Rashid Abdi interview on "The Price of Piracy," CNN, 9 May 2011.

[16] Peter Lehr, "A Western Armada Is Not the Way to Sink Somalia's Pirates," *The Guardian*, 18 November 2008: http://www.theguardian.com/commentisfree/2008/nov/ 19/piracy-somalia.

[17] For a succinct overview of all international antipiracy actors and their roles in the Gulf of Aden and the Indian Ocean, seeRobin Geiss and Anna Petrig, *Piracy and Armed Robbery at Sea: The Legal Framework for Counter-Piracy Operations in Somalia and the Gulf of Aden* (Oxford University Press, 2011), 17–35; Kraska, *Contemporary Maritime Piracy*, 59–68. See also Homan and Kamerling, "Operational Challenges to Counterpiracy."

[18] Geiss and Petrig, *Piracy and Armed Robbery at Sea*, 17–21.

accordingly launched several pre-emptive aerial and naval operations on land and the nearby waters.[19]

The US-led Combined Maritime Forces (CMT) had deployed Coalition Task Force 150 (CTF-150) for overall maritime security, especially for counter-terrorism, between the Red Sea and the Indian Ocean; it expanded its mandate to include counter-piracy in late 2008. In early 2009, it was replaced with Combined Task Force (CTF) 151 that was specifically mandated to combat piracy with the assistance of CTF 152, which had long been active in the Arabian Gulf.[20]

Several pre-existing and new, unilateral, multilateral, and international frameworks facilitated strategic planning, cooperation and coordination among the various naval forces deployed on counter-piracy missions. Among these were the Contact Group on Piracy off the Coast of Somalia (CGPCS), Shared Awareness and Deconfliction (SHADE), Maritime Security Center – Horn of Africa (MSCHOA), the International Maritime Bureau's Piracy Reporting Center (which predated Somali piracy), and others, many of which also worked on building local capacity. All of these were voluntary associations: the Contact Group was formed in response to a call in Security Council Resolution 1851 for international navies to work together and to coordinate their operations; SHADE was an information- and experience-sharing mechanism; and MSCHOA was an EU mechanism meant to aid Operation ATALANTA.[21]

In September 2008 the EU also set an Internationally Recommended Transit Corridor (IRTC) through which vessels could transit the high-risk area in groups or convoys under the close monitoring and protection of a series of foreign warships serving in rotation. In February 2009, the transit corridor was modified into wide east–west and west–east lanes parallel to the Yemeni coastline in the Gulf of Aden.[22] The International Maritime Bureau (IMB) and its Piracy Reporting Center served as

---

[19] Several individual countries – such as France and Indonesia – did so unilaterally and without an international sanction. See, for example, Angela Doland, "French Troops Attack Somali Pirates After 30 Hostages Freed," *The Washington Post*, 12 April 2008: http://www.washingtonpost.com/wp-dyn/content/article/2008/04/11/AR2008041103537.html; John McBeth, "Full Resolve: How Indonesia Took on the Somali Pirates," *Jakarta Globe*, 30 May 2011: http://www.thejakartaglobe.com/archive/full-resolve-how-indonesia-took-on-the-somali-pirates/.

[20] Geiss and Petrig, *Piracy and Armed Robbery at Sea*, 24–25; Murphy, *Somalia: The New Barbary?* 37–38. Also see the CMF website: https://combinedmaritimeforces.com/ctf-152-gulf-security-cooperation/.

[21] Geiss and Petrig, *Piracy and Armed Robbery at Sea*, 25–29.

[22] Kees Homan and Susanne Kamerling, "Operational Challenges to Counterpiracy Operations off the Coast of Somalia," in Ginkel and Putten (eds.), *The International Response to Somali Piracy*, 83–85; Robin Geiss and Anna Petrig, *Piracy and Armed Robbery at Sea: the Legal Framework for Counter-Piracy Operations in Somalia and the Gulf of Aden* (Oxford University Press, 2011), 17–21.

centers for investigation and for the gathering and dissemination of information.

A conglomerate of industry actors produced an effective manual on non-military "best management" practices (commonly referred to as BMPs) about avoiding, evading and resisting pirate attacks.[23] Currently in its fourth revision, this manual, *BMP4*, reifies a theoretical articulation of micro-level security tactics called situational crime prevention that rests on changing the immediate environment to dissuade or ward off the potential offender.[24] The BMPs recommend that sailors: increase vigilance; reduce ships' vulnerabilities; increase vessel speed and maneuver on encountering pirates; and avoid capture by hiding and disabling vessel in the event of being boarded. The limited available research on the topic indicates that some or all of the key aspects of these best-practice measures have been present in the majority of the more than 70 percent of failed pirate attempts globally and in close to 60 percent of those in the Horn of Africa).[25]

According to its own records, the Security Council authorized a loose-but-robust international mandate that made possible the above operations after the weak Transitional Federal Government (TFG) of Abdullahi Yusuf asked for it in a letter dated 27 February 2008.[26] Nevertheless, the TFG neither called on nor authorized the hard-to-regulate private military/security companies, whose advent into the Somali scene added to the mire, to combat piracy in Somali waters. With little uniformity, discipline or accountability, the widespread deployment of private military solutions in the Gulf of Aden and the western Indian Ocean further militarized the fragile region.[27] Under pressure from powerful ship-owners, business communities, and

---

[23] *BMP4: Best Management Practices for Protection against Somalia Based Piracy*, UKMTO-ICS (Edinburgh: Witherby Publishing Group Ltd., 2011).

[24] Jon M. Shane, Eric L Piza and Marissa Mandala, "Situational Crime Prevention and Worldwide Piracy: A Cross-Continent Analysis," *Crime Science*, vol. 4, no. 2 (2015): 1–13.

[25] Shane, Piza and Mandala, "Situational Crime Prevention and Worldwide Piracy," 5–7; Willow Bryant, Michael Townsley and Benoit Lecler, "Preventing Maritime Pirate Attacks: A Conjunctive Analysis of the Effectiveness of Ship Protection Measures Recommended by the International Maritime Organisation," *Journal of Transportation Security*, vol. 7 no. 1 (2014): 75–79.

[26] UN Security Council Resolution 1816, S/RES/1816 (2008), 2 June 2008: paragraph 9. Subsequent authorizations followed similar requests from the succeeding TFG of Sheikh Sharif Sheikh Ahmed.

[27] Kees Homan and Susanne Kamerling, "Operational Challenges to Counterpiracy Operations off the Coast of Somalia," in Ginkel and Putten (eds.), *The International Response to Somali Piracy*, 80–82. There are a number of cases when inexperienced private security guards shot at non-pirates in the high seas simply because they were armed with AK-47s; in a region where weapons are so rife, carrying such a gun is a sad normality.

international seafarers' associations demanding a robust response, the International Maritime Organization (IMO) removed one of the last restraints against the mushrooming private maritime security industry.[28]

In May 2011, IMO took the unprecedented step of tacitly approving the contracting with and use of private armed guards on board ships by issuing guidance and recommendations on how to do so.[29] Neither its first interim guidelines nor subsequent revisions openly endorsed the use of armed guards. In fact, all versions make it clear that IMO, "whilst not endorsing the use of privately contracted armed security personnel (PCASP), understands . . . " and goes on to offer guidance and recommendations on how to identify, contract and deploy good ones.[30]

Although sophisticated weapons of war have thus been deployed and used proactively, Douglas Guilfoyle argues that the counter-piracy mandates of international forces have been carefully couched in the language of law enforcement and not that of war.[31] Yet, the immediate effect of such a highly militarized response was to displace the problem into the wider Indian Ocean. As we saw in Chapter 3, pirates increasingly used mother ships that carried them and their attack boats far into the ocean, bringing them closer to unsuspecting preys upon whom they pounced.[32]

Meanwhile, there emerged a widely shared understanding within international policymaking circles that, according to Britanny Gilmer, located piracy at the intersection of underdevelopment and insecurity and revved up corresponding remedies; these proved to be misplaced and were only half-heartedly pursued in practice. The international community authorized the deployment of antipiracy naval armada in Somalia's waters and many powerful countries followed suit, but none were prepared to commit military assets on land in pursuit of security and development in order

---

[28] "Special Report: As Pirate Attacks Grow, Shipowners Take Arms," Reuters, 3 May 2011.

[29] IMO Circular, MSC.1/Circ.1405, "Interim Guidance to Shipowners, Ship Operators, and Shipmasters on the Use of Privately Contracted Armed Security Personnel on Board Ships in the High Risk Area," 23 May 2011. Available at: http://www.marad.dot.gov/documents/MSC.1-Circ.1405.pdf.

[30] Subsequent industry guidelines for such private security companies include Phillip Drew and Rob McLaughlin, *Handbook on the Use of Force for Private Security Companies* (Denver, CO: Oceans Beyond Piracy, 2016).

[31] Of Douglas Guilfoyle's numerous analyses of the laws of the sea, piracy and its suppression, see "International Law and Counter-Piracy in the Indian Ocean," in Weldemichael, Schneider and Winner (eds.), *Maritime Terrorism and Piracy in the Indian Ocean Region* (Routledge: 2015), 96–112.

[32] "According to the NATO Shipping Centre's description of piracy operations in the Gulf of Aden," reported the Monitoring Group, "mother ship supply ports exist at Al Mukallah and Al Shishr, Sayhut, Nishtun and Al Ghaydah on the Yemeni coast and Bossaso, Aluula and Mogadishu on the Somali coast." See Report of the United Nations Monitoring Group on Somalia, S/2008/769, 10 December 2008, paragraph 137.

to combat piracy. They opted for awareness-raising and development assistance, which they delegated to the United Nations Office on Drugs and Crime (UNODC) and other NGOs.[33]

Drawing on her experience working at the Nairobi regional office of the UNODC's Countering Piracy Program, Gilmer reflected critically on international non-military counter-piracy measures. To begin with, the new security–development framework marked the men in order "to criminalize or decriminalize bodies, mobilize or immobilize bodies, and produce developable and containable bodies in Somalia."[34] Potential pirates thus became "developable subjects," requiring alternative livelihoods. She went on to note that, following the captures of Maersk Alabama and Captain Phillips in the 2009s, "Somali pirate mania is being fueled by more than just a desire to prosecute those who commit crimes on the high seas. Rather, it is being fueled by a complex entanglement of personal profit motive, institutional machinations, and a desire to prevent and contain particular gendered and racialized bodies within Somalia, all under the banner of regional and global security."[35]

Other observers have also questioned the declared antipiracy intention of the international navies. The fact that other theaters, like the Libyan bombing and the Mediterranean refugee crisis, required the rotation of naval assets away from the Horn of Africa seem to give credence to the argument that counter-piracy was not in and of itself a pressing priority to world powers. While on the one hand the fear of piracy coalescing with terrorism seemed to have featured prominently in the thinking of international actors, on the other hand it has offered rival powers an ideal excuse to assert their presence in a region of far-reaching geopolitical and strategic significance.

The Specter of Piracy–Terrorism Nexus and Geostrategic Considerations

The 9/11 terrorist attacks on the United States spurred an aggressive – and often problematic – war on terror that involved the pursuit of terrorism suspects to the farthest corners of the world and hyper-vigilance against terrorist threats in any plausible theater. After the terrorist attack on the oil tanker MV *Limburg* in October 2002 in the Gulf of Aden (off the coast of Yemen), the antiterrorism rhetoric and disposition of global powers furnished a new normative comfort zone for security studies and

---

[33] Gilmer, *Political Geographies of Piracy*, offers a critical analysis of that aspect of international counter-piracy responses.
[34] Ibid., 12.   [35] Ibid., 13.

threat assessments that proved extremely profitable to some. Maritime piracy offered especially lucrative opportunities to insurance underwriters who furnished speculative hyperbole of threats of the piracy–terrorism nexus.

Lloyd's of London, the world's top maritime insurer, led the instilling of fear of a pirate-terror nexus through *Lloyd's List*, its publication that is widely read in the industry. Characterizing the phenomenon as a "ticking time bomb," a June 2004 article in that newsletter warned: "The global supply chain is in jeopardy. Pirates have evolved from clusters of commercial plunderers to a sinister and organised force that relishes the prospect of toying with the levers of the world economy."[36] In February 2005, David Osler's admonishment in *Lloyd's List* was characteristic: "We may think terrorist attacks are unlikely, but, if they happen, they will be devastating – and piracy is a real threat."[37] Around the same time John Burnett wrote an editorial entitled "The Next 9/11 Could Happen at Sea."[38] Shortly afterward, Lloyd's of London decided to cover both piracy and terrorism insurance under the same plan and reaped exorbitant profits.[39]

Similarly exaggerated security considerations, especially about a possible nexus between Somali pirates and Al-Shabaab, seem to have played a considerable role in the heavily militarized counter-piracy responses of the international community and those of individual powerful states. Donna Nincic observed early on that, in spite of "*prima facie* associations with state failure and maritime terrorism, there . . . [had] been little, if any, empirical attempt to explain systematically why contemporary maritime piracy occurs." She then went on to caution: "Without a sound understanding of the root causes of the problem, solutions remain *post facto*, and potentially haphazard and problematic."[40] Yet, Western military and intelligence sources have repeatedly asserted that there was in fact a nexus between pirates and terrorists. In a truncated document on WikiLeaks, for example, Commander Chris Dickinson of the Canadian warship HMCS *Ville de Quebec* that escorted WFP vessels in and out of

---

[36] Dominick Armstrong, "Maritime Terrorism Is a Ticking Timebomb," *Lloyd's List*, 22 June 2004, quoted in Jeremy Engels, "Floating Bombs Encircling Our Shores: Post-9/11 Rhetorics of Piracy and Terrorism," *Cultural Studies ↔ Critical Methodologies* vol. 7, no. 3 (2007): 326–349 [here 333–334]. Also see Currun Singh and Arjun Singh Bedi, "War on Piracy: The Conflation of Somali Piracy with Terrorism in Discourse, Tactic, and Law," *Security Dialogue* vol. 47, no. 5 (2016), 440–458.

[37] David Osler, "We Ignore Threats at Our Peril," *Lloyd's List*, 16 February 2005 quoted in Engels, "Floating Bombs Encircling Our Shores," 333–334.

[38] John S. Burnett, "The Next 9/11 Could Happen at Sea," *The New York Times*, 22 February 2005.

[39] Singh and Bedi, "War on Piracy," 447–448.

[40] Nincic, "State Failure and the Re-Emergence of Maritime Piracy."

Mogadishu between August and October 2008, claims that not only were the pirates and terrorists were joining forces but also that the Western-backed Transitional Federal Government (TFG) in Mogadishu was in cahoots with them.

Preeminent scholar of maritime affairs James Kraska wrote that a certain "Osen-Hunter Security Group shared its research with me that makes a strong case that the entry of Al-Shabaab into piracy represents the most insidious game changer yet."[41] There existed an inherent risk of piracy–terrorism collaboration and there was some level of coexistence whereby Al-Shabaab reportedly taxed successful pirate missions in areas under its control in central and southern Somalia.[42] Beyond that, there is little evidence so far to show organic ties between piracy and terrorism and none to show their operational cooperation – the insurance industry's hyperbole aside. The reasons for that are several.

"Innovation" has always been the trademark of terrorism, whether in choosing targets that had previously been considered taboo or in deploying previously unexpected methods. Accordingly, terrorists have used small boats as "floating bombs" to detonate their targets while at harbor (USS *Cole* in Aden in October 2000) or while sailing (the *Limburg* along the Yemeni coast in October 2002). They have also tried to take control of vessels at sea and ram them into other vessels or into strategic maritime infrastructures. While the possible targets and methods of maritime terrorism can be numerous, terrorism, as a tactic and weapon of the weak, generally deploys limited resources and targets the few in order to generate a disproportionately larger effect that draws the attention of many.[43] Peter Chalk, Martin Murphy and other experts have variously shown the logistical difficulty of staging such terrorist acts at sea. Even if they happened, the distance from the target audience denies the acts the "high symbolic and expressive value"[44] that terrorists expect. These two factors, the difficulty and the distance, help explain why maritime terrorism did not explode to the same extent as its overland counterpart, although terrorists could exploit the current technological advances to overcome this challenge.

In addition, fundamental ideological differences would make it impossible for the pirates and Islamist insurgents to cooperate beyond a tactical

---

[41] Kraska, *Contemporary Maritime Piracy*, 50.
[42] Personal conversations with Stig Hansen (25–27 May 2011, Hamburg); and with Somali intelligence and security sources (Galkayo, February and October 2012 and August 2015).
[43] Martha Crenshaw, "Thoughts on Relating Terrorism to Historical Contexts" in Martha Crenshaw (ed.), *Terrorism in Context* (Pennsylvania State University Press, 2007), 4.
[44] Ibid.

marriage of convenience. Ransom pirates splurged significant portions of their loot on luxury cars, alcohol, drugs, and prostitution, all forbidden in Islam. By contrast, Al-Shabaab strictly indoctrinates its fighters against those excesses and severely punishes those who stray, although it has tolerated the pirates' excesses so long as they generated badly needed funds. Al-Shabaab, its units or individual leaders have also clashed with the pirates.

Jay Bahadur, for example, reported in April 2009 that Al-Shabaab ambushed the notorious Puntland pirate linchpin Garad Mohamed as he led a heavily armed caravan of pirates from Garowe to Hobyo-Haradere (in the rival-held Galmudug region) to assist other pirates who had hijacked the MV *Faina* and were forced to anchor there. Al-Shabaab reportedly confiscated the cars and weapons of Garad Mohamed who managed to make it back to Puntland alive and to resume piracy.[45] Such hostility toward some pirates, however, has to be seen against the backdrop of Al-Shabaab's own aspirations to either lay its hands on the MV *Faina's* prized cargo of thirty-three tanks, other heavy artilleries, and ammunition, or at the very least to tax the pirates who were to land on its territory upon receiving ransom.[46]

There are only a few cases where Al-Shabaab became financially involved in piracy operations aside from their symbiosis where they physically overlapped in the Hobyo-Haradere area. It has become increasingly clear – since Al-Shabaab's takeover of pirate-dominated parts of Galmudug in late 2010 – that the Hobyo-Haradere pirates paid a part of their ransom proceeds to Al-Shabaab in levies of different forms.[47] In Puntland, however, only a few pirate groups are known to have – or are suspected of having – financial or logistical ties to Al-Shabaab. The pirate group of Fouad Warsame Said "Hanaano" is known to have had such close ties to Al-Shabaab. Although there is no evidence of his having organic roots in Al-Shabaab, Hanaano is known to have served, in at least one case, as a front for the Islamist group as he operated out of Lasqoray. Al-Shabaab is believed to have invested in the piracy mission that resulted in the 11 April 2009 capture of the American-owned, Italian-flagged tugboat *Buccaneer* with a crew of ten Italians, five Romanians and a Croatian. Of the reported USD 3 million extorted as ransom for the release of the tugboat and its crew four months later,

---

[45] Jay Bahadur, "The Pirate King of Somalia," *The Globe and Mail*, 26 April 2009: https://www.theglobeandmail.com/news/world/the-pirate-king-of-somalia/article4256243/.

[46] Unconfirmed sources indicate that there was a tense moment among the pirates of MV *Faina* when at least one of them wanted to pass on the cargo of heavy armaments to Al-Shabaab. That pirate was reportedly killed in the ensuing scuffle.

[47] Hansen, "The Dynamics of Somali Piracy," 528.

confidential intelligence sources indicate that the Islamist insurgent group collected a third.[48]

Other harder-to-corroborate claims of pirate–Al-Shabaab collaboration include the hijacking of the Italian chemical tanker *Enrico Ievoli* in late 2011.[49] There was also a 2012 case of Puntland pirates launching an operation out of Al-Shabaab–controlled Kismayo aboard a mother ship loaded with Al-Shabaab's illicit charcoal. Such earlier isolated incidences had led the Monitoring Group to report in 2010 that it had "found no evidence to support allegations of structured cooperation between pirate groups and armed opposition groups, including Al-Shabaab."[50] That assessment held until 2012 when piracy rates dropped to levels seen in the 1990s.

Most recently, Nairobi-based foreign sources claimed that pirates were complicit in Al-Shabaab's March 2016 amphibious landing of hundreds of its fighters in coastal locations in Puntland, namely at Gara'ad and Suuj-Garmal. They allege especially that the known pirate linchpin in the Galmudug region, Mohamed Osman Mohamed "Gafanje," rented his boats to Al-Shabaab. Nevertheless, several knowledgeable local sources not only dispute that assertion but they also point to non-pirate fishermen and businessmen who may or may not have known the purpose for which their boats were rented.

Contrary to the views of foreign observers and security experts, and perhaps ironically, in Puntland's remote and inaccessible area in the tip of the Horn, local government authorities sought the assistance of the notorious pirate Isse Yuluh against a breakaway Al-Shabaab group that in May 2016 occupied Qandala and declared loyalty to the Islamic State (IS). The fugitive pirate leader, who had instigated a bloody, drawn-out conflict between neighboring clan families, deployed his militia and heavy weapons in successfully fighting off the IS faction. Not only did his contribution lead to his family clan embracing him and his militia as their own, but it also led to the authorities tacitly dropping their pursuit of him. He lived openly in

---

[48] Confidential interview (26–27 February 2012, Galkayo). In addition to proceeds from ransoms for the release of a journalist and an aid worker in 2007 that helped set up Al-Shabaab in the northeast network in Galgala, the 2012 sum is believed to have been crucial in the consolidation of the position of that militant organization.

[49] "Pirates Hijack Italian Tanker with 18 on Board off Oman," *The Telegraph*, 27 December 2011: http://www.telegraph.co.uk/news/worldnews/piracy/8979120/Pirat es-hijack-Italian-tanker-with-18-on-board-off-Oman.html; "MT *Enrico Ievoli* Anchors off Dhinooda," *SomaliaReport*, 31 December 2011: http://piracyreport.com/index.php/post/2424/MT_Enrico_Ievoli_Anchors_Off_Dhinooda.

[50] Report of the Monitoring Group on Somalia, S/2010/91, 10 March 2010, paragraph 129.

Qandala until he killed one of his own men and fled the area to avoid being killed in revenge.[51]

A piracy–terrorism nexus has so far not come into existence in Somalia. Yet, the specter of one has not been removed; nor have the strategic security, economic and geopolitical concerns of the world's most powerful countries been allayed. High-profile hijackings such as those of the MV *Faina* and MV *Sirius Star* shortly after the Security Council's authorization of international military operations against piracy seemed to confirm the concerns of these powers. As mentioned earlier, in September 2008, Somali pirates had hijacked the Ukrainian cargo vessel, MV *Faina*. Its cargo of heavy weapons (thirty-three T-72 Tanks, various artillery pieces and ammunition all bound for South Sudan via Kenya) raised the alarm that Al-Shabaab may lay its hands on them despite the difficulties of security and logistics of offloading.[52] Less than two months later, in November, pirates hijacked the Saudi super tanker MV *Sirius Star*, which was fully loaded with a cargo of some two million barrels of crude oil worth at least USD 100 million.[53]

Counter-Piracy as a Means

Although the cases of MV *Faina* and *Sirius Star*, among many others that followed, spoke to the serious threat that pirates posed to the security, economy and energy resources of the most powerful countries in the region and the world, some analysts posit that there were additional geostrategic imperatives that moved the international community to a decisive and large-scale show of force against piracy. From a broad, geopolitical outlook Robert Kaplan concluded that the Indian Ocean was the twenty-first century's strategic theater of decisive global rivalry, and that the United States needed an approach that would allow an

---

[51] It is important to bear in mind that local political-cum-security imperatives contributed to clan-families' decisions to harbor or eject their wayward members in the context of piracy. Isse Yuluh was, for example, embraced back by his clan-family, which lacked a militia force to call its own in the context of local balance of power. Isse Yuluh's clan forgave him and secured government amnesty for him and his men because the government itself needed his fighters to combat radicalized fighters who claimed loyalty to IS.

[52] Xan Rice, "Somali Pirates Capture Ukrainian Cargo Ship Loaded with Military Hardwar," *The Guardian*, 26 September 2008: https://www.theguardian.com/world/20 09/feb/05/somali-pirates-free-military-shipPirates released MV *Faina*, reportedly, upon receiving a ransom of about $3.5 million.

[53] Robert F. Worth, "Pirates Seize Saudi Tanker off Kenya," *The New York Times*, 17 November 2008: https://www.nytimes.com/2008/11/18/world/africa/18pirates.html; "Hijacked Oil Tanker Nears Somalia," BBC, 18 November 2008: http://news.bbc.co.u k/2/hi/africa/7734733.stm. Pirates are believed to have released the *Sirius Star* upon the payment of $3 million in ransom.

"elegant decline" of its diminishing maritime superiority. While welcoming Indian and Japanese naval ascendancy to counter that of China, "U.S. military planners will have to invoke [common] challenges such as terrorism, piracy, and smuggling" in order to bring China into coalitions and joint policing roles, and thereby tame its military expansion; accordingly, a fitting force multiplier strategy for "the U.S. Navy should be a coalition builder supreme"[54] and "piracy has the potential to unite rival states along the Indian Ocean coastline."[55]

Focusing more specifically on piracy, Lee Willett analyzed the motives that compelled countries to dispatch their navies on counter-piracy missions and argued that combined regional, global and geostrategic factors weighed heavily in the calculation of powerful countries more than did a desire to rid the Indian Ocean of Somali pirates. He concluded that piracy had become "as significant for the international power play surrounding it, as for its direct threat to maritime security" because powerful countries seized "the political opportunities created by counter-piracy campaign to exert wider political presence in a region which is now the fulcrum of the global power balance."[56]

Accordingly, some countries (including the US, the UK and France) used involvement in coalition counter-piracy as a force multiplier in order to assert their presence in a region of geopolitical significance. Others (like France vis-à-vis the US) did so to counter-balance the preponderance of rival powers. Emerging and re-emerging naval powers similarly used counter-piracy commitments to promote their respective national interests by establishing (China) and re-establishing or seeking to re-establish (Russia) their presence.[57] Where many powerful countries would be quick to dismiss Willett's analysis, China's building of its first overseas military base in Djibouti gives his observations considerable weight.[58]

[54] Robert D. Kaplan, "Center Stage for the Twenty-first Century," *Foreign Affairs*, vol. 8, no. 2 (March/April 2009), 16–32 [here 25].

[55] Ibid.

[56] Lee Willett, "Pirates and Power Politics: Naval Presence and Grand Strategy in the Horn of Africa," *The RUSI Journal*, vol. 156, no. 6 (December 2012), 20–25 [here p. 24].

[57] Willett, "Pirates and Power Politics." For a different geopolitical analysis featuring the US, India, and China, see James R. Holmes, "The Interplay between Counterpiracy and Indian Ocean Geopolitics," in Ginkel and Putten (eds.), *The International Response to Somali Piracy*, 153–177.

[58] Geoffrey Aronson, "China to Open Its First Naval Base in Africa," Al-Jazeera, 22 December 2015: http://www.aljazeera.com/indepth/opinion/2015/12/china-opens-n aval-base-africa-151222141545988.html; Edmund Blair, "China to Start Work Soon on Naval Base in Djibouti-Guelleh," Reuters, 2 February 2016: http://uk.reuters.com/arti cle/uk-djibouti-china-idUKKCN0VB1Z6; "China Says Starts Construction of Djibouti Military Base," Reuters, 25 February 2016: http://www.reuters.com/article/china-dji bouti-idUSL3N1643RN; Kevin J. Kelley, "Djibouti Base Could Be Start of US–China Military Rivalry in EA," *The East African*, 28 November 2015: http://www.theeastafrican.

Somalis and some foreign observers have questioned the declared intentions of the international antipiracy armada off the coast of their country. Many Somalis hold powerful countries responsible for the origins of piracy in the first place or regard them as complicit in perpetuating it with the intention of justifying their military presence in Somali waters. That presence is necessary, according to these views, in order to exploit Somalia's maritime resources and to be strategically positioned in the geostrategic rivalry for the region as a whole.[59] Why else would one deploy the most advanced war ships to quash – or would one have such difficulty in quashing – a few, skinny young men on tiny skiffs? they ask.

Taken aback by the surveillance and firepower of an antipiracy NATO warship that he visited, a Somali intelligence officer related his experience and conclusions:

One time I have been on board NATO warship. They were 25 nautical miles off the coast. They showed us pictures of Eyl . . . Then they showed us live pictures of people moving around and asked us if we could recognize who the pirates were. They said they had the capacity to monitor the whole coast from where they were. Why then could they not solve the piracy problem? If they are serious and genuine about piracy, it is unbelievable that they could not end it and the young men in small skiffs continue to elude the best navies. They are using piracy as an excuse to continue pillaging/plundering Somalia and establish their presence. I have held long interviews with many pirates that convince me of this.[60]

Fishing and non-fishing coastal residents, educated townspeople, and highly informed officials in both governments and nongovernmental organizations in the Somali region have reached similar conclusions – that piracy was no more than an excuse. These suspicions are reinforced by the catch-and-release practices of some of the counter-piracy navy ships, the reluctance (or inability) of powerful Western countries to prosecute pirates while choosing instead to hand them over to third party jailers,[61] and the uninterrupted looting of Somali marine resources

co.ke/news/Djibouti-base-could-be-start-of-US-China-military-rivalry-in-EA/-/2558/29 76120/-/uw6ljx/-/index.html

[59] Some even claim that the warships were stealing maritime resources while others have claimed that military helicopters landed in the interior to either steal wild animals or to plant something among the wild herds.

[60] Interview with Lt. Col. Abdirizak Ismail Hassan (26 and 27 February 2012, Galkayo).

[61] Countries that have, at various times, agreed to pre-trial transfer of suspected pirates into their custody include Kenya, Mauritius and Seychelles. See, EU NAVFOR Somalia, "European Union Signs Prosecution Agreement with Kenya," 6 March 2009: http://eu navfor.eu/european-union-signs-prosecution-agreement-with-kenya/; "Agreement Between the European Union and the Republic of Mauritius on the Conditions of Transfer of Suspected Pirates and Associated Seized Property from the European Union-Led Naval Force to the Republic of Mauritius and on the Conditions of Suspected Pirates after Transfer," *Official Journal of the European Union*, L254/3,

by foreign ships; these observations lend credence to parallel analytical perspectives and conspiracy theories.

In 2011 a combination of these and other factors compelled Mogadishu-based Somali parliamentarians to reject external pressure to criminalize piracy and enact an antipiracy law.[62] In a broader examination of the impediments to Somalia's own antipiracy law, Afyare Elmi and Ladan Affi blamed the confusion on the gaping shortage of professional capacity in contemporary Somalia, a pervasive perception that Kenya was revving up to annex Somali territories and/or waters, and the belief that the West was exploiting Somali resources.[63] Yet, a veteran fighter of the Somali Salvation Democratic Front (SSDF), who went on to serve as a police colonel in Puntland, had the following to say: "Pirates posed all sorts of challenges to Somali society – security, cultural, religious – but we overlooked it because there was a bigger problem that preceded and caused piracy. We said let the two thieves fight it out. But the international community needs to be honest about their share . . . This can only be resolved when the truth is out and accounted for."[64] An important piece of truth that journalist reports, academic research and policy deliberations have not sufficiently accounted for is the fact that powerful, far-off countries have used counter-piracy efforts for purposes other than countering piracy as discussed above.

By contrast, African and Middle Eastern countries, which had been badly and more directly affected by piracy, had vested interest in ridding the region of the pirate menace. Members of the Arab League had taken up the matter in mid-2008 when the UN Security Council authorized the

30 September 2011: http://eur-lex.europa.eu/resource.html?uri=cellar:d437ef50-18ca-4883-b4fd-f043a9be1a86.0009.02/DOC_2&format=PDF. Also see, Seychelles Tourism Board-sourced report: "Seychelles and Mauritius Sign Pirates Transfer Agreement," 21 July 2011: https://www.eturbonews.com/47099/seychelles-and-mauritius-sign-pirates-transfer-agreement.
For a legal analysis of piracy prosecutions in Kenya before it terminated its pirate transfer agreements in late 2010, see James Thuo Gathii, "Kenya's Piracy Prosecutions," *The American Journal of International Law*, vol. 104, no. 3 (July 2010), 416–436. Also see Sellstrom, *Africa in the Indian Ocean*, 296-301.
[62] "Somalia Parliament Rejects Anti-Piracy Legislation," 19 January 2011: http://jurist.org/paperchase/2011/01/somalia-parliament-rejects-anti-piracy-legislation.php; "Somalia: Parliamentarians Accuse Foreign Warships of Supporting Pirates," 19 January 2011: http://allafrica.com/stories/201101190499.html. The Mogadishu-based federal parliamentarians flatly refused to legislate antipiracy law in defiant stand against foreign pressure, believing that the international community had granted foreign IUU fishers free rein while demanding that Somali authorities contain local responses against them.
[63] Afyare Elmi and Ladan Affi, "Barriers to Developing Anti-Piracy Law in Somalia" 20 November 2014: http://studies.aljazeera.net/en/reports/2014/11/201411201031052448.htm
[64] Col. Dahir (Focus group meeting with Knowledgeable Elders in Galkayo, 26 February 2012).

use of force and dispatched naval assets to the region. In December 2008 the Arab League called for the expansion of the mandate of the African Union Mission in Somalia (AMISOM) to include counter-piracy.[65] In pursuit of its call for Afro-Arab cooperation to combat piracy in 2009, the League mandated then-Libyan leader Mu'amar al-Gaddafi to help find a solution in his capacity as that year's chairman of the African Union (AU). He duly set up a taskforce to mobilize elders, to help with job creation, and to engage directly with pirate leaders, among other tasks. In September 2009, on Gaddafi's invitation, Mohamed Abdi Hassan "Afweyne" led an entourage of known pirates (kingpins and the rank and file) from central Somalia to Libya. When Gaddafi's tenure as AU Chairman ended in January 2010, the initiative fizzled under concerted pressure, possibly from Western powers.[66] The United Arab Emirates then proceeded to make unilateral security arrangements with Puntland as we have seen in Chapter 4.[67]

Outcomes and Missteps of International Counter-Piracy

The long-term effect of military responses to piracy is yet to be seen; many have, however, attributed the drop in pirate cases to international anti-piracy flotilla whose occasional public announcements of interdictions have been received with fanfare. The overall contribution of the foreign navies cannot be established precisely beyond those cases in which they were involved and they made public, but their overall role in the inter-mediate term cannot be dismissed. This was especially true in 2011 when the rate of successful hijackings was the lowest (at 28) despite the highest number of reported pirate incidents (237) that year. Nor can the role of

[65] "Statement by the Council of the League of Arab States at the Permanent Representatives Level at Its Extraordinary Session on the Developments in Somalia," Cairo, 4 December 2008.

[66] In March 2010, for example, the Monitoring Group reported to the UN Security Council that it was "concerned by reports that Afweyne, and possibly other pirate leaders, may have attracted the sympathy of the Government of the Libyan Arab Jamahiriya. Multiple media sources, as well as Monitoring Group contacts, reported Afweyne's presence in Tripoli as an invited guest . . . from 1 to 4 September 2009. On 23 September 2009, in his statement before the General Assembly of the United Nations in New York, the President of the Libyan Arab Jamahiriya, Mu'ammar Qadafi, acknowledged that he had met with Somali pirates, spoke in their defence and called upon States to respect Somalia's exclusive economic zone." Report of the United Nations Monitoring Group on Somalia, S/2010/91, 10 March 2010, paragraphs 135–156.

[67] UAE's less-targeted security arrangement with the federal government, however, became hostage to – and fell apart in April 2018 because of – the spiraling conflict between the Gulf Cooperation Council countries that pitted Saudi Arabia, UAE and Bahrain against Qatar. Qatar and its ally, Turkey, represent the largest foreign business and political interest in Mogadishu.

domestic antipiracy operations and activism be neglected in accounting for this decline, as discussed in Chapter 4.

The United Nations Security Council stated that the Somali Transitional Federal Government had asked for international assistance against piracy and had granted foreign powers the green light to combat piracy in its sovereign territory – on land and at sea.[68] Not all Somalis, however, supported the international naval presence that has done nothing to contain IUU fishing but has instead, in their view, resorted to methods and measures that are at best questionable. Perhaps tellingly, of 236 respondents in a February 2012 random survey conducted among Somali youth in Puntland, only six (2.5 percent) believed that continued and strengthened presence of EU and NATO warships could solve the problem of piracy.

Such views are reinforced by the missteps and nonchalance of the international navies and of private security guards on board the vessels or escorting them. These coalition, national, and private forces could not distinguish pirates from innocent fishermen; as a result, the latter became victims of antipiracy forces. After many such incidents, small-scale local fishermen feared venturing out to sea and many stopped doing so completely.

In the early hours of 1 May 2011, three known fishermen from Eyl, including Abdulgadir Al-Nur "Dadurow" and Nur Mursel Mohamed, went fishing as they did nearly seven days a week. They were never seen again. A week into their disappearance, Mayor Musa Osman Yusuf of Eyl telephoned Puntland Counter-Piracy Director General Abdirizak Mohamed Dirir in Garowe to inquire.[69] The Director General called his contacts in NATO's counter-piracy force, who told him that they had no knowledge of any incident involving fishermen around Eyl.[70] Residents of Bedey (the coastal half of Eyl) made frantic calls to their contacts along the coastline until five days later when the body of Dadurow washed up on the beach at Gaba'e.

With one hand zip-tied to the opposite leg and his back riddled with bullet holes, Dadurow's misconfigured body was discovered on the beach of Gaba'e in the morning of 13 May 2011. The villagers identified the body, sent the bad news to the village of the deceased and immediately buried the body due to its fragility and in accordance with Islamic tradition.[71] Dadurow was survived by his wife and children, four boys

---

[68] Ironically, as we have already seen, for the longest time the TFG itself had failed to promulgate an antipiracy law in spite of sustained international pressure to do so.

[69] Interviews (24 February 2012, Eyl) and (4 February 2012, Garowe).

[70] Confidential interview (4 February 2012, Garowe).

[71] Interviews with the two widows (22 February 2012, Eyl); Confidential interviews (4 February 2012, Garowe) and (24 February 2012, Eyl).

and a girl between the ages of four and fifteen years, who found closure.[72] Nur Mursel and the third fisherman were presumed to have met the same fate as Dadurow but their families have not had the same closure.[73]

Even though there are not enough such cases to establish a pattern or to identify who may have been behind these atrocities, sources privy to the grisly details of many such tragic incidents indicate they have observed a pattern, pointing to specific foreign navies in Somali waters. In 2010, in 'Aluula (near the tip of the Horn), an unidentified foreign warship strafed from close distance a Somali-rented Yemeni fishing vessel that had been loading the catch of local artisanal fishermen. The foreign sailors then boarded the fishing vessel and, on seeing what they had done, said "We thought you were pirates" and left without offering assistance to the injured.[74]

In July 2011, a warship, purportedly Danish, allegedly rammed an artisanal fishing boat near Bosaso, injuring the entire crew. The fishermen were not far from the coast and managed to send an SOS to their contacts on land, who rushed to their rescue. Similarly in late March 2012 an unidentified warship attacked the *Al-Qanim*, a Yemeni-registered, Somali-owned fishing vessel, and killed two of the ten Somali crew before letting the rest proceed with their journey back to Bosaso, the fishing boat's base of operations.[75] Scores of fishermen and officials relate that such killings were not uncommon.

Increasing numbers of artisanal fishermen continued to fish and started to sail farther into the ocean for better catches due to a combination of overfishing and competition with illegal foreign fishing vessels in the inshore waters. In doing so, the artisanal fishermen exposed themselves to several dangers. First, their old, small and poorly constructed fishing crafts were vulnerable to natural hazards in the strong waves of the ocean's open waters. Second, the commercial navies and the antipiracy flotilla – as well as the industrial-scale IUU fishing vessels – have generally been active in these richer fishing grounds off the Somali coast; this is where artisanal fishermen ventured later at the risk of being targeted by the international antipiracy navies and by the private armed guards that were on board or escorting transport or fishing vessels.

---

[72] Confidential interview (22 February 2012, Eyl).
[73] Nur Mursel left behind a wife and two children under two years of age, the youngest of whom was one week old when he went on that fateful fishing trip. When visited in February 2012, the two widows and their orphaned children still lived in the same run-down shacks by the water, surrounded by the spare fishing gear of their late breadwinners.
[74] Interview with Lt. Col. Abdirizak Ismail Hassan (26 and 27 February 2012, Galkayo).
[75] "Fishing Vessel Attacked by Naval Forces: Two Crew Members Killed in Attack," *SomaliaReport*, 26 March 2012: http://piracyreport.com/index.php/post/3152/Fishing_Vessel_Attacked_by_Naval_Forces.

Somali fishermen have lamented their lot at the hands of international and private antipiracy forces in the same way they have complained about the pirates. An unknown number of fishermen have been killed; others have been whisked off to overseas jails and many more have disappeared without a trace. Foreign national, international and private antipiracy missions have failed repeatedly to distinguish between pirates and non-pirates; the consequences of these missions have been deadly for innocent fisherman at sea and for civilians on land, but the actors have not been held to account. The incidence of fishermen killed by international or private antipiracy forces, wrongfully apprehended, or disappeared at sea is thus likely to be higher than what has been reported or than can be established with certainty.

As many Somalis are quick to point out, such targeting by the international antipiracy forces preceded the widespread misperception that all Somalis were either directly involved in piracy or benefited from it. Awad Yare, a fisherman in Bargal, told *SomaliaReport* that ever since "pirates started hijacking boats . . . everyone thinks even we are pirates . . . We have been having so much trouble, some international vessels have poured boiling water onto our boats and destroying boats which can cause injuries and even death."[76] Another fisherman in Lasqorey related how making a daily living left them in fear: "We are scared of both pirates and the international navies. We are scared that naval forces will arrest us because they are suspecting we are pirates."[77]

Some members of the Contact Group on Piracy off the Coast of Somalia (CGPCS) remained inadequately informed or were simply careless and equally callous about the treatment of suspected pirates at sea. In 2013, *The Guardian* reported that Danish ambassador Thomas Winkler, who led CGPCS's legal team, believed that prosecuting "more than 1,000 pirates [in more than 20 countries] and transferring them to Somali prisons, where conditions are grim, appeared to be having a preventive effect," quoting him as saying: "The number of active pirates is perhaps 3,000 . . . So if you put a thousand behind bars, and 300–400 die every year at sea from hunger (or) drowning . . . you will quickly come down."[78]

The morality of such talk aside, this claim is off the mark on several levels. First, it has never been possible to get a clear picture of the number

[76] Mohamed Beerdhige, "Pirates Hijack Vessel despite Gov Security Team. Iranian Dhow Fishing Legally with Support of Puntland Government," *SomaliaReport*, 25 January 2012: http://piracyreport.com/index.php/post/2618/Pirates_Hijack_Vessel_Despite_Gov_Securi ty_Team
[77] Ibid.
[78] "No Somali Pirate Hijacking in Nearly a Year, Says UN," *The Guardian*, 3 May 2013: https://www.theguardian.com/world/2013/may/03/somali-pirate-hijacking

of pirates at any given time because of the fluidity of the criminal enterprise. A German naval commander best captured the impermanence or even seasonality of the trade thus: "The ocean is not just an empty space. It is full of fishing boats and other kinds of merchant ships. The same person who is a pirate today may be a fisherman the next day, a trader bringing goods from Dubai to Kenya another day, or even a human smuggler heading to Yemen with a cargo of Somali migrants the day after that."[79] One, of course, has to add nomads to this list of licit and illicit professions and livelihoods. Second, as many Somali and non-Somali researchers have pointed out, for every pirate who was jailed or disappeared, there were many more ready to take his place; no analysis can afford to lose sight of this fact simply because the rate of attacks has gone down.

In 2010, UNODC estimated that a total of 200 to 300 pirates had disappeared after leaving on piracy missions.[80] While a few hundred are enough to generate a serious news storm in any society and more so in oral societies, all local estimates, coupled with my own experience traveling across Puntland, suggest that the above figures are minuscule.[81] This is especially likely in light of the low rate of pirate successes and their even lower chances of making it back home after the first failed attempt to capture a ship as the figures in Chapter 3 attest.[82] Winkler's assessment of 300 – 400 annual disappearances of suspected pirates may, therefore, be consistent with the widely held, very conservative estimates but his relegation of those disappearances to drowning does not seem tenable. Besides the innocent victims of international antipiracy operations, Somali pirates killed in the act of piracy,[83] during rescue operations,[84] and in retaliatory raids[85] have so far gone unaccounted.

[79] Quoted in Jatin Dua, "A Modern-Day Pirate's Port of Call," *Middle East Report* No. 256 (Fall 2010), 20–23 [here 22].

[80] Lang, *Report of the Special Adviser to the Secretary-General*, 14.

[81] A short field trip to Gara'ad in November 2012 found the one-time pirate hub abuzz with anticipation about the whereabouts of their loved ones.

[82] The rate of pirates' successful hijackings ranged between 31 percent in 2005 and 17 percent in 2012 with the exceptionally high 41 percent in 2011 and exceptionally low 11 percent in 2013.

[83] William McMichael reported that in mid-May 2011, "a U.S. naval helicopter opened fire on a pirate skiff as it was attacking a boat, likely killing all pirates onboard, and departed without verifying the condition of the pirates." See William McMichael, "Navy: Helo Fires on Pirate Skiff, Killing 4," *Navy Times,* 18 May 2011. Reproduced at https://blog .usni.org/posts/2011/05/19/now-youre-talking.

[84] On 21 January 2011, *The Guardian* reported that a South Korean rescue operation left eight pirates dead. Justin McCurry, "Eight Somali Pirates Killed as South Korea Rescues Freighter Crew," *The Guardian,* 21 January 2011, http://www.guardian.co.uk/world/20 11/jan/21/south-korea-rescue-somali-pirates

[85] Isolated French and Indonesian retaliatory raids have, for example, killed an unknown number of pirates. See "TNI: Four Pirates Killed in Gun Battle," reproduced at https://

In her report for the Oceans Beyond Piracy project, Kaija Hurlburt assembled some of these and other publicly available data for the first half of 2011 alone to find out that more than sixty pirates had reportedly been killed in the act. Even that figure does not take into account the unreported killings of pirates or those who were lost at sea. She rightly pointed out that the application of "consistent principles of law when dealing with both perpetrators and victims of criminal acts,"[86] requires that all piracy-related injuries and fatalities be accounted for. Doing so can also serve a more effective deterrent function by showing the real dangers of involvement in this criminal act to piracy's foot soldiers and potential recruits.

As it stands, however, the lack of clarity in mandate, operational uniformity, transparency and accountability of the unilateral, coalition and private counter-piracy forces that are operating in Somali waters precludes the possibility of establishing the exact number of such incidents. As Hurlburt puts it, there is no "official reporting on the numbers of Somalis killed by navy and coast guard personnel or by armed private security" in spite of military forces being required to report them.[87] Accidental deaths or injuries of Somali fishermen on the high seas as well as disappearances of pirates (that do not involve action of third parties) cannot be identified and isolated. As a result, Somalis are likely to relegate every disappearance in the high seas to the actions of the antipiracy forces or IUU fishers. With little to no communication between these forces and the Somalis on shore, a few cases among an oral society are enough to create an atmosphere whereby the exceptions – if these are in fact exceptions – become the rule in the eyes of the local people, leaving many artisanal fishermen too fearful to fish in the relatively richer fishing grounds within Somalia's waters.

Another inhumane penalty meted out to suspected pirates captured at sea is abandonment without any supplies to remain at sea for any amount of time nor the equipment needed to return to shore. In May 2010, for example, the Russian flotilla in the region captured ten suspected Somali pirates and set them adrift in a raft without supplies or navigation; they are

wikileaks.org/gifiles/docs/13/1359287_s3-indonesia-somalia-indonesian-army-kills-4-pirates-after.html.

    It is unknown if the Spanish commando raid in mid-November 2009 against the pirates who captured Alakrana resulted in any fatalities besides the capture of two pirates who were sailing away upon the payment of the ransom of over USD 3 million. "Somali Pirates Free Spanish Boat," BBC, 16 November 2009: http://news.bbc.co.uk/2/hi/africa/8364530.stm; "Somali Pirates Sentenced to 439 Years for Hijacking Spanish Fishing Boat," *The Guardian*, 3 May 2011: https://www.theguardian.com/world/2011/may/03/somali-pirates-sentenced-439-years

[86] Hurlburt, *The Human Cost of Somali Piracy*, 26.
[87] Hurlburt, *The Human Cost of Somali Piracy*, 11.

presumed dead.[88] In another extreme and particularly gruesome case purportedly involving the French navy and related by a self-declared pirate recruiter who spoke to one of the survivors, the caught-and-released pirates were handed knives and sent adrift without an engine:

> The French captured the pirates and released them in an engineless skiff and gave them knives to feed off each other. Of the ten onboard that skiff only three survived by eating the other seven. First they finished eating their clothes. Then members of one clan family attacked and ate the others. I met one of the survivors (a Saleeban from Hobyo) and asked him why he ate his friends. He replied: 'If you were in my position, you would have eaten me!'[89]

Although not all pirate accounts are to be trusted, incidences of cannibalism among stranded pirates in the high seas were mentioned several times in different locations during my fieldwork and with unrelated informants.

Somali fishermen have also fallen victim to Western counter-terrorism operations along the Somali coastlines. That was especially the case after August 2011. Following the streak of losses it suffered in south-central Somalia that culminated in its sudden retreat from Mogadishu, Al-Shabaab sought to reposition itself in the northeastern parts of the Somali region. In late 2011, intelligence sources suspected that a group of high-profile foreigners close to Al-Shabaab's top leaders was moving toward Puntland, either to cross over to Yemen or to help reinforce Al-Shabaab in the Northeast (ASNE), i.e. in Puntland. As a result, between January and March 2012, any boat seen moving along the surveilled Somali coastline became a target of Western counter-terrorism operations in the Horn of Africa. According to an intelligence source, half a dozen fishing boats were, in the process, hit with laser weapons that dug holes in the base of the boats, causing them to capsize.

Conclusion

To the extent that predatory ransom piracy off the coast of Somalia posed a threat to the internationally recognized right of passage through the strategic waters around the Horn of Africa, the international community had legitimate concerns about safety and security of maritime navigation in that strategic choke point. Nevertheless, the notion of piracy as an imminent threat stemming from state weakness or poverty exaggerates the capacity of the postcolonial Somali state (or generally of the

---

[88] "Freed Somali Pirates 'Probably Died' – Russian Source," BBC News, 11 May 2010, http://news.bbc.co.uk/2/hi/8675978.stm.
[89] Confidential interview (23 October 2012, Galkayo).

postcolonial African state for that matter); it also ignores the facts that poverty in Somalia predated its collapse and that piracy did not emerge until a decade and a half afterward. That view also conveniently ignores the causal relationship between foreign corporate crimes and violations by states on the one hand, and between legitimate local responses and the inherent potential of their abuse on the other.

Besides the many harmful developments associated with piracy and with the intra-clan tensions and bloody inter-clan conflicts that they triggered, Somali pirates brought about foreign government and private counter-piracy forces that have produced – locally and globally – the most consequential effects. In many instances, international navies and private security personnel did not follow clear and uniform codes of conduct nor have they accounted for their numerous errors, deliberate or accidental.

Many have attributed the gains against piracy to the international navies and foreign private security guards but have paid scant attention to the more dangerous and arduous work undertaken on the ground in piracy-infested coastal villages and towns by local communities and authorities – whatever the imperfections of their initiatives and however slow their effects. The fact that the incidence of pirate attacks – not just cases of successful hijacking – dropped in spite of foreign navies' lack of activities on land and their limited-to-no coordination with actors on land, speaks to the role of community-level mobilization and state-level security measures against piracy.

The welcome reprieve from piracy has brought into a sharper, retrospective focus the root causes of piracy that also raise the specter of its return. While state failure, the breakdown of law and order, rampant unemployment, greed, and wanton criminality contributed to the rise of piracy to epic proportions, IUU fishing remains the principal cause for piracy's emergence, a moral rationalization for its persistence, and a possible spur to its resurgence. To that extent, the divergent approaches of fixing Somalia on land or containing piracy at sea have, by and large, rested on incomplete diagnoses – and in some case complete misdiagnoses – of the root causes of the problems. To varying degrees, both have excluded or underestimated the role that illegal fishing played in the saga of Somali piracy. Treating piracy as a maritime security outgrowth of the turmoil on land, the prevalent discourse of a development–security nexus offered a normative frame to respond to it with military solutions. By doing so, however, the international community practically neglected piracy's maritime root causes and immediate contributory elements, i. e., land-based security and developmental factors. This book has laid bare the inaccurate diagnosis of international counter-piracy responses and the inadequate remedy that they represented.

Conclusion: IUU Fishing Is Back! Will Piracy Return?

Piracy off the coast of Somalia was not a natural extension of the conflict and lawlessness on land that precipitated and followed the collapse of the central government in Mogadishu in 1991. In other words, the gaping absence of the Somali state did not in itself cause piracy. Had that been the case, it would have been difficult – if not impossible – to explain the period between 1991 and 2005 when piracy off the coast of Somalia was no more a problem than was piracy off the west coast of Africa, in the Caribbean or the Strait of Malacca. For some years in the early 1990s, more piracy cases were reported off the coast of southern European than in the Horn of African waters. And the distinct feature of Somali piracy, holding hostages for ransom, is a uniquely post-2005 phenomenon.

The collapse of the central government contributed to the rise of piracy by disabling the country from reining in globally consequential corporate crimes of IUU fishing and waste dumping, and by removing the limited deterrence that even a weak state could exert against local and foreign criminality. These violations, especially IUU fishing, continued with impunity, initially forcing a necessity on those genuinely seeking to rid their waters of resource theft and environmental destruction. The impromptu local initiatives to fend off foreign exploitation in their waters took a life of their own and went woefully awry when foreign vessels readily paid rogue vigilantes rising ransoms and after unscrupulous and greedy local criminals hijacked the fishermen's initial responses for their personal ends.

Ransom piracy subsequently thrived because, on the one hand, foreign vessels kept fishing illegally in Somali waters and their companies continued to pay ransoms when these vessels were hijacked. On the other hand, the criminal enterprise thrived because on land the rampant poverty and joblessness, the vacuum of state authority, and the lapse in traditional authority were sufficient enablers. As piracy escalated off the coast of Somalia, ransoms for the release of hostage sailors and ships jumped from a few hundreds of thousands of US dollars per ship in the mid-2000s (with a few below $100,000) to millions of dollars (with two that exceeded ten million). Industry estimates indicate that, beyond the ransoms, pirates have cost the global economy billions of dollars in related costs. Although a few piracy linchpins and investors have amassed and retained large sums of ill-gotten fortunes, the vast majority of the pirates drained their shares in risky and transient pleasures that exacted a heavy toll on the local communities.

Besides the foreign hostages and their families, Somalis themselves carried the heaviest brunt of the consequent spiraling of piracy. The export-oriented Somali artisanal fishing hit rock bottom as the first casualty of predatory ransom piracy on top of the sustained onslaught from IUU fishers. In the immediate aftermath of the collapse of the Somali fisheries sector, rampant joblessness supplied the piracy industry with a seemingly endless reservoir of manpower, which was later reinforced by unpaid soldiers, young men from the interior, and townspeople who sought a shortcut to wealth. The thriving of piracy also contributed to the dramatic deterioration of security and safety among previously peaceful coastal communities, the erosion of their social values, the skyrocketing of consumer goods, the loss of job-creating investments, further militarization of the region, and the worsening image of Somali society and body politic that had already been tarred due to civil wars, disastrous international interventions, and attendant humanitarian crises (both natural and man-made).

Internationally, there has been rising attention to the global impact of piracy off the coast of Somalia, although this attention is still wanting and skewed. Journalist accounts and editorials sounded alarms about the broader consequences of piracy. Large-scale reports have made useful statistical estimates of the global economic and human costs of piracy in Somalia. International stakeholders have held numerous symposia and ongoing, intermittent, semi-informal multilateral consultations to combat piracy in the Gulf of Aden and the western Indian Ocean region. By foiling pirate attacks, rescuing ships under attack and/or repelling the pirates, the international navies and private security guards have also succeeded in pushing down the rate of successful hijackings. While national and coalition forces have publicized successful operations intermittently, proponents of private security solutions are quick to point out that no ship with armed guards on board has been attacked and successfully boarded, aside from a few embarrassing encounters early on. But with limited communication and coordination with local antipiracy efforts on land, the successes of foreign counter-piracy deployments at sea fail to adequately explain the simultaneous drop in the rate of attacks, which was due to the home-grown Somali initiatives against piracy.

Although many Somalis rejected ransom piracy as soon as large non-fishing vessels were brought to their coastal waters and foreign sailors were held hostage, a few years passed before their efforts bore fruit. Locally, several coastal communities rejected ransom piracy on moral, religious, economic and security grounds. Led by religious scholars, titled traditional elders, and elected office holders (in partnership with local authorities and international organizations), grassroots communities, local NGOs, women's organizations and youth groups launched aggressive awareness-raising campaigns. These campaigns, in collaboration with limited security measures by local administrations, proved effective in persuading many pirates to quit, dissuading others from joining in, and convincing many coastal communities to stop dealing with the remaining pirates. As a result, the rate of pirate attempts declined dramatically.

Not fully understanding – or opting to actively ignore – the fact that citizens led the charge against piracy and succeeded in spite of continued state frailty, many have continued to advocate the restoration of the state as a panacea to all security problems. Nevertheless, given that the crime of piracy is, to a large extent, an outcome of a bigger international crime, the dividends of putting the Humpty Dumpty state back together again would not guarantee an end to piracy unless the resuscitated state also succeeded in reining in the foreign corporate crimes in Somali waters. It is a testament to this that, in spite of Somalis' stand against piracy and of important gains against the pirates on land, continued international neglect of the maritime root causes of piracy has delayed a permanent solution and may be risking its resumption.

Not only is waste dumping still an unresolved international problem that continues to deal devastating blows on weakly governed or ungoverned spaces, but the IUU fishers also continue to receive astronomical subsidies from their respective governments that enable them to continue plundering already vulnerable coastal communities with impunity. The international community has failed to scrutinize these violations or to act decisively against the developmental factors that contributed to the emergence and growth of piracy. While a functional Somali state may not be impossible, its dividends in international security at sea, as on land, will not be forthcoming so long as illegal fishing and waste dumping remain rampant, in reality as well as in the perception of local communities.

Restoring the state can thus help to permanently end the scourge of maritime predation in Somali waters in all its forms only if the restoration succeeds in tackling the issue of IUU fishing that continues to be the bane of coastal communities in general and of artisanal fishermen in particular. Combating these international corporate crimes and assuaging real and perceived local grievances and misperceptions can also contribute toward creating livelihood opportunities and alleviating poverty, with the potential trickling up of security and political returns. Unfortunately, such a prospect is mired by the aggressive return of IUU fishers to the traditional preserve of Somali artisanal fishermen following the decline of piracy.

In the absence of the state, the rise of piracy served as a limited deterrent against illegal fishing in Somali waters; that fishing likely only withdrew farther into the vast ocean. Piracy may have even endangered fishing in the Somali EEZ and international waters, spurring European vessels to seek commensurate protection.[1] Only a few heavily armed vessels or those with local agents on the ground, who guaranteed their safety, continued to fish in Somali territorial waters throughout the piracy years.

Because the naval force that contributed to the suppression of piracy was not local and because foreign navies did not have a mandate against IUU fishing, illegal fishing returned audaciously on the heels of the retreating pirates. Foreign vessels resumed wreaking havoc on coastal communities and compromised the prospects of restoring the livelihoods of those communities. So intense has been the resumption of IUU fishing that regional fisheries authorities in Puntland, Galmudug, and Jubaland joined the federal government in Mogadishu in 2015 in an unprecedented unified position on the matter. They jointly compiled a detailed exposé of the illicit fishing activities of foreign vessels: the nationality and origins of vessels, the methods of their fishing, the time(s) they operated in Somali waters, and the legality or illegality of their operations; these details are documented with supporting evidence (documents, photographs and tracking imagery from the Automatic Identification System of trespassing vessels).[2]

Due to widespread corruption and a lack of capacity, only in a few cases have regional or federal Somali authorities managed to apprehend illegal foreign vessels in the act. In May 2013, PMPF apprehended several Iranian vessels with a total of seventy-eight sailors while the ships were illegally fishing in Somali waters.[3] In April 2015, the PMPF gave chase to one such

[1] "EU Fishermen Seek More Protection from Somali Pirates," *AFP*, 22 April 2009.
[2] Somalia, "Report on Presumed IUU Fishing Activities in the EEZ of Somalia," 27 April 2015: http://www.iotc.org/documents/report-presumed-iuu-fishing-activities-eez-somalia. In February 2018, all the autonomous states and the federal government reached a new agreement on their respective rights to issue fishing licenses. See "Somalia Leaders Reach Deal on Fishing and 2020 Polls," *Garowe Online*, 11 February 2018: https://www.garoweonline.com/en/news/somalia/somalia-leaders-reach-deal-on-fishing-and-2020-polls.
[3] "Somalia: Iranians Convicted of Illegal Fishing in Puntland State Waters," 19 May 2013. Reproduced at: https://neptunep2pgroup.com/somalia-iranians-convicted-of-illegal-fishing-in-puntland-state-waters/.

Iranian vessel, exchanging fire with its guards until the ship faced technical difficulties and the PMPF rescued those on board. The thirteen Iranian sailors, like those before them, were sent to prison in Bosaso and released upon the payment of a fine meted out by the court. Around the same time a similar arrest was made of another Iranian vessel off the coast of Hafun. The foreign sailors were released upon the payment of a fine that totaled USD 27,000, which was paid by intermediaries of the local agents. But generally nothing happens to the Somali guards on board because their membership in the local community guarantees their safety.

According to the local traditional and commercial fishermen, the return of so many foreign fishing ships to their waters has made the post-piracy period no different from the free rein that illegal fishers enjoyed before the explosion of ransom piracy in 2005. Because of such intensification of illegal fishing after piracy, the collusion of powerful local actors, and the alleged corruption of Somali officials, there are palpable signs that former pirates as well as would-be pirates may be lying in wait until the navies leave. Whereas the Somali state and regional authorities are still too weak to exert effective control, the Yemeni turmoil may not augur well for the continued safety of navigation in and through the waters that had been affected by Somali piracy.

A number of factors contribute to open popular support for the likely re-emergence of piracy. To begin with, rightly or wrongly, the public feels let down by the international community. Counting on other countries to assist in subduing IUU fishing, many Somali coastal communities openly mobilized against piracy, cajoling some pirates into renouncing that criminal enterprise and chasing away those who resisted. After piracy was nearly completely ended in 2012, however, IUU fishers resumed plundering Somali waters against the expectations of local communities that the world would now step up to rein in illegal foreign fishing operations. But as the international navies are tied by their national or coalition mandates and the national and international policy makers fail to make the protection of Somali resources and environment their concern, many Somalis feel betrayed and wish for pirates to return.[4] The former

---

[4] A year after operation ATALANTA went into effect, the European Union amended ATALANTA's mandate and vaguely alluded to ATALANTA contributing toward "the monitoring of fishing activities off the coast of Somalia." Council Decision No. 2009/907/ CFSP of 8 December 2009 Amending Joint Action 2008/851/CFSP on a European Union Military Operation to Contribute to the Deterrence, Prevention and Repression of Acts of Piracy and Armed Robbery off the Somali Coast, 2009 O.J. (L 322/2): http://eur-lex .europa.eu/LexUriServ/LexUriServ.do?uri=OJ:L:2009:322:0027:0027:EN:PDF.

Nevertheless, Thilo Neumann and Tim René Salomon argued that there were practical challenges that would make implementation of that mandate difficult even if it were to directly target IUU fishers in Somali waters. See Neumann and Salomon, "Fishing in

Puntland Director General for Counter-Piracy, Abdirizak Mohamed Dirir, believes that, if pirates returned, they would be considered as coast guards. He angrily added, as have others: "We want the navies to leave and we will face each other – the illegal fishers and us." He said that the people now believe that the foreign navies came to protect illegal fishing.[5] Additionally, the deteriorating economic situation across the country, the drought-induced worsening of poverty and hunger, the continued stranglehold on fisheries and shrinkage of the markets for it, and the prolonged non-payment of soldiers' monthly arrears contribute to an explosive situation.

Conclusion

The toxic mix of environmentally destructive resource theft at sea, lawlessness, unemployment and poverty on land, and the alacrity of resource pirates to pay rising fines have all served to send awry the haphazard defenses of Somali fishermen and to offer fertile ground for those claiming to defend Somali waters. The initial defensive measures escalated into a predatory ransom piracy to the long-term detriment of Somali political, economic, and security interests, and of the country's social and moral fabric. Pirate attacks dramatically declined in 2012 and 2013. The rate of piracy has remained at a record low since its epic explosion in the mid-2000s. That is in large part due to the Somali-owned, land-based, and peaceful as well as coercive counter-piracy initiatives that have gone unrecognized. The success of foreign coalition, national and private navies in foiling pirate attacks and reducing the rate of successful hijackings at sea have supplemented Somali accomplishments in deterring the pirates on land and in reducing the number of pirate missions launched from the coast.

Meanwhile, the root causes of piracy continue to escape serious deliberations among international stakeholders; efforts at combating them have, at best, been minimal. Similarly, the impact of piracy on coastal Somali communities, and of what these communities have done about it so far, are generally missing in the discourse as are the effects of international counter-piracy efforts. This book has tried to fill these important gaps by tracing the root causes of piracy off the coast of Somalia; by examining its dynamics and consequences on the ground; by amplifying the voices of local communities who have borne the heavier brunt of

Troubled Waters: Somalia's Maritime Zones and the Case for Reinterpretation," *Insights* vol. 16, no. 9 (15 March 2012): https://www.asil.org/insights/volume/16/issue/9/fishing-troubled-waters-somalia's-maritime-zones-and-case.
[5] Interview with Abdirizak Mohamed Dirir Duceysene (13 September 2015, Garowe).

foreign and domestic piracies and who took a stand against both of them; and by documenting the factors and initiatives that helped suppress Somali piracy while illegal fishing resumed unchecked. It has also shown that all the developmental factors that contributed to the explosion of piracy remain intact, while the international community continues to treat counter-piracy as a security project under Chapter VII of the UN Charter.

In light of piracy's local and regional destabilizing potential in volatile and geopolitically significant northeast Africa, the international community's security concerns and deployment of international navies may be understandable. But the continued prevalence of all the combustible factors that were at the heart of the emergence and spiraling of piracy render the militarized antipiracy solutions as ill-advised and unsustainable. Domestically, the state is still in tatters, law and order are absent, unemployment runs rampant, and poverty remains as high. Externally, the root causes of piracy – IUU fishing and waste dumping – continue unabated. Meanwhile, the power dynamics and attendant narratives perpetuate the West's erstwhile relations with the Global South and have determined the interactions between the world and a society that is war-ravaged, divided, conflict- and poverty-ridden, and that happens to be Muslim. With Somalia's sovereignty violated and its resources taken up for grabs and plundered by state-backed foreign corporate interests, Somali reactions were deemed criminal, warranting military repression.

Proper recognition and appropriate support of yet-uncelebrated Somali successes in combating piracy are crucial in order to stem the prospects of its future return. Somali coastal communities have made important gains against piracy with limited help from the state and from the outside world. In order to fortify local communities' antipiracy resolve, their gains must be capitalized by ending the repeated violation of their waters (at least of the inshore waters), by supporting them in overcoming its consequences, and by helping them restore a viable fisheries sector and identify and expand other sustainable livelihood alternatives.

Equally important would be the enactment of an international mandate through the United Nations against IUU fishing and waste dumping in Somalia. In November 2011, the UN Security Council passed Resolution 2020 urging states and competent international organizations "to positively consider investigating allegations of illegal fishing and illegal dumping, including of toxic substances, with a view to prosecuting such offences when committed by persons under their jurisdiction."[6] In following

---

[6] UN Security Council Resolution 2020, S/RED/2020 (2011), 22 November 2011, paragraph 24.

Figure C.1. The congested port of Bosaso is the only formal port across Puntland. (Photo by the author.)

through on this call, UN member states should expand the mandate of their navies in the Gulf of Aden and western Indian Ocean regions to include monitoring against waste dumping and IUU fishing. The international community should also assist coastal countries in the region to construct and maintain functioning waste management facilities so that passer-by vessels can dispose of the inevitable vessel-generated refuse responsibly during the course of their journey through the region's waters.

The protection of Somali resources on land and at sea, the rehabilitation of the marine environment, the restoration of livelihoods, and the creation of new sustainable jobs – all of which can progressively help people out of poverty – remain the final decisive steps to permanently ending piracy across the region. Attention needs to be diverted to strategic projects like restoring infrastructure, building roads, refurbishing the existing ports and developing some of the numerous natural harbors to ease pressure on the few functioning ones and to spread the benefits too. Job-creation projects should aim at expanding basic services, opening up and rehabilitating the economy through animal husbandry, processing of animal products, and the rehabilitation of the fishing sector, among other approaches.

Failing that, neither the 'fixing Somalia' nor the 'defeating piracy' approaches would suppress Somali maritime predation over the long term. As the late Mohamed Abshir Waldo put it, "The notorious [Somali] shipping piracy is unlikely to be resolved without simultaneously attending to the fraudulent IUU piracy."[7] In other words, only if the two approaches go hand in hand would it be possible to end the piracy problem off the coast of Somalia in a sustainable way and to address the immediate and long-term deleterious maritime and land-based consequences of both resource and ransom piracies. Anything short of that would only bring about a semblance of normalcy, thinly veiling the ominous systemic violence that will inevitably beget a form of counter-violence.

---

[7] Mohamed Abshir Waldo, "The Two Piracies in Somalia: Why the World Ignores the Other?" *Wardheer News*, 8 January 2009: http://somalitalk.com/2009/april/waldo.html.

Bibliography

Primary Sources: United Nations (UN), European Union (EU), Organization of African Unity/African Union (OAU/AU) and Somali Documents

"Agreement between the European Union and the Republic of Mauritius on the Conditions of Transfer of Suspected Pirates and Associated Seized Property from the European Union-Led Naval Force to the Republic of Mauritius and on the Conditions of Suspected Pirates after Transfer," *Official Journal of the European Union*, L254/3, 30 September 2011: http://eur-lex.europa.eu/resour ce.html?uri=cellar:d437ef50-18ca-4883-b4fd-f043a9be1a86.0009.02/ DOC_2&format=PDF.

Arab League, "Statement by the Council of the League of Arab States at the Permanent Representatives Level at Its Extraordinary Session on the Developments in Somalia," Cairo, 4 December 2008.

"Convention on the Rights of the Child (1989)" available at: http://www.unesco .org/education/pdf/CHILD_E.PDF.

Delegation of the Nogal Region, "Objective Discussions and Views on the Five Papers Prepared by UNOSOM for the Fourth Humanitarian Conference for Somalia in Addis Ababa On 29 November to 1 December 1993," Somalia.

European Union, "Council Decision No. 2009/907/CFSP of 8 December 2009 Amending Joint Action 2008/851/CFSP on a European Union Military Operation to Contribute to the Deterrence, Prevention and Repression of Acts of Piracy and Armed Robbery off the Somali Coast, 2009" *Official Journal of the European Union* L 322/2: http://eur-lex.europa.eu/LexUriServ/L exUriServ.do?uri=OJ:L:2009:322:0027:0027:EN:PDF.

Federal Republic of Somalia, "Proclamation by the President of the Federal Republic of Somalia," 30 June 2014.

Food and Agriculture Organization of the United Nations (FAO), *Fishery Country Profile: The Somali Republic* (January 2005).

Food and Agriculture Organization of the United Nations (FAO), *International Plan of Action to Prevent, Deter and Eliminate Illegal, Unreported and Unregulated Fishing* (2001).

International Court of Justice (ICJ). Case Concerning the Continental Shelf (Libyan Arab Jamahiriya v. Malta). Judgment of 3 June 1985.

International Court of Justice (ICJ). Concerning the Continental Shelf (Tunisia/ Libyan Arab Jamahiriya), Separate Opinion of Judge Jiménez de Aréchaga, 24 February 1982.

International Maritime Organization, "Interim Guidance to Shipowners, Ship Operators, and Shipmasters on the Use of Privately Contracted Armed Security Personnel on Board Ships in the High Risk Area," MSC.1/Circ.1405, 23 May 2011: www.marad.dot.gov/documents/MSC.1-Circ.1405.pdf.

Ministry of Maritime Transport, Ports and Counter Piracy, "Press Release," 2 August 2013: http://radiosahan.org/2013/08/3502/.

Ministry of Planning and International Cooperation (MOPIC), *Puntland Facts and Figures*, 4th ed. (Puntland State of Somalia, 2008).

Organization of African Unity, "Resolutions and Declarations of the Seventeenth Ordinary Session of the Council of Ministers Held in Addis Ababa, Ethiopia from 15 to 19 June 1971," Document CM/Res. 250 (XVII) and "Resolution on the Permanent Sovereignty of African Countries over Their Fishery Resources off the Shores of Africa": www.au.int/en/sites/default/files/decisions/9586-coun cil_en_15_19_june_1971_council_ministers_seventeenth_ordinary_session.pdf.

Presidency of the Somali Democratic Republic, Decree No. 14, "Instrument of Ratification," 9 February 1989.

President of the Supreme Revolutionary Council, Law No. 37 on the Somali Territorial Sea and Ports of 10 September 1972.

Puntland Ministry of Security and DDR, "Press Release: Somalia: Puntland Arrests 53 Al Shabaab and Piracy Suspects," 31 July 2012: http://halgan.net/ halgan/wp-content/uploads/2012/07/Halkaan-ka-eeg-Warsaxaafeedka-ka-soo-baxay-Wasaarada-amniga-Puntlland.pdf.

Report of the Secretary-General on the Protection of Somali Natural Resources and Waters, S/2011/611 (2011) 25 October 2011.

Report of the United Nations Monitoring Group on Somalia and Eritrea Submitted in Accordance with Resolution 1916, S/2011/433 (2010), 18 July 2011.

Report of the United Nations Monitoring Group on Somalia and Eritrea Submitted in Accordance with Resolution 2060, S/2013/413 (2012), 12 July 2013.

Report of the United Nations Monitoring Groups on Somalia and Eritrea Submitted in Accordance with Resolution 2111, S/2014/726 (2013), 15 October 2014.

Report of the United Nations Monitoring Group on Somalia and Eritrea Submitted in Accordance with Resolution 2182, S/2015/801 (2014), 20 October 2015.

Report of the United Nations Monitoring Group on Somalia pursuant to Security Council Resolution 1587, S/2005/625 (2005), 4 October 2005.

Report of the United Nations Monitoring Group on Somalia Submitted in Accordance with Resolution 1630, S/2006/229 (2005), 4 May 2006.

Report of the United Nations Monitoring Group on Somalia, S/2006/913, 22 November 2006.

Report of the United Nations Monitoring Group on Somalia Submitted in Accordance with Resolution 1811, S/2008/769 (2008), 10 December 2008.

Report of the United Nations Monitoring Group on Somalia Submitted in Accordance with Resolution 1853, S/2010/91(2008), 10 March 2010.

Sharci Lr. 6, "*Kuna Saabsan Xeerka Burcad-Badeed*" (Law No. 6, "The Law on Piracy"), 6 November 2010 in the *Official Gazette of the Puntland State of Somalia*, No. 12, 18 December 2010.

Somalia, Federal Ministry of Fisheries and Marine Resources, "Report on Presumed IUU Fishing Activities in the EEZ of Somalia," 27 April 2015: www.iotc.org/documents/report-presumed-iuu-fishing-activities-eez-somalia.

United Nations, "Security Council Authorizes States to Use Land-Based Operations in Somalia, as Part of Fight against Piracy off Coast, Unanimously Adopting 1851 SC/9541," 16 December 2008: www.un.org/pr ess/en/2008/sc9541.doc.htm.

United Nations Environmental Program, "After the Tsunami: Rapid Environmental Assessment," (2005): www.unep.org/tsunami/reports/TSUN AMI_report_complete.pdf.

United Nations Environmental Program, "Basel Convention on the Control of Transboundary Movements of Hazardous Wastes and Their Disposal," 22 March 1989.

United Nations General Assembly, "Interim Report of the Special Rapporteur on the Right to Food," A/67/268, 8 August 2012: www.srfood.org/images/stories/ pdf/officialreports/20121030_fish_en.pdf.

United Nations General Assembly Resolution 1803 (XVII), "Permanent Sovereignty over Natural Resources," 14 December 1962: www.ohchr.org/E N/ProfessionalInterest/Pages/NaturalResources.aspx.

United Nations General Assembly Resolution 2158 (XXI), "Permanent Sovereignty over Natural Resources," 25 November 1966: http://daccess-dd s-ny.un.org/doc/RESOLUTION/GEN/NR0/004/61/IMG/NR000461.pdf? OpenElement.

United Nations, "Convention on the Territorial Sea and the Contiguous Zone," Resolution 1307 (XIII), Article 1 (Geneva) 10 December 1958.

United Nations Security Council Resolution 733 (1992), 23 January 1992.

United Nations Security Council Resolution 1816, S/RES/1816 (2008), 2 June 2008.

United Nations Security Council Resolution 1838, S/RES/1838 (2008), 7 October 2008.

United Nations Security Council Resolution 1846, S/RES/1846 (2008), 2 December 2008.

United Nations Security Council Resolution 1851, S/RES/1851 (2008), 16 December 2008.

United Nations Security Council Resolution 1897, S/RES/1897 (2009), 30 November 2009.

United Nations Security Council Resolution 1918, S/RES/1918 (2010), 27 April 2010.

United Nations Security Council Resolution 1950, S/RES/1950 (2010), 23 November 2010.

United Nations Security Council Resolution 1976, S/RES/1976 (2011), 11 April 2011.

United Nations Security Council Resolution 2020, S/RES/2020 (2011), 22 November 2011.

United Nations Somalia and Eritrea Monitoring Group (SEMG) Report, 9 February 2011.

United Nations, United Nations Convention on the Law of the Sea, 10 December 1982.

United States Navy and Marine Corps Public Health Center, "Naples Public Health Evaluation, Volume III: Public Health Summary," May 2011.

Primary Sources: Interviews, Consultations and Focus Group Meetings

Confidential conversations with Puntland fisheries official (February 2012, Bosaso).

Confidential Interview (August 2011, Nairobi).

Confidential Interview (August 2015, Galkayo).

Confidential Interview (August 2015, Galkayo).

Confidential Interview (February 2012, Bosaso).

Confidential Interview (February 2012, Bosaso).

Confidential Interview (February 2012, Bosaso).

Confidential Interview (February 2012, Bosaso).

Confidential Interview (February 2012, Eyl).

Confidential Interview (February 2012, Eyl).

Confidential Interview (February 2012, Eyl).

Confidential Interview (February 2012, Eyl).

Confidential Interview (February 2012, Eyl).

Confidential Interview (February 2012, Eyl).

Confidential Interview (February 2012, Galkayo).

Confidential Interview (February 2012, Galkayo).

Confidential Interview (February 2012, Galkayo).

Confidential Interview (February 2012, Galkayo).

Confidential Interview (February 2012, Galkayo).

Confidential Interview (February 2012, Garowe).

Confidential Interview (February 2012, Garowe).

Confidential Interview (February 2012, Garowe).

Confidential Interview (February 2012, Garowe).

Confidential Interview (February 2012, Garowe).

Confidential Interview (February 2012, Garowe).

Confidential Interview (February 2012, Garowe).

Confidential Interview (February 2012, Garowe).

Confidential Interview (January 2012, Garowe).

Confidential interview (July 2011, Germany).

Confidential Interview (November 2012, Garowe).

Confidential Interview (November 2012, Garowe).

Confidential Interview (November 2012, Garowe).

Confidential Interview (November 2012, Garowe).

Confidential Interview (November 2012, Garowe).

Confidential Interview (October 2012, Galkayo).
Confidential Interview (October 2012, Galkayo).
Confidential Interview (October 2012, Galkayo).
Confidential Interview (October 2012, Galkayo).
Confidential Interview (October 2012, Galkayo).
Confidential Interview with a Government Official with Intelligence and Fishing Knowledge (February 2012, Bosaso).
Confidential Interview with a Knowledgeable Government Official (August 2015, Galkayo).
Confidential interviews (March 2017, Garowe).
Confidential Interviews (October 2012, Galkayo).
Confidential Interviews (October 2012, Galkayo).
Confidential Interviews (Summer 2014, Garowe).
Confidential Interviews (Summer 2014, Garowe).
Consultations with John Steed (March–April 2017, Nairobi).
Conversations with Abdiwahid Mohamed Hersi "Jo'ar" (14 February 2012, Bosaso).
Conversation with Ali Farah Ali (between 2012 and 2017, Garowe).
Conversations with Burhaan Daahir (13 November 2012, Garowe).
Conversations with Former Deputy Minister of Interior of Puntland Ali Yusu Ali "Hoosh" (31 January 2012, Garowe).
Conversations with Naeem Sarfraz (25–27 July 2012, Halifax, Nova Scotia).
Focus Group Meeting with Knowledgeable Elders in Galkayo (26 February 2012).
Focus Group Meeting with Residents of Eyl (5 September 2015).
Focus Group Meeting with Residents of Eyl (6 September 2015).
Interview with a Somali Woman Activist (6 November 2012, Garowe).
Interview with Abdirahman Jama Kulmiye (11 September 2015, Galkayo).
Interview with Abdirahman Mohamed Farole (14 August and 12 September 2015, Garowe).
Interview with Abdirizak Mohamed Dirir Duceysene, former head of Puntland's Counter Piracy Directorate (4 February 2012 and 13 September 2015, Garowe).
Interview with Abdiweli Mohamed Ali "Gas" (21 October 2012, Galkayo).
Interview with Abshir Abdullahi Abdule "Boyah" (8 and 15 June 2014, Garowe).
Interview with AGfish Company (27 February 2012, Galkayo).
Interview with Al-Shaab33 Fishing Company (19 February 2012, Bosaso),
Interview with Andrew Mwangura (8 January 2012, Mombasa, Kenya).
Interview with Asha Abdulkarim Hersi (24 February 2012, Eyl).
Interviews with Brig. Gen. Abdirizak Sheikh Osman "Ali Baadiyow" (February and October 2012, Galkayo).
Interview with Colonel Abdirizak Ahmed "Gantal" (26 March 2017, Garowe).
Interview with East African Fishing Company (5 February 2012, Garowe).
Interview with former prime minister of the Transitional Federal Government, Abdiweli Mohamed Ali (21 October 2012, Galkayo).
Interview with Head of Puntland's Counter Piracy Directorate, Abdirizaq "Duceysene" Mohamed Dirir (4 February 2012, Garowe).

Interview with Lt. Col. Abdirizak Ismail Hassan (26 and 27 February 2012, Galkayo).

Interview with Mayor of Bargal, Abubakar Ahmed Yusuf (28 August 2015, Galkayo).

Interview with Mayor of Eyl, Musa Osman Yusuf (24 February 2012, Eyl).

Interview with Mayor of Bandar Bayla, Saed Adan Ali (11 February 2012, Garowe).

Interview with Mohamed Abdirahman "Farole" (12 June 2014, Garowe).

Interview with Mohamed Ali Yusuf "Gagab" (11 September 2015, Galkayo).

Interview with Mohamed Daylaaf (8 August 2011, Nairobi, Kenya).

Interview with Mohamud Abdulkadir "John" (27 February 2012, Galkayo).

Interview with One of Abdullahi Yusuf's Former Bodyguards (28 October 2012, Galkayo).

Interview with PMPF Commander, Admiral Abdirizak Dirie Farah (13 August 2015, Garowe).

Interview with Puntland's Attorney General Mohamed Hassan (12 February 2012, Garowe).

Interview with Shire Haji Farah (28 March 2017, Garowe).

Interview with Two Former Pirates Serving Time in the Bosaso Prison (20 February 2012, Bosaso).

Interview with Two Former Pirates Serving Time in the Bosaso Prison (5 June 2014, Bosaso, Puntland).

Interviews with Two Widows (22 February 2012, Bedey, Eyl).

Personal communication with John Steed (February 2018).

Personal conversations with John Steed and Abdirizak Mohamed Dirir (January–March 2017).

Personal conversations with Somali intelligence and security sources (February and October 2012 and August 2015, Galkayo).

Personal conversations with Stig Hansen (25–27 May 2011, Hamburg).

Secondary/Media Sources: News Reports and Analyses (no author listed)

"11 Indian Sailors on Small Boat Hijacked off Somali Coast," *Arab News*, 3 April 2017: http://www.arabnews.com/node/1078481/world.

"Afweyne Big Mouth and the Somali Pirates," CCTV Faces of Africa, 2014.

"Aid Workers Kidnapped from Kenya's Dadaab Camp near Somalia," BBC, 29 June 2012: www.bbc.co.uk/news/world-africa-18644745.

"As Deadline Approaches, Pak to Raise Money for MV *Albedo* Crew's Release," NDTV, 14 April 2012 : www.ndtv.com/world-news/as-deadline-approaches-pak-to-raise-money-for-mv-albedo-crews-release-476663.

"At Least 11 Dead as Ship Held by Pirates Sinks off Somalia," Reuters, 8 July 2013: http://uk.reuters.com/article/uk-somalia-pirate-ship-idUKBRE9670QU20130708.

"Auditor-General's Life at Risk Following Investigations into Illegal Fishing," Somali Agenda 21, January 2015: https://somaliagenda.com/auditor-generals-life-at-risk-following-investigations-into-illegal-fishing/.

"Brits Arrested in Somalia with '£2.2 Million Ransom for Pirates,'" *The Telegraph*, May 26, 2011: www.telegraph.co.uk/news/worldnews/piracy/8539 542/Brits-arrested-in-Somalia-with-2.2-million-ransom-for-pirates.html.

"China Says Starts Construction of Djibouti Military Base," Reuters, 25 February 2016: www.reuters.com/article/china-djibouti-idUSL3N1643RN.

"Crew of FV *Naham 3* Released by Pirates after Over 4 1/2 Years in Captivity," Oceans Beyond Piracy, 22 October 2016: http://oceansbeyondpiracy.org/som ali-pirates-release-crew-fv-naham-3.

"Danish Family Yacht Captured by Pirates," YachtPals, 1 March 2011: http:// yachtpals.com/pirates-dutch-yacht-9206.

"The Devil and the Deep Blue Sea: Four Thai Fishermen Watched Their Friends Die and Suffered Brutal Assaults during Five Years of Captivity at the Hands of Somali Pirates," *Bangkok Post*, 22 March 2015: www.bangkokpost.com/print/ 503918/.

"Dutch Marines Abseil on to a Hijacked Cargo Vessel to Rescue Its Crew and Arrest 10 Somali Pirates," *Daily Mail*, 7 April 2010: www.dailymail.co.uk/ne ws/article-1263960/Dutch-marines-abseil-deck-ship-MV-Taipan-freeing-cre w-Somali-pirates.html.

"EU Fishermen Seek More Protection from Somali Pirates," *AFP*, 22 April 2009, reproduced at: www.capitalfm.co.ke/business/2009/04/eu-fishermen-seek-pro tection-from-pirates/.

"EU Naval Force Helicopter Overflies MV *Albedo* and FV *Naham 3*," European Union Naval Force Somalia – Operation Atalanta 18 July 2013: http://eunavfor .eu/update-eu-naval-force-helicopter-overflies-mv-albedo-and-fv-naham-3/.

"Exclusive: High-Level Corruption in Somalia Facilitates Illegal Fishing," Somali Agenda, 2 April 2015: https://somaliagenda.com/illegal-fishing/.

"Fishermen Freed," Maritime Security Review, 16 March 2011: www.marsecre view.com/2011/03/fishermen-freed/.

"Fishing Vessel Attacked by Naval Forces: Two Crew Members Killed in Attack," Somalia Report, 26 March 2012: http://piracyreport.com/index.php/ post/3152/Fishing_Vessel_Attacked_by_Naval_Forces.

"Freed Somali Pirates 'Probably Died' – Russian Source," BBC News, 11 May 2010: http://news.bbc.co.uk/2/hi/8675978.stm.

"German-Owned Ship Paid 1.1. Mln USD Ransom to Somali Pirates," *Xinhua*, 12 September 2008, reproduced at: www.somalinet.com/forums/viewtopic.p hp?t=184311.

"Hijacked Oil Tanker Nears Somalia," BBC, 18 November 2008: http://news.b bc.co.uk/2/hi/africa/7734733.stm.

Italian Ministry of Foreign Affairs, "Press Release: Release of Italian Ship the *Enrico Ievoli*," 23 April 2012: www.esteri.it/mae/en/sala_stampa/archivionoti zie/comunicati/2012/04/20120423_ievoli.html.

"Marine Insurers Re-Draw High Risk Area in the Indian Ocean," Mint, 16 December, 2015: .

"MT *Enrico Ievoli* Anchors Off Dhinooda," *SomaliaReport*, 31 December 2011: http://piracyreport.com/index.php/post/2424/MT_Enrico_Ievoli_Anchors_Off_ Dhinooda.

"MV *Albedo* Sinks after Nearly 3 Years in Captivity," MS Risk, 12 July 2013: www.msrisk.com/somalia/mv-albedo-sinks-after-nearly-3-years-in-captivity/.

"MV *Rim* Abandoned," Maritime Accident, 4 June 2010: http://maritimeacci dent.org/tags/mv-rim/.

"NATO Ends Anti-Piracy Mission in Indian Ocean," *Voice of America*, 24 November 2016: www.voanews.com/a/nato-ends-anti-piracy-mission-in-i ndian-ocean/3609724.html.

"Navy, Coast Guard Destroy Somali Pirate Vessel," *Deccan Herald*, 29 January 2011, www.deccanherald.com/content/133143/navy-coast-guard-destroy-somali.html.

"No Somali Pirate Hijacking in Nearly a Year, Says UN," *The Guardian*, 3 May 2013: www.theguardian.com/world/2013/may/03/somali-pirate-hijacking.

"Pakistani Crew Held by Somali Pirates Reaches Home," *Dawn*, 2 August 2012: www.dawn.com/news/739203/pakistan-crew-held-by-somali-pirates-reaches-home.

"Pictured All Smiles on Their Yachting Holiday, the Family of Five Somali Pirates Are Now Threatening to Kill," *Daily Mail*, 2 March 2011: www.daily mail.co.uk/news/article-1361691/Somali-pirates-threaten-kill-family-5-pic tured-yachting-holiday.html.

"Pirate Will Free Family if He Can Marry Girl, 13" *National Post*, 30 March 2011: news.nationalpost.com/news/pirate-will-free-family-if-he-can-marry-girl-13.

"Pirates Attack Oil Tanker near Bab al-Mandab," *Al-Arabiya*, 27 October 2016: http://english.alarabiya.net/en/News/middle-east/2016/10/27/Pirates-attack-oi l-tanker-near-Bab-al-Mandab.html.

"Pirates Hijack Greek-Owned Tanker off Oman," Reuters, 11 May 2012: www .reuters.com/article/us-somalia-piracy-idUSBRE84A0B820120511.

"Pirates Hijack Italian Tanker with 18 on Board off Oman," *The Telegraph*, 27 December 2011: www.telegraph.co.uk/news/worldnews/piracy/8979120/P irates-hijack-Italian-tanker-with-18-on-board-off-Oman.html.

"Pirates vs the People: Somali Hijackers Turn against Civilians," SomaliaReport, 23 December 2011: www.piracyreport.com/index.php/post/2384/ Pirates_vs_The_People.

"Product Tanker *Aris 13* Hijacked by Somali Pirates in Gulf of Aden," *Maritime Herald*, 14 March 2017: http://www.maritimeherald.com/2017/tanker-aris-13-hijacked-by-somali-pirates-in-gulf-of-aden/.

Royal Thai Consulate-General, "Consul-General of Thailand to Mumbai Visits the Original Crews of Vessel *Prantalay 14*," 9 February 2011: www.thaiem bassy.org/mumbai/th/news/443/18413-กงสุลใหญ่-ณ-เมืองมุมไบ เยี่ยม ลูก เรือ ประมงพรานทะเล-1.html.

"The Saga of the MV *Iceberg*," *Neptune Maritime Security*, 27 June 2012.

"Seychelles and Mauritius Sign Pirates Transfer Agreement," Eturbonews, 21 July 2011: www.eturbonews.com/24134/seychelles-and-mauritius-sign-pir ates-transfer-agreement.

"Shipowners Turn to AK-47s to Halt $2.4 Billion of Piracy Off Africa, India," *Bloomberg*, 17 May 2011: www.bloomberg.com/news/2011–05-17/armed-gua rds-fighting-somali-pirates-to-rise-trade-group-says.html.

"Somali Pirate 'Big Mouth' Arrested in Belgium," *Al-Jazeera*, 14 October 2013: www.aljazeera.com/news/africa/2013/10/somali-pirate-big-mouth-arrested-be lgium-2013101416231617270.html.

"Somali Pirates Free Greek-Owned Bulk Carrier," Reuters, 11 December 2010: http://af.reuters.com/article/energyOilNews/idAFLDE6BA09D20101211.

"Somali Pirates Free Japan Tanker," BBC News, 12 December 2007: http://ne ws.bbc.co.uk/2/hi/africa/7139897.stm.

"Somali Pirates Free Spanish Boat," BBC, 16 November 2009: http://news.bbc .co.uk/2/hi/africa/8364530.stm.

"Somali Pirates Free Thai fishermen Held for Four Years," BBC News, 27 February 2015: www.bbc.com/news/world-asia-31664266.

"Somali Pirates Release Danish Hostages," *The Guardian*, 7 September 2011: www.theguardian.com/world/2011/sep/07/somali-pirates-release-danish-hostages.

"Somali Pirates Release Fishermen Held for Five Years," *Al-Jazeera*, 27 February 2015, www.aljazeera.com/news/2015/02/somali-pirates-release-fi shermen-held-years-150227094729606.html.

"Somali Pirates Sentenced to 439 Years for Hijacking Spanish Fishing Boat," *The Guardian*, 3 May 2011: www.theguardian.com/world/2011/may/03/somali-pir ates-sentenced-439-years.

"Somali Tsunami Victim Toll Rises," BBC, 5 January 2005: http://news.bbc.co .uk/2/hi/africa/4147097.stm.

"Somalia: Iranians Convicted of Illegal Fishing in Puntland State Waters," Garowe Online, 19 May 2013. Reproduced at: https://neptunep2pgroup.co m/somalia-iranians-convicted-of-illegal-fishing-in-puntland-state-waters/.

"Somalia Leaders Reach Deal on Fishing and 2020 Polls" *Garowe Online*, 11 February 2018: www.garoweonline.com/en/news/somalia/somalia-leaders-reach-deal-on-fishing-and-2020-polls.

"Somalia Parliament Rejects Anti-Piracy Legislation," Jurist, 19 January 2011: http://jurist.org/paperchase/2011/01/somalia-parliament-rejects-anti-piracy-le gislation.php.

"Somalia: Parliamentarians Accuse Foreign Warships of Supporting Pirates," *AllAfrica*, 19 January 2011: http://allafrica.com/stories/201101190499 .html.

"Somalia Piracy Began in Response to Illegal Fishing and Toxic Dumping by Western Ships off Somali Coast," Democracy Now: www.democracynow.org/ 2009/4/14/analysis_somalia_piracy_began_in_response.

"Somalia: Pirates Attack UN Aid Ship, Prompting Call for Action," UN News, 20 May 2007: www.un.org/apps/news/story.asp?NewsID=22609&Cr=Somali a&Cr1#.UTDXW6X3A_M.

"Somalia: Pirates Seize Fishing Ship off the Coast of Puntland," *Garowe Online*, 24 March 2017: http://www.garoweonline.com/en/news/puntland/somalia-pir ates-seize-fishing-ship-off-the-coast-of-puntland.

"Somalia: Puntland Captures North Korean Flagged Vessel Dumping Waste," Garowe Online, 18 November 2012: www.somalinet.com/forums/viewtopic.p hp?t=317824.

"Somalia: Puntland Forces Pursue Aid Worker Kidnappers Linked to Al Shabaab," Garowe Online, 12 July 2012: https://allafrica.com/stories/201207 130007.html.

"Somalia: Puntland Leader Speaks out on Illegal Fishing, Calls It 'a National Disaster,'" *Garowe Online*, 2 June 2013.

"Somalia: UN mission to Puntland on Toxic Waste in the Coastal Areas of Somalia," Relief Web. 7 October 2005: http://reliefweb.int/node/186918.

"Special Report: As Pirate Attacks Grow, Shipowners Take Arms," Reuters, 3 May 2011.

"SSDF Group Seizes Two Taiwan Fishing Boats," *AFP*, 6 April 1992.

"TNI: Four Pirates Killed in Gun Battle," *The Jakarta Post*, 2 May 2011: www .thejakartapost.com/news/2011/05/02/tni-four-pirates-killed-gun-battle.html.

"UN Envoy Decries Illegal Fishing, Waste Dumping off Somalia," Hiiraan Online, 25 July 2008: www.hiiraan.com/news4/2008/July/7409/un_envoy_de cries_illegal_fishing_waste_dumping_off_somalia.aspx.

"Verdict in Somali Hijacking Case: Court Rules in Germany's First Modern-Day Piracy Trial," *Spiegel Online*, 19 October 2012: www.spiegel.de/interna tional/germany/hamburg-court-hands-down-somali-pirate-sentences-a-862350 .html.

"Weekly Piracy Report: Thirteen Pirates Killed by US, Drama of Seized Ransom in Mogadishu," SomaliaReport, 30 June 2011: www.piracyreport.com/index .php/post/892/Weekly_Piracy_Report.

"Xiang Hua Men Freed by Iranian Naval Commandos. High Profile Pirate Leader Garaad Captured in the Operation," SomaliaReport, 6 April 2012: ht tp://piracyreport.com/index.php/post/3219/XIANG_HUA_MEN_Freed_By_ Iranian_Naval_Commandos.

"Yacht Tanit Attacked by Pirates – Sailing Crew Taken Hostage," YachtPals, 7 April 2009: http://yachtpals.com/pirates-yacht-4130.

Secondary Sources: Media, News Reports and Analyses (by author)

Abdi, Ahmed and Robert Young Pelton. "The Negotiators: The Business Side of Pirate Ransoms." *SomaliaReport*, 03 May 2012: http://piracyreport.com/index .php/post/3308/The_Negotiators.

Abdi, Rashid (Interview), "The Price of Piracy," CNN, 9 May 2011.

Ahmed, Abdalle. "Somalia: Puntland Bans Illegal Fishing, Warns Foreign Vessels," 11 March 2014: http://www.raxanreeb.com/2014/03/somalia-punt land-bans-illegal-fishing-warns-foreign-vessels/.

Aronson, Geoffrey. "China to Open Its First Naval Base in Africa." *Al-Jazeera*, 22 December 2015: www.aljazeera.com/indepth/opinion/2015/12/china-open s-naval-base-africa-151222141545988.html.

Bahadur, Jay. "Pirates, Inc." *The Financial Times*, 23 June 2010: www.ft.com/co ntent/e5f60614-7d23-11df-8845-00144feabdc0.

Bahadur, Jay. "The Pirate King of Somalia." *The Globe and Mail*, 26 April 2009: www.theglobeandmail.com/news/world/the-pirate-king-of-somalia/arti cle4256243/.

Beerdhige, Mohamed. "Pirates Hijack Vessel despite Gov Security Team: Iranian Dhow Fishing Legally with Support of Puntland Government." *SomaliaReport*, 25 January 2012: http://piracyreport.com/index.php/post/2618/ Pirates_Hijack_Vessel_Despite_Gov_Security_Team.

Blair, Edmund. "China to Start Work Soon on Naval Base in Djibouti." *Reuters*, 2 February 2016: http://uk.reuters.com/article/uk-djibouti-china-idUKKCN0VB1Z6.

Bridger, James M. "The Rise and Fall of Somalia's Pirate King." *Foreign Policy*, 17 November 2013.

Burnett, John S. "The Next 9/11 Could Happen at Sea," *The New York Times*, 22 February 2005.

Chalk, Peter. "Somali Piracy [Is] All about Economics." *USA Today*, 10 October 2013: www.usatoday.com/story/opinion/2013/10/10/captain-phil lips-somali-pirates-column/2962329/.

Charter, David. "$3M Ransom Paid to Free Danish Yachting Family Held Hostage for Six Months by Somali Pirates." *The Australian*, 8 September 2011: www.theaustralian.com.au/news/world/m-ransom-paid-to-free-danish-yacht ing-family-held-hostage-for-six-months-by-somali-pirates/news-story/ 39dd68022210eb30f87a7a1efae4a1e6.

Cretu, Virgil (Interview), Associated Press; video clip available at: https://www .youtube.com/watch?v=6aQ9rk5oZCg&t=21s.

Crilly, Rob. "Somali Pirates on 'Benzene Bomb' Threaten to Kill Hostages." *The Times*, 12 December 2007: www.thetimes.co.uk/tto/news/world/africa/arti cle2593380.ece.

Doland, Angela. "French Troops Attack Somali Pirates after 30 Hostages Freed." *The Washington Post*, 12 April 2008: www.washingtonpost.com/wp-d yn/content/article/2008/04/11/AR2008041103537.html.

European Union Naval Force (EU NAVFOR): Somalia, "Crew of the Hijacked MV *RIM* Retake Control from Pirates, EU NAVFOR Warship SPS *Victoria* Gives Medical Support," 2 June 2010: http://eunavfor.eu/crew-of-the-hijacke d-mv-rim-retake-control-from-pirates-eu-navfor-warship-sps-victoria-gives-m edical-support/.

European Union Naval Force (EU NAVFOR): Somalia, "European Union Signs Prosecution Agreement with Kenya," 6 March 2009: http://eunavfor.eu/eur opean-union-signs-prosecution-agreement-with-kenya/.

Feo, Gianluca di and Claudio Pappaianni. "Bevi Napoli e Poi Muori, l'Inchiesta-choc degli USA." *l'Espresso*, 13 November 2013: http://espresso.repubblica.it/ inchieste/2013/11/13/news/bevi-napoli-e-poi-muori-1.141086?refresh_ce.

Freeman, Colin. "Abandoned at Sea – The Forgotten Hostages of the Somali Pirates." *The Telegraph*, 29 August 2012: www.telegraph.co.uk/news/world news/africaandindianocean/somalia/9507047/Abandoned-at-sea-the-forgot ten-hostages-of-the-Somali-pirates.html.

Freeman, Colin. "Why a Retired British Army Colonel Has Become the Last Hope for Somalia's Forgotten Hostages." *The Telegraph*, 26 March 2015: www .telegraph.co.uk/news/worldnews/africaandindianocean/somalia/11495268/W hy-a-retired-British-army-colonel-has-become-the-last-hope-for-Somalias-for gotten-hostages.html.

Freeman, Colin and Mike Pflanz. "Somali Pirates Release Crew after Nearly Four Years in Captivity." *The Telegraph*, 7 June 2014: www.telegraph.co.uk/news/ worldnews/piracy/10883414/Somali-pirates-release-crew-after-nearly-four-ye ars-in-captivity.html.

Gettleman, Jeffrey. "In Somali Civil War, Both Sides Embrace Pirates." *The New York Times*, 1 September 2010: www.nytimes.com/2010/09/02/world/africa/0 2pirates.html.

Gettleman, Jeffrey. "Lessons from the Barbary Pirate Wars." *The New York Times*, 12 April 2009: www.nytimes.com/2009/04/12/weekinreview/12gettleman.html.

Gettleman, Jeffrey. "Q. & A. With a Pirate: 'We Just Want the Money.'" *The New York Times*, 30 September 2008: https://thelede.blogs.nytimes.com/2008/09/3 0/q-a-with-a-pirate-we-just-want-the-money/.

Gridneff, Ilya. "Somalia Questions Deal Giving Ex-U.K. Soldiers Fish Rights." *Bloomberg Business*, 23 December 2014: www.bloomberg.com/news/articles/2 014-12-23/somalia-questions-deal-giving-ex-u-k-soldiers-all-fish-rights.

Harding, Andrew. "Postcard from Somali Pirate Capital." *BBC*, 16 June 2009: http://news.bbc.co.uk/2/hi/africa/8103585.stm.

Hassan, Abdisalam Warsameand Awet T. Weldemichael. "Somalia Airspace and Waters' Control Must Be Reclaimed: UN May Owe Millions in Unaccounted For Air Navigation Charges." *African Argument*, 14 June 2012: http://africanar guments.org/2012/06/14/somalia-must-reclaim-control-over-airspace-and-wa ters-as-un-may-owe-somalia-millions-in-unaccounted-for-air-navigation-char ges-by-abdisalam-warsame-hassan-and-awet-t-weldemichael/.

Hickman, Andy. "Somalia Cracks Down on Illegal Fishing," *Al Jazeera*, 24 Sept 2014: https://www.aljazeera.com/news/africa/2014/09/somalia-cracks-down-il legal-fishing-201492320535275716.html.

Hurlburt, Kaija and Boberta Spivak. "The Fishing Sector in Somalia/ Somaliland." *Shuraako*, 9 January 2013: http://shuraako.org/sites/default/files/ documents/The%20Fishing%20Sector%20in%20SomaliaSomaliland.pdf.

International Consortium of Investigative Journalists (ICIJ), "Spain Doles Out Millions in Aid Despite Fishing Company's Record," 2 October 2011: https:// www.huffingtonpost.com/2011/10/02/spain-doles-millions-fishing-compa ny_n_989246.html.

Kelley, Kevin J. "Djibouti Base Could Be Start of US-China Military Rivalry in EA." *The East African*, 28 November 2015: www.theeastafrican.co.ke/news/D jibouti-base-could-be-start-of-US-China-military-rivalry-in-EA/-/2558/29761 20/-/uw6ljx/-/index.html.

Khalif, Abdulkadir. "Somalia: How Illegal Fishing Feeds Somali Piracy." *The East African*, 15 November 2005: https://allafrica.com/stories/200511150675 .html.

Kulmiye, Abdirahman Jama. "Militia vs Trawlers: Who Is the Villain?" *The East African Magazine*, 9 July 2001: www.ecop.info/e-news/e-news-01-07-9.htm.

Lehr, Peter. "A Western Armada Is Not the Way to Sink Somalia's Pirates." *The Guardian*, 18 November 2008: www.theguardian.com/commentisfree/2008/n ov/19/piracy-somalia

MacGuire, Eoghan. "'Resurrection' of Somali Pirate Attacks Feared after Tanker Shootout." NBC News, 20 November 2016: www.nbcnews.com/news/world/ resurrection-somali-pirate-attacks-feared-after-tanker-shootout-n685731.

MacKenzie, Debora. "Toxic Waste Adds to Somalia's Woes." *New Scientist*, 19 September 1992: www.newscientist.com/article/mg13518390.400-toxic-w aste-adds-to-somalias-woes-/.

Majumder, Sanjoy. "Indian Navy Seizes Pirates' Indian Ocean Mothership." BBC News, 6 February 2011: www.bbc.co.uk/news/world-south-asia-12376695.

Mazzetti, Mark and Eric Schmitt. "Private Army Formed to Fight Somali Pirates Leaves Troubled Legacy." *The New York Times*, 4 October 2012: www.nytim es.com/2012/10/05/world/africa/private-army-leaves-troubled-legacy-in-soma lia.html?_r=2&smid=tw-share&.

McBeth, John. "Full Resolve: How Indonesia Took On the Somali Pirates." *The Jakarta Globe*, 30 May 2011: www.thejakartaglobe.com/archive/full-resolve-h ow-indonesia-took-on-the-somali-pirates/.

McCurry, Justin. "Eight Somali Pirates Killed as South Korea Rescues Freighter Crew." *The Guardian*, 21 January 2011: www.guardian.co.uk/world/2011/jan/ 21/south-korea-rescue-somali-pirates.

McMichael, William. "Navy: Helo Fires on Pirate Skiff, Killing 4." *Navy Times*, 18 May 2011, reproduced at: https://blog.usni.org/posts/2011/05/19/now-you re-talking.

Milmo, Cahal. "Dumped in Africa: Britain's Toxic Waste. Children Exposed to Poisonous Material in Defiance of UK Law." *The Independent*, 17 February 2009: www.independent.co.uk/news/world/africa/dumped-in-afr ica-britain8217s-toxic-waste-1624869.html.

Mwangura, Andrew. Seafarers Assistance Programme website: http://www.ecop .info/english/e-sap-net.htm

Narayan, V. "Somali Pirates Wanted $27M for *Prantalay*." *The Times of India*, 9 February 2011: http://timesofindia.indiatimes.com/city/mumbai/Somali-pir ates-wanted-27m-for-Prantalay/articleshow/7455661.cms?referral=PM.

Nuxurkey, Mohamed. "Kenyan Aid Workers Kidnapped near Galkayo." *SomaliaReport*, 11 July 2012: http://piracyreport.com/index.php/post/3509/ Kenyan_Aid_Workers_Kidnapped_Near_Galkayo.

Osler, David. "Svitzer Tug Hijacked off Somali Coast." *Lloydslist*, 4 February 2008: https://lloydslist.maritimeintelligence.informa.com/L L073042/Svitzer-tug-hijacked-off-Somali-coast.

Pala, Christopher. "Billions in Subsidies Prop Up Unsustainable Overfishing." IPS, 8 November 2012: www.ipsnews.net/2012/11/billions-in-subsidies-prop-up-unsustainable-overfishing/.

Pelton, Robert Young. "Terrorists, Pirates or Fishermen? Part Two: Land Based Anti-Piracy." *SomaliaReport*, 20 April 2012: http://piracyreport.com/index.ph p/post/3257/Terrorists_Pirates_or_Fishermen.

Pew Charitable Trusts, "When Crime Pays: How the EU Subsidises Illegal Fishing," 8 March 2011: www.pewtrusts.org/about/news-room/press-releases-and-state ments/2010/03/11/when-crime-pays-how-the-eu-subsidises-illegal-fishing.

Puntland Ministry of Security and DDR, "Press Release: Somalia: Puntland Maritime Police Forces Deploy in Strategic Coastal Towns," 8 June 2012: ht tps://pmpf.files.wordpress.com/2012/06/pr_08june2012_en1.pdf.

Rice, Xan. "Somali Pirates Capture Ukrainian Cargo Ship Loaded with Military Hardware." *The Guardian*, 26 September 2008: www.theguardian.com/world/ 2008/sep/27/3.

Richards, Sue. "Somalia Hostages – Danish Family Free." *Noonsite.com*, 7 September 2011: www.noonsite.com/Members/sue/R2011-09-07-1.

Saul, Jonathan. "Ships More at Risk after First Somali Pirate Attack in Years: Officials." *Reuters*, 8 November 2016: www.reuters.com/article/us-shipping-p iracy-somalia-idUSKBN1331UJ.

Schwartz, Jan. "German Court Convicts 10 Somalis of Piracy." *Reuters*, 19 October 2012: www.reuters.com/article/us-germany-somalia-pirates/ger man-court-convicts-10-somalis-of-piracy-idUSBRE89I0YX20121019.

Scudder, Brian. "Pirate King Turns Law Enforcer." *African Business*, Issue 256 (Jul/Aug 2000), reproduced at: www.thefreelibrary.com/Pirate+king+turns% 3A+law+enforcer.-a063825769.

Shapira, Ian. "Blackwater Founder Erik Prince Goes to War against a Former Business Partner." *Washington Post*, 1 January 2015: www.washingtonpost.co m/local/blackwater-founder-erik-prince-goes-to-war-against-a-former-busi ness-partner/2015/01/01/23385e8a-6f39-11e4-893f-86bd390a3340_story.ht ml?utm_term=.f7a8712056c8.

Shapira, Ian. "Blackwater Founder Erik Prince Prevails in Legal Battle with Ex-Business Partner." *Washington Post*, 8 December 2017: www.washingtonpost .com/local/blackwater-founder-erik-prince-prevails-in-legal-battle-with-ex-busi ness-partner/2017/12/08/e0f3d26a-dbc9-11e7-a841-2066faf731ef_story.html? utm_term=.72ea5487b63b.

Tharoor, Ishaan. "How Somalia's Fishermen Became Pirates." *Time*, 18 April 2009: www.time.com/time/world/article/0,8599,1892376,00.html.

Tsai, Michelle. "Why the Mafia Loves Garbage: Hauling Trash and Organized Crime." *Slate*, 11 January 2008: www.slate.com/articles/news_and_politics/ex plainer/2008/01/why_the_mafia_loves_garbage.html.

Verini, James. "Escape or Die: When Pirates Captured a Cargo Ship, Its Crew Faced One Desperate Choice after Another." *The New Yorker*, 20 April 2015: www.newyorker.com/magazine/2015/04/20/escape-or-die.

Vidal, John. "Toxic 'E-waste' Dumped in Poor Nations, Says United Nations," *The Guardian*, 14 December 2013: www.theguardian.com/global-develop ment/2013/dec/14/toxic-ewaste-illegal-dumping-developing-countries.

Wabala, Dominic. "Ex-UK Soldiers Based in Nairobi Carried Tebbutt Ransom to Adado." *The Star*, 23 March 2012: https://allafrica.com/stories/201203231 364.html.

Waldo, Mohamed Abshir. "The Two Piracies in Somalia: Why the World Ignores the Other?" *Wardheer News*, 8 January 2009: http://somalitalk.com/2009/april/ waldo.html.

Worth, Robert F. "Pirates Seize Saudi Tanker off Kenya," *The New York Times*, 17 November 2008: https://www.nytimes.com/2008/11/18/world/africa/18pir ates.html.

Yamaguchi, Mari. "Seized Crew of Japan Tanker Believed Safe." Associated Press, 11 December 2007: www.washingtonpost.com/wp-dyn/content/article/ 2007/12/11/AR2007121100098.html.

Yardley, Jim. "A Mafia Legacy Taints the Earth in Southern Italy." *The New York Times*, 29 January 2014: www.nytimes.com/2014/01/30/world/europe/beneat h-southern-italy-a-deadly-mob-legacy.html.

Yuen, Laura. "Former Minnesotan Arrested on Suspicion of Assisting Pirate Ringleader," *MPRNews*, 23 October 2013: https://www.mprnews.org/story/2 013/10/23/mohamed-aden-arrested-belgium.

Yusuf, Khalid. "Somalia Government Signs Landmark Coastal Protection Contract," Horseed Media, 30 July 2013: https://horseedmedia.net/2013/07/ 30/somali-government-signs-landmark-coastal-protection-contract/.

Secondary Sources: Industry, Think Tank, NGO and Activist Reports

Ali, Nimo-Ilhan. *Going on Tahriib: The Causes and Consequences of Somali Youth Migration to Europe*. Nairobi: Rift Valley Institute, 2016: www.raxanreeb.com /2014/03/somalia-puntland-bans-illegal-fishing-warns-foreign-vessels/.

Andreone, Gemma. "The Exclusive Economic Zone" in Donald R. Rothwell, Alex G. Oude Elferink, Karen Scott, and Tim Stephens (eds.), *The Oxford Handbook of the Law of the Sea* (Oxford University Press, 2015), 163–164.

Bellish, Jonathan. *The Economic Cost of Somali Piracy 2012*. One Earth Future Foundation Working Paper: http://oceansbeyondpiracy.org/sites/default/files/ attachments/View%20Full%20Report_3.pdf.

Bowden, Anna and Shikha Basnet. *The Economic Cost of Somali Piracy 2011*. One Earth Future Foundation Working Paper: http://oceansbeyondpiracy.org/sites/ default/files/economic_cost_of_piracy_2011.pdf.

Bowden, Anna, Kaija Hurlburt, Eamon Aloyo, Charles Marts and Andrew Lee. *The Economic Cost of Maritime Piracy*, 2010. One Earth Future Working Paper, December 2010: http://oceansbeyondpiracy.org/documents/The_Economic_ Cost_of_Piracy_Full_Report.pdf.

Coffen-Smout, Scott. "Pirates, Warlords and Rogue Fishing Vessels in Somalia's Unruly Seas." 1999: www.chebucto.ns.ca/~ar120/somalia.html.

Drew, Phillip and Rob McLaughlin. *Handbook on the Use of Force for Private Security Companies*. Denver, CO: Oceans Beyond Piracy, 2016.

Environmental Justice Foundation. *Pirates and Profiteers: How Pirates Fishing Fleets are Robbing People and Oceans*. London: Environmental Justice Foundation, 2005.

Fritz, Hermann M. and Jose C. Borrero. "Somalia Field Survey after the December 2004 Indian Ocean Tsunami." *Earthquake Spectra*, Vol. 22, No. S3 (June 2006).

Geopolicity. "The Economics of Piracy: Pirates Ransoms and Livelihoods off the Coast of Somalia." May 2011: http://oceansbeyondpiracy.org/sites/default/file

s/geopolicity_-_the_economics_of_piracy_-_pirates__livelihoods_off_the_ coast_of_somalia.pdf.

Glaser, Sarah M., Paige M. Roberts, Robert H. Mazurek, Kaija J. Hurlburt and Liza Kane-Hartnett. *Securing Somali Fisheries*. Denver, CO: One Earth Future Foundation, 2015.

Greenpeace. The Toxic Ships: The Italian Hub, the Mediterranean Area and Africa. Greenpeace Italy Report, June 2010: www.greenpeace.org/italy/Global/ italy/report/2010/inquinamento/Report-The-toxic-ship.pdf.

High Seas Taskforce. "Closing the Net: Stopping Illegal Fishing on the High Seas. Final report of the Ministerially-led Task Force on IUU Fishing on the High Seas." March 2006: http://www.oecd.org/sd-roundtable/papersandpubli cations/39375316.pdf.

Hurlburt, Kaija. *The Human Cost of Somali Piracy*. One Earth Future Foundation, 2011: http://oceansbeyondpiracy.org/sites/default/files/human_cost_of_soma li_piracy.pdf.

ICC International Maritime Bureau. "Piracy and Armed Robbery against Ships: Annual Report, 1 January–31 December 2005." January 2006 [and all subsequent annual reports].

Indian Ocean Tuna Commission. "IOTC Circular 2014–59." 31 May 2014.

International Consortium of Investigative Journalists (ICIJ). "Spain Doles out Millions in Aid Despite Fishing Company's Record." 2 October 2011: www.huf fingtonpost.com/2011/10/02/spain-doles-millions-fishing-company_n_989246 .html.

Lang, Jack. *Report of the Special Adviser to the Secretary-General on Legal Issues Related to Piracy off the Coast of Somalia*. January 2011.

Maritime London, "Piracy: A Tax for Shipping?" 26 June 2009: www.maritime london.com/london_matters29june09.htm#1.

Maritime Resources Assessment Group Ltd. (MRAG). "Review of Impacts of Illegal, Unreported and Unregulated Fishing on Developing Countries. Final Report." July 2005: http://webarchive.nationalarchives.gov.uk/200904221813 06/http://www.dfid.gov.uk/pubs/files/illegal-fishing-mrag-report.pdf.

Maritime Resources Assessment Group Ltd. (MRAG) and Fisheries Ecosystems Restoration Research, Fisheries Centre, *The Global Extent of Illegal Fishing*. University of British Columbia. April 2008: www.mrag.co.uk/Documents/Ext entGlobalIllegalFishing.pdf.

Puntland Development Research Center (PDRC). *Somali Customary Law and Traditional Economy: Cross Sectional, Pastoral, Frankincense, and Marine Norms*. Garowe, Puntland: PDRC, 2003.

Qayad, Mahdi Gedi. "Assessment Mission to Somalia in Connection with Alleged Dumping of Hazardous Substances." May–June 1997.

Schroeer, Anne, Courtney Sakai, Vanya Vulperhorst and Andrzej Białaś. "The European Union and Fishing Subsidies." September 2011: http://oceana.org/ sites/default/files/reports/EU_Subsidies_Report_FINAL_FINAL-1.pdf.

Shortland, Anja. "Treasure Mapped: Using Satellite Imagery to Track the Developmental Effects of Somalia Piracy." Chatham House Africa Programme Paper: AFP PP 2012/01, 2012.

Somali Maritime Resource and Security Strategy, Fisheries Working Group. "Communiqué of the Somali MRSS Fisheries Working Group." 2–6 April 2014, Beau Vallon, Seychelles: http://oceansbeyondpiracy.org/sites/default/files/attach ments/Apr-6-Somali-Fisheries-Working-Group-Communique.pdf.

UKMTO-ICS. *BMP4: Best Management Practices for Protection against Somalia Based Piracy*. Edinburgh: Witherby Publishing Group Ltd., 2011.

World Bank. *Pirate Trails: Tracking the Illicit Financial Flows from Pirate Activities off the Horn of Africa*. Washington, DC: The World Bank, 2013.

World Bank. "Somalia: From Resilience towards Recovery and Development. A Country Economic Memorandum for Somalia." Report No. 34356-SO, 11 January 2006: http://documents.worldbank.org/curated/en/693021468112 737015/Somalia-From-resilience-towards-recovery-and-development-a-Cou ntry-Economic-Memorandum-for-Somalia.

World Bank. "The Pirates of Somalia: Ending the Threat, Rebuilding a Nation." 2013: http://documents.worldbank.org/curated/en/182671468307148284/Th e-pirates-of-Somalia-ending-the-threat-rebuilding-a-nation.

Yusuf, Abdinasir M. *The Rako Peace Process: Intra-clan Reconciliation Progress*. Report of the Mobile Audio Visual Unit of Puntland Development Research Center, April 2012.

Secondary Sources: Scholarly Papers, Articles, Chapters, Books, and Lectures

Adama, Onyanta and Chidi Nzeadibe (eds). *Dealing with Waste: Resource Recovery and Entrepreneurship in Informal Solid Waste Management in African Cities*. Trenton, NJ: Africa World Press, 2017.

Affi, Ladan and Afyare Elmi. "Avoiding Somalia: What Prevents Onshore Solution to Piracy?" *Global Affairs* 1:3, (2015): 305–314.

Agnew, David J. John Pearce, Ganapathiraju Pramod, Tom Peatman, Reg Watson, John R. Beddington and Tony J. Pitcher, "Estimating the Worldwide Extent of Illegal Fishing," *PLoS ONE* 4(2) (2009): www.plosone .org/article/info:doi/10.1371/journal.pone.0004570.

Al-Qasimi, Sultan Ibn Muhammad. *The Myth of Arab Piracy in the Gulf*. London and Dover, NH: Croom Helm, 1986.

Alpers, Edward A. *East Africa and the Indian Ocean*. Princeton: Markus Wiener, 2009.

Alpers, Edward A. "Piracy and the Indian Ocean," *Journal of African Development* 13 (2011): 15–38.

Alpers, Edward A. *The Indian Ocean in World History*. Oxford and New York: Oxford University Press, 2014.

Antoniotto, Roberto. "The Fishing Settlement at Baraawe: Notes on Cultural Adaption," in Hussein M. Adam (ed.), *Somalia and the World. Proceedings of the International Symposium held in Mogadishu, October 15–21, 1979 Vol. Two*. Mogadishu: Second Haglan Publication: 237–250.

Bahadur, Jay. *Deadly Waters: Inside the Hidden World of Somalia's Pirates*. London: Profile Books, 2011.

Bahadur, Jay. *The Pirates of Somalia: Inside Their Hidden World.* (New York: Pantheon Books, 2011.

Baldacci, Giulio. "The Promontory of Cape Guardafui." *The Journal of the Royal African Society*, Vol. 9, No. 33 (October 1909).

Bateman, Sam. "Maritime Security and Port State Control in the Indian Ocean Region," in Awet T. Weldemichael, Patricia Schneider and Andrew C. Winner (eds.). *Maritime Terrorism and Piracy in the Indian Ocean Region.* London and New York: Routledge, 2015: 82–95.

Bateman, Sam. "Maritime Security Implication of the International Shipping Recession." *The Australian Journal of Maritime and Ocean Affairs*, Vol. 1, No. 4 (December 2009): 109–117.

Bradbury, Mark. *Becoming Somaliland.* London: Progressio, 2008.

Braudel, Fernand. *The Mediterranean and the Mediterranean World in the Age of Philip II, Vol. 2.* New York: Harper & Row, 1972.

Brilmayer, Lea and Natalie Klein. "Land and Sea: Two Sovereignty Regimes in Search of a Common Denominator." *N.Y.U. Journal of International Law and Politics*, Vol. 33, No. 703 (2000/2001): 703–768.

Bryant, Willow, Michael Townsley and Benoit Lecler. "Preventing Maritime Pirate Attacks: A Conjunctive Analysis of the Effectiveness of Ship Protection Measures Recommended by the International Maritime Organisation." *Journal of Transportation Security*, Vo. 7 No. 1 (2014): 69–82.

Bueger, Christian. "Drops in the Bucket? A Review of Onshore Responses to Somali Piracy." *WMU Journal of Maritime Affairs* 11 (2012): 15–31.

Bueger, Christian. "NATO's Fight against Somali Pirates: The End of an Unsung Success Story." *Piracystudies.org.* 21 December 2016: http://piracy-studies.org/natos-fight-against-somali-pirates-the-end-of-an-unsung-success-story/.

Bueger, Christian. "Piracy Studies: Academic Responses to the Return of an Ancient Menace." *Cooperation and Conflict* 49, 3 (2014), 383–406.

Cassanelli, Lee V. "Explaining the Somali Crisis" in *The Struggle for Land in Southern Somalia: The War Behind the War*, Catherine Besteman and Lee V. Cassanelli eds. London: Westview Press, 1996.

Cassanelli, Lee V. *The Shaping of Somali Society: Reconstructing the History of a Pastoral People, 1600–1900.* Philadelphia: University of Pennsylvania Press, 1982.

Casson, Lionel (ed. and trans.). *The Periplus Maris Erythraei.* Princeton University Press, 1989.

Chalk, Peter. "The Evolving Dynamic of Piracy and Armed Robbery at Sea in the Modern Era: Scope, Dimensions, Dangers and Policy Responses." *Maritime Affairs*, Vol. 5 No. 1 (Summer 2009): 1–21.

Chaudhuri, K.N. *Trade and Civilization in the Indian Ocean: An Economic History from the Rise of Islam to 1750.* Cambridge: Cambridge University Press, 1985.

Crenshaw, Martha. "Thoughts on Relating Terrorism to Historical Contexts," in Martha Crenshaw (ed.). *Terrorism in Context.* University Park, PA: The Pennsylvania State University Press, 2007.

Daniels, Christopher L. *Somali Piracy and Terrorism in the Horn of Africa.* Plymouth, UK: Scarecrow Press, 2012.

de Waal, Alex. "A Social Science in Africa Fit for Purpose" (Keynote address, 2015–2016 Next Generation Social Sciences in Africa, Addis Ababa,

Ethiopia): http://nextgen.ssrc.org/fellows/spotlight/towards-a-social-science-i n-africa-fit-for-purpose/.

de Waal, Alex. *The Real Politics of the Horn of Africa: Money, War and the Business of Power.* Cambridge: Polity Press, 2015.

Dua, Jatin. "A Modern-Day Pirate's Port of Call." *Middle East Report* No. 256 (Fall 2010), 20–23.

Dua, Jatin. "A Sea of Trade and a Sea of Fish: Piracy and Protection in the Western Indian Ocean." *Journal of Eastern African Studies* Vol. 7, No. 2 (2013), 353–370.

Dua, Jatin. "After Piracy? Mapping the Means and Ends of Maritime Predation in the Western Indian Ocean." *Journal of Eastern African Studies* Vol. 9, No. 3 (2015), 505–521.

Dua, Jatin and Ken Menkhaus. "The Context of Contemporary Piracy." *Journal of International Criminal Justice* 10 (2012): 749–766.

Durrill, Wayne K. "Atrocious Misery: The African Origins of Famine in Northern Somalia, 1839–1884." *The American Historical Review*, Vol. 91, No. 2 (April 1986): 287–306.

Eichstaedt, Peter H. *Pirate State: Inside Somalia's Terrorism at Sea.* Chicago: Lawrence Hill Books, 2010.

Elmi, Afyare Abdi. *Understanding the Somalia Conflagration: Identities, Political Islam and Peacebuilding.* New York: Pluto Press, 2010.

Elmi, Afyare and Ladan Affi. "Barriers to Developing Anti-Piracy Law in Somalia." Al Jazeera Centre for Studies, November 2014: http://studies.alja zeera.net/en/reports/2014/11/2014112010310522448.htm.

Engels, Jeremy. "Floating Bombs Encircling Our Shores: Post-9/11 Rhetorics of Piracy and Terrorism." *Cultural Studies: Critical Methodologies*, Vol. 7 No. 3, (2007): 326–349.

Fielding, P. J. and B. Q. Mann. "The Somalia Inshore Lobster Resource. A Survey of the Lobster Fishery of the North Eastern Region (Puntland) between Foar and Eyl during November 1998." IUCN Eastern Africa Programme (June 1999).

Finley, Carmel. *All the Fish in the Sea: Maximum Sustainable Yield and the Failure of Fisheries Management.* Chicago: University of Chicago Press, 2011.

Finley, Carmel and Naomi Oreskes. "Food for Thought. Maximum Sustained Yield: A Policy Disguised as Science." *ICES Journal of Marine Science*, 70: 245–250.

Forni, Elizabetta. "Woman's New Role and Status in the Baraawe Settlement," in Hussein M. Adam, *Somalia and the World: Proceedings of the International Symposium held in Mogadishu, October 15–21, 1979. Vol. Two.* Mogadishu: Second Halgan Publication, 1979: 251–264.

Freeman, Colin. *Kidnapped: Life as a Hostage on Somalia's Pirate Coast.* London: Monday Books, 2011.

Gathii, James Thuo. "Kenya's Piracy Prosecutions." *The American Journal of International Law*, Vol. 104, No. 3 (July 2010), 416–436.

Geiss, Robin and Anna Petrig. *Piracy and Armed Robbery at Sea: the Legal Framework for Counter-Piracy Operations in Somalia and the Gulf of Aden.* Oxford University Press, 2011.

Gilmer, Brittany. *Political Geographies of Piracy: Constructing Threats and Containing Bodies in Somalia*. New York: Palgrave MacMillan, 2014.

Guilfoyle, Douglas. "Counter-Piracy Law Enforcement and Human Rights." *The International and Comparative Law Quarterly*, Vol. 59, No. 1 (Jan., 2010): 141–169.

Guilfoyle, Douglas. "Interdicting Vessels to Enforce the Common Interest: Maritime Countermeasures and the Use of Force." *The International and Comparative Law Quarterly*, Vol. 56, No. 1 (Jan., 2007): 69–82.

Guilfoyle, Douglas. "International Law and Counter-Piracy in the Indian Ocean," in Awet T. Weldemichael, Patricia Schneider and Andrew C. Winner (eds.) *Maritime Terrorism and Piracy in the Indian Ocean Region*. London and New York: Routledge, 2015: 96–112.

Guilfoyle, Douglas. "Piracy off Somalia: UN Security Council Resolution 1816 and IMO Regional Counter-Piracy Efforts." *The International and Comparative Law Quarterly*. Vol. 57, No. 3 (Jul., 2008), 690–699.

Haakonsen, Jan. "Somalia's Fisheries: Case Study." Food and Agriculture Organization of the United Nations (FAO): Rome, Italy, 1983.

Haid, Yusuf Mohamed. *Out of Mogadishu: A Memoir of the Civil War in 1991*. N. P.: 2016.

Hamdun, Said and Noel King. *Ibn Battuta in Black Africa*. Princeton: Markus Wiener Publishers, 2010.

Hansen, Stig Jarle. *Al-Shabaab in Somalia: The History and Ideology of a Militant Islamist Group, 2005–2012*. London: Hurst & Company, 2013.

Hansen, Stig Jarle. "Debunking the Piracy Myth: How Illegal Fishing Really Interacts with Piracy in East Africa." *The RUSI Journal*, Vol. 156, No. 6 (December 2012): 26–30.

Hansen, Stig Jarle. *Piracy in the Greater Gulf of Aden: Myths, Misconceptions and Remedies*. Oslo: Norwegian Institute for Urban and Regional Research, 2009.

Hansen, Stig Jarle. "The Dynamics of Somali Piracy." *Studies in Conflict & Terrorism*, 35:7–8:523–530.

Harper, Mary. *Getting Somalia Wrong? Faith, War and Hope in a Shattered State*. London: Zed Books, 2012.

Holmes, James R. "The Interplay between Counterpiracy and Indian Ocean Geopolitics," in Bibi van Ginkel and Frans-Paul van der Putten, eds. *The International Response to Somali Piracy: Challenges and Opportunities*. Leiden and Boston: Martinus Nijhoff Publishers, 2010: 153–177.

Homan, Kees and Susanne Kamerling. "Operational Challenges to Counterpiracy Operations off the Coast of Somalia," in Bibi van Ginkel and Frans-Paul van der Putten, eds. *The International Response to Somali Piracy: Challenges and Opportunities*. Leiden and Boston: Martinus Nijhoff Publishers, 2010: 65–103.

Issa-Salwe, Abdisalam (ed.). *Abdirazak Haji Hussein: My Role in the Foundation of the Somali Nation-State, a Political Memoir*. Trenton, NJ: Africa World Press, 2017.

Jennings, Todd. "Controlling Access in the Absence of a Central Government: The Somali Dilemma." *Ocean Yearbook Online*, Vol. 15, Issue 1 (2001).

Kaplan, Robert D. "Center Stage for the Twenty-first Century." *Foreign Affairs*, Vol. 8 Issue 2 (March/April 2009): 16–32.

Kapteijns, Lidwien. *Clan Cleansing in Somalia: The Ruinous Legacy of 1991*. Philadelphia: University of Pennsylvania Press, 2013.

Khaldun, Ibn. *The Muqaddimah: An Introduction to History*. Franz Rosenthal (trans.). Princeton and Oxford: Princeton University Press, 1969.

Kraska, James. *Contemporary Maritime Piracy: International Law, Strategy and Diplomacy at Sea*. Santa Barbara, CA: Praeger, 2011.

Kraska, James. "Freakonomics of Maritime Piracy." *Brown Journal of World Affairs*, Vol. XVI, Issue II (Spring/Summer 2010): 109–119.

Lehr, Peter and Hendrick Lehmann. "Somalia – Pirates' New Paradise," in Peter Lehr (ed.). *Violence at Sea: Piracy in the Age of Global Terrorism*. New York: Routledge, 2007: 1–22.

Lewis, I. M. *A Modern History of the Somali: Nation and State in the Horn of Africa*. Athens: Ohio University Press, 2002.

Lewis, I. M. *Understanding Somalia and Somaliland: Culture, History, Society*. New York: Columbia University Press, 2011.

Liss, Carolin. "Maritime Piracy in Southeast Asia." *Southeast Asian Affairs*, Vol. 2003: 52–68.

Liss, Carolin. "The Roots of Piracy in Southeast Asia." APSNet Policy Forum, 22 October 2007: http://nautilus.org/apsnet/the-roots-of-piracy-in-southeast-asia/.

Little, Peter D. *Somalia: Economy without State*. Oxford: James Currey, 2003.

Marchal, Roland. "Somali Piracy: The Local Contexts of an International Obsession." *Humanity*, Vol. 2, No. 1 (Spring 2011): pp. 31–50.

Marchal, Roland. "Warlordism and Terrorism: How to Obscure an Already Confusing Crisis? The Case of Somalia." *International Affairs*. Vol. 83, No.6 (November 2007): 1091–1106.

May, R. De. *Narrative of the Sufferings and Adventures of Henderick Portenger, A Private Soldier of the Late Swiss Regiment de Mueron, who was Wrecked on the Shores of Abyssinia in the Red Sea*. London: Sir Richard Phillips and Co., 1819.

Menkhaus, Ken. "Dangerous Waters." *Survival*, Vol. 51, no. 1 (2009): 21–25.

Menkhaus, Ken. "Governance without Government in Somalia: Spoilers, State Building, and the Politics of Coping." *International Security*, Vol. 31, No. 3 (Winter 2006/07): 74–106.

Menkhaus, Ken. "Somalia and Somaliland: Terrorism, Political Islam, and State Collapse," in Robert I. Rotberg (ed.). *Battling Terrorism in the Horn of Africa*. Cambridge, MA: World Peace Foundation, 2005: 23–47.

Menkhaus, Ken. *Somalia: State Collapse and the Threat of Terrorism*. London and New York: Routledge, 2004.

Middleton, Roger. "More Than Just Pirates: Closing the Space for Somali Pirates through a Comprehensive Approach." in Bibi van Ginkel and Frans-Paul van der Putten (eds.). *The International Response to Somali Piracy: Challenges and Opportunities*. Leiden and Boston: Martinus Nijhoff Publishers, 2010: 13–30.

Moorthy, Shanti and Ashraf Jamal. "Introduction: New Conjunctures in Maritime Imaginaries," in Shanti Moorthy and Ashraf Jamal (eds.). *Indian Ocean Studies: Cultural, Social, and Political Perspectives*. New York: Routledge, 2010.

Murphy, Martin N. *Small Boats, Weak States, Dirty Money. Piracy and Maritime Terrorism in the Modern World*. London: Hurst & Company, 2010.

Murphy, Martin N. *Somalia: The New Barbary? Piracy and Islam in the Horn of Africa*. New York: Columbia University Press, 2011.

Neumann, Thilo and Tim René Salomon. "Fishing in Troubled Waters: Somalia's Maritime Zones and the Case for Reinterpretation." *Insights* Vol. 16, Issue 9 (March 15, 2012): https://asil.org/insights/volume/16/issue/9/fishing-troubled-waters-somalia%E2%80%99s-maritime-zones-and-case.

Nincic, Donna. "Maritime Piracy in Africa: The Humanitarian Dimension." *African Security Review* 18.3 (2009).

Nincic, Donna. "State Failure and the Re-Emergence of Maritime Piracy," (presented at the 49th Annual Convention of the International Studies Association, March 26–29, 2008, San Francisco, CA). Reproduced as "Statskollaps og sjørøveriets tilbakekoms," *Internasjonal Politikk* 67 (1)(January 2009).

Onuoha, Freedom C. "Piracy and Maritime Security off the Horn of Africa: Connections, Causes, and Concerns." *African Security*, 3 (2010): 191–215.

Pearson, Michael. *The Indian Ocean*. London and New York: Routledge, 2003.

Persson, Lo, Alasdair Lindop, Sarah Harper, Kyrstn Zylich and Dirk Zeller. "Failed State: Reconstruction of Domestic Fisheries Catches in Somalia, 1950–2010" The University of British Columbia Fisheries Center: Working Paper #2014–10, 2014: www.seaaroundus.org/doc/publications/chapters/2015/Persson-et-al-Somalia.pdf.

Pham, J. Peter. "Putting Puntland's Potential into Play." World Defense Review, 24 September 2009.

Pham, J. Peter. "Putting Somali Piracy in Context." *Journal of Contemporary African Studies*, Vol. 28, No. 3 (July 2010), 325–341.

Pham, J. Peter. "The Failed State and Regional Dimensions of Somali Piracy," in Bibi van Ginkel and Frans-Paul van der Putten, eds. *The International Response to Somali Piracy:Challenges and Opportunities* . Leiden and Boston: Martinus Nijhoff Publishers, 2010: 31–64.

Potgieter, Thean and Clive Schofield. "Poverty, Poaching and Pirates: Geopolitical Instability and Maritime Insecurity off the Horn of Africa." *Journal of the Indian Ocean Region* Vol. 6, No. 1 (June 2010): 86–112.

Prestholdt, Jeremy. "Locating the Indian Ocean: Notes on the Postcolonial Reconstitution of Space." *Journal of Eastern African Studies*, Vol. 9, No. 3 (2015): 440–467.

Puntland Development Research Center. *Dialogue for Peace: Peacemaking at the Crossroads. Consolidation of the 1993 Mudug Peace Agreement*. Garowe, Puntland: Interpeace, September 2006.

Rejeb, Lotfi Ben. "Barbary's 'Character' in European Letters, 1514–1830: An Ideological Prelude to Colonization." *Dialectical Anthropology* Vol. 6, No. 4 (June 1982): 345–355.

Rembe, Nasila S. *Africa and the International Law of the Sea: A Study of Contribution of the African States to the Third United Nations Conference on the Law of the Sea*. Alphen/Rijn, The Netherlands: Sijthoff and Noordhoff, 1980.

Rothwell, Donald R., Alex G. Oude Elferink and Karen N. Scott. *The Oxford Handbook of the Law of the Sea*. Oxford University Press, 2015.

Rumley, Dennis, Sanjay Chaturvedi, and Vijay Sakhuja. "Fisheries Exploitation in the Indian Ocean Region." in Rumley, Chaturvedi, and Sakhuja (eds.). *Fisheries Exploitation in the Indian Ocean: Threats and Opportunities*. Singapore: ISEAS Publishing, 2009: 1–17.

Samatar, Abdi I. *The State and Rural Transformation in Northern Somalia, 1884–1986*. Madison: University of Wisconsin Press, 1989.

Samatar, Abdi Ismail. *Africa's First Democrats: Somalia's Aden A. Osman and Abdirazak H. Hussen*. Bloomington: Indiana University Press, 2016.

Samatar, Ahmed I. *Socialist Somalia: Rhetoric and Reality*. London: Zed Books, 1988.

Samatar, Abdi I, Mark Lindberg and Basil Mahayni. "The Dialectics of Piracy in Somalia: the Rich versus the Poor." *Third World Quarterly* Vol. 31, No. 8 (2010), 1377–1394.

Samatar, Said S. *Somalia: A Nation in Turmoil*. London: Minority Rights Group, 1991.

Schmidt, Elizabeth. *Foreign Intervention in Africa: From the Cold War to the War on Terror*. Cambridge: Cambridge University Press, 2013.

Schnepel, Burkhard. "Piracy in the Indian Ocean (ca. 1680–1750)," (working paper, Max Planck Institute for Social Anthropology, Working Paper No. 160), 2014.

Schraeder, Peter J. "US Foreign Policy in an Altered Cold War Environment." *Middle East Journal* 46 (Autumn 1992), 571–593.

Sellstrom, Tor. *Africa in the Indian Ocean: Islands in Ebb and Flow*. Leiden and Boston: Brill, 2015.

Shane, Jon M., Eric L Piza and Marissa Mandala. "Situational Crime Prevention and Worldwide Piracy: A Cross-Continent Analysis." *Crime Science*, Vol. 4, No. 2 (2015): 1–13.

Singh, Currun and Arjun Singh Bedi. "War on Piracy: The Conflation of Somali Piracy with Terrorism in Discourse, Tactic, and Law." *Security Dialogue* Vol. 47(5) (2016), 440–458.

Sjoblom, Kirsti-Liisa and Gordon Linsley. "Sea Disposal of Radioactive Wastes: The London Convention 1972." *IAEA Bulletin*, 2/1994: www.iaea.org/sites/d efault/files/publications/magazines/bulletin/bull36-2/36205981216.pdf.

Smith, Nicholas W. S. "The Machinations of the Majerteen Sultans: Somali Pirates of the Late Nineteenth Century?" *Journal of Eastern African Studies*. Vol. 9, No. 1 (2015): 20–34.

Sumaila, U. Rashid and Mahamudu Bawumia. "Fisheries, Ecosystem Justice and Piracy: A Case Study of Somalia." *Fisheries Research* 157 (2014): 154–163.

Sumaila, U. Rashid, Ahmed S. Khan, Andrew J. Dyck, Reg Watson, Gordon Munro, Peter Tydemers and Daniel Pauly. "A Bottom-up Re-estimation of Global Fisheries Subsidies" (working paper, Fisheries Centre, University of British Columbia, Working Paper # 2009–11 (2009).

Vagg, Jon. "Rough Seas? Contemporary Piracy in Southeast Asia," *British Journal of Criminology* . vol. 35 no. 1 (Winter 1995), 63–80.

War-Torn Societies Project. *Rebuilding Somalia: Issues and Possibilities for Puntland*. London: HAAN Associates, 2001.

Weldemichael, Awet T. *Dalhousie Marine Piracy Project: When Elephants Fight, the Grass Suffers: A Report on the Local Consequences of Piracy in Puntland*. Marine Affairs Program Technical Report #12, 2014: https://cdn.dal.ca/content/dam/dalhousie/pdf/faculty/science/marine-affairs-program/Technical_series/Dalhousie-Marine-Affairs-Program-Technical-Report-%2312.pdf.

Weldemichael, Awet T. "Maritime Corporate Terrorism and Its Consequences in the Western Indian Ocean Region: Waste Dumping, Illegal Fishing and Piracy in 21st Century Somalia." *Journal of the Indian Ocean Region* Vol. 8, No. 2 (December 2012), 110–126.

Weldemichael, Awet T. "Ransoming in Contemporary Northeast Africa: Piracy in Puntland." *African Economic History* 42 (2014): 215–237.

Weldemichael, Awet T. "The Law of the Sea and Il/Legal Fishing in Somalia," *The Nautilus IX* (August 2018), 29–52.

Weldemichael, Awet T., Patricia Schneider and Andrew C. Winner. *Maritime Terrorism and Piracy in the Indian Ocean Region*. London and New York: Routledge, 2015.

Willett, Lee. "Pirates and Power Politics: Naval Presence and Grand Strategy in the Horn of Africa." *The RUSI Journal*, Vol. 156, No. 6 (December 2012): 20–25.

Yassin, Mohamed. "Somali Fisheries Development and Management." June 1981: http://ir.library.oregonstate.edu/dspace/bitstream/1957/6400/1/Mohamed_Yassin_ocr.pdf.

Yohannes, Okbazghi. *The United States and the Horn of Africa: An Analytical Study of Pattern and Process*. Boulder, CO: Westview Press, 1997.

Yusuf, Aweys Warsame. "Somali Enterprises: Making Peace their Business," in Jessica Banfield, Canan Gunduz, and Nick Killick (eds.), *Local Business, Local Peace: The Peacebuilding Potential of the Domestic Private Sector* (London: International Alert, 2006): 469–507.

Zalinge, N.P. van. "Summary of Fisheries and Resources Information for Somalia." Rome: FAO, 1988.

Zedner, Lucia. "Pre-crime and Post-criminology," *Theoretical Criminology*, vol. 11, no. 2 (2007): 261–281.

Index

'Aadde Muse (Mohamud Hirsi Muse),
    89–91, 95–97, 157–158, 159
Abdallah, Ahmedou Ould, 29–30
Abdi, Mohamed ("Garfanje"), 86–88
Abdi, Rashid, 100
Abdi Isse clan family, 75–78
Abdiweli Mohamed, Ali "Gas," 56–57,
    75–78, 130, 136–138, 162n.76
Abdullahi, Farah, 88
ab initio doctrine, 32–35
Abshir, Mohamed, 11–12, 70
Academy for Peace and Development
    (APD), 17–18
Affi, Ladan, 33n.44, 186–187
African countries, anti-piracy initiatives
    and, 187–188
African Union (AU), 32–35
African Union Mission in Somalia
    (AMISOM), 187–188
"Afweyne" (Mohamed Abdi Hassan),
    81–82, 86–88, 127–132, 187–188
Ahlu Sunna Wal Al-Jamaa, 10–11
Ahmed, Sharif Sheikh, 89–91, 132
Ahmed "Saneeg," 86–88
Aidid, Mohamed Farah, 9–10, 52
air-dropping of ransoms, 110, 126–127
alcohol consumption, smuggling by pirates
    linked to, 145–150
"Ali Baadiyow" Abdirizak Sheikh Osman,
    75–78
Ali Farah, Ali, 27–28, 43–44, 46n.103
Al-Itihad Al-Islami, 9–10
Alpi, Ilaria, 26n.22, 53n.57
Al-Qanim fishing vessel, warship attack on,
    189–191
Al-Shabaab
    ideological differences with pirates,
        182–183
    pirates' links to, 121, 166–169,
        180–181
    threat to Somalia from, 10–11, 94, 159
'Aluula, 169

ancillary trades, ransom piracy and rise of,
    104–115
anti-piracy initiatives
    abandonment of pirates at sea and,
        193–194
    best management practices, 177
    decline in piracy and, 197–198
    emergence of, 20
    geopolitics and, 184–188
    grassroots initiatives, 162–166
    international measures, 20, 171–195
    local antipiracy responses, 157–158
    militarization of, 102–103, 171–173,
        175–176, 178–179
    non-military measures, 178–179
    outcomes and missteps of, 188–194
    piracy-terrorism nexus and, 179–184
    recommendations involving, 201–203
    regional governments, 158–162
    Somali criticism of, 186–187
    Union of Islamic Courts and, 85–86
    violence against Somalis from,
        191–194
antiterrorism tactics
    anti-piracy initiatives and, 179
    violence against Somali fishermen from,
        193–194
Arab, Salah Hashi, 70
Arab League, 187–188
ARA Fisheries, 57–59
Aris XIII tanker, 169
arms traffic in Somalia, 157n.65
artisanal fishermen in Somalia
    collusion in IUU by, 51–62
    foreign violence against, 189–191
    growth of, 40–41
    IUU intensification and demise of, 2,
        44–46, 47–48
    predatory piracy adopted by, 78–88
    Puntland as center for, 65–68
    yields of, 41–42
Asayr II fishing dhow, 169

229

Atlantic Marine and Offshore Group, 55–56
Awdal trawler, 52–53

Bahadur, Jay, 102–103, 182–183
*Bakeyle, 88
Bateman, Sam, 27
"Battle of Hul," 165
"bemboweyne," reducation of pirates to,
    111–113
best management practices, counterpiracy
    initiatives and, 177
BMP4 manual, 177
Boqor Abdullahi ("King Kong"), 70
Boyah (Abshir Abdullahi Abudule), 72–74,
    75–88, 111, 164–166
Buccaneer tugboat, hijacking of, 182–183
Bueger, Christian, 171
burcad badeed (bandits of the sea), 13

Camorra, waste dumping activities of,
    24–25
Cantrill, Richard, 102–103
car accidents, pirate drivers as cause of,
    143–146
Cassanelli, Lee, 8–9
catch-and-release anti-piracy tactic,
    119–122, 186–187, 193–194
Central Regions State, formation of,
    10–11
Chalk, Peter, 181
Chandler, Paul and Rachel, 125–127
children in piracy, 152–153
China
    fishing in Somalia by, 41–42
    fishing subsidies in, 37
    geopolitics of piracy and, 185–186
Citizen's Police Liaison Committee
    (CPLC) (Pakistan), 127–131
"Clan Cleansing," 7–8
clan networks and identity
    conflict within, 143–146
    economic and political impact of, 8–9
    elders' authority in, piracy's erosion of,
        153–155
    investment in piracy by, 91–92
    IUU fishing and, 62–63
    livestock exports and conflicts in,
        139n.20
    pirate-caused conflicts and, 155–157
    protection of pirates and, 95–97, 184n.51
    security against piracy and, 74–78
    Somali National Movement and, 9–10
    Somali state collapse and, 9
    transition to predatory piracy and,
        81–82, 86–88

turmoil in Puntland and, 89–91
Coffen-Smout, Scott, 49–51, 52–53,
    72–74, 161
Cold War
    fishing industry in Africa and, 41–42
    Somalia and, 7–8
colonialism
    collapse of Somali fishing industry and
        impact of, 44–46
    population movements in Somalia
        and, 8–9
    Somali civil war and, 7–8
Combined Maritime Forces (CMT),
    176
Combined Task Force (CTF), 176
conflict mediation, pirate-caused clan con-
    flict and, 155–157
consumer goods, piracy and cost increases
    for, 135, 136–138
Contact Group on Piracy off the Coast of
    Somalia (CGPCS), 49–51, 176,
    191–194
corporate predatory practices
    IUU fishing and, 35–36
    piracy linked to, 14–16
    waste dumping in Somalia as, 26–30
corruption, IUU fishing and, 51–62, 198–201
CPO *Korea* hijacking, 169
Cretu, Virgil, 119–122, 122n.72
criminal activity
    financing for piracy from, 91–92
    impact on Somali fishing of, 64–65
    Somali piracy linked to, 4
    upsurge in, 166–169
    waste dumping and involvement of,
        24–30

"Dadurow" (Abdulgadir Al-Nur), 189–191
Darod clan, 7–8, 9–10, 89–91, 95–97,
    156n.64
debt burdens of pirates, 111–114, 122–124,
    138–139
defensive piracy
    fishermen vigilantes and, 69–74
    rise of, 4, 12
    transition to predatory piracy, 78–88
    weakness of security initiatives against,
        74–78
Dickinson, Chris, 180–181
Dirir, Abdirizak Mohamed, 130,
    189–191, 201
Distance Water Fishing Nations (DWFNs)
    destructive methods and violent activities
        of, 48–49, 64–65, 72–74
    government subsidies of, 36–37, 62–63

IUU fishing and, 35–36, 45–46, 115
partnerships with Somali fisheries,
  41–42, 70
predation of Somali resources by, 45–46,
  115n.51, 115
private security protection of, 75
distant water fishing nations (DWFN),
  piracy linked to, 2
diya system (blood money), 155–157
Dua, Jatin, 79–80, 93, 115–119

economic conditions
  debt burden of pirates and, 138–139
  impact of piracy on, 14–16, 72–74, 135,
    196–201
  job-creation and humanitarian aid losses
    from piracy and, 141–143
  livestock business losses and, 139–140
  in post-civil war Puntland, 65–68
  support for piracy as result of, 83–84,
    196–201
  trickling down of insurance costs and
    trade declines, 136–138
Edwards, Leslie, 129n.99
elders, authority of
  grassroots antipiracy initiatives and,
    162–166
  piracy's erosion of, 153–155
electronic waste, dumping of, 25
Elmi, Afyare, 33n.44, 186–187
Enrico Ievoli chemical tanker, hijacking
  of, 183
environmental destruction, by Distance
  Water Fishing Nations, 48–49
EU Common Fisheries Policies, 37
EU NAVFOR, 102–103, 122
European Union (EU)
  fishing subsidies in, 37
  international counter piracy measures
    and, 173–174
  waste dumping by, 25
European Union Naval Force, 175–176
exclusive economic zone (EEZ)
  lack of Somali declaration of, 30–31
  UNCLOS provisions on, 33–34
Eyl
  catch-n-release activity near, 119–122
  children as pirates in, 152–153
  counter-piracy measures in, 83–84,
    157–158, 162–166
  economic impact of piracy in, 134–135
  fishing industry in, 47, 59–60, 66–67,
    72–74, 81–82
  governance in, 158–162
  IUU fishing near, 48–49

IUU violence near, 189–191
khat industry in, 148–150
predatory piracy around, 88–93,
  169
violence by pirates in, 143–146

Failed State Index (FSI), piracy linked
  to, 94
failure rates for ransom piracy, 103–104,
  192–193
family structure, piracy's impact on, 150–152
Farah, Abdirizak Dirie, 162
Farah, Abdulkadir Nur "Gacmay,"
  164–166
Farah, Isse Haji, 52–53, 54
Farah, Nur, 59–60
Farah, Shire Haji, 54, 57–59
Farole, Abdirahman Mohamed, 45–46,
  92–93, 94–97, 126n.84
  antipiracy initiatives of, 158–162,
    162n.76
Finley, Carmel, 31n.37
fishing industry in Somalia
  anti-terrorism violence against, 193–194
  foreign partnerships with, 41–42, 64–65
  foreign violence against, 48–49, 64–65,
    72–74, 189–191
  government restrictions on, 43–44
  piracy and collapse of, 89–91, 134–135,
    196–201
  privatization of, 43–51
  in Puntland, 10, 65–68
  state collapse and rise of, 14–16, 20,
    38–43, 44–46
  technological advances and, 31–32
  tsunami devastation of, 80–81
Five Year Development Plan (Somalia),
  40–41
Food and Agriculture Organization (FAO)
  on IUU fishing, 45–46
  Somali fishing data from, 39
  sustainable fishing practices and, 35n.56
foreign partnerships with Somalia
  fishing industry and, 41–42, 64–65
  piracy and decline of, 136–138
Freeman, Colin, 128
FV Al-Amal, 59–60
FV Jaber hijacking, 129, 130
FV Naham 3 hijacking, 129, 130
FV Poseidon, 59–60
FV Siraj hijacking, 129, 130

Gaddafi, Mu'amar al-, 187–188
Galkayo Medical Center, resources directed
  toward pirate violence by, 145–146

Galmudug
  formation of, 10–11
  piracy operations in, 94
"Gantal" Abdirizal Ahmed, 126–127
Gara'ad
  Al-Shabaab presence in, 183
  catch-n-release near, 119–122
  clan authority in, 153–155
  counter-piracy initiatives in, 162–166
  fishing industry in, 66–67, 72–74, 75
  IUU fishing near, 48–49
  governance in, 158–162
  khat industry in, 148–150
  predatory piracy in, 88, 92, 115,
    143–146
Garad Mohamed, 88, 107–108, 182–183
Garowe Psychiatric Center, 145–150
Geneva Convention on the Territorial Sea
  and the Contiguous Zone, 31–32
geopolitics
  counter-piracy measures and, 171–173,
    184–188
  piracy-terrorism nexus and, 179–184
Gilmer, Brittany, 22–23, 178–179
global economy, cost of piracy to, 196–201
Global South, foreign infringement on fishing in, 32–35
government subsidies for fishing
  global impact of, 31–32
  IUU fishing linked to, 36–37, 62–63
grassroots antipiracy initiatives, 162–166
Greenpeace, 25, 26
grievance, as piracy motivator, 14–16
Guilfoyle, Douglas, 178–179
"guns-for-fish" agreements, 41–42

Haakonsen, Jan, 39, 40–41
Habar Gidir sub-clan, 9–10
Hansen, Stig Jarle, 3, 30–31, 64–65, 81–82
Hart Group security services, 75–78
Harti sub-clan, 96
Hawa Mohamed, Mrs., 145–150
Hawiye clan, 7–8, 9–10, 156n.64
HDMS Esbern Snare hijacking, 114–115
Heeb state, formation of, 10–11
Hersi, Abdiwahid Mohamed "Jo'ar," 70,
  75–78
High Seas Task Force, 38, 45–46
Himan state, formation of, 10–11
Hirsi, Abdulkadir Musse, 119–122
HMCS Ville de Quebec, 180–181
Hobiyo-Haradhere cartel, 81–83, 85–86,
  182–183
hostage negotiators, ransom piracy raids
  and, 106

hostages' fate in ransom piracy, 115,
  127–132
humanitarian aid, piracy and loss of,
  141–143
Hurlburt, Kaija, 193
Hussein, Aden Abdirizak "Aden Sanjab,"
  110, 122–124

illegal, unregulated and unreported (IUU)
  fishing
  corporate predatory practices and, 35–36
  current intensification of, 1, 198–201
  decline of piracy and expansion of, 55–56
  defensive piracy against, 72–74
  financial and environmental costs of, 38
  flouting of Somali restrictions by, 75
  geography of Somali coastline and,
    62–63
  global challenge of, 30–38
  grassroots efforts against, 164–166
  impact in Somalia of, 30–38, 43–51,
    62–63, 68
  local factors in Somalia and, 51–62
  piracy collusion with, 2, 14–16, 20,
    166–169
  ransom piracy proliferation and, 97–98,
    196–201
  recommended international actions
    against, 201–203
  resource piracy and, 4
  Somali state collapse and rise of, 11–12,
    43–51, 62–63
  subsidies as catalyst for, 36–37, 62–63
  vigilante targeting of, 69–74
  violence against Somali fishermen and,
    48–49, 64–65, 72–74, 189–191
The Independent, 25
Indian Ocean
  geopolitics in, 184–185
  piracy expansion across, 99–104
Indian Ocean Tuna Commission, 34–35
inflation, piracy as cause of, 135
infrastructure failure, piracy and, 94–95
Ing sailing yacht, hijacking of, 125–127
INS Cankarso, 118
INS Tir, 118
insurance industry
  anti-piracy initiatives and, 180
  cost increases linked to piracy in,
    136–138
intermediaries, in ransom piracy operations,
  104–115
internally displaced population (IDP)
  piracy's impact on, 150–152
  in Puntland State, 10, 65–66

International Civil Aviation Organization (ICAO), administration of Somali airspace by, 49–51
International Consortium of Investigative Journalists, 37
international counter-piracy measures, 20
International Court of Justice (ICJ), 32–35
international law
  counterpiracy measures and, 171
  IUU fishing as violation of, 49–51
International Maritime Bureau (IMB)-Piracy Reporting Center, 18–19
  anti-piracy initiatives and, 176
  data on mother ships from, 100–102
  definition of piracy by, 22–23
  piracy data from, 74, 82–83, 103–104
International Maritime Organization (IMO), 173–174
  militarization of anti-piracy initiatives and, 178–179
International Peace-Building Alliance (Interpeace), 17–18
International Recommended Transit Corridor, 119–122, 176
investment in piracy
  risks and scams in, 113–114
  sources for, 91–92
Iranian fishing vessels, IUU fishing and, 54, 198–201
Islamic State (IS), theat to Somalia from, 155–157, 183–184
Issaq clan, 7–8
Isse, Islan, 164–166
Isse Mohamud clan family, 74, 96, 164–166
Isse Yuluh, Mohamoud Yussuf, 88, 94–95, 107–108, 126–127, 155–157, 183–184

Japan, fishing subsidies in, 37
Jennings, Todd, 49–51, 72–74
Jental, Abdirizak Sanof Ina, 92–93
job creation, piracy and loss of, 141–143
Johansen, Jan, 125–127

Kapteijns, Lidwien, 7–8
Khan, Jawaid, 129
Khan, Shahnaz, 129
khat consumption, piracy and, 102–103, 148–150
kidnappings, upsurge in, 166–169
Kraska, James, 180–181
Kulmiye, Abdirahman Jama, 39, 44–46, 47, 166–169

Lang, Jack, 16, 30–31, 141–143
Latin American countries, fishing industry growth in, 31–32
"Law on Somali Territorial Sea and Ports," 33
legitimate defense, as piracy motivator, 14–16
Lehr, Peter, 175–176
Le Ponant hijacking, 125–127
Letter of Credit system, livestock exports and, 139–140
licenses for fishing
  DWFNs' defiance of, 75
  proceeds of sales of, 52–53
  Puntland moratorium on, 56–57
Lindberg, Mark, 4, 13, 14–16
Liss, Carolin, 78n.44
livestock exports, piracy and decline in, 139–140
Lloyd's List, 111–113, 180
Lloyds of London, insurance costs of piracy and, 136–138
local antipiracy responses, 157–158
"Looyan" (Mohamed Said Baafe), 107–108
Lynn Rival sailing yacht, hijacking of, 125–127

Maersk Alabama hijacking, 178–179
Mafia, waste dumping activities of, 24–25
Mahayni, Basil, 4, 13, 14–16
Mahdi, Ali, 52–53
maritime insurance, fluctuations in, 1
Maritime Resources Assessment Group (MRAG), 36–37
Maritime Security Center – Horn of Africa (MSCHOA), 176
marriages, piracy's impact on, 150–152
Mejerten sub-clan, 7–8, 9–10, 89–91, 95–97, 153–155
Menkaus, Ken, 3, 13–14, 93
mental illness in Somalia, 145–150
merqan (khat high), 102–103
Middle East
  anti-piracy initiatives and, 187–188
  Somali fishing partnerships with, 47–48, 54, 65–68
  militarization of anti-piracy initiatives, 102–103, 171–173, 175–176, 178–179, 180–181
  outcomes and missteps of, 188–194
military troops, entry into piracy by, 89–91
militia formation, Somali nation-state collapse and, 9

Ministry of Fisheries and Maritime
    Resources (Somalia), 40–41
Mohamed, Mohamud Abdulkadir "John,"
    72–74
Mohamed Osman Mohamed
    "Gafanje," 183
mother ships, pirates' use of, 100–102
MT *Enrico Ievoli*, 107–108
MT *Smyrni*, 107–108
Munyo, Hassan, 52–53, 74
    as SSDF target, 70
Murphy, Martin N., 3–4, 13–14,
    70–71, 181
Muse Saleban clan, 155–157
MV *Albedo* hijacking, 127–131
MV *Bahari Hindi* hijacking, 72–74
MV *BBC Trinidad* hijacking, 113–114
MV *Chios* hijacking, 118
MV *Danica White* hijacking, 111–113
MV *Dover* hijacking, 126–127
MV *Eleni P* hijacking, 113–114
MV *Faina* hijacking, 182–183, 184
MV *Feisty Gas* hijacking, 82, 111
MV *Golden Nori* hijacking, 111
MV *Iceberg* hijacking, 122–124, 130
MV *Limburg* hijacking, 179, 181
MV *Melati Satu* hijacking, 169
MV *Pompei* hijacking, 132
MV *Rim* hijacking, 95–97, 108–109,
    119–122
MV *Sembow* hijacking, 141–143
MV *Semlow* hijacking, 82–83, 141–143
MV *Shen Kno II* hijacking, 70–71
MV *Sirius Star* hijacking, 184
MV *Taipan* hijacking, 104n.13
MV *Victoria* hijacking, 107–108, 142
Mwangura, Andrew, 106, 113–114

"National Volunteer Coast Guard,"
    82–83, 88
'Ndrangheta, waste dumping activities of,
    24–25
negotiations schema in ransom piracy,
    104–115, 138–139
    double-crossings and absence of trust in,
        106–109
    Prantalay hijacking and, 117
    profits from, 106
"The Next 9/11 Could Happen at Sea"
    (Bennett), 180
Nincic, Donna, 13–14, 94, 135, 141–143,
    180–181
nomadic culture in Somalia, 8–9
non-military counter-piracy measures,
    178–179

North Atlantic Treaty Organization
    (NATO), 173–174
Northeast Fishing Company (NEFCO),
    52–62
Nur Mursel Mohamed, 189–191

OCEANA, fishing subsidies research by,
    37
Oceans Beyond Piracy, 111–113,
    136–138, 193
Omar Mohamud clan family, 74, 96
One Earth Future Foundation, 38
Operation Allied Protector, 173–174
Operation ATLANTA, 175–176
Operation Ocean Shield, 173–174
Organization for the Protection of Somali
    Coastline (*Ururka Badbaadinta
    Xeebaha Somaliyeed*, UBAXSO),
    70–71
Organization of African Unity (OAU), 32–35
Osman Mohamud sub-clan, 89–91, 96,
    126n.84, 157–158

Pakistan, MV *Albedo* hijacking negotiations
    and, 127–131
Peace and Development Research Center
    (PDRC), 17–18, 48–49, 162–166
Pearson, Michael, 16
pelagic fish grounds, tuna fishing use of,
    46n.103
Pelton, Robert Young, 18–19
Pham, J. Peter, 5n.15
Phillips, Michael, 45–46, 69
*Phillips (Captain), 178–179
piracy
    children in, 152–153
    clan conflicts caused by, 155–157
    collapse of fishing sector as consequence
        of, 89–91, 134–135
    data collection on, 78n.44, 82–83
    defined, 22–23
    deteriorating conditions for, 20
    erosion of social values linked to,
        153–155
    failure rates of, 103–104, 192–193
    fluctuations in, 1
    global decline in, 85–86
    impact on families and marriages of,
        150–152
    impact on Somalia of, 20, 133–134,
        196–201
    Indian Ocean expansion of, 99–104
    inflation and price hikes as result of, 135
    insurance costs and trade impacts of,
        136–138

inter-clan pirate groups, 143–146
IUU fishing expansion and decline of,
  55–56
job-creation and humanitarian aid losses
  from, 141–143
loss of life for pirates and, 192–193
overview of research on, 3–4
public perceptions of, 86–88, 142
recommended solutions to, 201–203
research methodology in approaches to,
  16–19
scholarly research on, 12–16
state collapse and growth of, 22–23,
  196–201
substance abuse rates among pirates,
  145–150
terrorism and, 179–184
typologies of, 4
political piracy, in Somalia, 4
Port State Control (PSC), regulation
  mechanisms of, 27
poverty, piracy linked to increase in,
  138–139
power relations
  anti-piracy initiatives and role of,
    171–173, 201–203
  geopolitics of anti-piracy and, 184–188
Prantalay vessels, 115
pre-crime concept, counterpiracy and, 173
predations-resistance frame, piracy scholarship and, 13
predatory piracy
  defensive piracy transition to, 78–88
  proliferation of, 88–93
  Somali state collapse and rise of, 12
  Somali support for, 83–84
price increases
  debt burden of pirates and, 138–139
  piracy linked to, 135, 136–138
Prince, Erik, 18–19, 160n.69, 162
private security providers
  anti-piracy measures and use of, 178–179
  Puntland contracts with, 75–78
  Somali suspicion of, 186–187
prostitution, piracy linked to, 150–152
PT Interfisheries, 115
public perceptions of piracy, 142, 153–155
Puntland Development Research Center
  (PDRC), 162–166
Puntland Marine Police Force (PMPF),
  59–60
  inter-clan conflict and, 126n.84,
    155–157
  IUU fishing and, 198–201
  piracy and, 94–95

UAE training for, 160–161
  waste dumping and, 29–30
Puntland State of Somalia
  antipiracy initiatives in, 158–162
  collaboration with piracy in, 95–97
  displaced refugee migration to, 10, 65–66
  economic impact of piracy in, 89–91,
    136–138
  formation of, 9–10, 11–12
  IUU fishing and corruption in, 53–62
  livestock exports decline in, 139–140
  mental illness in, 145–150
  post-civil war entrepreneurship in, 65–66
  semi-autonomy of, 4
  tsunami devastation in, 80–81
  weakness of security initiatives in, 74–78

"Qandala Hafun network," 88
Qayad, Mahdi Gedi, 26, 45–46

Rajbhar, Rajoo, 128
ransom delivery systems, 109, 138–139
ransom piracy
  defined, 4
  fate of hostages in, 131–132
  financing sources for, 91–92
  initial low profile of, 86–88
  negotiations schema in, 104–115
  proliferation of, 88–93, 196–201
  rival groups involved in, 86–88
  share allocations (saami) from, 92–93,
    111–113
  state collapse and rise of, 10–11, 12,
    14–16, 20
  support in Somalia for, 83–84
  ungovernable terrain and absent govern-
    ment and, 93–97
rape, piracy linked to increase in, 150–152
Rapid Response Unit (Puntland), 126–127
Ras Asir trawler, 52–53
recruitment of pirates, 114–115, 134–135
Reer Mahad clan family, 75
regional governments
  antipiracy initiatives of, 158–162
  IUU fishing and corruption in, 53–62
rescue operations, limits of, in ransom
  piracy attacks, 104–115
resource piracy
  disinterest in, 12
  IUU fishing and, 4
risk assessment, cost-benefit analysis of
  piracy and, 102–103

Sa'ad clan family, 81
Saeed, Mohammed Mussa "Aargoosto," 88

safety and security in Somalia, piracy and
  deterioration of, 143–146
Said, Fouad Warsame "Hanaano," 88,
  182–183
Salama Fikira International, 109
Saleebaan clan family, 81
Samatar, Abdi, 4, 13, 14–16
Santiago Declaration on the Maritime
  Zone, 31n.38
Saracen International, 160–161, 162
Sarfaz, Naeem, 129
Seabourne Spirit hijacking, 173–174
Seafarers Assistance Program (SAP),
  104–115
Secure Fisheries Project, 38
security initiatives against piracy
  piracy-terrorism nexus and, 179–184
  state weaknesses concerning, 74–78
share allocations *(saami)* of pirate groups,
  92–93, 111–113
Shared Awareness and Deconfliction
  (SHADE), 176
Sharmarke, Abdirashid Ali, 6–7
Shibin, Mohamed Saalil, 107
ship communication systems, pirates' control of, 104–115
Shortland, Anja, 14–16
Siad Barre, Mohamed, 6–7, 10, 65–66
  fishing industry development under,
    40–41
  foreign partnerships with, 41–42
socioeconomic conditions
  erosion of social values, piracy linked to,
    153–155
  piracy linked to, 4, 143–146
  refugee migration patterns and, 8–9
Somalia
  absence of anti-piracy laws in, 186–187
  acceptance of piracy in, 13, 198–201
  clan-families in, 8–9
  consequences of piracy in, 20, 133–134
  exclusive economic zone established by,
    34–35
  fishing industry in, historical overview,
    38–43
  foreign actors in civil war in, 11–12
  governance without government in, 3
  hazardous waste dumping in, 26–30
  historical overview of events in, 6–12
  illegal, unregulated and unreported fish-
    ing in, 30–38, 43–62
  impact of piracy in, 20, 133–134,
    196–201
  local anti-piracy initiatives in, 157–158,
    197–198

privatization of fishing industry in,
  43–51
Puntland State semi-autonomy in, 4
regulation of fishing industry in, 43–44
state decay and collapse in, 10–11
state restoration efforts in, 1, 198–199
suspicion of anti-piracy initiatives in,
  186–187
Somalia and Eritrea Monitoring Group
  (SEMG), 18–19
Somalia Fisheries Protection Force, 55–56
Somalia Fishguard Ltd, 55–56
SomaliaReport, 18–19, 108–109,
  134–135, 191
Somali-Canadian Coast Guard (SomCan),
  75–78
SOMALIFISH company, 41–42
Somali High Seas Fishing Company
  (SHIFCO), 41–42, 52–53, 70, 74
Somaliland
  civil war and, 7–8
  displaced refugee migration to, 65–66
  fishing industry in, 39
  SNM break with, 9–10
  state formation in, 9–10, 11
Somali National Movement (SNM)
  annulment of Somaliland-Italian Somalia
    union and, 9–10
  civil war and, 7–8
  political piracy and, 4
Somali Salvation Democratic Front
  (SSDF), 186–187
  civil war and, 7–8, 9–10
  divisions within, 11–12
  security initiatives of, 75–78
  vigilante groups and, 69–74
SOMITFISH company, 41–42
South Korea, 37
  IUU fishing in Somalia by, 54,
    57–59
sovereignty issues
  fishing industry and, 31–32
  IUU fishing and, 49–51
Soviet Union
  fishing industry in Africa and, 41–42
  Somali dictatorship and, 6–7
spendthrift lifestyles of pirates, 111,
  113–114, 122–124, 138–139,
  143–146, 182–183
state decay and collapse
  collapse of Somali fishing industry and,
    44–46
  history of, 9
  local antipiracy responses, 157–158
  ransom piracy in wake of, 93–97

Somali piracy linked to, 4, 13–14, 22–23,
    196–201
Steed, John, 130
substance abuse, smuggling by pirates
    linked to, 145–150
SV Quest hijacking, 107, 108–109,
    125–127
SV Tanit hijacking, 125–127

telecommunications, piracy and, 94–95
terrorism
    piracy and, 179–184
    use of boats as weapons in, 181
Third World countries
    fishing industry growth in, 31–32
    waste dumping in, 25
Thongchai Tavanapong family, 116
Tolba, Mostafa, 26
Towfiq Export Company, 141–143
trade activity, piracy's impact on, 136–138
Transitional Federal Government (TFG)
    allegations of terrorism links to, 180–181
    antipiracy initiatives and, 161, 173–174,
        177–178
    formation of, 89–91
    skepticism of anti-piracy initiatives
        in, 189
translators-cum-negotiators, ransom piracy
    and emergence of, 106–109
"Treasure Mapped" (Shortland), 14–16
Tromp (Dutch frigate), 104n.13
Tsunami of 2004
    exposure of waste dumping by, 28
    transition to predatory piracy and, 80–81
200-nautical-mile territorial waters, Somali
    claim of, 30–31

Union of Islamic Courts (UIC), 85–86
    political ascendancy of, 89–91
United Arab Emirates (UAE), 160–161
United Kingdom
    influence in fishing industry of, 31n.37
    waste dumping by, 25
United Nations Conference on the Law of
    the Sea (UNCLOS I), 31–32, 33–34
United Nations Environmental Program
    (UNEP), 26, 35n.56
United Nations Office on Drugs and Crime
    (UNODC), 130, 178–179
United Nations Security Council (UNSC),
    13–14
    IIU fishing investigations and, 30–31,
        62–63
    international counterpiracy measures
        and, 173–174

Puntland antipiracy initiatives and,
    159–162
Resolution 1851, 173–174
Resolution 1976 for protection of
    Somalia's resources, 49–51
Somali Transitional Federal Government
    and, 177–178
    waste dumping investigations and, 29–30
United Somali Congress (USC), 7–8,
    9–10
United States
    anti-piracy measures by, 176
    fishing industry in Africa and, 41–42
    influence in fishing industry of, 31n.37
    Somali dictatorship and, 6–7
    surveillance of waste dumping by, 24–25
University of British Columbia Fisheries
    Centre, IUU fishing research by, 36–37
UN Monitoring Group
    on alleged Al-Shabaab-pirate connec-
        tions, 183
    on anti-piracy measures, 175–176
    data on mother ships from, 100–102
    IUU fishing and, 53–62
    negotiators' profits data from, 106
    piracy-state collaboration and, 95–97
    on pirate-IUU collusion, 166–169
    predatory piracy incidents and, 78,
        85–86
    ransom delivery data from, 110
USS *Cole*, 181

van Zalinge, N. P., 41–42
vigilante groups
    defensive piracy and, 69–74
    state collapse and rise of, 14–16, 20
    transition to predatory piracy by, 78–88
violence
    by anti-piracy groups, Somalis as victims
        of, 191–194
    Distance Water Fishing Nations perpe-
        tration of, 48–49, 64–65, 72–74,
        189–191
    by pirates, 143–146

Waldo, Mohamed Abshir, 204
waste dumping
    continuation of, 198–199
    global challenges of, 24–30
    international duplicity in, 29–30
    piracy linked to, 2, 14–16, 20
    recommended international actions
        against, 201–203
Willett, Lee, 185–186
Winkler, Thomas, 191

women
  grassroots antipiracy initiatives and role
    of, 165
  in khat trade, 102–103, 148–150
  piracy and violence against, 150–152
World Bank, Somali fisheries data from, 39
World Food Program (WFP)
  international counter piracy measures
    and, 173–174
  pirate hijacking of vessels from, 141–143

Xiang Hua Men hijacking, 108n.24

Yare, Awad, 191
Yassin, Mohamed, 41–42
Yemeni fishing industry

hijacking of ships from, 85–86
IUU fishing in Somalia by, 47–48, 54,
  56–57
Yere, Abdullahi, 88, 92
Yusuf, Abdinasir, 155–157
Yusuf, Abdullahi (Col.), 177–178
  clan politics and, 75
  as emerging leader, 9–10, 11–12, 30–31
  growth of piracy and, 70–71
  IUU fishing and, 52–53, 54
  as Transitional Federal Government lea-
    der, 89–91
Yusuf, Aweys Warsame, 65n.5
Yusuf, Musa Osman, 189–191

Zedner, Lucia, 173